D1552679

Farm Workers
and the
Churches

Number Eight: Fronteras Series

Sponsored by Texas A&M International University

José Roberto Juárez, General Editor

Farm Workers

and the

Churches

The Movement in California and Texas

Alan J. Watt

Texas A&M University Press

College Station

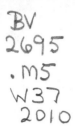

This paper meets the requirements of ANSI/NISO z39.48-1992 (Permanence of Paper).
Binding materials have been chosen for durability.

Library of Congress Cataloging-in-Publication Data

Watt, Alan J., 1956–
    Farm workers and the churches : the movement in California and Texas / Alan J.
Watt. — 1st ed.
        p. cm. — (Fronteras series ; no. 8)
    Includes bibliographical references and index.
    ISBN-13: 978-1-60344-174-2 (cloth : alk. paper)
    ISBN-10: 1-60344-174-3 (cloth : alk. paper)
    ISBN-13: 978-1-60344-193-3 (pbk : alk. paper)
    ISBN-10: 1-60344-193-x (pbk : alk. paper)   1. Church work with migrant labor—
California—History—20th century. 2. Church work with migrant labor—Texas—
History—20th century. 3. Solidarity—Religious aspects—Christianity. 4. Church
and social problems—California—History—20th century. 5. Church and social
problems—Texas—History—20th century. 6. Mexican American migrant agricultural
laborers—California—History—20th century. 7. Mexican American migrant agricultural laborers—Texas—History—20th century. 8. California—Church history—
20th century. 9. Texas—Church history—20th century. 10. National Farm Workers
Association—History. 11. United Farm Workers Organizing Committee—History.
12. United Farm Workers—History. 13. Chávez, César, 1927–1993. I. Title. II. Series:
Fronteras series ; no. 8.
    BV2695.M5W37 2010
    277.3′082088305563—dc22

                                                                        2009031571

To

Sydney and Philip

Contents

Acknowledgments

This work was successfully completed due to many persons who helped me at various stages. My thanks to Mary Lenn Dixon and others at the Texas A&M University Press for many editorial labors and to Dawn Hall for copyediting. Thanks, too, to my academic mentors at Vanderbilt University, namely, John Fitzmier, Dale Johnson, the late Howard Harrod, Eugene TeSelle, and Samuel McSeveney. I thank my friend and former fellow student, Douglas Sweeney, for his support and for directing me to pertinent resources, and to Don Huber of Trinity Lutheran Seminary as well. Thanks also go to the many archivists for their assistance: Kathy Schmeling at the Walter P. Reuther Library of Labor and Urban Affairs; Jane Boley, formerly of the Special Collections Department, at the University of Texas, Arlington; William Brock, formerly at the Stitt Library Archives of Austin Presbyterian Seminary; Jeffrey Burns at the Archives of the Archdiocese of San Francisco; Edward Loch, S.M., at the Archives of the Archdiocese of San Antonio; L. Dale Patterson at the General Commission on Archives of the United Methodist Church, Madison, New Jersey; William John Shepherd Sr., at the Archives of The Catholic University of America, Washington, D.C.; Amy J. Roberts and others at the Presbyterian Historical Society, Philadelphia; Sr. Catherine Louise La-Costa at the Archives of the Diocese of San Diego; and Peter Whidden of Special Collections of Stanford University Libraries. Others who were helpful include the staff at the Chancery Offices of the Diocese of Fresno, Don Vlasak and Jean Piccirelli for translating articles, Steve Davis, and Lynn Thompson of the New Braunfels Public Library. Thanks are in order as well for those farm workers and ministers I interviewed and with whom I corresponded. Last, my gratitude to the members of my family for their constant encouragement and support throughout this long effort. Special thanks go to my wife Deborah Hoermann Watt.

Farm Workers

and the

Churches

Chapter 1: Introduction

The contest for property and profit [in the United States West] has been accompanied by a contest for cultural dominance. Conquest also involved a struggle over languages, cultures, and religions, the pursuit of legitimacy in property overlapped with the pursuit of legitimacy in way of life and point of view.

PATRICIA N. LIMERICK, *The Legacy of Conquest*

On 1 April 1994, nearly 750 people assembled in the vineyards of Delano, California, about thirty miles north of Bakersfield. Before beginning a 330-mile march to the state capital in Sacramento, they celebrated a morning mass. During this service of worship, farm workers laid offerings on an altar adorned by a statue of La Virgen de Guadalupe, patroness saint of Mexico. Then they set out on their march, carrying the United Farm Workers' flag—a black Aztec eagle set against a red background. Along the way they sang "De Colores," a Mexican folk song celebrating spring colors in the countryside. One of the marchers was a woman whose wrinkled face and brown, downcast eyes suggested a life of sadness and hardship. She shouldered a large, wooden cross. A white, broad-rimmed hat shielded her eyes from the rays of the morning sun.[1]

A Comparative Study

This three-week march began on the sixty-seventh anniversary of the birth of farm labor leader César Chávez and ended on 23 April 1994, the first anniversary of his death. Organizers marked it as a pilgrimage, a *peregrinación*. They even described it as a penitential march. Dolores Huerta, longtime leader in the farm worker movement, and Arturo Rodriguez, new president of the United Farm Workers, identified the event's purpose as twofold: first, to encourage farm laborers and supporters to recommit themselves to unionizing efforts; and, second, to provide a means for these same people to do penance for having failed their "brother and founder"

César Chávez. Rodriguez, a holder of a master's degree in social work and son-in-law of Chávez, said, "[All] of us let César carry the responsibility for organizing the union on his shoulders. Now the burden for fulfilling César's dreams and our own rests squarely on each of us."[2]

In short, UFW officials were seeking to recapture the mood and momentum of the first farm workers' march held in March and April of 1966. Using the very same symbols—and invoking the name of Chávez as well—they were trying to reawaken the feelings and visions that Chávez had inspired twenty-eight years earlier. At that time the grape strike and boycott, or *La Causa* as it came to be known, had entered its seventh month. Greater visibility was crucial, and the union needed more members. So Chávez and others proposed a daring event—a civil rights march with a cultural twist.[3] A one-page paper, titled "Peregrinación, penitencia, revolución," was written and circulated. In it Chávez gave the upcoming march a triple meaning: it was a Mexican religious pilgrimage, a Lenten penitential procession, and an act of defiance, all in one. It was an opportunity, on the one hand, for the marchers to celebrate their spiritual heritage. It also served as a vehicle to express contrition, to do "public penance for the sins of the strikers, their own personal sins as well as their yielding perhaps to feelings of hatred and revenge" toward the growers. On the other hand, the protest elements of the event were undeniably clear. It signaled the Chicana/o's[4] demand for "justice, freedom, and respect from a predominantly foreign cultural community in a land where he was first."[5]

The 1966 march was a great success. The National Farm Workers Association recruited many new members and supporters and gained much needed news coverage. In addition, Schenley Industries, one of the companies against which the union was striking, bowed to the media exposure and capitulated to union demands. Chávez's creative use of religious and nationalist symbols associated with Mexican devotional Catholicism had accomplished its purposes. Over the next four years Chávez employed similar strategies that, along with other factors, led to the historic 1970 contract between the union and the Delano grape growers.

The term *Mexican devotional Catholicism* needs to be explained. It refers to a subcategory of what theologian Orlando Espín has called Latina/o popular Catholicism. He has written: "Its roots are planted in the medieval type of Christianity that preceded [the Reformation and the Council of Trent] and in the Iberian Reconquista process that formed the

Spanish character. However, it is not understandable without the sacral worldview and histories of the Amerindian, African, and mestizo people of Mesoamerica and the Antilles."[6] Although Latina/o[7] popular Catholicism sometimes seems synonymous with symbols such as an exaggerated crucifix and traditions such as home altars, Espín asserts it cannot be reduced to a "collection . . . of rituals and devotions."[8] Here is one definition he has offered:

> By its centuries-old history, Latino popular Catholicism can be characterized as an effort by the subaltern to explain, justify, and somehow control a social reality that appears too dangerous to confront in terms and through means other than the mainly symbolic. However, this popular religion is founded on the claim that the divine (identified by the people as the Christian divine) has been and is encountered by them in and through the symbols (ritual, ethical, and doctrinal) of popular Catholicism.[9]

I apply this definition to the more specific manifestation of "Mexican devotional Catholicism," in which symbols such as La Virgen de Guadalupe have originated. In short, Mexican devotional Catholicism is one expression of a New World interaction of Iberian, pre-Tridentine Christianity with the beliefs of oppressed indigenous Amerindians and Mexicans. It is a Catholicism that has been shaped by laypersons living primarily in rural settings.

Farm union developments outside California, particularly in Texas, did not go as well. Just a few months after the beginning of the West Coast conflict, melon pickers in the Lower Rio Grande Valley of Texas announced a wildcat strike. In the end it failed miserably, although the melon workers' strike somewhat mirrored events in California. For instance, in the grueling summer months of 1966 a pilgrimage/protest march made its way from Rio Grande City to the state capitol in Austin. Led by a Mexican American[10] Catholic priest and a Mexican American Baptist minister, it finally reached its destination on Labor Day. But the leadership, organization, and aims of the march compared poorly with the tight control and strategy of the California *peregrinación*.

The marches in California and Texas revealed an important religious dimension that came to characterize La Causa in the 1960s. Some of the most colorful and memorable elements of each pilgrimage—the *mestiza*[11] features of La Virgen de Guadalupe, the morning masses held in Mexican American Catholic parishes, and the mariachi music that gave the eve-

nings a festive atmosphere—attested to the importance and vitality of a
particular cultural-religious tradition. At the same time, however, Anglo[12]
priests and nuns and Anglo Protestant clergy often marched alongside
the farm workers. The traditions that those priests, nuns, and ministers
represented, respectively, the institutional Roman Catholic Church and
liberal Protestantism, also made up a vital part of the spiritual story of La
Causa.

This work is an examination of how the aforementioned religious dimensions interacted with one another and with the farm worker movement as a whole. This work is an exploration of the complex of religious
traditions, responses, and relationships that significantly affected the
farm worker movements through the 1960s. By comparing the interactions of these dimensions as events unfolded both in California and in
Texas, I hope to shed further light on the roles of religion in La Causa.
I seek to answer questions such as the following: How did the ethnic
makeup of Catholics in each state influence how bishops, priests, and others responded to the activities of the farm workers' unions? And: What
part did the prevailing Protestant ethos of each state play in the outcome
of the two strikes? The answers to these questions and others will illustrate
the importance of differences between California and Texas, not only in
terms of economics, politics, and demographics, but also of religious identity and strength.

In addition to highlighting the lay spirituality of Chávez and his creative use of Mexican devotional Catholicism, I will recount the roles of
the Roman Catholic Church in labor history as it has related to Mexican
Americans, Chicanas/os, and, to a lesser extent, Filipino Americans who
comprised a small but significant bloc within the union.

For instance, at the end of World War II a special organization, the
Bishops' Committee for the Spanish-Speaking, was created to oversee
work among Mexican Americans. Members of the Catholic hierarchy also
served as arbiters between the grape growers and the union, which led to
the first major contract for farm workers in the continental United States.
This victory occurred even as the national labor movement and its traditional support from the Catholic Church were already in decline.

Mainline Protestantism also played an important part in the unfold-
ing of La Causa. As early as the 1920s the ecumenical Council of Women
on Home Missions had developed summer programs among Mexican
and Mexican American farm laborers in California. A network of Anglo

women had spearheaded and maintained this work, which slowly evolved from a traditional ministry of mercy into one of advocacy. By the mid-1960s a further shift had occurred in which staff members placed themselves at the beck and call of Chávez's nascent farm worker union. Many of them were "new-breed" ministers who were active in the social and political issues of the day. These ministers' responses to La Causa represented one of the last major undertakings of liberal Protestantism in the late twentieth century.

After the Texas melon-workers' strike commenced in June of 1966, a number of individuals and groups became deeply involved in that arena. A longtime advocate of labor, the archbishop of San Antonio aided the strikers. Then the pan-Protestant Texas Council of Churches entered the conflict as well. Ultimately, however, the churches in Texas steered a middle course between growers and workers. Before 1970, both Catholic and Protestant leaders had already scaled back their efforts among farm workers. The actions of these religious groups reflected the realities of a state more conservative than those on the West Coast. Farm worker unionism survived in California and continued to fight hard-won battles through the 1970s. In Texas it left the fields and found expression as a general movement among young Chicanas/os.[13]

The farm worker movement was national in scope, even international at times.[14] This book, however, is limited to events in California and Texas. There are a number of reasons for setting these boundaries. First, the respective strikes in the vineyards and melon fields occurred nearly simultaneously. The Delano conflict began in September of 1965, the Rio Grande Valley struggle in June of 1966. Both strikes also were essentially resolved by 1970. In contrast, union leaders in other regions undertook efforts somewhat later. Another reason to confine the project to California and Texas is that these two states have long been regarded as especially suited for various comparisons. As specific subregions of the West, both are steeped in borderlands history, where the cultures of Native Americans, Mexicans, Mexican Americans, Anglos, and others have met and often clashed. Furthermore, California and Texas also have been known as "imperial states," exercising an economic influence far beyond their political borders. As geographer D. W. Meinig observed a generation ago:

Interestingly, in many parts of the West, the greatest resentment is not directed against "Easterners," but against Californians or Texans. In neither case is this feeling based primarily upon a strong sense of obvious cultural differences . . . rather it is a fear of an aggressive entrepreneurship backed by great wealth and vigorously growing and restless populations. Residents of neighboring regions see a kind of insidious, relentless imperialism, the one spreading over the entire Pacific Slope, the other north and west over Colorado and New Mexico, expressed in a wave of activities: speculators buying farm and ranch lands, choice urban sites, huge suburban tracts, entire recreational districts; financiers investing in retail chains, banks, newspapers, and broadcasting stations; people pouring in as vacationers, hunters, seasonal sojourners, and students.[15]

Yet the chapters that follow reveal that significant economic, political, and social differences set apart both states. For example, for all practical purposes California became part of the United States with the Gold Rush of 1849. Obviously, this phenomenon was international in scope. It immediately ushered in one of the most culturally and racially diverse populations the world has ever seen. In addition to Anglo-Americans, many other groups were represented. This commingling of races and languages helped to establish more of a pattern of cosmopolitanism in much of California. In contrast, Texas developed from the armed resistance of a predominantly Anglo-American group of settlers from the Lower and Upper South. Shouting "Remember the Alamo!" Sam Houston and others won independence from Mexico in 1836. Although a number of racial minorities eventually settled in Texas, the stamp of the Anglo-American tradition of the South left its impress for generations to come. As an extension of the South, Texas remained a bastion of provincialism well into the twentieth century. The rise of commercial agriculture in each state highlights another fundamental difference: Before the turn of the twentieth century, California was well on its way as the pacesetter for large farms and the growth of agribusiness. Not until the 1920s, however, did Texas begin to see family farmers, hired hands, and sharecroppers falling victim to "factories in the field." Urbanization rates illustrate at least a third difference: The growth of San Francisco and Los Angeles has long characterized much of California as urban, while Houston, Dallas, Fort Worth, San Antonio, and El Paso did not become major metropolitan areas until the 1960s and 1970s. This difference proved significant for La Causa, which found much of its regional support in the cities. Even as Texas was becoming a more urban state, many of its new city dwellers still held conservative rural values.[16]

The religious patterns of both states differed as well. For example, Protestant missionaries answered the call to go to California and minister to the men who had left home to search for fame and fortune in the gold fields. Such missionaries came primarily from the East and the Midwest, especially Congregationalists, Northern Presbyterians, and Northern Methodists. Inheriting strong theological and political traditions, they believed in religion as a positive force in society. By the end of the nineteenth century they also believed deeply in the ecumenical movement. For instance, San Francisco boasted one of the first and largest councils related to the Federal Council of Churches. In the 1960s this same local organization, a stronghold for liberal Protestantism on the West Coast, was among the first to support the grape strike.[17] Irish American Catholics represented another early cultural-religious group in San Francisco. They robustly entered local politics and were in the forefront of union efforts among teamsters and other workers. In the late 1800s San Francisco already enjoyed a reputation as a center of organized labor in the United States. Moreover, by the 1930s the Association of Catholic Trade Unionists had established a San Francisco chapter, and courses on the church and labor were regularly taught at the diocesan seminary. Significantly, a local Irish American priest passed on to César Chávez this tradition of church support for labor.[18]

The religious scene in Texas was a far cry from that in the San Francisco Bay area, although it resembled some conservative enclaves in Southern California. The Southern counterparts of the major Protestant faiths—Methodists, Baptists, and Presbyterians, all of them organizationally distinct from the Northern churches—dominated Texas towns and cities. European Protestants, especially German Lutherans and Czech Moravians, were scattered throughout the central part of the state. Political and social conservatism marked all of these groups, Prohibition serving as one of the few divisive issues. Unlike California, the ecumenical movement was anemic. For example, the Texas Council of Churches was not even founded until 1954, forty years after the creation of the California Council.[19] The Roman Catholic Church in Texas was equally conservative. After Texas passed into Anglo-American hands in 1836, a French-based missionary order rose to the challenge of reestablishing the Catholic Church in Galveston, Houston, San Antonio, Brownsville, and other locations. Although many sites were dedicated to Spanish-speaking Catholics, the arrival of new immigrants soon redirected the energies of the missionaries.

Organizing and funding parishes for Germans, Poles, Czechs, and others led to the relative neglect of Mexican Americans. Only in the post–World War II era did the Church undertake major efforts to improve both the spiritual and material well-being of Tejana/o[20] Catholics.[21]

In summary, twentieth-century California has resembled some of the social, economic, and political features of the Northeast. In certain respects, including religion, it was liberal in nature and helped to contribute to the overall success of La Causa in that locality. To be sure, California, on the one hand, has evidenced more than its share of racial prejudice and reactionary movements even as it has been characterized as a fairly tolerant and progressive state. On the other hand, Texas has shared many affinities with the South, namely, a heritage of conservative politics, right-to-work laws, and overt racism. The states' religious organizations have predictably followed the lead of other conservative institutions. Thus the failure of the farm worker movement in the Lower Rio Grande Valley should have come as no surprise to anyone. The real surprise was that some churches in Texas ever supported the workers at all.

The "Old" New Western History

This book's comparison of La Causa in California and Texas is interpreted in part by a methodology known as the New Western History. Since the 1960s historical studies of the U.S. West have undergone an extensive revision, which is well suited for understanding the farm worker movement. Two major themes of the New Western History, that is, economic dominance and ethnic conflict, lend themselves particularly well to the topic of La Causa. Put briefly, this revision issues from a broader historiographical shift that commenced in the 1950s. At that time some scholars of the U.S. West began to question the claims of the revered historian Frederick Jackson Turner. In the 1980s students of these postwar academicians laid to rest the Turner thesis, which regarded the frontier primarily as a westward movement that ended in the 1890s. Chief among these scholars has been Patricia Nelson Limerick, whose synthesis, *The Legacy of Conquest*,[22] created a sensation among historians. In both this work and others, secondary themes such as rugged "individualism, self-reliance, practicality, optimism, and a democratic spirit" as characteristic of the frontier have been debunked.[23] Furthermore, the New Western History focuses not only on economic power and ethnic conflict but also on a host of other issues. For example, most historians now regard the West less as a process and more as a geographical location, that is, the region lying roughly between the one-hundredth meridian and the West Coast. The related themes of aridity, environmental concerns, the role of the federal government, and mining and agriculture also are included as defining characteristics of the West. Last, these themes are no longer regarded as limited to the nineteenth century or even early 1900s but as extending well into the twentieth century, indeed to the present. As the newer scholars of the U.S. West readily acknowledge, the social history emerging in the 1960s has had a fundamental impact on their historical research and writing. It has tended to splinter the field into a number of subspecialties, for instance, cultural, women's, and urban studies, while eschewing an older generation's celebration of supposed frontier virtues. In this sense the New Western History has been compared favorably to newer interpretations of Southern history, in the sense that the former also admits its own dark past. Now that this revisionism of the West has been promoted for an entire generation, it may appropriately be identified—as it has been by its signature proponent—as the "Old" New Western History.[24]

At the same time, critics of this revisionism have charged that qualifying remarks by Frederick Jackson Turner in his later essay, "The Significance of the Section in American History," have been overlooked. In it he supplemented his original thesis with an understanding of the frontier as one of three major geographical regions in the United States, namely, the West, the other two being the North and the South.[25]

> [I]t must be clearly borne in mind that as the West grew in power of population and in numbers of new [U.S.] senators, it resented the conception that it was merely an emanation from a rival North and South; that it was the dependency of one or another of the Eastern sections; that it was to be so limited and controlled as to maintain an equilibrium in the Senate between North and South. It took the attitude of a section itself.[26]

This analysis of sections so convinced twentieth-century theologian, H. Richard Niebuhr, that he appropriated it to explain the phenomenon of U.S. denominationalism. He supposed that one frontier Protestant faith, distinct from and often opposed to sophisticated, urban churches in the East, characterized much of Western religiosity.[27] In the present work I also employ this concept of sections, but in a non-Turnerian fashion. In other words, I demonstrate that various groups migrating westward from the North and the South—and northward from Mexico—not so much created or embraced a new frontier faith as they transported with them their respective religious views and practices. Historian Earl Pomeroy, an early critic of Turner, generally regarded the West as imitative of the East. Writing in 1955 about the Pacific Slope, Pomeroy highlighted the continuities between the Northern East and the Far West. In terms of economics, politics, and culture, he asserted that the West was nearly as Eastern in outlook as the East itself. For example, he welcomed a then recent shift among scholars from stereotyped views of "fanatical and anti-intellectual" Western ministers trying to convert "immoral" lay people: "The current generation of church historians is coming to describe the western clergy less as promoters of an orgiastic expression of cultural primitivism than as major ties to the older way of life left behind in the East."[28]

Focusing mainly on the Pacific Rim, however, Pomeroy failed to take into account religious variety in the United States, East or West.[29] He may have well operated from the then popular premise that the legacy of New England Puritanism virtually defined Christianity, if not religion as a whole, in the United States. Obviously, numerous studies from the 1980s have concentrated on pluralistic themes. In his essay, "Regionalism and Religion in America," Jerald C. Brauer suggested reframing religious historiography to include not one but at least two Protestant visions. He identified a Northern vision, acting in the shadow of its Puritan heritage, as trying to realize the transfiguration of the United States into a "truly Christian nation, a righteous empire," in which "society as well as the individual" would undergo a glorious spiritual renewal. In contrast, "Southern evangelicals eschewed changing the world of economic and political power and settled for transforming and disciplining the individual."[30] I appropriate this thesis, holding that the Northern, urban vision especially extended into the Western subregion of the Pacific Slope, which is dominated by California. Conversely, the Southern, rural vision principally advanced into the subregion known as the Southwest, dominated by Texas. East Coast–West Coast religious ties helped to produce a liberal Protestantism first in Northern California and later in the southern part of the state, which, in tandem with the pro-labor wing of the Roman Catholic Church, supported the grape workers' strike and boycott in the late 1960s. Moreover, this Northern Protestantism and institutional Catholicism joined hands with a resurgent Latina/o popular religion issuing from south of the U.S. border. Combining various symbols and practices of Mexican devotional Catholicism with key elements of the civil rights movement, César Chávez consolidated all of these resources in behalf of La Causa. In short, this religious phenomenon expressed a late twentieth-century, half-secularized attempt to remold society according to a particular cluster of Judeo-Christian beliefs.

In contrast, the Southern vision extended its reach into Texas. Anglo Methodists, Presbyterians, and Baptists from the South peopled much of the state in the second half of the nineteenth century, eventually overwhelming Mexican American Catholics. Economically, politically, and culturally, Southern white Protestants shaped and promoted a way of life in Texas that conformed to that in much of the South. Religious institutions sought to convert individuals, but not society as a whole. Although Northern Protestantism and pro-labor Catholicism gained a foothold in the Lone Star State and came to the aid of the melon workers in the Rio Grande Valley, these outsiders eventually retreated from their partisan support and attempted a more traditional reconciliation between laborers and agribusiness. Notably, liberal Protestants and Catholics in Texas had no local, indigenous figure with the charisma and skills of Chávez to coordinate their efforts.

Other Methodologies

In the context of the New Western History, *Farm Workers and the Churches* relies heavily on this regional comparison of California and Texas. This book also uses several other methodologies, such as the sociological model known as resource mobilization theory. Essentially, this theory holds that the success of social movements stands or falls on identifying potential sources of support and then recruiting and maintaining them or, if you will, even exploiting them. For example, César Chávez and other union leaders appealed to a wide array of individuals and groups to respond to the plight of the farm workers. These individuals and groups not only included those that were religious in nature but also Anglo and Chicana/o college students, civil rights organizations, established labor unions, the media, and even a Chicana/o theater troupe. Chávez intuitively knew how to present La Causa in ways that were both general and specific enough in nature to strike a chord with all of the aforementioned sources of support, that is, until the times of the tumultuous 1960s and early 1970s exhausted themselves. Meanwhile, farm workers in South Texas failed to tap adequately enough similar resources.[31]

Among the resources to which Chávez turned were some of the symbols and practices of Mexican devotional Catholicism. Mentioned earlier was the march to Sacramento, which carried different meanings for different groups of people. Even the use of the banner of La Virgen de Guadalupe generates a rather complex, even ambivalent, message. As a *mestiza,* she is readily identified as an ethnic-national-religious image. But she also stands in solidarity with the poor and can even become a rallying point for the empowerment of Mexican American women. This book will seek, then, to examine the various shades of meaning of this symbol, including the points of view of several feminists, or *mujeristas.*[32]

Last, throughout this work, I offer vignettes or brief biographies of key religious figures who played major roles in the farm worker movement. Admittedly, this element of my work is more art than methodology and reflects a deeply held belief that the faith commitments of individual persons can be strong enough to spur slow-moving bureaucracies into action, if only for brief periods of time. As a longtime historian of religion in the U.S. West has noted: "although the twentieth century has often been viewed as an age of impersonal institutions, I believe that human activity lies at the heart of any meaningful historical narrative."[33]

Conclusion

The following chapters witness the drama of La Causa from the panoramic view of the New Western History, that is, from the twin perspectives of economic struggle and ethnic diversity. Looking at the farm worker movement as a whole, I will refer occasionally to its social, political, and economic dynamics. La Causa may thus be likened to a great play whose overarching theme I will return to from time to time. Its stage was set in California and Texas. Its cast of characters included commercial growers, multinational corporations, and their legal counsel and public-relations consultants. Other actors were farm workers, trade-union members, and labor leaders, as well as liberal politicians, left-leaning college students, and other supporters. Since this work is fashioned as a two-act play, the agricultural valleys of Southern and Central California and, at times, San

Francisco and Los Angeles serve as the settings for act 1. The backdrop for act 2 is South Texas, including the Lower Rio Grande Valley. Those whom I spotlight were the religious players, who often stood in the center of the stage and interacted with other characters. Each chapter—each scene, so to speak—presents a close-up of these changing religious players as the farm worker drama unfolded first in California and then in Texas.

Again, the following chapters are divided into two parts—California and Texas. So chapter 2, "The Church, Home Missions, and Farm Labor in California, 1920–40," examines the interactions of Roman Catholic bishops and priests, representatives of mainline Protestantism, and Mexicans and Filipinos in the Golden State, and especially within the context of organized labor. Chapter 3, "From Service to Advocacy, 1940–64," highlights a subtle but significant shift from traditional ministries of mercy toward a more assertive strategy of churches on behalf of farm workers. This chapter focuses on groups such as the Bishops' Committee on the Spanish Speaking, the Spanish Mission Band of San Francisco, and bureaucrats in the National Council of Churches. In chapter 4, "Religion and La Causa in California, 1962–70," the grape workers' strike is reenacted, including portrayals of Chávez, other union leaders, the staff of the California Migrant Ministry, and the Catholic priests who served as arbiters between the strikers and the grape growers.

Part 2 concentrates on Texas. Chapter 5, "Churches, Mexicans, and Farm Labor in Texas, 1930–60," recounts the building and expansion of the Catholic Church in the post-Mexican period, the nature and growth of major Protestant groups, and their interactions with one another and Mexican Americans, particularly in light of organized labor. In chapter 6, "The Church and the Farm Worker Movement in South Texas, 1966–69," I turn mainly to the Lower Rio Grande Valley and events leading up to and including the melon workers' strike. As in California the participants were quite colorful. On one side was a flamboyant but inexperienced Anglo organizer. Another labor leader spoke English with a strong Spanish accent, sported a long moustache, and wore a black hat, shirt, and trousers. A padre imagined himself a Latino version of Martin Luther King Jr., while an outspoken Irish American priest had flown combat missions in World War II. Another cast member was a quiet but energetic pastor of the Texas Migrant Ministry. On the other side of the stage were WASP (white Anglo-Saxon Protestant) growers, other conservative Anglos, and a strike-breaking captain of the Texas Rangers who had a white cowboy hat on his head, a cigar in his mouth, and a pearl-handled .45 in his holster. Valley clergy and church executives in San Antonio and Austin often stood in the middle of the stage, wringing their hands and wishing that the conflict were nothing more than a bad dream. Finally, a conclusion follows act 2/part 2, exploring further the place of this work in the historiography of religion in the U.S. West and, more importantly, how the Christian elements in the farm worker struggle influenced the broader Chicana/o civil rights movement.

Part 1: California

Chapter 2: The Church, Home Missions, and Farm Labor in California, 1920–40

The business of the church is divine. To seek the things of the next world, not of this. . . . Christ did not found the Church to be a mere humanitarian institution. The Church is a teacher. She works to bring God's grace to the souls of men. . . . She has, in fact, plenty to do to attend to her own business.

The Tidings, CATHOLIC ORGAN OF THE
ARCHDIOCESE OF LOS ANGELES, 1937

In the Treaty of Guadalupe Hidalgo in 1848 Mexico ceded most of the present-day states of New Mexico, Colorado, Arizona, Nevada, and California to the United States, officially opening California to further Anglo-American immigration. The following year miners discovered gold near Sacramento, and one of the greatest mixtures of humanity in world history descended on the northern part of what soon became the thirty-first state. In the 1870s a real-estate boom commenced in Southern California, and Anglos and others began settling in that region. Several religious traditions soon followed them, competing for the souls of gold seekers frequenting saloons and brothels in San Francisco and homesteaders searching for the good life in Los Angeles. Not surprisingly, the religious groups that prevailed were Irish American Catholics and Anglo-American Protestants, particularly Northern Methodists, Presbyterians, Episcopalians, and Congregationalists. Although Catholics were numerous in the Bay Area and WASPs in Los Angeles, each group became well established in both locales. Anglo Protestants quickly dominated regional economic life, while, at least in San Francisco, Irish Catholic labor countered with its own strength. In any event, the way of life of the indigenous Californios, that is, the *criollo* landowners who eventually sold or lost their land to Anglo businessmen, disappeared before the cultural and economic onslaught of these newcomers. The Mexican Revolution of the 1910s, however, brought a new generation of Spanish-speaking people to California, many of whom worked in agriculture.

This chapter examines the arrival, growth, and interaction of the aforementioned groups in California: Irish Catholic and Anglo Protestant institutions, Mexicans, and, to a lesser extent, Filipinos. It also explores the nature of popular religion among Mexicans and Filipinos. I then turn to the farm labor unrest of the late 1920s and 1930s, noting the tenuous positions in which various ministers of migrant workers often found themselves. The Roman Catholic Church in the United States also developed substantial ministries among Mexicans and less significantly among Filipinos, but in both instances only as religious subjects and not specifically as organized workers. Prior to the late 1940s such support occurred only in rare, isolated cases. This state of affairs persisted not because Mexicans and Filipinos were not involved in farm labor organizing. Indeed, they founded a number of unions and desperately needed the resources of the Catholic Church. Instead, other factors were at play. First, the Catholic Church in the Far West initially lacked institutional strength and functioned primarily as a frontier entity. Bishops struggled to establish parishes, schools, and basic social services that were well developed in the East. Second, cultural differences served as a major obstacle. Irish American clergy unfamiliar with Mexican and Filipino socioreligious traditions tried to impose a more formal Catholicism on their charges. In short, these priests often concentrated on the fundamentals of the faith as they understood them, administering the sacraments of the Eucharist, baptism, confirmation, and last rites. Little time and energy remained to address labor issues. Third, the political and social conservatism following World War I discouraged Catholic support for organized workers. Although the crisis of the Great Depression revitalized the labor movement, the Catholic Church extended its aid mainly to Euro-Americans, such as Irish American longshoremen in New York, German American factory workers in Milwaukee, and Polish coal miners in Pennsylvania. In contrast, the hierarchy in California avoided applying the social encyclicals *Rerum Novarum* (1891) and *Quadragesimo Anno* (1930) to the plight of Mexican and Filipino farm workers. Local prelates were acutely aware of the fear, distrust, and hostility of xenophobic Anglos and less aware of their own racial prejudices. So the Catholic Church in California was content to seek to transform Mexicans, Filipinos, and other immigrants into so-called good citizens. Suspicions of socialistic and communistic influences in farm labor unions also served to justify this approach.

Although nativism was a staple of life in Southern California, some Anglo Protestants nevertheless reached out to the increasing numbers of brown-skinned immigrants. Proponents of a moderate Social Gospel, Northern Methodists, Presbyterians, and Baptists founded Mexican home missions as early as the late nineteenth century. Spanish-speaking churches multiplied as Mexican refugees inundated Los Angeles and its environs in the 1910s. Protestants opened chapels, settlement houses, schools, and health clinics. In competition with the Catholic Church, mainline congregations not only tried to turn Mexicans into so-called good Americans but also into good, Bible-believing evangelicals. As in the case of their Roman Catholic counterparts, however, Protestants did not support West Coast immigrants as organized farm workers. On the contrary, individual denominations hardly ministered among agricultural laborers, concentrating instead on the urban scene. Protestant leaders left such work to the ecumenical Council of Women on Home Missions, even as Catholic authorities recruited women's religious orders to tend to the needs of immigrants based in rural communities.

Prologue 1: The Catholic Church and Home Missions in California, 1850–1920

In the 1840s, the Catholic Church in California was in a sorry state of affairs. The Franciscan missions had been secularized after Mexico won its independence from Spain, and Mexico City had all but neglected to send new priests to the far-flung province. In 1840 Francisco García Diego y Morena had been appointed bishop of a newly created diocese, which stretched all the way from present-day Northern California to the southern tip of Baja California. Father Diego took up residence at the old mission in Santa Barbara, but contracted tuberculosis and died in 1846.[1] A vicar general managed a handful of priests until a new bishop was assigned to the area. A firsthand account related the desperate straits in which the diocese found itself:

> There are but three Priests for the entire Southern District of California embracing a coast of some 500 miles. Of these there is but one who appears

to render any service whatever, and his character is so notoriously profligate that his influence and respect is [*sic*] entirely gone; he is a Spaniard, old and somewhat infirm and has been 29 years in this country, his name is Blaz Ordaz. The other, Antonio Rosales, quite a young man, well educated, but constantly sick (hypochondriac) and confined to his house, these are the only officiating Priests from this to some two hundred miles below. The other, Jose Maria Himenez is also a young man of unsteady mind constantly urging the people of the country to resort to violent measures to rid themselves of the American authorities. . . . I can not give you the exact situation in the upper country but am informed that it is even in a worse condition than this section.[2]

In 1850 the Vatican named Joseph Sadoc Alemany, O.P., as the new bishop. A native of Spain, he had labored a decade in the Ohio River Valley. Three years after his elevation to the bishopric, Baja California reverted to Mexico and Alemany's new see became known as the Diocese of Monterey. Yet a suffragan bishop was soon appointed to manage local affairs, while Alemany relocated to San Francisco, which became designated as an archdiocese. Once there he founded and strengthened religious institutions in order to meet the spiritual needs of gold seekers and others. As in Southern California, the Catholic Church in the northern part of the state was almost nonexistent. Only one parish in San Francisco, a former mission overseen by a Mexican priest, was open for mass. The vicar general of the Diocese of Oregon and one of his priests built a second parish in the city.[3]

Alemany quickly began searching for missioners from a number of sources. He secured fellow Dominicans from continental Europe; priests from All Hallows College in Dublin, Ireland; Jesuits who later founded colleges in San Francisco and Santa Clara; and a host of women religious. At least one priest, who later became known as "the Gold-Rush Bishop," was recruited from the mines. Throughout the archdiocese, several large churches were constructed, and Alemany sought to supply the largest groups of Catholic immigrants with priests who spoke their languages, mostly Irish, French, and German. Sadly, the Spanish speaking—like the Chinese—were essentially banned from the mines and also were ostracized in San Francisco. Only one parish in the city was established for Spaniards and their New World descendants, although Alemany opened up several others in Northern California.[4] In the meantime, women's religious orders opened and staffed a number of convent schools, orphanages, and hospitals. They included the Dominican Sisters, the Daughters of Charity, the Sisters of Notre Dame, and the Sisters of Mercy. This last group was especially distinguished by the work of Mary Baptist Russell, who later earned the title, "the Mother of San Francisco." Exemplifying the good servant in the twenty-fifth chapter of Matthew, she ministered among victims of the cholera epidemic, housed teenaged girls, visited the incarcerated, and befriended new immigrants. Yet one more order, the Sisters of the Holy Family, was founded in San Francisco and focused on tending to the poor, giving catechetical instruction to Catholic children who attended public schools, and offering child care to working-class parents. By the time Alemany retired in 1884, the Archdiocese was blessed with "over 200,000 Catholics with 175 priests, hundreds of women religious and more than 125 parishes."[5]

Alemany's successor, Patrick W. Riordan, enlarged upon this foundation. Educated in the Midwest and Europe, he taught a few years in Illinois and then served several parishes, most notably a large church in Chicago. Known as a "builder," he was then tapped to continue the work of Alemany. Among his projects were constructing a cathedral, establishing new parochial schools, and multiplying ministries of mercy. The founding of St. Patrick's Seminary in 1898 was his signal achievement. Its completion ushered in a new era, insofar as the archdiocese no longer needed to rely as heavily on priests from Europe and the eastern United States. A number of Catholic organizations also were established, such as mutual aid societies and social groups for young men and women. The San Francisco earthquake and fire of 1906, however, decimated much of Riordan's program of institutional growth. He spent most of the remainder of his tenure raising funds to repair the seminary, a hospital, and many parish buildings.[6] Yet as far as numbers are concerned, he left an extensive legacy, for instance, the following:

> There are 149 churches, 17 stations, 56 chapels, 276 priests, 1 theological seminary, 7 colleges and academies for boys, and 21 for girls, 1 Normal school, 37 parochial schools with 14, 822 pupils, 4 orphan asylums with 1,505 inmates, 1 infant asylum, 2 industrial schools, 1 protectory for boys, 1 deaf mute asylum, 6 hospitals and 6 homes for the aged poor.[7]

As in Alemany's time, certain ethnic groups benefited more than others, especially the Irish. Italian and Portuguese immigrants, who began landing at the docks in the 1880s, also fared well. Although not initially warmly received by either longtime Catholics or Anglo Protestants, they were nevertheless treated with much less prejudice than the small enclaves of Chinese and Japanese Catholics. Spanish-speaking Catholics in the archdiocese had all but disappeared.[8]

Californios continued to dominate life in the southern part of the state—at least for another generation. When Alemany moved to San Francisco, another Spaniard, Thaddeus Amat y Brusi, C.M., was assigned as suffragan bishop in Monterey. The latter served in that position from 1853 until his death in 1878. He and the Mexicans under his charge often clashed with one another. An early and prolonged controversy had to do with a struggling college in Santa Barbara. Born from the secularization of the local mission, the college was maintained by a handful of Mexican Franciscans. Amat designed, however, to replace the college with a regular parish and send the monks to evangelize among some of the remaining indigenous peoples. The monks and townspeople objected, and both sides appealed to Rome. In the end, Amat enjoyed a partial victory: even though the college survived, the Franciscans were removed. Two historians have remarked that the bishop frowned on the public processions and other practices of popular religion. He regarded them not only as unorthodox but also as potentially harmful to the future of Catholicism in Southern California, inasmuch as its churches might thus be further isolated by the growing Anglo Protestant population.[9]

In 1859 Amat moved to Los Angeles, and his see was renamed the Diocese of Monterey–Los Angeles. It was from there, with sixteen priests, that he began carving out a new Catholic presence. For example, the Vincentians began a school in Los Angeles. Even earlier, however, the Daughters of Charity had established their own work in Southern California, just as they had in San Francisco. They founded orphanage schools for Native American children and others in both Santa Barbara and Los Angeles. The Daughters also "opened the first medical dispensary" in Los Angeles, which later housed smallpox patients. In the 1870s ten nuns from another order, the Daughters of the Immaculate Heart, set up academies in Gilroy and San Luis Obispo, California.[10]

One of the best-known clergy in the early years of the diocese was Peter Verdaguer y Prat. In the early 1860s Amat had recruited him from his own native province in Spain. Verdaguer ministered among Native Americans in San Bernadino County, who affectionately called him El Padre Pedro.

After Amat's death in 1878, he was transferred to the plaza church in Los Angeles. A dozen years later, the pope named him the vicariate apostolic of Brownsville, Texas, and the Spanish speaking of Southern California lost one of the few priests who sympathized with their plight as a minority within their own church. The second and last bishop from Spain did little to stem this tide, not even residing at the old plaza church but instead at the new cathedral in the Anglo district of Los Angeles.[11]

The first Irish American bishop of Southern California was George T. Montgomery. He assumed his post in 1897, having already served in the diocese for four years. His time as the bishop in Los Angeles was brief, however, for he returned to the Archdiocese of San Francisco as coadjutor in 1902. Nevertheless, he made his mark on the diocese, and its institution building continued unabated. In 1890 the Sisters of Mercy organized a hospital in San Diego, followed by health clinics in El Centro and Oxnard. In 1908, in Santa Barbara, the Franciscan Sisters of the Sacred Heart also founded a hospital. Meanwhile, the Missionary Sisters of the Sacred Heart arrived to minister among the increasing numbers of Italians. Mother Frances Cabrini surveyed Southern California and secured some property for the order, which soon opened an orphanage and a school for girls. Eventually a shrine was built on a site in the San Fernando Valley, accompanied later by an academy.[12]

Parishes in the diocese grew at an exponential rate, aided to no small degree by the Catholic Church Extension Society. Founded in 1905 and based in Chicago, it had a mandate, among other things, to provide funds "to build, remodel and furnish thousands of chapels, catechetical centers, rectories and parochial utility buildings." By 1924 the society was responsible for nearly a dozen parishes in the Diocese of Monterey–Los Angeles, at least two of which were Spanish-speaking congregations. The organization also helped to maintain a Native American school in Banning, California, as well as a mission for Japanese Catholics in Los Angeles.

The Catholic Church and Immigrant Mexicans, 1910–30

In the late nineteenth century, most Catholic bishops initially distrusted the labor movement in the United States. Yet Pope Leo XIII upheld labor's right to exist as expressed in his famous social encyclical *Rerum Novarum* (1891). While doubtless designed as a conservative document, it nevertheless marked the Vatican's first positive response to the dramatically changed relations between workers and employers since the onset of the industrial revolution. Over the next thirty years a number of priests argued passionately for a liberal interpretation of *Rerum Novarum.* Many of them served working-class parishioners in the urban East and Midwest.[13] A notable exception was Peter C. Yorke, a diocesan priest in San Francisco. Raised and educated in Ireland, Yorke was ordained in 1888 and sent to the Archdiocese of San Francisco to minister among his countrymen. Although a number of ethnic groups converged on the city following the Gold Rush, the Irish were particularly well represented. They became employed in the building trades and quickly proved themselves able workers. In the relatively egalitarian society of late nineteenth-century San Francisco— for white, English-speaking persons, that is—they soon dominated social and political life. By the time Yorke reached the Bay Area, Irish American unions had already gained substantial power. For example, Denis Kearney, who was known as "the people's dictator," had already founded the Workingmen's Party in 1877. It advocated "the eight-hour day, compulsory education, statewide schools, banking reform, tax restructure and direct election of [state] senators." By the early 1900s, then, the city boasted over 180 labor organizations, distinguishing San Francisco as the center of unionism in the largely nonunion West. In this context, Yorke served as a mouthpiece for Irish Americans in general and unionism in particular. During the San Francisco Strike of 1901 he authored pro-labor essays and spoke at fundraising events. In later years he continued to support organized labor, often using his Irish nationalist paper, *Leader,* as a public platform for his views. Opposing socialist arguments in favor of unionism, he relied on workers' rights as explicated in *Rerum Novarum.* Yorke, of course, never spoke out in favor of Mexican or Filipino workers. On the contrary, he would have regarded them as a threat to Irish American interests. Yet his legacy may have ultimately influenced unionism among Mexican agricultural workers. A priest who inherited this pro-labor tradition passed on its precepts to César Chávez in the early 1950s.[14]

Edward J. Hanna, Archbishop of San Francisco from 1915 to 1935, dealt directly with Mexican labor on at least one occasion. As president of the California Commission on Immigration and Housing, he once called for limits on the influx of Mexicans. Reeling from the post–World War I recession, established unions feared the new immigrants as potential strikebreakers. In the name of organized labor—Irish American, German American, and Italian American, that is—the Catholic Church found itself in the awkward position of opposing one of its own constituencies. Mexican immigration from the 1910s to 1930s is an ironic and complicated story, some of which revolves around the relationships between Mexicans and the Catholic Church in Southern California.[15]

Beginning in 1910, a flood of individuals and families poured into the U.S. Southwest in order to escape the ravages of the Mexican Revolution and to seek economic betterment. One historian has noted that they came not only from the northern states along the international border but also "from such central plateau states as Jalisco, Guanajuato, and Michoacán," often depending on a vast network of railroads leading into the United States.[16] One account has estimated the numbers of Mexicans and other Spanish-speaking people in San Francisco and Los Angeles at 7,000 and 125,000, respectively. John J. Cantwell, the prelate of the consecutive Dioceses of Monterey–Los Angeles and Los Angeles–San Diego and the Archdiocese of Los Angeles from 1917 to 1947, faced a formidable task in meeting the needs of these new Catholic residents.[17] Despite the challenges confronting him, he responded surprisingly well. Building on a system of charitable services begun by his predecessor, he oversaw an ambitious construction of social welfare. Ultimately known as the Catholic Welfare Bureau, this agency recruited, trained, and deployed a remarkable number of professionals and volunteers:

> Within two years after its establishment, the association reported cash expenditures for its vast programs totaling $140,178.71. That figure, impressive as it was, excluded entirely the donated services of thirty-six physicians, twenty-five lawyers, fifteen volunteer workers and nurses and twenty child caseworkers. By 1923, thirty-seven professionally-trained [sic] persons were employed to direct and supervise twenty-eight institutions throughout the diocese.[18]

Mexican refugees benefited from much of this charitable work. The archdiocese established the Immigrant Welfare Department and the educational Confraternity of Christian Doctrine to address their needs. Community centers soon began offering "year-round recreational, educational, and social programs for Mexican-Americans, along with courses in homemaking and athletic and club activities for the younger generation."[19]

While these services were limited mostly to residents of greater Los Angeles, some aid also was available in outlying areas. A few women's religious orders tended mainly to the needs of rural Mexicans, particularly Our Lady of Victory Noll Sisters, better known as the Missionary Catechists. Founded in 1915, the Missionary Catechists specialized in ministry among Mexicans in the U.S. West. Primarily educators, members of the order also provided food, clothes, and medical care to farm workers. The Catechists became prominent in remote border communities such as Brawley, Calipatria, Calexico, and El Centro—all in the Imperial Valley of California. Of course, these relief efforts predictably included programs of Americanization, for church leaders assumed that rapid acculturation was in everyone's best interest. By the end of the 1920s the archdiocese directed over half of its welfare budget to Mexicans in Southern California. As early as 1919, Cantwell had assigned the assistant director of Catholic Charities, Jesus Ramirez, to oversee this task. Administrators also placed exiled Mexican clergy and founded new missions and parishes. In gratitude, the Catholic Church in Mexico invited Cantwell to participate in the 1940 Pan American ceremonies in Mexico City.[20]

Still, the work of the Roman Catholic Church seldom extended to Mexicans—and Filipinos—as members of labor unions. Understandably, the California Catholic Church had to concentrate first on basic relief efforts. Second, many clergy also were unacquainted with or ignored liberal interpretations of workers' rights as given in *Rerum Novarum*. Third, unlike other Catholic immigrants in the United States, most Mexicans did not receive ministrations from indigenous clergy, that is, those who were both Spanish speaking and intimately familiar with their religious culture and needs. Last, the Catholic Church had to assist its Mexican constituency discreetly so as not to strain further its own relations with a largely antilabor, antiradical, and antiforeign Anglo Protestant majority. Cantwell, for example, was not above muzzling priests who espoused pro-labor views. A case in point was Robert E. Lucey, a one-time director of the diocese's welfare bureau. As a seminarian in San Francisco, Lucey was exposed to the works of Catholic social theorist John Ryan. Later, in Los Angeles, Lucey unabashedly promoted his teachings. Confronted with the plight of Los Angeles' unemployed and underemployed workers, he critiqued economics through a liberal reading of *Rerum Novarum* and, later, *Quadragesimo Anno*. He then regularly disseminated these views on a church-sponsored radio show. On the pretext of financial constraints,

however, Cantwell eventually cancelled the program, an act Lucey regarded as blatant censorship.[21]

Prologue 2: The Protestant Church in California, 1850–1920

When world adventurers converged on Northern California in the mid-
nineteenth century, local Protestant clergy understandably felt overwhelmed. Nevertheless, they struggled to rise to the evangelistic challenges
before them. Northern Methodists, Presbyterians, Baptists, Congregationalists, Episcopalians, and Unitarians preached and founded churches
in the San Francisco Bay Area and as early as 1849 had established a cluster
of congregations between San Francisco and Sacramento and a number of
mission points as well. Many of these pastors were nurtured and educated
in the evangelical tradition of New England. They felt a moral obligation
to minister among gold seekers in order to dissuade them from the vices of
drinking, gambling, prostitution, and violence. In contrast, other clerics
moved to Northern California as a geographical springboard from which
to launch missions in the Far East. Yet others, especially lay preachers,
arrived for the same reason as most newcomers, that is, to take their turn
at panning for gold. In time, Protestant groups also founded missions
among other ethnic populations, for example, the Chinese. Little evidence
currently exists, however, in regard to work among Mexicans. Ministers
from New England, the Mid-Atlantic States, and the growing Midwest
were preoccupied with adapting a once familiar and morally settled way
of life to a completely new set of circumstances.[22]

Mexican missions were more successful in the "Southland," which, as
Anglos began inhabiting the region from the 1870s, became the popular
name for Southern California. So many of these new residents were midwesterners that, by the 1920s, Los Angeles was known pejoratively as the
"Sea Coast of Iowa," "Iowa with palm trees," and "Double Dubuque."[23]
They were "the middle-aged from the middle class of the middle west
[sic]."[24] The first wave of this migration followed the laying of tracks for
the Southern Pacific Railroad in the 1870s and 1880s. Ranchos were soon
replaced by wheat fields, truck gardens, and sheep pastures. Real-estate
promoters later stereotyped local Mexicans and restricted them to particular neighborhoods, while promoting greater Los Angeles to Anglos from

the East. The latter group congregated in distinctive enclaves. Outsiders could even identify these communities by religious denomination by simply noting their respective educational institutions. Occidental College was Presbyterian, Pomona College was Congregational, and the University of Redlands was founded by the American Baptists.

> . . . Los Angeles was emerging based upon its conservative political and social outlook. The region remained more or less a Protestant community, perpetually boosterish in outlook. Materialistic as well, it celebrated long-held Anglo-Saxon values in its clubs, churches, and schools.[25]

These Protestants usually treated their Catholic neighbors with misunderstanding, indifference, and intolerance. As increasing numbers of Anglo-Americans settled in the Los Angeles basin, early cooperative efforts among Protestants, Catholics, and Jews succumbed to sectarian posturing. For example, Bishop Thaddeus Amat reacted quickly to Presbyterians who were proselytizing members of his Mexican flock. He established parochial schools not only for educational purposes but also to limit social interaction between Catholics and Protestants, thereby hoping to discourage mixed marriages. Temperance served as another divisive issue, not to mention other moral crusades. While attempts by Anglo-Saxon Progressives to prohibit alcohol were defeated in heavily Catholic San Francisco, the Women's Christian Temperance Union prevailed in the more homogeneous suburbs encircling Los Angeles. Protestants were even able to force the retirement of Amat's successor. The next bishop had to found a local chapter of the Catholic Truth Society to counteract the propaganda of Anglo Protestant groups, such as the American Protective Association.[26]

Most Anglo Protestants in Southern California especially ignored or deplored a particular group of Catholics, namely, the ever-growing Mexican population. A handful of evangelists, however, responded positively to the new group of immigrants. Influenced by the moderate arm of the Protestant Social Gospel, a few religious leaders began launching ambitious service programs. Home mission boards apportioned funds and recruited Anglo supervisors who were theologically trained and had previously served as missionaries in Latin America. In seminary some of these pastors had enrolled not only in courses on theology and the Bible but also in sociology, social work, and economics. So, church leaders supplemented conventional practices such as preaching stations and Sunday school classes with charitable activities. These activities often centered on Americanization efforts and so also served as conscious attempts to maintain a Protestant culture in an increasingly pluralistic nation.[27]

The Northern Baptists began coordinating Mexican home missions in Southern California in 1911. The Presbyterian Church, U.S.A., followed in 1913, assigning former missionary Robert McLean to head the newly created Mexican Department of Home Missions. In 1918 his son, Robert N. McLean, succeeded him, evidencing a trend toward greater professionalism. The younger McLean accelerated the shift from traditional evangelism to social and educational programs, opening six Homes of Neighborly Service as well as establishing night classes, an employment agency, a dental clinic, and children's summer camps. More than any other Protestant denomination, the Northern Methodists excelled in work among Mexican immigrants. Their Women's Home Missionary Society founded the Frances DePauw Home of Los Angeles in 1898, which held sewing classes and club activities for Mexican girls and women. The Spanish-American Institute opened its doors in 1913. The Plaza Community Center in Los Angeles quickly followed, holding the honor as the largest Methodist institution dedicated to home missions among Mexicans. Located on East Sunset Boulevard, it housed an employment agency, a medical clinic, a welfare department, a health club, and other ministries. More than any other individual, Vernon M. McCombs shined as Methodism's guiding light for early Mexican projects in California. A former missionary in Peru, he led work among Mexican, Filipino, Portuguese, and Italian immigrants. He epitomized the home missionary who bridged two distinct traditions: he exuded an old-fashioned, heartfelt faith but also embraced the new bureaucratic style, complete with academic degrees from Drew Theological Seminary and New York University as well as extensive training in Mexico and Central America.[28]

> McCombs was a son of missionaries and had seminary during the period when the social gospel movement was the major religious trend of the time. He represented an interesting transitional blend of missionary evangelism and social-gospel ideology. In defining the objects of his attention, he was the traditional missionary, with what might be called a vocation for one particular people—the Mexicans. . . . And in common with other Protestant missionaries who had preceded him, he employed Mexican and Mexican American evangelists.[29]

The 1910s and 1920s thus marked the advent of the segregated period of Protestant home missions among Mexicans, which persisted into the 1950s. These Mexican-Protestant congregations typically held fundamentalist views, regardless of denominational affiliation. This state of affairs was perpetuated by the inferior education of local shepherds who shared the ghettoized experiences of their spiritual sheep. Traditionally Catholic Mexicans and middle-class Anglo Protestants alike shunned them. Community centers provided some cultural interaction between Mexicans and Anglos, but underscored only too well the gaping inequities that divided them.[30]

Mexican Devotional Catholicism and Filipino Catholicism

While some Mexicans joined the Protestant faith, the vast majority remained in the fold of the Catholic Church. Yet the religion they knew departed from or was even at odds with much of U.S. Catholicism. Mexicans and Mexican Americans have often expressed their spirituality in very personal, artistic, and experiential ways. In contrast, Catholics of Irish, German, and French descent were likelier to follow official practices, such as solemnizing marriage by means of church weddings, regularly attending confession, and encouraging holy orders. In part, scholars of the Latin American church attribute these differences to the transmissions of two kinds of Catholicism to the New World. On the one hand, Catholics in Northern and Central Europe had accepted and implemented the reforms of the Council of Trent (1545–64), which proscribed glaring church abuses while also consolidating ecclesiastical authority and standardizing liturgical practice. This newer Catholicism was eventually transported to most of North America. On the other hand, an older Catholicism that was fundamentally medieval and pre-Tridentine in nature prevailed in Spain. Having recently defeated and expelled the Moors, the Spanish Crown exported its unapologetically crusading faith to Latin America. Tridentine Catholicism stressed a more rational approach to religion, while much of Spanish Catholicism appealed to the senses and emotions. One expression produced "mass-and-sacraments" Catholics, while the other continued to cultivate the faith through oral traditions, dramatic rituals, and religious art.[31]

Still, the introduction of pre-Tridentine Catholicism hardly explains all of the peculiarities of the Latin American church. Other factors also have shaped the spirituality of the indigenous peoples and the descendants of their conquerors, such as antecedent religions and the dynamics of the Conquest itself. In other words, the *indios* could not understand much less accept the new faith imposed on them unless it could somehow be localized and so become their own. This phenomenon occurred in Mexico in 1531 when the Indian peasant Juan Diego encountered La Virgen de Guadalupe on the hill at Tepeyac, a place where the Nahuatl goddess Tonantzin was once worshipped. Immediately he noticed the Virgin's dark features and realized that, like him, she too was an *india*. The miraculous imprint of her image on his *tilma,* or cloak, convinced the bishop that a shrine should be built in her honor. Thus a conquered people both accepted the faith of their new masters and reinterpreted it to meet their own needs.

The veneration of La Morenita, as the Virgin also is called, has ultimately surpassed devotions of other Marian apparitions—both in the Old and New World—for she has held an extraordinarily revered place in the hearts of her devotees. For example, other expressions of Mary in Latin America too have received a great deal of devotion, such as Nuestra Señora de la Garidad del Cobre (Cuba), La Virgen de la Providencia (Puerto Rico), La Virgen de la Cisne (Ecuador), and even in Mexico itself, namely, Nuestra Señora de la Lagos. Yet Guadalupe has eclipsed them all, holding a special place in Latina/o communities in the United States. Historically Mexican *mestizos,* such as revolutionaries Father Miguel Hidalgo and Emiliano Zapata, claimed her, as did much of the *criollo* propertied class.[32] Yet chiefly the indigenous population has felt the deepest affinity for La Virgen. Theologian Virgilio Elizondo writes:

> For a people whose tragic existence began with conquest and rape, the only real beginning could take place in an event which was of equal or greater magnitude than the trauma they had suffered. Only in an event which clearly originated in heaven could the conquest and rape of Mexico be reversed, and a people truly proud of their new existence begin a "raza" who had been born not out of a violated person but out of a pure and inviolate mother. This compassionate mother would "remedy" the worst of all miseries, pains and lamentations caused by the conquest with its subsequent illegitimate birth.[33]

As with many symbols, La Virgen de Guadalupe has experienced a multitude of meanings over the years. Not only do they include the continuum from gentle comfort to political independence for Mexicans, Mexican Americans, and others in general, but for Latinas in particular. Feminists and *mujerista* theologians have focused on how various meanings ascribed to La Virgen have alternately served, on the one hand, to keep Latinas stereotyped as submissive, sacrificial wives to, on the other, empowering them to resist and perhaps even break the cultural, economic, and political chains that have enslaved them. This theme will be considered at length in chapter 4.[34]

Closely associated with devotion to La Virgen has been the Mexican people's acknowledgment of and identification with the suffering Christ, often known as the Man of Sorrows, or El Nazareno. As in the case of Mary, Mexicans and other Latin Americans inherited this image from Europe but typically exaggerated it as evidenced, for example, in graphic crucifixes.[35] A third emphasis of Latina/o popular religiosity, of which Mexican devotional Catholicism is a subcategory, has been its display of colorful rituals. Once again, this tendency has not been unknown in Europe, particularly in Spain. Yet in Latin America it reached new heights. For example, pilgrimages to various shrines have been legendary, either to produce cures for physical ailments or as gestures of gratitude for prayers already answered. Dramatically portrayed events in the liturgical calendar also have evolved, such as Las Posadas and Los Pastores at Christmas and the reenactment of the Passion on Good Friday (El Vía Crucis).

Popular religiosity has permeated family life as well, such as devotions centered on home altars (*altarcitos*). These intimate worship spaces can be simple or elaborate and almost always are maintained by women. Mexican women usually have been responsible for nurturing and sustaining faith in the family.[36] This religious role of women may stem in part from their identification with La Virgen. It may also reflect a fourth characteristic of Mexican Catholicism, namely, the perennial shortage of priests. Although pastoral oversight was sufficient in urban settings, rural communities were in constant need of resident priests. One of the reasons for the low numbers of clergy lay in the fact that the Catholic Church was reluctant to recruit candidates from the ranks of *indios* and *mestizos*. This policy unfortunately helped to divide clergy and laity along the lines of race and class. Intellectuals exposed to the ideals of the Enlightenment and peasants alike resented the prestige of the priests and the Catholic Church as a whole. A type of anticlericalism festered that eventuated in the persecution of the church from 1911 to 1937.[37]

As Mexicans carried their faith with them as they streamed into the U.S. Southwest in the 1910s and 1920s, the beliefs and rituals often clashed with those of Tridentine Catholicism. Irish American and French American priests were appalled at many Mexican religious customs, scorning them as rife with superstition and syncretism. These clergy were also disappointed that Mexicans neglected mass and failed to fulfill other religious duties. The poverty of their new parishioners evoked antipathy as well. By the same token, the new immigrants often felt repelled by clerical attitudes of superiority and authoritarianism. Racism played its part, too. Occasional church signs instructing Mexicans to sit in pews in the rear of the sanctuary hardly endeared them to their co-religionists. In spite of these obstacles, however, a number of priests, nuns, and laypersons ministered faithfully among the Spanish speaking. These missionaries cultivated an attitude of *simpático,* a Spanish term connoting warmth, compassion, and dedication.[38]

In addition to Mexico and the rest of Latin America, Iberian Catholicism accompanied Spain's conquest of the Philippines. Consequently, Filipinos have shared some affinities with Mexican Catholicism, for instance, relative neglect stemming from an inadequate supply of priests. At the same time, several features distinguished the colonizations and evangelizations of Filipinos and Mexicans. First, since the Philippines were among the last and most far-flung of the Spanish conquests, a more sophisticated, streamlined, and tolerant bureaucracy ruled over the islands. In essence, the governors subjected the indigenous peoples to less disruption and cruelty than Latin American groups suffered, an approach emulated by various religious orders. A second difference lay in the challenge of communication in each colony. Although by no means the lingua franca of Mexico during the Conquest, Nahuatl nevertheless served as a convenient medium for government business in New Spain. Dialects in the Filipino archipelago were even more numerous and dispersed. So Augustinians, Franciscans, and other Catholic missionaries had to learn not only the dominant Tagalog tongue but also many other languages throughout the coastlines, the lowlands, and the mountains. Preservation of local languages necessarily led to some preservation of local customs and mores, including those that missionaries wanted to abolish. A third trait distinguished Mexico and the Philippines, namely, the level of preexisting cultures. The Spanish Crown and the Catholic Church, with great difficulty, adapted some of the hierarchical nature of highly developed Aztec law, religion, and culture to their own. Filipino tribes meanwhile relied on kinship networks for governance and customs. These localized and ever-changing expressions of influence retarded the advance of Western notions of centralized power. Filipinos ultimately did not receive the catechetical instruction of the missionaries in toto but were even more selective and discriminating than Mexicans in blending their new faith with the beliefs of their ancestors. Hence, the assessment of historian John Leddy Phelan that the "Hispanization" of the Philippines, including Catholic conversion, was more "indirect" than in Mexico. Moreover, the United States limited early Filipino immigration to single males, many of whom never married. This phenomenon may help to explain another peculiarity of the Filipino Catholic Church in the United States, that is, its relatively small size. It has had parishes in the agricultural communities of Salinas, Stockton, and Watsonville, as well as some in San Francisco, Oakland, Sacramento, and San Diego.[39]

California Agribusiness, Migrant Workers, and Labor Strikes

In the 1920s and 1930s, many Mexicans and Filipinos in California lived and labored in the cities. A number of them also were migrant farm workers. Exploitation and despair often characterized their experiences. Yet they hoped and fought for a better life, occasionally even reaching across racial and cultural barriers toward that end. In order to place their struggles in context, however, a description of the growth of California agribusiness is first necessary.

A geographical wonderland, California consists of coastal canyons, mountain chains, valleys, and deserts. Spanning several hundred miles, the Great Central Valley stretches from north of Sacramento to Bakersfield in the south.[40] Its two subregions, namely, the Sacramento Valley and the San Joaquin Valley, first underwent commercial cultivation in the 1860s. After the gold mines played out, entrepreneurs obtained California land grants through legal and extralegal maneuvers.[41] These speculators then converted these ranchos into a succession of agricultural concerns. First came the wheat farms, then an array of fruit orchards, and finally cotton in the 1910s. Meanwhile, the Coastal Salinas Valley became renowned as the lettuce capital of the world. Lettuce also was produced in the newly irrigated Coachella and Imperial valleys in Southern California, as well as cantaloupes, tomatoes, asparagus, and nuts.[42] They all required labor-intensive cultivation. From 1870 to 1920 Anglo growers systematically recruited racial minorities to harvest the crops. The first workers were members of landless Native American tribes, followed by Chinese immigrants who had been banished from the gold and silver mines or had finished building railroads. In 1900 growers imported Japanese laborers and then Sikhs a few years later. Crossing the border to escape civil war and economic hardship, Mexicans soon followed. Finally, commercial farmers shipped workers from the Philippines. The vast majority of California agriculture never knew the intimate owner-hired hand relationship that prevailed on family farms in the East and Midwest. Independent labor contractors recruited workers, who were then supervised by local foremen. Absentee growers living in San Francisco or Los Angeles were not uncommon. Built on the backs of foreign labor, this large-scale agriculture eventually propelled California beyond all would-be competitors. Technology, of course, played its own part in the form of extensive irrigation systems and the invention of the refrigerated railroad car. New markets opened up, stimulating crop specialization, the construction of process plants, and the creation of new distribution companies. Growers founded associations as early as the 1880s and soon became powerful players in local, state, and regional politics.[43] For example, public taxes largely financed several irrigation projects, representing one of agribusiness's early lobbying achievements. An economic historian has noted: "By 1910, the foundations of modern California agriculture had been firmly laid."[44]

Farm workers were almost always the losers in these "factories in the field." Their economic status, migratory lifestyle, and identities as racial minorities constantly set them apart from others in rural society. Yet they periodically rebelled against the treatment suffered at the hands of employers and other Anglos. In an early and rare display of interethnic cooperation, Mexican and Japanese sugar-beet workers called a strike in 1903. In that same year farm laborers organized a union in San Jose.[45] The most spectacular clash occurred in 1913 in the Sacramento Valley. Known as the Wheatland Riot, it broke out at a hops ranch during harvest time. The owner had resorted to the common ploy of over-advertising for laborers and thereby depressing wages. Furthermore, he refused to provide even remotely decent living and working conditions—a perennial practice in migrant agricultural work. Labor representatives objected, violence broke out, and two workers and two law enforcement officers were killed. Several laborers were subsequently tried and convicted of murder.[46]

In the late 1920s, farm workers, particularly Mexicans and Filipinos, were willing once again to fight for higher wages and better working conditions. Self-help groups played a pivotal role. Known as *mutualistas,* these organizations provided their members modest financial assistance and social opportunities like celebrations of national and cultural holidays. These organizations later served as the basis for fledgling unions. For instance, agricultural laborers founded La Union de Trabajadores del Valle Imperial in 1928.[47] It was concentrated in several border towns in the Imperial Valley, which was originally a desert transformed into an agricultural breadbasket by intense, early twentieth-century land promotion. The union's membership of approximately twelve hundred asked for concessions from cantaloupe growers. When farmers denied their requests, a spontaneous strike followed. Local law enforcement quickly suppressed it, arresting labor leaders, closing establishments frequented by union members, and threatening deportation. Although a failure, the strike nevertheless signaled a new resolve among workers. Mexican unionists not only realized the need to develop better organizing techniques but also to overcome a reluctance to join ranks with other groups.[48]

Opponents branded La Unión de Trabajadores as a front for communists. Yet it was actually a politically conservative organization. Ironically, communists thereafter did become involved in unionizing efforts among migrant farm workers. When growers began slashing wages as early as 1930, communist labor organizers appeared and intervened in strikes already underway. Preoccupied with bread-and-butter issues, Mexican workers simply ignored or were even unaware of the political orientation of their Anglo strike leaders. The latter first tried to capitalize on the Brawley lettuce strike of January 1930 and, in the spring, in a nearby cantaloupe strike. Organized as a local of the Agricultural Workers Industrial League, this group held out in both strikes for only a few weeks. In order to broaden its base, it later recruited cannery-shed workers. Relocating to more promising sites, it initiated strikes in 1933 in Northern California and then Tulare, Oxnard, and San Diego in the southern part of the state. While these strikes were usually peaceful and enjoyed modest success, others were marred by vigilante-inspired violence. Farmers physically evicted cherry pickers in San Jose, grape harvesters in Fresno and Lodi, and cotton pickers near Bakersfield. Some workers complained so desperately that the Los Angeles chapter of the American Civil Liberties Union investigated their claims. Vigilantes in the Imperial Valley soon kidnapped one of its representatives, roughed him up, and dumped him off at the county line. Groups like the Associated Farmers meted out this frontier justice. Local law enforcement unofficially supported them by arresting union organizers whom Anglo juries then convicted and Anglo judges sentenced. By 1934 these sanctions had destroyed the union. The Imperial Valley thus aptly earned its nickname as "the Cradle of Vigilantism."[49]

Mexican women were seldom involved in these episodes of violence. Their gender-specific duties of preparing food, caring for children, and other camp activities usually kept them out of harm's way. Yet *mexicanas* occasionally accepted more direct and dangerous roles, for example, in a cotton strike in 1933. Employing a not unknown practice in Mexico, strike leaders sent women to the picket lines, assuming that substitute workers in the fields would be less likely to assault females. This ploy, however, sometimes led to mixed results, especially when the women themselves incited the physical encounters:

> They threatened and cajoled strikebreakers, using the female issue of food: confronting scabs at the Hanson ranch [in Corcoran, California], the women warned them, "Come on out, quit work, we'll feed you. If you don't, we'll poison you." Exhortations turned to threats and then to violence. Some women, armed with lead pipes and knives—evidently in expectation of using methods more persuasive than verbal appeals—attacked the pickers. The male strikebreakers retaliated. One woman was brutally beaten.[50]

Filipino farm workers suffered the same privations and indignities as Mexicans and, since the prospect of returning to their homeland was dim, they perhaps bore their suffering with greater pain. They were originally shipped to the West Coast after the U.S. Congress imposed severe immigration restrictions on other foreign workers. Following the Spanish-American War the Philippines had become a protectorate of the United States, which afforded California growers a legal means to circumvent the spirit of the new immigration law. Although fewer than 6,000 Filipinos had entered the mainland at the beginning of the 1920s, over 45,000 did move to the United States by 1930—most of them less than thirty years of age. Some labored in Alaska's salmon canneries and others took menial jobs in the restaurant and hotel industries. Yet the vast majority worked in California agriculture. They were especially well represented in Stockton, Salinas, Fresno, and the Imperial Valley. As young, single males they were regarded as a social problem by xenophobic Anglos. The Filipinos frequented bars and dance halls to seek out female companionship. The specter of miscegenation ever present, local Anglos often reacted by vilifying them as sexual predators and ne'er-do-wells. Two such incidents, one each in 1929 and 1930, led to mob attacks. Anglo vigilantes, such as the Native Sons of the Golden West, also intimidated Filipinos who participated in agricultural strikes.[51]

Many Filipinos first worked on sugar plantations in Hawaii and so were already acquainted with labor organizing. After several abortive attempts in California, they finally organized in earnest toward the end of the 1920s. Filipino lettuce workers unionized in the Imperial Valley in 1928, paralleling both efforts and failures by Mexicans. In the winter of 1933/34, Filipinos joined Mexicans and demanded work and wage improvements, each group accepting the aid of the communist-led Cannery and Agricultural Workers Industrial Union. By the summer of 1934, however, vigilantes and hostile government authorities had all but broken the back of the union. In the Salinas Valley, Filipino lettuce workers fared somewhat better. In 1933, D. L. Marcuelo of Stockton founded the Filipino Labor Union. It soon held a strike, which growers quickly destroyed by using Mexicans, Sikhs, and other strikebreakers. The following year, an Anglo packing-shed union and the Filipinos held simultaneous strikes. Growers again resorted to threats and violence, culminating in the shooting of two Filipino pickets. As in the Imperial Valley, local law enforcement intimidated the strikers. Such actions, however, merely emboldened Filipinos to make even greater demands. Unfortunately, dissension between them and the packing-shed workers grew, and ties were eventually severed. Vigilantes then concentrated their attacks solely on Filipinos, including not only those in Salinas but also those in several other communities. Furthermore, growers once more recruited Mexican laborers to complete the harvest. A scant month after the beginning of the strike, it fell apart. The Filipino union managed to secure some modest concessions, but a desertion of more than 50 percent of its members rendered these gains virtually meaningless.[52]

Mexican and Filipino farm labor unions won few victories in the 1930s. Yet at least one historian has asserted that these temporary ties between the two racial groups, which were based on common goals, opened the door to future cooperation.[53]

The Migrant Ministry, 1926–38

The Catholic Church responded meekly to the dozens of agricultural strikes convulsing California in the 1930s. A few priests supported workers and tried to mediate between them and growers. The Missionary Catechists also persevered in their work in the Imperial Valley. As a whole, however, the Catholic Church in California avoided the thorny issue of agricultural unions, strikes, and vigilante violence. In contrast, a Protestant group commanded a much stronger presence in the tumultuous 1920s and 1930s. Like the Missionary Catechists, it too was a women's group—the Council of Women for Home Missions. It was founded in 1908, the same year as the Home Missions Council and the Federal Council of Churches. These pan-Protestant organizations all evolved from the late nineteenth-century trend toward social service and ecumenism. Some historians hold that these groups developed as a result of an unconscious attempt to retain or regain "a Protestant hegemony" in the face of an increasingly pluralistic culture. While the other two aforementioned organizations were dominated by male church executives and prominent laymen, the Council of Women, which initially resembled an expanded version of a female religious society, was, of course, headed by laywomen. It practiced hands-on work among racial minorities, a specialization carved out during the days of foreign missions. In turn, the council provided ministerial opportunities for professional white women barred from the possibility of ordination in their respective churches. Like their male counterparts, the members of the Council of Women were committed to Social Gospel ideals, such as inevitable progress based on an optimistic view of human nature.[54] One of their chroniclers has written:

> The historical roots of cooperation among American church women are to be found in their missionary societies of the nineteenth century. The development of these societies may be seen as part of the broader women's movement of that era, concerned with temperance, anti-slavery, prison reform, suffrage, and the role of women in higher education, industry and the professions. Within the churches, women found their early opportunity for expression chiefly in connection with the rising interest in missions. While

the denominations were founding the general boards of missions, women were starting local groups with quaint names like "Female Society for Missionary Purposes" or "Pious Female Praying Society." There were hundreds of "female mite societies," raising their modest funds by selling butter and eggs, homemade quilts and rugs, and contributing the proceeds to the general boards.[55]

The Council of Women focused on agricultural laborers as early as 1914, when it publicly deplored the working and living conditions of Italian immigrant women and children harvesting cranberries in New Jersey. In 1920 the Council officially adopted this work, christening it the Migrant Ministry. It quickly expanded services to other groups, such as Poles, Lithuanians, and African Americans, all of whom found seasonal employment in the fruit, vegetable, and canning operations of the Mid-Atlantic States. In 1924, the Migrant Ministry's first full-time director sent home missionaries to the West Coast. They compiled information about housing, infant mortality rates, recreational opportunities, public education, and social relationships. On a trial basis, the Council sent a Spanish-speaking health worker to the region. Commissioned to establish and operate stations in two border towns, she sought out the support of local women's missionary societies, the Imperial Valley Ministerial Association, chambers of commerce, and fraternal clubs. In essence, the Migrant Ministry founded a rural version of community centers that offered basic health care, food, clothes, and vacation Bible school. Two important elements distinguished it, however, from most urban programs. First, not only did women exclusively conceive, organize, and manage it, but it also was truly interdenominational. Churchmen were apparently content that women had assumed the task of overseeing the even more difficult mission field that included migrant farm workers.[56]

In October of 1926, the Council of Women appointed Adela J. Ballard as its first Western Supervisor for Farm and Cannery Migrants. A native of the urban East, she was rudely awakened by rural life in California. The Imperial Valley in particular shocked her. Land companies had promoted it at the turn of the century, and it was still a newly settled area. Physically and socially isolated from coastal communities, it especially evidenced a racist relationship between Anglos and minorities. The Council of Women's report concluded that the Valley perpetuated some of the more unsavory features of frontier society, confirming its notoriety as the Cradle of

Vigilantism. Ballard concurred but nevertheless remained cheerful about the region's prospects:

> Then the Imperial [Valley] with its border psychology—its racial antago-nisms and its economic problems and its struggling churches! Our worker has spent the year trying to create the mood which would make advance possible. The difficulties discouraged people at the outset! A bit of visual ed-ucation proved a happy thought. A series of Nationality Nights brought each race [that is, Filipinos, Mexicans, Japanese, and African Americans] in the Valley into intimate contact with the [Anglo] people of the community.[57]

Simultaneously, the Migrant Ministry reached out to workers in the orchards, farms, and canneries near San Francisco. The organization also entered the vineyards and cotton fields of the San Joaquin Valley. Since its programs required ongoing financial support, Ballard began contacting Protestant leaders. She met with local chapters of the Women's Federated Missionary Society, denominational heads in Los Angeles, Mexican pas-tors in Stockton, and YMCA managers. She also scheduled fundraising events during her return trips from the annual conferences of the Council of Women. In 1929 she spoke at missionary society meetings at presti-gious urban churches in New York, Philadelphia, Washington, Chicago, St. Paul, Minneapolis, Denver, and other cities. Offerings poured in on the World Day of Prayer, the Council of Women's single largest fundraiser of the year. As Western Supervisor from 1926 to 1938, Ballard conducted several of these trips, always searching for new benefactors even as she continued to call on old friends and acquaintances. Tirelessly she devoted time, energy, and money to strengthen the Migrant Ministry.[58]

Priorities in California eventually shifted from the Imperial Valley to the San Joaquin Valley. Possibilities in border towns appeared so dim by 1929 that Ballard considered shutting down the Council's entire program in that region. She cited problems of church comity as the official culprit, but labor unrest probably discouraged her. She suggested that local Anglos blamed the Migrant Ministry for contributing to a feeling of dissatisfac-tion among laborers:

> . . . all California [mission] fields will be continued—with the possible excep-tion of the Imperial [Valley]—cooperation of the C[hamber] of C[ommerce] of Brawley is still hanging fire—there has been a trifle more cooperation

from local groups—[the town of] Calipatria says frankly—"We do not want any [mission] work—we do not want the workers stirred up to different ways of living"—work of course should be done! But it will take a special type of worker to do it![59]

A lay minister on the scene confirmed Ballard's assessment, bemoaning that "positive goodness that reaches out helpful and beneficent hands and restrains evil and builds constructively to conserve the good, this is totally absent in industry, education, religion, politics and social life."[60] After 1930, Ballard no longer reported on the Imperial Valley, suggesting that the Migrant Ministry had indeed withdrawn from that field.

The outlook in the San Joaquin Valley appeared brighter. A local ministerial association voted to maintain work among grape harvesters, and Protestants in another town agreed to help nearby cannery workers. Chapters of the Women's Federated Society supported a presence among cotton pickers in Fresno. Yet these community programs faced their own obstacles, including lukewarm support among many churches. Ballard accepted these problems as inevitable bumps in the road. After the stock market crash of 1929 and the ensuing economic depression, however, a formidable pall was cast over the work of the Council of Women. The financial crisis affected agriculture as much as any other segment of the economy, perhaps more. Even in good years growers often faced less than adequate prices for their crops. As the depression deepened, the demand for California's specialty fruits, vegetables, and nuts plummeted. Prices for staple produce also fell. So commercial growers cut production costs where they always had—in labor.[61]

Meanwhile, a related phenomenon was set into motion, namely, the large-scale deportation and repatriation of tens of thousands of Mexicans. In the early 1930s, local law enforcement often rounded them up in both the cities and countryside. The U.S. Secretary of Labor, William N. Doak, coordinated this national directive, operating by means of the Immigration and Naturalization Service. Leaders of Mexican labor strikes and other so-called troublemakers were particularly singled out. Two historians have estimated the special focus on driving out Mexicans from the border states: "During the period from 1930 to 1939, Mexicans constituted 46.3% of all the people deported from the United States. Yet Mexicans comprised less than 1% of the total population." The majority of deportees was loaded onto trains and returned to the border, while others traveled by cars and trucks and even ships. Family members often bid farewell to one another, younger adults taking their chances and choosing to remain in the only country they had ever known. As U.S. citizens, Mexican Americans also felt torn in their allegiances. They identified with those with whom they shared a common homeland, history, and culture. Yet they feared illegal deportation or at the very least felt the pressure to move voluntarily to Mexico.[62]

Mexicans, Mexican Americans, and Filipinos who remained in California, including farm workers, often lost their jobs to another casualty of the depression, namely, dust bowlers from Oklahoma, Texas, Arkansas, and Missouri. They quickly displaced minority farm workers. These economic and social disruptions naturally strained the adaptive powers of the Migrant Ministry. For instance, lower prices for farm produce also translated into lower donations. Furthermore, bad weather wreaked havoc on staple crops, forcing the Migrant Ministry to terminate several longstanding projects. Another factor that affected the work of the Council of Women were shifts in government policy. In 1936 the Federal Security Administration built a migrant labor camp in a community where the Migrant Ministry had maintained a presence for nearly a decade. Then the next year the Council of Women relinquished its work in two other counties. This expanded federal role in migrant work was driven by the growing stream of dust bowlers into California. The arrival of Okies and Arkies finally brought the evils of agricultural migrant labor into the national spotlight. The general public took notice only as large numbers of old-stock Anglo-Americans appeared in the fields, orchards, and vineyards of California, especially after the publication of John Steinbeck's *The Grapes of Wrath*. As one historian has noted: "Long had [a college professor, i.e., Paul Taylor of the University of California] labored to publicize the plight of California's farm labor force. Now he discovered the empathetic value of white skin."[63]

In general, however, longtime Valley residents felt little empathy for the dust bowlers. On the contrary, local Anglos felt so threatened by the appearance of seemingly endless carloads of indigent whites that they categorized them less in terms of class than race: "The content of anti-Okie prejudice was a composite of the most negative characteristics attributed by rural Californians to Negroes, Filipinos, Mexicans, and Orientals . . . [a] stereotype of the Okie as a naturally slovenly, degraded, primitive subspecies of white American."[64] The new migrants were dismayed to discover that they were identified with minority groups toward which they themselves held deeply racist attitudes. Okies who had worshipped all their lives as Methodists or Baptists were now regarded with scorn by their coreligionists. As a result, Okies and Arkies often left their former denominations for Pentecostal sects that welcomed them with open arms.[65]

While adapting to the dust bowlers, the Migrant Ministry encountered a number of problems. In the unusual strike year of 1934, police evacuated nurses from camps that allegedly harbored communist agitators and then tear-gassed the facilities. At other times farm managers accused the health workers of subversive behavior. Migrant Ministry staff also had to learn to contend with Anglo clients who, on the whole, seemed less cooperative than other groups.[66] Yet in spite of all of these challenges Adela Ballard and her co-workers maintained a positive attitude. Whenever one door of ministry closed, another seemed to open. Notwithstanding economically hard times and a continuing public fear of farm labor unions, finances remained relatively stable. Even so, Ballard knew that the Migrant Ministry faced fundamental changes, especially as public health agencies assumed greater responsibilities. Always the optimist, she remained confident about the future of the ministry. Unfortunately, she did not live to take part in its transformation. She soon suffered a physical collapse, was hospitalized, and later was moved to a convalescent center. A short time later, in the spring of 1938, she died. The years of traveling, fundraising, staff training, and responding to various crises had exacted their toll.[67]

The Social Action Department in the 1920s and 1930s

The Catholic Church's work among Mexicans and Filipinos as farm laborers paled by comparison to the Migrant Ministry. A national Catholic organization, however, soon recognized those needs more clearly. Known as the Social Action Department of the National Catholic Welfare Conference and directed by social theorist John A. Ryan, it sought to include farm workers in the overall struggle for fair wages and good working conditions. The U.S. hierarchy commissioned it in 1919, the same year that Ryan authored the extremely influential "Bishops' Program of Social Reconstruction." This document finally signaled the commitment of national Catholic leaders to institutionalize Leo XIII's social encyclical *Rerum Novarum,* which included support of organized labor. Hence the establishment of the Social Action Department, by which Ryan planned to spearhead programs of economic assistance among working-class Catholics. The nation's postwar swing to conservatism, however, soon deflated the high hopes of the Bishops' Program. Undaunted, Ryan and several colleagues persevered. They struggled to sponsor industrial conferences, found labor schools, and monitor legislation on economic issues. By the end of the 1920s, circumstances began to shift in their favor. The stock market crash and the Depression, Pius XI's new social encyclical *Quadragesimo Anno* (1930), and the first stage of the New Deal helped to breathe new life into the Social Action Department. Its report of 1931–32 revealed an upsurge in activity. Priests requested more literature. Protestants as well as Catholics inquired about the role of religious institutions in the world of work. By the late 1930s organized labor had regained a foothold in industry, and many recognized the Catholic Church as one of labor's major allies.[68]

Despite preoccupation with many other groups and issues, the Social Action Department began addressing concerns of farm labor. Surprisingly, the department focused initial efforts not in California or Texas but in Colorado.[69] Moreover, a laywoman, Linna E. Bressette, acted as the chief catalyst. Formerly a factory inspector, that is, until local manufacturers forced her resignation, she had gained a reputation as a staunch advocate for the rights of women workers. She also had spearheaded legislation to restrict child labor and organized night school classes for local Mexicans. Friends and foes alike knew her as "the Velvet Hammer." She joined the Social Action Department in 1921 and pioneered the first Catholic study about Mexicans in the United States. She also coordinated a number of industrial conferences, a role that introduced her to labor organizing among Colorado beet workers.[70]

Simultaneously, Robert E. Lucey was quickly becoming a major figure among Catholics in the Southwest. He had served as the first director of Catholic charities in Los Angeles, where he squarely encountered the so-called Mexican problem. The Vatican soon recognized his administrative skills, commitment to the papal encyclicals, and familiarity with social conditions among Mexicans and Mexican Americans. In 1934 he was appointed bishop of the Diocese of Amarillo, Texas. Even then, perhaps, Rome was grooming him to succeed the archbishop in San Antonio. Besides raising overall standards in his new see, he helped to organize summer labor schools sponsored by the Social Action Department. Lucey and close friend Raymond A. McGowan, assistant director of the department, created the regional Bishops' Committee for the Spanish Speaking in 1945. This organization marked a major shift in strategy and scope in Mexican American ministry.[71]

Conclusion

Catholic and Protestant church leaders in California did not relate to Mexicans and Filipinos as farm workers intent on labor organizing. Instead, these leaders were often preoccupied with establishing and maintaining traditional ministries. Of course, other factors like limited budgets and constantly shifting populations all influenced how, when, and where churches would approach and serve agricultural laborers. In 1900 the Catholic Church in California and indeed the entire U.S. West frankly existed as a frontier institution. Missionary bishops struggled to secure funds and attract priests and nuns for their newly created dioceses. Members of religious orders faced hardships unknown in the East. By the 1920s, however, the Catholic Church in California exhibited a greater degree of maturity, sophistication, and stability. Unfortunately, the constant stream of impoverished immigrants flowing into the state sorely strained its resources. Racial prejudice, cultural differences, lack of indigenous clergy, and mass repatriations during the Great Depression merely compounded the problem. The Catholic Church was poorly prepared to provide basic spiritual care and social services to Mexicans, Filipinos, and other immigrant groups. So it is hardly surprising that church leaders usually turned a deaf ear to the cries of organized farm labor, in spite of the fresh, bold approach of the Bishops' Program of 1919. Although prelates, priests, and nuns recognized the economic and social inequities between Anglo-Americans on the one hand and Mexicans and Filipinos on the other, most accepted these differences as inevitable facts of life. Of course, the Missionary Catechists continued their ministry among agricultural migrants, and a few priests openly defended those who fought for better wages and working conditions.[72] Yet bishops wanted to maintain cordial if tense relations with Anglo Protestants in the xenophobic and antiunion climate of Southern California. Moreover, prelates themselves were often suspicious of organized labor. The Catholic Church strongly opposed communism and refused to support groups with alleged ties to its political ideology. As

Charles Buddy, one-time bishop of San Diego, wrote: "The real danger to the Mexicans is not Protestantism, but communism." Bishops preferred to concentrate on noncontroversial assistance to immigrants, as well as build new parishes, schools, and hospitals.[73]

Through the 1930s, California Protestants established a modest social ministry mixed with traditional soul-winning evangelism. They established Spanish-speaking churches, community centers, and health clinics. Male clergy and laity tended to the urban scene, while the interdenominational Council of Women on Home Missions served rural communities. A handful of Methodists, Presbyterians, Northern Baptists, and others ministered faithfully if paternalistically among Mexicans and others, perhaps lending credence to this period as the golden age of Protestant home missions.[74] A leavening agent, the Social Gospel inspired men and women to respond to both the spiritual and physical needs of immigrants. Church leaders occasionally arbitrated during union strikes or otherwise spoke on behalf of the working poor. For example, Presbyterian Robert N. McLean wrote several articles criticizing Mexican repatriation, and a fact-finding group that included pastors pursued workers' complaints of vigilante violence. A similar contingent investigated grievances of cotton workers in the San Joaquin Valley. At best, however, most Protestant churches offered ameliorative services. Depending on the time and place, of course, these activities were controversial. Gradually a few practitioners of the Social Gospel embarked on the path of farm worker advocacy, their numbers growing in the 1940s. They consolidated their strength in the 1950s in response to a new exploitation of agricultural laborers—the Bracero Program. Catholic, Protestant, and secular organizations all waged a protracted legal war against it, prompting not only a shift from service to advocacy but also from advocacy to outright servanthood.[75]

Chapter 3: From Service to Advocacy, 1940–64

Surely this is the time when our ministry, the Church's ministry, His ministry must mean something more than paints and dolls, films and hymn singing. For what good are all of these when you have no job and there is hunger in the house [sic]. Surely now the Church must speak in a voice that will be heard in high places and in low places. Surely the Church cannot keep silent . . .

MIGRANT MINISTRY STAFF, 1953

As a result of World War II, a number of Mexican Americans realized significant economic gains in the 1940s and 1950s. The enrollment of minorities in the armed forces helped to weaken racial obstacles and open up new opportunities for them. A few Mexican Americans also took advantage of the G.I. Bill and attended college. Others worked as civil employees at military bases. Still others held on to factory jobs that became available during the wartime manufacturing boom, especially in cities like Los Angeles. A small percentage of Mexican Americans thereby entered the ranks of the working class and some even the middle class. As a sign of their newfound status, a handful of men with Spanish surnames ran for political office on local, state, and national levels—notably Edward Roybal in California, Dennis Chavez in New Mexico, and Henry B. Gonzalez in Texas. New self-help organizations, such as the American G.I. Forum, were founded as well.[1]

Despite these gains, the majority of Mexican Americans continued to suffer from poverty and racial prejudice. Most of them remained in urban barrios. Others, like their parents before them, labored in the fields. By the 1950s, a significant percentage of Mexican Americans had built permanent homes in farm communities. They were no longer migrants, but tended nearby specialty crops and worked at odd jobs in the off-season. Most Filipino men were less fortunate, resigned to a nomadic existence of endlessly traversing the breadbasket of California. Still, they were arguably better off than Mexican nationals. Growers increasingly used the latter in World War II, under the auspices of the new government-sponsored Bracero Program, which, after 1951, was known as Public Law 78. Composed of groups such as "the American Farm Bureau Federation, the Vegetable Growers Association of America, the Amalgamated Sugar Company, the National Cotton Council, and others," the farm lobby originally persuaded the U.S. Congress to enact the program as an emergency wartime measure.[2] Growers liked it so much, however, that they convinced lawmakers to extend it in various forms into the early 1960s. Finally, on the lowest rung of the agricultural ladder were undocumented Mexicans, whom growers could summon and dismiss at will. Most of the *braceros* and undocumented nationals toiled on farms near the border. So Mexican Americans were forced to move to agricultural communities in central and northern California. Even there, however, *braceros* eventually appeared in the fields and orchards, once again displacing domestic workers who both resented yet identified with them. A harsh assessment of postwar realities for Mexican Americans in general was certainly accurate for farm laborers in particular:

> It is a historical truth that, while the United States fought World War II to free the world from fascism, neither that country nor western Europe planned to extend the benefits of democracy to people of color, at home or abroad. The Western world never intended to abolish colonialism . . . Mexican Americans and other minorities returned to a racist society, separate and unequal.[3]

Religious liberals, civil rights organizations, and labor unions opposed the Bracero Program. Roman Catholics and mainline Protestants led the charge among faith groups, evidencing a growing trend of advocacy on behalf of farm workers. Priests steeped in the social encyclicals had risen to positions of leadership. They strongly supported the labor movement, which not only recovered but also surpassed earlier gains. Catholic clergy in the Northeast and Midwest had endorsed labor in the building trades, manufacturing, and mining. A small but vocal group of Catholic clergy felt compelled to apply the same principles to migrant labor in the Southwest and far West. Robert E. Lucey, Archbishop of San Antonio and executive chair of the new Bishops' Committee for the Spanish Speaking (BCSS), set this goal high on his list of priorities. Representatives in two other Catholic organizations fired off a steady stream of letters and newspaper columns in opposition to Public Law 78. Finally, several priests in northern California founded a *bracero* ministry that actually evolved into a labor organization.

Catholics were not alone in challenging commercial agriculture. The Migrant Ministry also foresaw the consequences of the Bracero Program. In 1951 its new parent body, the National Council of Churches of Christ (NCCC), issued a major policy statement on migrant labor. Locally, the California branch of the Migrant Ministry virtually underwent a metamorphosis. By the mid-1950s it was experimenting with a new model of ministry, acknowledging that many farm workers had established permanent homes in rural communities. This newfound stability opened up the possibility of community organizing, prompting the Migrant Ministry to select sites, recruit indigenous leaders, and solicit support from local churches. Short-term objectives included neighborhood improvements such as paved streets and water/sewer service. As its long-term goal, the California Migrant Ministry strived for farm worker empowerment.[4]

This chapter charts a gradual but crucial transformation in several religious organizations. On national, regional, and local levels church groups discernibly shifted from a ministry of service to one of advocacy. Opposition to the Bracero Program often served as the catalyst for this redirection. New church leaders who held advanced degrees not only in theology but also in social work and economics had become more sophisticated about social systems, the political process, and economic power. Certainly the growing civil rights movement inspired them. In headquarters in New York and Washington, DC, both mainline Protestants and Catholics devised national strategies, which in turn had a major impact in California.[5]

The Bishops' Committee for the Spanish Speaking

By the late 1930s the painstaking work of the Social Action Department began to yield measurable results. Commissioned in the wake of the Bishops' Program of Social Reconstruction of 1919, it had survived the onslaught of the conservative 1920s. It persevered despite retreats in the labor movement, researching and publicizing a variety of issues. The department grappled not only with the topic of organized labor but also with citizenship education, social work, rural problems, international peace, and family life. Above all else, director John Ryan and his lieutenants disseminated papal social thought among priests and rank-and-file Catholics. In the late 1930s the tide finally turned in favor of labor organizing. President Franklin Delano Roosevelt and other New Dealers passed laws that, in effect, legitimized unionism. The Wagner Act, for example, recognized the right of collective bargaining and instilled new hope in the movement. World War II was another major factor. As millions enlisted in the U.S. Army and U.S. Navy, the ranks of factory workers were decimated. Groups like the American Federation of Labor and the Congress of Industrial Organizations (AFL-CIO) seized this opportunity to display their strength and solidify recent gains. In both good and bad times, then, the Social Action Department had remained steadfast in its commitment to unionism. By the late 1940s it felt gratified for its contributions to labor's victories.[6]

In World War II the department also accelerated efforts among Mexicans and Mexican Americans, particularly by sponsoring high-profile seminars. Initially, these seminars were partly underwritten by the government to strengthen ties with nations to the south. In 1942, Associate Director Raymond A. McGowan brought together Catholic leaders from the United States and Latin America. Bishops, authors, politicians, and college presidents and professors gathered in Washington, D.C., to discuss social and economic matters. The next year McGowan and Archbishop Robert E. Lucey organized a conference in San Antonio that focused on the challenges the Catholic Church faced among the Spanish-speaking populations of the Southwest. More than seventy religious leaders deliberated over evangelism, religious education, and farm labor. Subsequent meetings led to the birth, in 1945, of the Bishops' Committee for the Spanish Speaking. The new organization encompassed a large territory, including the archdioceses of San Antonio, Denver, Santa Fe, and Los Angeles. Soon afterward "the Lucey-McGowan Blueprint" appeared. These two men conceived a comprehensive program to uplift the spiritual, social, and economic conditions of Mexican nationals and Mexican Americans. Lucey and McGowan foresaw the establishment of community centers in urban and rural locations, which would be staffed by trained priests and laypersons. Publicity directors would spread news about these projects to all of the faithful. Then seminaries would attract more Mexicans to the priesthood, who in turn would build more Catholic schools for Spanish-speaking children. Padres would accompany migrant field workers on their annual treks, offering nighttime masses and nurturing devotional exercises. Clergy also would encourage Mexicans to join labor unions and then urge unions to welcome them. Finally, Catholic lay leaders would lobby for protective legislation for agricultural laborers, as well as public housing and Social Security benefits.[7]

If fully implemented, this grand plan may have indeed elevated the overall status of Mexican Catholics in the Southwest. Yet even the influence, energy, and resourcefulness of individuals like Lucey and McGowan could not overcome the inertia of religious institutions, not to mention other variables. As always, a basic problem was adequate funding. The American Catholic Board of Missions committed much less than the requested amount of $100,000. So staffing for the neighborhood centers had to be drastically reduced. The greater impediment, however, may have been Lucey's fellow bishops. They respected him for his organizational skills and his support of New Deal liberalism, but regarded him as overbearing and egotistical. Not only did the sees of Denver, Santa Fe, and Los Angeles resent his assertiveness, but also his own suffragan bishops. They all feared that Lucey would use the BCSS to impose his episcopal will on the entire Southwest. His colleagues thus hesitated to endorse a comprehensive program. They voted instead to allow each diocese to determine for itself the use of funds earmarked for Mexican ministry. Bishops who preferred to build churches and schools could thereby bypass controversial activities like farm worker advocacy. This regional autonomy dimmed Lucey and McGowan's vision of an integrated ministry stretching from San Antonio to New Mexico, Colorado, Arizona, and Southern California. If anything, Lucey and McGowan never realized their plan beyond Texas. Even then the program varied greatly from one diocese to another. A pattern of lackluster performance prompted critics to charge the Bishops' Committee as long on official resolutions but short on concrete results. On the positive side, the committee did accomplish several of its objectives. First, it coordinated the schedules of Mexican priests who accompanied *braceros* during the harvests. It also encouraged voter registration among farm workers. Last, the BCSS served as the midwife for modest physical improvements in several South Texas neighborhoods.[8]

The Spanish Mission Band and Farm Labor Strikes

The BCSS often resembled the Social Action Department in terms of its educational and persuasive functions. In other words, the committee served as a leavening agent that spread the social views of church leaders and thereby influenced a number of Catholics. One of the committee's annual conferences even inspired two priests to enter full-time work among migrant farm laborers. In 1948 Donald McDonnell and Ralph Duggan attended the Fifth Regional Conference of the Bishops' Committee for the Spanish Speaking. They represented not the Los Angeles Archdiocese with its large population of Latinas/os, but instead the Archdiocese of San Francisco. McDonnell and Duggan had witnessed the recent growth of barrios in San Jose and Stockton. They also knew that local farms were employing more and more *braceros*. McDonnell, Duggan, and two other priests—Thomas McCullough and John Garcia—had all studied the social encyclicals in seminary. Furthermore, McCullough had been raised in a pro-labor family. These priests ultimately linked the Bay Area's tradition of Irish Catholic unionism to the needs of Mexican field workers. Initially, however, these young clerics never intended to become involved in labor organizing. Their desire was simply to minister among *braceros* and other Spanish-speaking Catholics. So they sought permission to leave the confines of parish life and, in effect, become home missionaries to field workers. The archbishop granted their wish, dividing them among four counties outside of San Francisco. Known as the San Francisco Mission Band or, simply, the Spanish Mission Band, the priests quickly set to work. They made door-to-door visits, held open-air masses, taught religious classes, and performed other pastoral duties. They helped laborers to establish credit unions and find affordable housing. McCullough also opened a *bracero* center in Stockton, while McDonnell focused on Mexican Americans in east San Jose.[9]

A five-year evaluation revealed both the missionaries' accomplishments and failures. In spite of their faithfulness, they had made only modest headway. The seemingly endless multiplication of Mexican nationals overwhelmed the band. McDonnell and McCullough eventually took another tack, identifying and attacking a root cause that demoralized the Mexican apostolate—the Bracero Program itself. A moral problem was that the *braceros* were separated from their parents, wives, and children.

Bereft of traditional family life, the farm workers were more susceptible to the temptations of drinking, gambling, and prostitution. Like Filipino men, they lived in cultural exile. *Braceros* faced the prospect of giving up many of their customs but never truly acclimating to their new social environment. The Bracero Program negatively affected Mexican Americans as well. Although the government expressly forbade the use of *braceros* whenever domestic workers were available, many growers routinely ignored this provision of the law. Growers were also intimately involved in price fixing for *braceros,* whose pay scale was often lower than a living wage for domestic workers. This practice forced Mexican Americans to migrate elsewhere or completely abandon agricultural work. Furthermore, commercial farmers built camps designed for men only, intentionally neglecting new housing for Mexican American farm families. Economic considerations aside, Mexican Americans feared that their own recent gains as legitimate citizens in the United States would again be undercut by this new immigration. Still, *braceros* seemed the most vulnerable; they were usually a source of tractable labor, and if they even whispered about organizing for better pay and working conditions, growers threatened to deport them.[10]

Nevertheless, some farm workers unionized and staged strikes, particularly from 1947 to 1952 and 1960 to 1961. The National Farm Labor Union (NFLU) led much of the earlier activity, while the Agricultural Workers' Organizing Committee (AWOC) protested in the twilight years of the Bracero Program. Multiracial in composition, both groups had affiliated with the American Federation of Labor. Two figures who later played major roles in the grape strike of the 1960s, namely, Mexican American Dolores Huerta and Filipino Larry Itliong, served as organizers for the AWOC. Earlier the NFLU had recruited Okies and others who were still working the crops, and in October of 1947 it struck against one of the area's largest growers—the DiGiorgio Fruit Company. The union held extensive picket lines, which vigilantes tried to break up. Meanwhile, DiGiorgio imported scabs from other parts of California and even from Texas. The conflict dragged on and deteriorated into a protracted public-relations war. Eventually the fruit corporation's resources outlasted union reserves, and a lawsuit ended the strike in 1950. Other attempts included a work stoppage in the cotton fields of Fresno, a cantaloupe strike in the Imperial Valley, union organizing in a Delano vineyard, and a strike by Filipino workers that Chris Mensalvas and Ernesto Mangaoang led in the asparagus fields of Stockton. Complaints usually focused on low wages and the use of *braceros* and undocumented Mexicans. While the union occasionally won battles with growers, it ultimately lost the war against California agriculture. After 1952 the NFLU concentrated efforts elsewhere, for example, in the sugarcane fields of Louisiana.[11]

A few religious individuals and organizations supported the aforementioned efforts, including disparate groups like Okie preachers and the Los Angeles Ecumenical Council. Mexican workers relied on the ubiquitous Virgen de Guadalupe, who smiled serenely from wall posters in union offices and halls. Strikers received very little help, however, from the institutional Catholic Church, at least until the creation of the Spanish Mission Band. In September of 1950 McCullough and McDonnell witnessed their first farm labor strike. They were ministering to tomato pickers in Tracy, a community between San Jose and Stockton. Poor working and living conditions had disheartened the *braceros* who approached McCullough for advice. According to Catholic social thought, he said, they had an inviolable right to organize. But their supervisor forbade any such plans, and the discouraged *braceros* simply returned to Mexico. In 1954, however, Mexican American field workers requested help in starting a union. This time McDonnell sought the permission of the auxiliary bishop to share church teachings on such matters. The bishop granted McDonnell's request, concurring with the proposed use of neutral terms like "association" instead of "union," and McDonnell serving as a "consultant" instead of a "labor organizer."[12]

McDonnell and McCullough soon inched more and more toward direct social action. They devised a two-pronged offensive in which they openly criticized Public Law 78 and organized workers. McCullough wrote letters to local newspapers, spoke on radio programs, and testified at legislative hearings. He and McDonnell also scheduled more house meetings and introduced field laborers to various grassroots organizations. As early as 1952 McDonnell had become acquainted with Fred Ross, a community organizer who had previously worked in Los Angeles. Ross had founded the Community Service Organization (CSO), which was loosely related to the Industrial Areas Foundation headed by Chicago activist Saul Alinsky. It was McDonnell who gave Ross the name of César Chávez as a potential recruiter. Then a resident of east San Jose, Chávez quickly embraced community organizing, eventually working for Ross. McCullough introduced Ross to Dolores Huerta as well, who later joined Chávez in organizing farm workers.[13] McDonnell and McCullough also appealed to various trade unionists to take up the cause of domestic agricultural laborers, such as packinghouse workers, meat cutters, and longshoremen. The two Mission Band members even traveled across the country to plead their case to AFL-CIO President George Meany—all to no avail. McCullough and McDonnell thus faced a dilemma. According to church practice, the priests were customarily limited to teaching the social encyclicals and sometimes arbitrating between management and labor. Occasional advocacy also was acceptable. Direct organizing, however, was strictly the province of the laity. Yet no trade unions would sponsor the farm workers. So McCullough and McDonnell decided to violate church tradition. In tandem with Ross and Huerta, they founded the Agricultural Workers Association in late 1958. Its members soon wrote their own constitution, established a workers' cooperative, and set up a dues system and several standing committees.[14]

Then, in a strange turn of events, the AFL-CIO reversed itself and created its own organizing committee. Labor organizer Norman Smith arrived in Stockton and met with McCullough, Ross, Huerta, researcher-activist Ernesto Galarza, and others. McCullough dutifully turned the reins over to Smith, and union members transferred to the new AFL-CIO affiliate. Although armed with a war chest and a high profile, Smith lacked familiarity with the world of farm laborers. He tried to organize them as if they were factory workers. Ignoring house meetings, he concentrated on recruiting casual workers congregating on Stockton's skid row. He succeeded in enlisting some Filipinos and Anglos, but attracted few Mexican Americans. Later he committed an even greater blunder, relocating the entire operation to the Imperial Valley in Southern California. This move belied his ignorance of the especially repressive history of the region. He opened an office and cooperated with the local packing shed union. By late 1960 he was organizing the area's domestic workers, and on 3 January 1961, announced a strike against one of the growers. Smith soon extended the strike to a total of twenty growers. The government forced some farms to remove *braceros,* but those who actually left the fields were small in number. So Smith resorted to physical intimidation, sending hired toughs to labor camps to assault Mexican nationals. Dynamite was also planted at one of the camps. Reacting to the union's strong-arm tactics, the Mexican consul called for the removal of all *bracero* workers. Yet the strike ultimately backfired, for union leaders, facing a host of charges, were arrested and indefinitely incarcerated. Legal fees mounted, and AFL-CIO head Meany grew increasingly impatient with the new farm labor affiliate.[15]

As the strike unfolded, McCullough and McDonnell drove down to the Imperial Valley. They met first with the local bishop, who granted McCullough permission to pray at a union rally. The local press reported, however, that the two priests were serving as the bishop's official representatives while allegedly fomenting discontent among farm workers. Although McCullough and McDonnell denied both claims, their relationship with the local bishop became severely strained. Furthermore, the chancellor of their diocese, who disliked the Mission Band, used the controversy as a pretext to terminate the organization. He soon reassigned McCullough, McDonnell, and others to traditional ministries.[16]

As crucial as it was, the Imperial Valley episode was only one of several factors that led to the demise of the Spanish Mission Band. Structural changes in the Catholic Church also played a role. For example, the Bay Area had recently been divided into three new dioceses. Transitions were taking place on the national level as well. The Bishops' Committee for the Spanish Speaking encouraged dioceses to set up their own councils, which would then integrate both urban and rural ministry among Latinas/os. In effect, this reorganization rendered the Mission Band obsolete. Such factors notwithstanding, the lettuce strike incident probably served as the coup de grâce. Catholic growers and their parish priests had complained for years about McCullough and McDonnell. Although not a liberal, the archbishop had firmly defended the actions of the Band. In face-to-face encounters, he told angry farmers that the mission padres were merely upholding Catholic doctrine. Circumstances in Southern California, however, were quite different. The bishop of San Diego ostensibly supported trade unionism but discouraged any direct church participation. He was very sensitive toward long-standing Anglo attitudes that identified union activity with communism. Two outside priests making newspaper headlines especially embarrassed him. He wrote to Robert Lucey:

My thinking is that both the [Bishops' Committee on the Spanish Speaking] field inspectors and the priests in charge of *bracero* camps ought to confine their activities altogether to the spiritual. Otherwise, the field inspectors and the chaplains are regarded as rabble-rousers and trouble-makers, so much so that after a visit from the regional representative, some of the camp supervisors refused to permit our chaplains to re-enter the camps.[17]

Catholic Opposition to Public Law 78

Even as the days of the Spanish Mission Band were numbered, the Catholic Church accelerated efforts to close down the Bracero Program. The triumvirate of Robert E. Lucey, George G. Higgins, and James A. Vizzard were the major figures in this movement. Chair of the BCSS, Lucey regularly spoke out against the use of Mexican nationals. His archdiocesan newspaper ran front-page stories opposing Public Law 78. Furthermore, Monsignor George G. Higgins, Director of the Social Action Department in Washington, also deplored the inequities of the *bracero* system in "The Yardstick," a weekly column appearing in Catholic papers throughout the nation. Last, a representative of a third Catholic agency worked tirelessly to abolish the Bracero Program. James Vizzard, S.J., coordinated advocacy efforts for the National Catholic Rural Life Conference. Founded in 1923, its purpose was to preserve the values and quality of life for Catholic families in the agricultural heartland of the Midwest. By the 1950s, however, it became increasingly involved in issues related to agricultural migrant workers. A native of the Bay Area, Vizzard was yet another priest who had grown up in the tradition of Irish Catholic activism. Thoroughly versed in the plight of farm laborers, he constantly pressured members of the U.S. Congress to repeal or at least amend Public Law 78. Elite Catholic leaders like Vizzard, Higgins, and Lucey—all of whom had attended graduate school—ultimately joined hands with liberal Protestants, Jews, union leaders, civil rights organizations, and a select group of politicians to end the Bracero Program. In late 1961 they finally began seeing results. While lawmakers extended the program another two years, it was quietly allowed to expire at the end of 1964.[18]

The Migrant Ministry and the National Council of Churches, 1945–55

The Council of Women for Home Missions had criticized farm labor legislation as early as the late 1930s. Executive Secretary Edith E. Lowry, who also served as the director of the Migrant Ministry, depicted the travesty of migrant agricultural labor in her book *They Starve That We May Eat.* This trend toward advocacy continued after the 1940 merger of the Council of Women with the Home Missions Council. While worker shortages

during World War II temporarily improved conditions for migrant laborers, the late 1940s saw a return to business as usual. Ironically, the lives
of migrant workers regressed in spite of the growth and expansion of the
Migrant Ministry. Offerings from the annual World Day of Prayer multiplied fivefold from 1942 to 1946, and the Home Missions Council secured
other funds as well. The Migrant Ministry even boosted its staff to twenty
permanent employees and two hundred summer workers. It bought new
supplies, such as portable altars, folding organs, Bibles, hymnbooks, type-
writers, movie projectors, record players, and other recreational materials. In conjunction with the twenty-fifth anniversary of working with
migrants in the Pacific Coast states, the Western Area purchased its first
station wagon and christened it the "Western Harvester." By 1948 two
more station wagons began making rounds among the migrants. Simultaneously, however, other factors adversely affected the farm workers. As
Okies left the fields for factory jobs in Los Angeles, Oakland, and Seattle,
growers inconspicuously bought aging government camps and charged
higher rents to Mexican Americans and Filipinos. Public health agencies
also curtailed their services. Most importantly, the Bracero Program kept
wages stagnant and swelled unemployment among domestic workers.
Once again the well-being of farm workers was no longer a "white" or
"Anglo" priority. Western Migrant Supervisor Velma Shotwell noted:

> The progress made in improved housing, health and education, notably
> those administered by the federal government, have been completely lost.
> Coincident with these losses came the continued use of imported Mexican
> Nationals, even after the war emergency was over, and increasing use of the
> "wetbacks." Three questions are forcibly presented at this point: (1) Why was
> the use of imported laborers begun as a temporary measure and allowed to
> continue as a permanent one? (2) How are the prevailing wage and the cer-
> tification of need determined within a given area? (3) Why cannot domestic
> workers be given contracts assuring them the same guarantees extended to
> imported workers?[19]

Deeply aware of these setbacks, the Migrant Ministry, now under the
auspices of the new National Council of the Churches of Christ in the
U.S.A. (NCCC), cast about for fresh strategies. This ecumenical agency
opened its doors on 1 January 1951. A highly complex organization, it soon
turned to its tasks focused on interchurch cooperation and impact on society. Nine months later the agency's Division of Home Missions, formerly

the Home Missions of North America, produced a brief policy statement, "The Concern of the Churches for Migratory Farm Laborers." Echoing the results of President Truman's Commission on Migratory Farm Labor, this pronouncement called for limits on imported workers, a minimum wage, federal housing codes for labor camps, health and welfare services, regulations for transportation of workers, and broader exclusion of child labor. In 1954 the Division of Home Missions issued yet another statement, "The Wetbacks: America's Displaced Persons Problem," in which some of the same concerns were reiterated. Both statements stopped short, however, of endorsing farm laborers' right to organize. While the Division continued to publicize the migrant problem, coordinate strategy with Washington-based agencies, and alert politicians to new developments, it sought no direct action. In contrast to prophetic stands often taken by the Federal Council, the National Council of Churches communicated a spirit of moderation. One historian has written: "The explanation for the council's caution is to be found partly in the pronouncedly conservative, pro-business attitudes that prevailed among most rank-and-file churchmen in the '50s." Only in the tumultuous 1960s would it act as well as speak out on social issues.[20]

The Rural Fringe Ministry in California, 1956–61

While Protestant leaders laid the foundation of the new National Council of Churches, the Migrant Ministry continued its traditional program of religious and educational activities. Yet changes were quietly afoot, especially in California. In 1950 two teachers, Douglas and Hannah Still, began working for the Migrant Ministry in Bakersfield. Their supervisor encouraged them to introduce new methods among migrant children. But local school administrators disapproved of their efforts. Frustrated, Douglas Still finally left to study theology at Union Theological Seminary and community organizing at the New York School of Social Research. Several years later he returned as the new director of the California Migrant Ministry, outfitting and launching a concept that he called rural fringe ministry.[21]

Rural fringes were recognized as a growing, postwar phenomenon. Agricultural laborers had slowly but steadily inhabited a variety of locales. Some of these rural slums appeared near major agricultural centers such

as Bakersfield, Fresno, and San Jose. Others were founded outside the industrial neighborhoods of smaller communities, particularly in the San
Joaquin Valley. Small, unincorporated towns constituted yet a third type
of rural fringe. At least one hundred such settlements dotted the California
landscape. Although these clusters of tents, shacks, and cabins confirmed
the ongoing poverty of farm workers, they also reflected a deep longing for
stability and self-determination. In 1956 the California Migrant Ministry
devised a method to take advantage of this new state of affairs. Douglas
Still and others proposed a total of three pilot programs, one for each type
of settlement. A team of three staff members—a social worker, a teacher,
and a minister—would service each rural fringe. Trained in community
organizing, the social worker would forge stronger bonds among residents
and then help them press for local improvements like water and sewage
service. The teacher would hold classes in literacy, citizenship, and home
economics. The minister would counsel or encourage residents and later
lead worship services and offer religious instruction. By 1958 several of
these projects were underway. The California Migrant Ministry soon oversaw at least five such ministries, each of which was supported by a particular religious denomination. The Methodists and Disciples of Christ
maintained separate programs in Fresno County, while the Augustana Lutheran Church and the Congregationalists underwrote projects in greater
Bakersfield. The United Presbyterian Church sponsored a rural fringe in
the Imperial Valley town of Brawley, which, not surprisingly, was the weak-
est site, especially since growers and camp managers constituted much of
the membership of the local church. An evaluation concluded that all of
the other ministries were making measurable gains, thanks in large part to
Still's supervision and intentionality. The assessment also highlighted the
need of the Migrant Ministry to learn more about Pentecostal churches,
which were conspicuous in the rural fringes. The report noted too that progressive school officials might serve as potential allies. All in all, it hailed
community organizing as the wave of the future.[22]

Developments in the National Council
of Churches, 1958–64

As the Migrant Ministry in California experimented with a new mission
strategy, significant changes also were taking place at the New York head-

quarters of the National Council of Churches. First, the General Board finally approved a sweeping statement on issues in American agriculture. Second, the board sponsored several resolutions related to farm labor. Most importantly, the Migrant Ministry celebrated its fortieth anniversary in 1960, a milestone that served as an opportunity both to reflect on the past and chart a path for the future. Since 1926 Edith E. Lowry had faithfully navigated the course of the Migrant Ministry. In fact, her name had become virtually synonymous with the organization. Growing up in a family of American Baptist clergy, Lowry had graduated from Wellesley College in 1920. From 1926 to 1929 she served concurrently as the assistant both to the executive secretary of the Council of Women and the director of the Migrant Ministry. She then headed the Migrant Ministry from 1929 to 1936 and the entire Council of Women from 1936 to 1940, a post in which she continued following a merger in 1940. Twice in the 1950s she oversaw yet two more reorganizations. In 1958, partly as a cost-cutting measure, Lowry consolidated the Midwestern and Western regional directorships. Later that year she stepped down as the executive secretary of the Division of Home Missions of the National Council of Churches, although she remained head of the Migrant Ministry.[23]

Slowly but surely men assumed control over a religious agency that women had conceived, founded, and built into an impressive organization, a fact hardly lost on those who had devoted years of service to the Migrant Ministry. The new director of the Division of Home Missions, Jon L. Regier, epitomized the male theologian-turned-bureaucrat. Thirty-six years old, he held master's degrees from McCormick Theological Seminary and the University of Michigan School of Social Work. From 1949 to 1957 he directed a neighborhood ministry in Chicago, taught at McCormick, belonged to a dozen local boards and commissions, and moderated the Presbytery of Chicago. He also served on several national committees. An "organization" man, he stressed the new business professionalism. He called for a greater sense of purpose, constantly pressing fellow staff and board members to articulate their visions and formulate plans of action. As the 1960s unfolded, the division continued to ask itself what constituted authentic mission, evangelism, and witness. Regier also encouraged closer ties to other entities within the National Council of Churches. In particular, he sought a stronger relationship with the Department of the Church and Economic Life.[24] It had existed a number of years before the NCCC, but had only begun addressing agricultural issues

in the late 1940s. Eventually that office and the Migrant Ministry cosponsored conferences on farming, agribusiness, and rural life. The department
also drafted a study document in 1952—"The Churches and Agricultural
Policy." In 1958 the National Council finally adopted a refined version.
Titled "Ethical Goals for Agricultural Policy," it included a section on
farm labor and reiterated points from an earlier statement of the Division
of Home Missions about workers' coverage and benefits. For the first time,
however, the department specifically referred to union activity:

> A violation of the Christian concept of justice exists in the fact that wage
> workers in agriculture are denied most of the legal and economic protections
> long accorded to wage workers in industry. We believe that, with adapta-
> tions required for their practical application to the business of farming (as
> in the enactments on social security), the principles of workmen's and un-
> employment compensation, minimum wage laws, and the right to organize
> and bargain collectively under the National Labor Relations Act should be
> extended to wage workers in agriculture.[25]

Resolutions soon followed that addressed more traditional concerns
such as child labor and the use of Mexican nationals. But the NCCC's
outright endorsement of farm worker unionization clearly signaled a de-
parture from earlier pronouncements. For the first time, the NCCC was
speaking more directly about the plight of farm workers. In turn, dis-
pleased lay people quickly relayed their own message. A major contributor
to the California and Arizona Migrant Ministries withdrew a large dona-
tion, while several other corporate sponsors threatened to follow suit. The
Migrant Ministry soon learned the cost of farm worker advocacy.[26]

> Some of the concern is focused on the matter of general uneasiness about
> communism in the Protestant churches. We cannot overlook, however, the
> honest difference of opinion of some of our colleagues concerning Council
> positions stimulated by the Division, dealing with the area of agricultural
> life and work. These primarily focus around questions of *bracero* laborers, of
> union organization of farm labor, and a general feeling on the part of some
> persons that the Migrant Ministry is becoming too deeply involved in ex-
> pressing its concern for the dignity and rights of the migrant. These financial
> losses add to our fiscal problem. Of greater concern to all of us I am sure is
> the fact that we continue to have many persons in this nation who are un-
> willing to see the full Gospel proclaimed and lived by all persons, regardless
> of race or status."[27]

In tandem with its new professionalism, the Division of Home Missions began recruiting more highly trained staff for the Migrant Ministry. The Division also established working relationships with other units in the NCCC. Last, the fortieth anniversary of the Migrant Ministry provided the perfect opportunity to celebrate the past and set goals for the future. In 1959 Edith Lowry laid out plans for the anniversary, which would be a major public-relations event. In November of 1960 the NCCC hoped to host a luncheon in Washington, D.C., at which President Eisenhower would serve as the keynote speaker. An open or closed television circuit would broadcast his speech to luncheons held simultaneously in various state capitals. More important than the anniversary itself, however, was the momentum it could build for years to come. In the end, the celebration was never realized on a grand scale. Nevertheless, the Migrant Ministry revised its goals for the future:

1. Presentation of the Christian faith and call to discipleship;
2. Reduction of agricultural migrancy to a minimum;
3. Elimination of foreign farm labor importation programs;
4. Provision of basic education and vocational training opportunities for farm workers;
5. Extension of educational opportunity for the children of migratory families;
6. Improvement of living and traveling conditions for farm workers;
7. Elimination of legal exemptions and discriminations;
8. Social acceptance and inclusion in the life of the local community;
9. Responsible and democratic organization for economic and civic self-help;
10. Flexibility and adaptability in goals and policy to meet the rapid changes taking place in the agricultural economy.

The Migrant Ministry had pursued some of these points ever since its inception, most notably evangelistic efforts, improvement of living conditions, and education of migrant children. These concerns highlighted its service approach from 1920 to 1940. Attempts to repeal discriminatory laws and the Bracero Program marked the second stage in the life of the Migrant Ministry, which began in the late 1930s and continued into the 1960s. This strategy displayed the trend toward legislative solutions, which began with the New Deal. The ninth goal expressed the Migrant Ministry's new and direct commitment to aid farm workers in their struggle for self-determination. Objectives to achieve this goal included greater opportunities for citizenship education and community organizing. Moreover, the New York headquarters encouraged state and local staff "consistently [to] study and assess the validity and responsibility of all attempts to organize farm workers into unions, cooperatives, and other forms of labor associations; where such attempts are found to meet criteria of democratic and responsible operation, *they should be supported.*" Three years later events in California and then in Texas would test this directive head-on.[28]

Conclusion

In the 1940s and 1950s, California's agricultural workers once more faced seemingly insurmountable obstacles in their struggle for a better life. As the United States entered World War II and Okies and Arkies left the fields, the federal government lost interest in the welfare of farm workers. Mexican Americans, Filipinos, and some Anglos nevertheless organized and held strikes against great odds—occasionally holding out for extended time periods. Meanwhile, the Roman Catholic Church and mainline Protestants gradually shifted from a ministry of service to one of advocacy. Beginning in the 1910s, both religious groups had established settlement houses, community centers, and welfare bureaus in cities in the Southwest and on the West Coast. By the late 1920s special missionaries—mostly nuns belonging to religious orders and women in the Migrant Ministry—tended to health, educational, and spiritual needs in rural areas. These missionaries devoted themselves selflessly to alleviate hardships among farm workers. Following World War II, however, men began to dominate this ministry. Priests in the Social Action Department, the Bishops' Committee of the Spanish Speaking, and the National Catholic Rural Life Conference coordinated new efforts, pushing for legislative reforms on behalf of field laborers. By the 1950s the Migrant Ministry followed a similar path. Men trained in graduate school slowly replaced the women who had pioneered a unique ministry spanning both coasts. The bureaucratically minded National Council of Churches of Christ was a far cry from the personal warmth exemplified in the Council of Women on Home Missions. Yet some of the ethos of the Migrant Ministry survived.

The Division of Home Missions sponsored many of the same programs and pursued the same legislative issues over which Edith Lowry and others had labored. When Jon Regier took over the reins, however, he set the Migrant Ministry on a new course.[29]

While these changes were underway on a national scale, a new set of innovative ministries surfaced in California. As in the 1910s and 1920s, Catholic and Protestant expressions of these changes occurred simultaneously—one in northern California and the other in the San Joaquin Valley. The Spanish Mission Band of the Archdiocese of San Francisco initially encouraged a casual version of community development. Donald McDonnell led house meetings among Mexican Americans in east San Jose even as he met Fred Ross and learned about the strategies of the Community Service Organization. Several hundred miles away, schoolteacher Douglas Still had hit on a very similar idea, namely, organizing residents of rural fringe areas. It was no coincidence that these two new ministries unfolded simultaneously in California. Leading the nation in commercial agriculture, the state had spawned the greatest number of rural *colonias* in which the seeds of community organizing would find fertile soil. Ethnic and economic history also played their part. McDonnell and Thomas McCullough had grown up in the shadow of San Francisco, a city well known for its Irish American populace and pro-union sympathies. These priests had cultivated at home and seminary an appreciation for organized labor. By the same token, Douglas Still represented a long-standing tie between Protestant liberals on the East Coast and West Coast. He ministered among farm workers in California, but received his training at Union Theological Seminary in New York—a school profoundly shaped by the social ethics of Reinhold Niebuhr. Still also deepened relationships with the staff of the Division of Home Missions at the nearby headquarters of the NCCC. The division eventually recruited students from the liberal seminary, a number of whom served as summer interns in California. In fact, another Union graduate eventually succeeded Still as director of the California Migrant Ministry.

As the farm worker movement grew in the 1960s, both Protestants and Catholics in California contributed substantially to the success of César Chávez and his labor association. In particular, the Migrant Ministry shifted its focus once again. Building on its strategy of community organizing, the Migrant Ministry consciously moved from advocacy to what it later called servanthood.

Chapter 4: Religion and *La Causa* in California, 1962–70

The seventeenth of March
  First Thursday morning of Lent
  César walked from Delano
  Taking with him his faith.

When we arrive in Fresno
  All the people shout
  Long live César Chávez
  And all who follow him.

Now we reach Stockton
  The mariachis sing to us
  Long live César Chávez
  And the Virgin who guides him.

Listen Señor César Chávez
  Your name is honored
  On your breast you wear
  The Virgin of Guadalupe.

"El Corrido de César Chávez"

Several factors led to the 1970 contract between the United Farm Workers and the table grape growers of California. Chief among them was the growing self-awareness of Mexican Americans as a political force. President Lyndon B. Johnson's War on Poverty stimulated some of this awakening. Newly established government programs, many of which aggressively recruited workers from minority populations, publicly acknowledged the inequities between Anglos and other racial groups. The Chicana/o youth movement played an even greater role in consciousness-raising. First-generation college students from Kingsville, Texas, to Santa Barbara, California, united in protest against racism in social attitudes, economics, and public policies. More assertive and anti-assimilationist than their parents, they shunned older self-help groups, such as the League of the United Latin American Citizens (LULAC) and the American G.I. Forum. Regarding such entities as "agents of social control," younger Mexican Americans opted for a host of new organizations. These new groups were identified by acronyms such as MAPA, MAYO, and MECHA, and through them Chicanas/os pursued "an ideology of confrontation." In Denver Rudolfo "Corky" Gonzales rallied others to form a short-lived political bloc. In Northern New Mexico Reies López Tijerina founded a grassroots organization in an attempt to reverse long-standing land-grant judgments. In South Texas the Raza Unida Party emerged from the efforts of people such as José Ángel Gutiérrez. In East Los Angeles the Brown Berets became a force with which to be reckoned.[1]

Another new group, the United Farm Workers Organizing Committee (UFWOC), represented a transition between the older and younger generations of Mexican Americans. Perhaps it was in a classification all its own. Its president, César Chávez, belonged neither to the accommodationist, older Latina/o groups nor the newer, unapologetic Chicanas/os who promoted racial separateness. On the contrary, he welcomed the support of people of various colors, creeds, and backgrounds. In response, liberal politicians such as presidential candidate Robert F. Kennedy advocated for the farm workers. So did many other individuals and associations, such as trade unions and civil rights groups. Walter P. Reuther of the United Auto Workers cheered on the Chavistas and underscored his words with generous donations. Martin Luther King Jr. applauded their nonviolent struggle. Anglo students at college campuses across the nation joined La Causa, mailing newsletters and marching in demonstrations. Sympathetic consumers boycotted supermarkets from coast to coast. All of this external support and Chávez's ability to promote and direct it constituted an invaluable and necessary factor in the success of the California farm worker movement.[2]

Mainline Protestants and Roman Catholics also participated in this original "rainbow" coalition, to use a popular phrase. In fact, the California Migrant Ministry identified so completely with the movement that one labor historian called it "a virtual subsidiary of the union."[3] Indeed, liberal Anglo Protestants everywhere lent their support. Denominational executives committed funds. Bishops and other ecclesiastical authorities publicly affirmed La Causa, while pastors and laypeople formulated discussion groups and action committees. Yet a number of Protestants and Catholics opposed the movement. On the whole, pastors and priests reflected more liberal trends. Younger ministers especially downplayed individual sins, while accusing agribusiness of corporate evil. Politically and socially active, they quickly earned the title "the new breed," which distinguished them from older and more moderate clergy. Age and educational differences likewise revealed fissures among Anglo laity. Younger adults who had attended college were more likely to support La Causa than either their parents or working-class peers. Geographical location was another significant factor. Urban Protestants and Catholics in the Midwest, Northeast, and Mid-Atlantic States supported the grape boycott, of course, at little or no cost to their own economic well-being. In general, the same held true in West Coast cities such as San Francisco and Los Angeles. The vast majority of churches in California's agricultural heartland, however, condemned César Chávez and the farm workers. Fearing economic, political, and social change, such rank-and-file church members often opposed the movement. Their ministers sometimes echoed their outcry, but most often remained silent on the controversy. Catholics in particular were divided. Many of the grape growers were children and grandchildren of Italian or Slav immigrants. They were not absentee landlords but lived on the farms they operated. These growers belonged to local Catholic parishes and contributed heavily to their budgets. Most of the Mexican American and Filipino American field workers also were Catholics. Further complicating matters, a largely Irish American clergy ministered among this ethnically diverse flock. Growers, farm workers, priests, and other Catholics constantly pressured California bishops to choose sides. Prelates officially took a neutral stand however, which liberals and conservatives alike regarded as cowardice or even betrayal. Yet behind closed doors church leaders ultimately pursued negotiations that benefited the workers.[4]

This chapter first outlines the formation, structure, and ethos of the National Farm Workers Association (NFWA). Then it turns to the crucial roles played by the Migrant Ministry on behalf of the union. Third, it examines Chávez's creative use of Mexican popular religiosity and methods that he borrowed from the civil rights movement. The chapter finally concludes with the arbitration efforts of the Roman Catholic Church.

The National Farm Workers Association

César Chávez had long wished to organize agricultural laborers. This desire may have stemmed largely from the fact that his own family had once
owned a farm in Arizona. An Anglo grower bought it in the late 1930s
before Chávez's father could repay a bank loan. In other words, the family was cast adrift and forced to join the migrant stream still pouring into
California. This traumatic event had a lasting effect on the then young
Chávez. He once reminisced:

> I missed that house. When I was living there we had all kinds of space—it
> seemed like the whole world belonged to us. In the cities I couldn't get used
> to the fences. We couldn't play like we used to. On the farm we had a little
> place where we played, and a big tree in there was ours and we played there.
> We built bridges and we left everything there and found it in the same place
> the next morning.[5]

After coming of age, Chávez served in the U.S. Navy in World War II.
A few years later, in east San Jose, he met Father Donald McDonnell of
the Spanish Mission Band and learned about the social teachings of the
Catholic Church. He also was introduced to community organizing—via
social activist Fred Ross. Chávez joined the staff of the Community Service Organization (CSO), which focused on issues such as voter registration, neighborhood projects, and legislative action both in local communities and the state capitol in Sacramento. In 1958, in Oxnard, California,
Chávez led his first successful strike with farm workers. But the CSO
refused to assign him to work permanently with agricultural laborers. So
after repeated pleas he resigned in frustration. Still wanting to organize
farm workers, he rejected several lucrative job offers and in 1962 moved
to the community of Delano. He chose the town for several reasons: its
central location, its population of stable domestic workers, and not least
of all the fact that some family members already lived there. Establishing it as a base of operations, he visited farm workers throughout the San
Joaquin Valley. Employing the proven techniques of community organizing, he drew laborers to house meetings and invited them to share
their struggles, disappointments, and dreams. Still, recruitment remained
difficult, in spite of advertising not as a union per se but as a mutual-aid
society. His diligence finally paid off, however, and the first convention of

the National Farm Workers Association was held in Fresno, California, on 30 September 1962. One hundred and fifty delegates attended the meeting. Chávez was elected president, Dolores Huerta and Gilberto Padilla as vice presidents, and Antonio Orendain as secretary-treasurer. Huerta and Padilla had long known Chávez, having worked with him in the CSO. Growing up in Stockton, Huerta had attended college and operated her own business. Assertive and independent, she represented one of the few Chicana voices in La Causa. She later negotiated directly with the growers. Gil Padilla was a former farm worker who had participated in field strikes since the late 1940s. A native of northern Mexico and a one-time migrant worker, Tony Orendain later organized efforts in South Texas. In addition to officer elections, the convention established a credit union, a cooperative, and a funeral insurance program. By 1964 one thousand members had been recruited. In 1965 a total of seventeen hundred families had joined the organization. Its newfound bargaining power even led to some modest wage increases for workers.[6]

Chávez crafted a union singular in structure and character. He purposely avoided the hierarchical, top-down style of business unionism. Based on the model of community organizing, the NFWA was designed as a democratic, grassroots phenomenon that projected a self-consciously Mexican American ethos. For example, delegates at the constituting convention chose "Viva La Causa" as their slogan. In Fresno they also witnessed the unveiling of the group's banner—a large black Aztec eagle encircled in white and set against a red background. Accompanying this pre-Columbian image were other ethnic/nationalistic symbols and events. When Filipino workers went on strike and asked for support, Chávez scheduled an association meeting on 16 September 1965—Mexican Independence Day. He hoped to capitalize on the occasion, thereby eliciting a positive vote from union members. He and others used religious images as well. In the spring of 1965, for instance, rose-flower workers fought for a wage increase and better working conditions. In order to dissuade them from abandoning their goals, leaders "had a pledge ceremony on Sunday, the day before the strike started. Dolores [Huerta] held the crucifix, and the guys put their hands on it, pledging not to break the strike." Timely application of nationalistic and religious symbols—combined with other means to evoke feelings of pride, dedication, even guilt and shame—became a trademark of La Causa.[7]

The California Migrant Ministry and the National Farm Workers Association, 1962–65

While Chávez and others quietly organized farm workers in the San Joaquin Valley, changes also were afoot in the California Migrant Ministry. Several of these changes issued from the hands of its new director, Wayne "Chris" Hartmire Jr. A graduate of Princeton University, he had first worked for the Civil Engineer Corps of the U.S. Navy. He then enrolled at Union Theological Seminary, New York, and specialized in New Testament studies. A Migrant Ministry internship in the summer of 1959 exposed him to the plight of farm workers, alerting him to some of the challenges and opportunities that later awaited him.[8]

Hartmire's leadership epitomized a further shift in Protestant ministry among agricultural laborers. The first change occurred in the 1940s as Migrant Ministry leaders increasingly turned from the first stage of ameliorative services to the second stage of advocacy on behalf of farm workers. Then, in response to the growing rural fringes, the third stage of grassroots organizing commenced in the mid-1950s. Staff members were trained in community work and supported indigenous leaders. This last stage Hartmire called servanthood ministry, a term that envisioned the Christian Church less as a bearer of religious tradition in society and more as a servant on behalf of the world at large. He and others based this new mission approach on the example of Jesus, who purportedly did not impose his religious agenda on others but responded freely to their needs. Hartmire also was inspired by the prophetic literature of the Old Testament and the philosophical movement of existentialism. Most of all, the Union Seminary graduate relied on Dietrich Bonhoeffer's view that the Christian Church might have to die so the world could live. The Christian Realism of Reinhold Niebuhr, a longtime professor of social ethics at Union Seminary, may have played its part as well. The religious principles set forth by Hartmire in his position papers suggested a transition from Niebuhrian neo-orthodoxy to liberation theology. His most important statements were "The Church and the Delano Grape Strike—A Partial Report" and "The Church and the Emerging Farm Worker's Movement." Always the spokesperson, he constantly interpreted to others the roles of the Migrant Ministry vis-à-vis La Causa.[9]

Hartmire initially concentrated on strengthening ties with Chávez and with member churches of the California Migrant Ministry. He also expanded the rural fringe ministries in Dos Palos, Lamont, Mendota, Fresno, Corcoran, and Goshen—all in the San Joaquin Valley—which led to open confrontations with local citizens. These conflicts may have been unavoidable as staff shifted from offering basic services to practicing advocacy and servanthood. Typically, personnel helped to organize indigent residents in each selected community—usually Mexican Americans or African Americans—who in turn sought improvements for their neighborhoods. Predictably, this newfound assertiveness usually offended local Anglos who then withdrew financial support for the ministry.[10]

The Goshen project was a case in point. In 1961 the United Church of Christ suggested the possibility of a rural fringe ministry in that location. Originally a settlement of Dust Bowl Okies and Arkies, it had grown into a community of 2,500 residents, 60 percent of whom were Anglos, 30 percent Mexican Americans, and 10 percent African Americans. While Goshen became the home of several Pentecostal churches and a Catholic parish, no mainline Protestant denominations were represented. So Congregationalists in a neighboring town served as local sponsors. Although enjoying a recent population spurt and economic stability, Goshen still lacked a sense of identity and cohesiveness. In particular, it had no physical facility for social activities. In tandem with a local board, the California Migrant Ministry and the United Church of Christ purchased land for a community center. James Drake accepted the call to serve as the director of the new ministry. A native of Southern California and a graduate of Occidental College and Union Seminary, he believed a countywide ministry among farm workers would help to bring about positive change. He moved to the area and joined other Migrant Ministry staff, all of whom were trained and experienced in community organizing. They soon established a small mutual-aid group modeled on Chávez's organization. Drake and others confronted head-on the issues of welfare eligibility, wage disputes, adequate housing, and voter registration. Not surprisingly, their actions threatened local Anglos, which spelled an end to local support. In January of 1965 the sponsoring Congregational church cut off funds to the project.[11]

Nevertheless, the Migrant Ministry further trod a path leading to the Delano grape strike. In April 1965 members of the union in Goshen voted to affiliate with the NFWA, tying Migrant Ministry staff more directly to Chávez. One month later union members walked off the job at flower nurseries south of Delano. The Migrant Ministry helped them win a wage increase and then immediately turned to help vineyard workers on strike in a neighboring county. Drake and others played an even more active role in a third and ultimately successful conflict—a rent strike. Residents of two farm labor camps withheld rent payments to protest a large rate increase. Owners had raised the rent in spite of the fact that the shelters had been condemned. Tenants even marched to the county courthouse. Although the housing authority tried to evict them, a local court ruled that the rent increases were illegal.[12]

The Beginning of the Delano Grape Strike

Filipino farm laborers called the grape strike in September of 1965. They were single men who had immigrated to the United States mainland in the 1930s. A small, tightly knit group, they followed the table grape harvest as it moved northward from the Coachella Valley. They were protesting a legal loophole that temporarily allowed growers to hire Mexican nationals. The Filipinos especially objected that the minimum wage for the Mexicans did not also apply to them. As members of the virtually defunct Agricultural Workers Organizing Committee (AWOC), the Filipinos contacted fellow countryman Larry Itliong. A seasoned organizer, he quickly drove down from Stockton and led a successful strike. As the harvest moved to Kern County, workers again demanded a wage increase, but backed down when growers threatened to recruit local Mexican Americans. In September the Filipino laborers once more demanded higher wages—this time in Delano. The stakes were now considerably higher since the camps in Delano, which were owned by local growers, served as the winter home for the workers. Instead of reporting to crew leaders, strikers stayed in their cabins. So camp managers turned off the utilities and padlocked the doors. In defiance, about twelve hundred workers then picketed the fields. When Mexican Americans began replacing them, Itliong appealed to the NFWA. Although Chávez knew that his people lacked maturity and strength, he nonetheless scheduled a meeting for 16 September 1965, the one hundred forty-fifth anniversary of Mexican independence from Spain. Members would vote whether to join the Filipinos. That evening over one thousand workers packed the parish hall of Our Lady of Guadalupe Church. Alongside images of saints, the union displayed its banner of the black Aztec eagle and posters of the Mexican revolutionary Emiliano

Zapata. Organizer Tony Orendain led cheers of "¡Viva La Causa!" Gil Padilla also stirred the workers. Finally Chávez stepped onto the platform. He retold the glories of the Mexican Revolution, invited participants to share their own struggles, and swore a strict vow of nonviolence if workers participated in the strike. Overwhelmingly the crowd voted to join the Filipinos. Soon, however, enthusiasm dissipated as the union actually began challenging growers. Other problems followed. Al Green, head of the AWOC, initially resisted the overtures of the Mexican Americans. So Chávez and his organization worked independently and picketed other Delano growers. In effect, the two labor groups temporarily conducted parallel strikes. This arrangement held until the fall of 1966, at which time Chris Hartmire and AFL-CIO organizer Bill Kircher mediated so the two unions could merge into a new multiracial group—the United Farm Workers Organizing Committee (UFWOC). Chávez became the president, while Dolores Huerta and Larry Itliong were elected as vice presidents. Other Filipino officers included Andy Imutan, Philip Vera Cruz, and, later, Peter Velasco. Both sides had considered the dangers and pitfalls of a merger. Itliong in particular feared that the Filipinos would be swallowed up by the more numerous Mexican Americans. Still, he saw the potential benefits that a merger could bring to all farm workers, regardless of background. Yet his fears of Mexican American domination were ultimately confirmed, and in 1971 he resigned in protest. Ironically, a central chapter in labor history inspired by Filipinos became bereft of their leadership only a few years later.[13]

For its part, the NFWA faced a number of obstacles at the beginning of the strike. First, pickets had to cover a strike area of fifteen by twenty miles. They also suffered from harassment and occasional violence. In the meantime, grower attorneys filed injunctions against them, often forcing strikers to leave the fields to attend court proceedings. Growers imported scabs from Mexico and Texas as well. Furthermore, employers and labor contractors created several phony unions, the first of which was the Tulare-Kern Independent Farm Workers. Perhaps the greatest problem of all for the strikers was securing adequate funds. The union quickly depleted its modest reserves, and some strikers had to search for other employment. Fortunately, the union capitalized on media exposure to build up its base of support. Sympathizers in San Francisco, Los Angeles, Sacramento, and even Fresno and Bakersfield responded with generous donations. College students in Berkeley and elsewhere volunteered both money and time. Longshoremen, Teamsters, and members of other unions refused to handle shipments of table grapes. Much to the consternation of George Meany of the AFL-CIO, fellow labor leader Walter P. Reuther unreservedly endorsed La Causa and committed substantial funds. Then, in the spring of 1966, a subcommittee of the U.S. Senate held hearings on the strike. News coverage of the hearings reflected poorly on the growers.[14]

Religious groups and individuals also championed the strike. Jim Drake began working full time for the union. Hartmire recruited other ministers to walk the picket lines, preferably wearing their clerical collars. Their presence in the fields and arrests for trespassing further helped to publicize La Causa. They made newspaper headlines and appeared on magazine covers, such as on *Time* magazine. They also acted as peacekeepers during tense confrontations between workers and growers and, in general, provided moral support.[15] Hartmire later credited religious institutions and individuals for the strategic role they played in the first several months:

> Support for the strike in its early days came from a variety of sources. The most important were students, SNCC and CORE, the churches, the California Center for Community Development (CCCD), and some parts of the labor movement. *As a matter of historical fact the churches were the single most important source of support in the first ninety (90) days of the Huelga. César Chávez has spoken of this fact many times."*[16]

Hartmire spoke at numerous churches and wrote to denominational offices to secure strike relief. Of course, many religious groups and organizations opposed the strike. Congregations in local communities had previously withdrawn aid to the California Migrant Ministry. On discovering its role in Delano, several other churches lodged formal complaints. Pastors and laity throughout the San Joaquin Valley protested bitterly about the so-called unchristian actions of Hartmire, Drake, and others. In particular, the Delano Ministerial Association expressed its shock and disgust. It questioned the Migrant Ministry's involvement in matters it regarded as economic rather than moral or spiritual in nature. One pastor, an African American, denied reports of racial tensions. On the contrary, he described Delano as an ethnic melting pot, a "Little United Nations" of California in which Anglos, Japanese Americans, Mexican Americans, African Americans, and others all lived in perfect harmony. Hartmire and Drake dismissed these claims as nothing more than wishful thinking.[17]

Another incident further exacerbated feelings. In December of 1965 a religious fact-finding mission descended on Delano, an event orchestrated by James L. Vizzard, S.J., of the National Catholic Rural Life Conference, and William J. Quinn of the Bishops' Committee for the Spanish-Speaking. Chávez, Hartmire, and labor organizer Al Green had pleaded with Vizzard to press local Roman Catholics for a public show of support. A native Californian familiar with the farm worker scene, Vizzard knew the futility of such a request. He knew that the bishop of the Monterey-Fresno Diocese, A. J. Willinger, enjoyed long-standing relationships with growers. So Vizzard and Quinn took a different tack. They contacted several national leaders and, without advance notice, visited the site of the strike. Beforehand, Vizzard tipped off the Jesuit periodical *America*. He also prepared a press release. On 13 December 1965, Vizzard, Quinn, representatives of the National Council of Churches of Christ, several mainline denominations, the Synagogue Council of America, and various Catholic groups arrived in Delano. While area ministers resented the intrusion, no one was more furious than the local Catholic bishop. He was so angry he even publicized excerpts of a reprimand Vizzard later received from a supervisor. Headlines on the front page of the diocesan weekly referred to Vizzard as "The Horn Blower of Delano." Although severely criticized, he judged his strategy a success. The fact-finding mission kept the Delano strike in the national spotlight and helped to generate more sympathy for the workers.[18]

As the strike dragged on into 1966, California's Protestants felt pressured to take a stand. Would they side with the growers or champion the cause of the farm workers? Would they condemn the efforts of the California Migrant Ministry or applaud them? Most religious judicatories held annual assemblies in May and June. Many of them had already produced statements that were equivocal or, at best, mildly supported the strike. Others clearly went on record as opposed to the Migrant Ministry, for example, the San Joaquin Diocese of the Episcopal Church. The Fresno Area Council of Churches penned a more restrained document that simply questioned the tactics of the Migrant Ministry. In contrast, the Northern California–Nevada Conference of the Methodist Church, the Pacific Southwest Synod of the Lutheran Church in America, and especially the Northern and Southern California Conferences of the United Church of Christ stood squarely behind the strikers and the Migrant Ministry.[19]

The stances taken by individual churches and their judicatories were usually determined by their degree of economic interest. Districts, presbyteries, and dioceses in agricultural valleys disapproved of the actions of Hartmire, Drake, and their colleagues, although over twenty valley clergy formed an independent organization in support of the strike. San Francisco judicatories generally voted in favor of the Migrant Ministry and the strikers. Protestants in Southern California were more evenly divided and often split on the issue. The United Presbyterian Church was an example of such tensions. Representing one extreme was the Presbytery of San Joaquin, which unsuccessfully introduced a resolution at the spring session of the synod referring to Migrant Ministry actions as "coercive" and "unwholesome." Earlier, however, San Francisco Presbyterians endorsed the boycott. The Los Angeles Presbytery took a middle position, narrowly defeating unqualified support for the California Migrant Ministry.[20]

La peregrinación

By February of 1966 the strike was once more in danger of losing momentum. The union desperately needed a stimulus to reinvigorate La Causa. So leaders considered a method often used in the civil rights movement, that is, a march. It was a tactic Chávez first used when briefly organizing farm workers in Oxnard, California, in the late 1950s. In the grape strike he and others originally thought about walking all the way from California to New York City, the latter of which was the headquarters of one of the agribusinesses they opposed. But distance and cost ruled it out. So they chose the more manageable goal of marching to the state capitol in Sacramento, an event designed to accomplish several objectives. First, it would help to keep the strike in the eyes of the general public. It also would be a means by which to organize other workers in the San Joaquin Valley. Third, the march would challenge Governor Edmund "Pat" Brown to take a stand one way or the other. Last, the march would serve as a positive outlet for potentially violent strikers. Workers were angry that an airplane pilot for the Schenley Corporation, which owned one of the vineyards, had sprayed pesticide on a picket line. Many of them vowed to take revenge. Union leaders knew that retribution could have spelled an end to support from liberal Anglos. So Chávez and others promoted the event not only as a protest march but also as an act of penance. They even scheduled it to coincide with the second half of the Lenten season, including Holy Week. Chávez likened it to a *peregrinación,* a religious pilgrimage in the tradition of devotional Catholicism. But the march also appealed to supporters for other reasons. Its eclectic nature soon characterized La Causa as a whole, for nearly everyone could identify with some aspect of the march—Catholics, Protestants, Chicanas/os, liberal Anglos, Mexican American farm workers, college students, and others. The religious aura of the march, however, disturbed a number of union leaders. Many who were not Catholic saw no need for penance among the farm workers. Strike captain Epifanio Camacho, an evangelical Protestant, balked at the proposed use of Catholic symbols and subsequently resigned his post. He especially objected to using the banner of La Virgen de Guadalupe. A significant contingent of Pentecostals bolted from the union altogether. When asked about the decision to display the banner, Dolores Huerta simply commented: "The question was brought up at a special meeting. We put the Virgin to a motion, and virginity won." Still others rejected outright the idea of a march, including Al Green of the predominantly Filipino union.[21]

Sixty-five to seventy-five *peregrinas/os* set out from Delano on 17 March 1966, led by farm laborer Roberto Bustos. One worker held high a banner of La Virgen, while others followed with flags of the union, the United States, Mexico, and the Philippines. Participants sported red armbands and hatbands etched with the black Aztec eagle. The very last *peregrino* carried a wooden cross draped in black cloth. The daily walk inched its way northward, stepping through an archipelago of small agricultural towns. The entourage eventually reached a major highway taking it to Fresno and the heart of the San Joaquin Valley. Proceeding in an orderly fashion, marchers were strictly prohibited from the use of any alcohol. Monitors also instructed them to ignore hecklers and underscored the event's religious nature to all new arrivals. Every night an upbeat program, a fiesta, rejuvenated the spirits of the weary marchers. It often resembled a religious revival, the techniques of which Chávez had witnessed years before at a Pentecostal rally. Farm workers and others joined in an array of songs, ranging from traditional union hymns like "Solidarity Forever" and Woody Guthrie's "Pastures of Plenty" to Mexican favorites such as "De Colores" and "Tu Reinaras." A song about spring flowers in the countryside, "De Colores" on the one hand has been strongly associated with the Latina/o Cursillo movement. On the other hand, "Tu Reinaras" was the anthem of the Cristero Movement in Mexico in the 1920s. Song sheets also included "El Picket Sign" by Augustine Lira, "Huelga en General" by Luis Valdez, "Brown-Eyed Children of the Sun," the African American spiritual "Go Down, Moses," and the protest songs "The Times They Are a-Changing" and "Blowin' in the Wind." This music from various sources revealed again that the march was designed to appeal to the greatest number of supporters. Later Luis Valdez and his drama company, El Teatro Campesino, entertained marchers with melodramatic depictions of growers as villains and workers as virtuous underdogs. He often followed with a reading of *El Plan de Delano,* which was reminiscent of the manifesto authored by early twentieth-century Mexican revolutionary Emiliano Zapata. Rallies always ended with singing "We Shall Overcome" in Spanish. Both exhausted and reinvigorated, marchers then slipped away to find places in which to sleep. Early every morning they gathered for mass and afterward set out on another day's journey. The discipline of the march and the emotional release of the rallies thus forged an unbreakable bond among participants.[22]

In Fresno the march attracted a greater following. Over one thousand supporters packed a rally at the Azteca Theater. On Palm Sunday the marchers then entered Stockton, where the bishop-elect of the new Fresno Diocese said a morning mass. That evening more than 2,500 people crowded into a fiesta at a local park. More priests, nuns, college students, and trade unionists joined the swelling procession. On Good Friday marchers reenacted the Stations of the Cross. Saturday afternoon the original *peregrinas/os* and their supporters filed into West Sacramento and, that night, held a bonfire ceremony. Finally, on Easter morning, an estimated eight to ten thousand marchers converged on the state capitol. Governor Brown was conspicuously absent, purportedly having already scheduled the holiday with friends in Palm Springs. Yet several other public figures greeted the weary, foot-blistered farm workers. Often interrupted by thunderous applause, Dolores Huerta spoke passionately about the new power of Mexican Americans. In contrast, Chris Hartmire chided the churches for their complacency and lack of costly discipleship. He quoted extensively from French existentialist Albert Camus. That afternoon the local bishop presided at a special worship service, which was followed by a fiesta in a nearby park. However, a persistent, drizzling rain eventually thinned out the crowd. The protest march, the act of penance, the pilgrimage had come to an end.[23]

Reactions to *La peregrinación* varied considerably. On the whole,

Chicanas/os felt a new sense of pride, for dignitaries at the capitol rally had relinquished their seats of honor to the original marchers. Farm worker and *peregrina* María Saludado de Magaña, for instance, experienced a newfound self-confidence and self-respect. Liberal Anglos also were jubilant about the power of the march. Schenley Corporation, a large company that owned vineyards in Delano, had capitulated to the demands of the union. Farm workers, Chicanas/os, and others believed that a new day had finally dawned. Meanwhile, growers regarded the march with a mixture of scorn, cynicism, and alarm. They resented the expansion of the table grape conflict into a civil rights issue. They also accused Chávez of profaning the holiest day in the Christian calendar. One newspaper advertisement read: "Easter Sunday in Sacramento was ugly. God and the Virgin must have felt very sad. The Lady of Guadalupe must have wept to see her friends set her aside. Now that Schenley [Corporation] had chosen César and his friends to work for them, they no longer spoke to her." Accusations that the union was exploiting religion were not entirely baseless. Yet it was a long-standing tradition for Mexican reformers and revolutionaries to rely on La Virgen to legitimate their causes. Chávez creatively blended this time-honored symbol with other powerful images, some of which were overtly spiritual and others that were not. The testimony of inside religious supporters, such as Jim Drake and LeRoy Chatfield, have offset a jaded view of the march. They knew Chávez intimately and witnessed his deep, intense spirituality.[24] Organizer Bill Kircher, who first became acquainted with Chávez during the march, offered the most balanced assessment of the union's appropriation of Mexican devotional Catholicism:

> Chávez knew more than anybody else, he knew more about where the thing [the farm workers' movement] had to go, he knew more about what problems the workers faced and he knew that to approach the organization of these people like an organizer going into an auto plant some place, was ridiculous. They had no frame of reference, they were people who had been born in Mexico and the United States. While Chávez directed their attention to the economic needs, he pulled them together through this common denominator, the cultural religious form.
>
> I'll never forget one night, we were talking. It was toward the end of the march. He held his two hands in fists, like they were holding something, palms up, fingers closed. He looked at one closed hand and said, "Today we must have the Eagle and Our Lady of Guadalupe; when we get the contracts we won't need Our Lady" and he opened one hand. It wasn't that he was taking advantage of the Church, it's as if he knew that to get from where the

farm workers were to where they had to go, they needed help. He is a guy
who knows what he ultimately wants and he knows he can't get there in the
traditional ways. Radical? Sure, in the sense of being different.[25]

The Fast

Chávez walked in the march, but tried to keep a low profile. He did not
personally lead it, and he refrained from speaking to the thousands of on-
lookers at the state capitol. He wished not to publicize himself but rather
La Causa. Yet the farm workers often exclaimed, "¡Viva, César!" They also
chanted a song about him, titled "El Corrido de César Chávez." Later
he forged an event that could not help but propel him further into the
spotlight—his public fast in February of 1968. By then the strike and boycott had survived for over twenty-eight months. The union had won contracts with several vintners, including Perelli-Minetti, Gallo, and Franzia.
Yet the Delano grape growers still refused to recognize the workers. Strikers once more felt demoralized, angry, and frustrated. They believed that
peaceful methods had produced little more than a stalemate. Some workers threatened to destroy property and physically attack their opponents.
Union leaders feared that widespread violence would lead to criminal
convictions and a loss of aid from liberal Anglos. In addition to defusing
the possibility of farm worker violence, the union needed once more to
expand the boycott and raise funds. It had affiliated with the American
Federation of Labor–Congress of Industrial Organizations (AFL-CIO)
in 1967, whose support was vital. Nevertheless, the farm workers required
more money for their steadily growing operations. Perhaps Chávez was
seeking a fresh, new medium to broaden the union's base of support.[26]

One night at Delano's Filipino Hall, Chávez announced to other leaders that he had been fasting for several days. He described it as an act of
penance in response to the feelings of discouragement, impatience, and
hatred among strikers. He then left the hall and walked to the union headquarters known as Forty Acres. Witnesses were dumbfounded. Chávez's
press secretary, LeRoy Chatfield, quickly recovered from the shock and set
about preparing a proper environment for the fast. The union office, which
had been converted from an old service station, was again transformed.
Pictures of La Virgen and Mahatma Gandhi had long adorned the walls.
Filipinos soon designed an even more religious atmosphere by painting the

windows to resemble stained glass. The garage soon operated not only as an administrative office but also as a worship center. Visiting farm workers flocked to the temporary chapel. Celebrating mass every night of the fast, Franciscan priest and union chaplain Mark Day observed:

> It really looks good—the huge banner of the Union is against the wall, and the offerings the people make are attached to the banner, pictures of Christ from Mexico, two crucifixes, a large picture of Our Lady of Guadalupe— the whole wall is covered with offerings. There is a permanent altar there (a card table) with votive lights, almost like a shrine.[27]

Almost? A nearby storage room was converted into "a monastic cell" for Chávez. Lying on a cot, he both meditated and tended to union matters. As his physical condition weakened, he was no longer able to walk and thereafter remained in the room. Yet he continued to receive hundreds of visitors, many of whom revered him as a living saint. Meanwhile, Chatfield organized a tent city at the headquarters, and Chávez's brother, Richard, constructed a large outside cross. Nearly ten thousand people traveled to the pilgrimage site. The following description of one pilgrim was not unusual:[28]

> [A]n elderly Mexican-American woman dropped to her knees in the dirt about 200 feet from a small room in Delano where César Chávez, the controversial farm union leader, was ill in bed.
>
> She was one of a crowd of workers, students and others who had been waiting to see Chávez, to ask his advice and to pray for his recovery from a back ailment which had kept him bedridden . . .
>
> The crowd hushed as the woman, in tears, crawled the entire distance in the dirt on her knees to Chávez' side. In Spanish, she blessed him as a martyr of the Catholic Church and a hero of the poor."[29]

On Sunday, 11 March 1968, Chávez finally ended his penitential discipline, which he had endured twenty-five days. A great ceremony marked the occasion. A throng of supporters congregated at the city park. Robert F. Kennedy even left his presidential campaign in Los Angeles to attend the mass. A participant recounted the sight:

> Delano's Memorial Park was overflowing with men, women and running children. Estimates of the gathered crowd vary from eight to ten thousand persons. Most of the thousands who tramped through the park were farm

workers. The entire scene was a kaleidoscope—a festival, religious procession, political gathering, church social and family reunion.

At noon, a procession stretching for nearly a mile began to snake through the main entrance of the park. The people marched slowly, two by two. Priests, nuns, farm workers, union officials, and Senator Robert Kennedy marched behind the thunderbird flag and the Our Lady of Guadalupe banner. Most of the marchers near the front ranks of the line carried cardboard boxes heaped with shiny gold-colored loaves of semita (Mexican [pastry] bread).

The procession ended in front of a flatbed truck that had been converted into an altar and speaker's platform. Standing on the truck were priests, a rabbi, ministers, and several union officials. The improvised altar was surrounded by Valley flowers of red and yellow and blue. Two overstuffed chairs were placed in front of the altar side of the truck; César Chávez sat huddled in one and Robert Kennedy in the other. Two farm workers hoisted a large Union flag over Chávez, forming a canopylike [sic] shade from the warming Valley sun. The celebrating began.[30]

Two aides read a short but moving speech written by Chávez, who was too weak to address the crowd himself. Union Vice President Julio Hernandez read the text in Spanish, while Jim Drake read it in English. Then Kennedy spoke to the assembly. An official of the United Auto Workers followed him and presented a $50,000 check to the farm workers. Chicano activist Reies López Tijerina also stood at the podium. A personal letter of encouragement was read from Martin Luther King Jr. As always, a fiesta concluded the day's activities.[31]

Like the march, reactions ranged from awe and inspiration to dismay. Farm workers earlier had extolled Chávez. Now they nearly exalted him. Friends and foes alike admired his ingenuity, determination, and intuitive ability to cast the strike in terms of a religious crusade. Legal counsel Jerry Cohen marveled at the efficacy of the fast: not only did it ward off the threat of worker violence, but it also functioned as another organizing tool. He later orchestrated a public event tied to the fast. Halfway through his self-imposed ordeal, Chávez was scheduled to appear at the Kern County Courthouse. The Guimarra Company had charged the UFWOC with violating a picket injunction. Cohen and Chatfield helped the weakened Chávez begin ascending the massive steps of the building. Meanwhile, hundreds of farm workers silently encircled the square, stood on either side of the steps, and also lined the hallway leading into the courtroom. The workers then kneeled and prayed. On account of Chávez's physical condition, the judge postponed the hearing. Although infuriated, the Giumarra family recognized the success of the ploy and later asked for dismissal of the charge.[32]

Visitors to Forty Acres returned home and convinced fellow farm workers to join the movement. In contrast, growers and many other outsiders condemned the fast as simply another attempt to manipulate the public. Some asserted that Chávez did not really forego food at all. Fellow union officers, especially Tony Orendain, were among his severest critics. In protest, strike leader Epifanio Camacho, a few Anglo volunteers, and others left the union. Inside detractors claimed Chávez suffered from a martyr complex.[33]

The Spirituality of César Chávez

As in the case of the Sacramento march, the social fast was both an authentic act *and* a calculated move.[34] Chávez had fasted privately on a number of occasions, long before the Lenten season of 1968. During the 1950s Donald McDonnell of the Spanish Mission Band had introduced him not only to labor history and Catholic social teaching, but also to the life of Mahatma Gandhi. Although Chávez's formal schooling ended with the eighth grade, he was nevertheless self-educated and read voraciously. In Gandhi's struggles Chávez recognized the moral value of fasting. Closer to home he observed the power of nonviolence in the African American civil rights movement. He had also read about the self-denial of St. Francis and the tradition of civil disobedience through figures such as Henry David Thoreau. The example of the gentleness of Chávez's mother may have further predisposed him toward nonviolence."[35]

Chávez also had learned much about Christian manliness through the movement of El Cursillo de Cristiandad, a Spanish Catholic retreat that became popular among working-class Mexican Americans in the 1950s and 1960s, which, in California, were often led by Franciscan priests. At these events participants first received a refresher course on Catholic doctrine. Themes included Christian anthropology, divine grace, the Church, and the nature and efficacy of the sacraments. Then *cursillistas* were encouraged to interpret their faith through their own experiences and express it in their own words. This exercise often proved life changing for men, who had previously assumed that spirituality was the exclusive preserve of priests, nuns, and laywomen. Last, retreat leaders challenged participants to practice their renewed faith in everyday life. Although the *cursillo* was originally intended as a conservative type of religious renewal,[36] Chávez used it as an organizing tool for La Causa, as evidenced in the following excerpt:

> While it may have been easy to experience God during these meetings, it is more important to see him at home. We must labor for God, forget ourselves and work with the people. Your responsibility is to let the world know that there is a Savior. There must be a change in the social order—we must make our faith influence the social order through unions, organizations, classes, etc.[37]

Another element to which the union leader turned was the concept of suffering in Mexican religious piety. Many Mexicans attached redemptive value to personal suffering. Accustomed to hardship and tragedy, they easily identified with the tribulations of the crucified Jesus. No one needed to explain to most farm workers the significance of the fast. They instinctively interpreted it as an act of self-sacrifice. This understanding effectively muted another Mexican custom, namely, machismo. Chávez concluded the speech at the end of the fast with his own definition of true manliness: "To be a man is to suffer for others. God help us to be men!"[38]

Chávez's mental and physical suffering during the fast was real. He experienced nightmares, nausea, and chronic back pain. In the long run, however, the social fasts hindered Chávez not only physically but also strategically. In comparison to the success of the 1968 Lenten discipline, subsequent fasts in 1970, 1972, and 1973 turned out to be dismal failures. Jim Drake commented on the mixed blessings of the 1968 fast, which virtually elevated Chávez to the status of sainthood: "After that he was a guru instead of a general. . . . After that he could not make mistakes."[39]

Chávez's tendency to draw his spirituality from many sources mirrored his penchant for recognizing, recruiting, combining, and implementing a number of strategies. Sociologists refer to this phenomenon as resource mobilization, a skill that Chávez thoroughly mastered. It fitted well with his eclectic religiosity,[40] which often permitted others to project onto him whatever most appealed to them. For many Catholics he was a modern-

day champion of the working class. For mainline Protestants he was an-
other Dietrich Bonhoeffer who exemplified the cost of true discipleship.
For leftists he was an anticapitalist. For union members he was a fellow
Mexican American and field laborer.[41] One farm worker who practiced
Native American religion attributed all of these qualities to him:

> César was an exceptional man who generated great motivation in people.
> To me and many other [*sic*] he was as close to goodness as any hu-
> man could be. . . . Cesars [*sic*] beliefs were intense and his commitment to
> campesino workers made me fill [*sic*] humble in his presence. Since César
> was Indio and claimed it, I endorsed his spirituality wholeheartedly as well
> as his commitment to humanity and nonviolence, with great affection for
> the man and his actions.[42]

Chávez indeed seemed a modern-day embodiment of Juan Diego, the
sixteenth-century Indian peasant who, through his encounter with La
Virgen de Guadalupe, served as the conduit for the Christian conversion
of the indigenous peoples of Mexico. Yet union insiders also knew Chávez
as a taskmaster, an overly stubborn idealist, and a manipulator. For example, he later refused to alter the status of staff from volunteer to salaried
positions. He insisted that they continue to subscribe to a virtual vow
of poverty and receive only room and board and five dollars per week.
Another indication of his desire to maintain an ascetic lifestyle among
staffers was the transfer of the union headquarters from Forty Acres in
Delano to a rural retreat-type setting outside of Bakersfield, known as La
Paz. In later years he was described as an authoritarian who may even have
suffered from paranoid tendencies. This side of his personality especially
manifested itself from the late 1970s, when he briefly became enamored
of "The Game," an intense, encounter-group experience developed by the
quasi-religious, self-help cult Synanon. "The Game" was supposed to reveal dishonest behavior among union staff and so ferret out potential en-
emies from within. Some volunteers and paid workers soon complained
that Chávez equated internal criticism with a lack of commitment to La
Causa. In other words, those who dared to question the decisions of senior
leadership were summarily branded as traitors. The accused were often
Anglo intellectuals or "lefties" whom Mexican American leaders resented.
Abuse and purges of such persons—ultimately even longtime supporter
Chris Hartmire—revealed a serious discrepancy between the public

persona and private character of Chávez. His first office secretary, Susan Drake, penned a cynical poem about him:

> *Farm workers*
> > *All races*
> > *Ages*
> > *Flannel-suiters*
> > *Hollywood stars*
> > *Singers internationally known*
> > *César tucks them so neatly*
> > *Into the pocket*
> > *Of the movement.*[43]

Latina Leadership and *Mujerista* Theology

That image that Chávez promoted contrasted sharply to the stereotype of Mexican manhood. Another union official, Dolores Huerta, also defied the social conventions of the day. She refused to play the part of "the quiet, long-suffering" Mexican wife and mother. Factors such as family, education, work experience, and personal temperament all prepared her for very active and visible roles in La Causa.[44]

This section will examine the leadership styles of Huerta, Helen Chávez, and others and how they may or may not be interpreted in light of the academic field known as *mujerista* theology.[45]

Huerta's background departed from that of many Mexican American women who worked in the fields and vineyards. For example, her parents were born not south of the border but in New Mexico, and her mother grew up in a family that enjoyed modest economic success. Furthermore, both Huerta's mother and grandmother had divorced and remarried in an era that strongly sanctioned such behavior. In the early years of the Great Depression, when Huerta and her brother were still small children, they moved with their pregnant mother to Stockton, California. Initially, their mother was forced to work in a nearby cannery and wait tables at restaurants. Eventually, however, her fortune changed. She remarried, co-managed a hotel with her new husband, divorced him after World War II, and soon was operating a second hotel. Both of these establishments were patronized by migrant farm workers and other seasonal laborers, whom Huerta's mother and third husband often befriended.[46]

As a result of her upbringing, Huerta spent her later childhood in a middle-class home filled with high expectations. She graduated from high school, attended Stockton Junior College, and received a two-year degree—at that time a high level of education for a Mexican American woman. After marriage, the birth of two children, and the dissolution of her first marriage, she returned to school to pursue a teaching degree. In 1955 she remarried, had several more children, and divorced her second husband in 1963. Throughout these years she not only duplicated her mother's marital relationships but her employment patterns as well. Instead of becoming a traditional, full-time homemaker, Huerta worked outside of the home—first as an office secretary and later as a teacher. Yet she felt much more fulfilled as a volunteer in several of Stockton's social and charitable organizations. In 1955 Fred Ross of the CSO recruited her, which, in turn, led to her employment in a farm labor union. She soon resigned, however, and rejoined the CSO as a salaried worker. She lobbied tirelessly for working-class groups, thereby gaining invaluable experience as a public speaker and learning about the inner workings of governmental institutions.[47]

In the early 1960s, Huerta and others later helped Chávez to found the National Farm Workers Association, even as she remained in her relatively secure job in community organizing. Yet she eventually resigned her position and served as an unpaid recruiter for the new farm labor group. Short of money, she left some of her children with relatives and relocated with Chávez and others to Delano. This arrangement continued when she began living with Chávez's brother, Richard, with whom she eventually had four more children. When the grape strike was announced, she increasingly juggled the roles of administration, picketing, recruiting, fundraising, and public speaking. Foremost among her activities was negotiating labor agreements with fruit companies and wineries. For instance, she represented the union in its first major contract—Schenley Industries. She was especially instrumental in talks leading to the contracts with Guimarra Vineyards and other Delano grape growers in 1970. Furthermore, she temporarily led boycott efforts in New York and San Francisco. Last, she lobbied for state legislation that was crucial for California farm labor in the 1970s and 1980s.[48]

Dolores Huerta was influenced by the then unconventional examples of her mother and grandmother. She also benefited from a college education and work experience that prepared her for the rigors of farm labor activism. Ultimately, however, her strong personality and communication skills were the factors that enabled her to survive in a world dominated by men. Growers, their legal counsel, and others in agribusiness naturally resisted her as a spokesperson for the union. So did fellow union leaders. Some of them particularly criticized her style of motherhood. In any event, she served as an inspiring role model for a number of young Chicanas who joined La Causa.[49]

In contrast, Helen Chávez resembled more the traditional image of the Mexican wife and mother. Yet she also contributed significantly to La Causa. In addition to maintaining a home for her family, she kept records for her husband César, picked crops to support the family as he organized farm workers, and occasionally marched and picketed in the fields. Later she also managed the United Farm Workers' credit union. She fulfilled these duties, however, at her husband's direction and so conformed to the stereotype of the obedient, compliant wife. She served as the more acceptable example for the vast majority of Latinas who, with their husbands, joined the union. So it was for most of the women who left their homes to boycott grapes in far-off cities; they were, in fact, following their husbands.[50]

How may these models of Latina activists in the farm worker movement be informed by *mujerista* theology? Arguably, this theology may not apply to Huerta as an individual. In contrast to César Chávez, she did not seem to cast her leadership in terms of any religious ideology but, if anything, approached her union work from a secular frame of reference. In contrast, Helen Chávez and most other Mexican American women may have been somewhat characterized by several understandings of La Virgen de Guadalupe or Nuestra Señora de Guadalupe, or, simply, Our Lady. *Mujerista* theologians have often commented on the positive part that Our Lady has played in the lives of Latinas. For instance, and first, many Mexican American women have shared the view that they regard Our Lady as a sympathetic mother, a mediator, and role model who listens to their prayers and inspires them. She is the one to whom they have turned in times of fear, disappointment, or despair. Thus Latina theologians, activists, and artists regard Our Lady not only in stereotypical terms such as *submissive* or *passive* but also as an empowering figure. This phenomenon begins with identification with the physical features of Nuestra Señora: "Our Lady of Guadalupe expresses a Mexican-American woman's values of being female, a mother, brown-skinned, mestiza." This identification has been instrumental for women who have too often experienced low status in society, due to the sexism from which all women suffer, racism, and finally "sexism within [their own] culture."[51]

Second, while Our Lady conveys qualities such as submissiveness and passivity, one must be aware of the inherent ambiguities in this Marian image. In one study, for example, Mexican American "women perceived Our Lady of Guadalupe as being both meek and strong-willed, independent and dependent, assertive and shy—all at the same time."[52] Third, a few advocates of Latinas have even referred to Our Lady as "subversive" in nature.[53] Some scholars have illustrated how such perspectives of Our Lady have played out on the historical scene. For example, women's devotional groups dedicated to Our Lady:

> By identifying with the love of Nuestra Señora for the community, Mexican American women had a role model that helped them to move beyond their roles within the family and become social activists. It was also through the *sociedades guadalupanas* [Guadalupe societies] that Mexican American women were given opportunities to develop leadership skills for both the church and society . . . the women were also able to create a bridge between the realm of religious ritual that expressed their faith in Nuestra Señora and the realities of the daily lives of their communities. . . . The dual benefits of membership in the *societies*—religious leadership and community activism—cannot be dismissed.[54]

Although the UFW was a heavily chauvinistic union in the 1960s,[55] its use of the image of Our Lady of Guadalupe helped to serve as a catalyst for Latina empowerment as evidenced in activist groups such as that of Las Hermanas, which was founded by Catholic women in 1971. Similar organizations have developed over the years and witnessed to a multifaceted interpretation of Our Lady.[56]

Protestants and the Grape Boycott

More conventional leaders in La Causa had first called for a boycott against the Schenley and DiGiorgio conglomerates. In August of 1967 the union leveled its sights on the Guimarra Vineyards Corporation, which was California's largest producer of table grapes. By December of that year the Guimarra strike had escalated into a boycott. The company tried to defeat it in several ways, such as filing lawsuits against picketers. The Guimarras also began selling their grapes under the labels of other growers. This tactic forced the union to declare a boycott against all table grape growers, including smaller, more vulnerable farmers. Meanwhile, most large groceries still carried the grapes, prompting the union to resort to a secondary boycott.[57]

Religious figures again played an important role. As early as October of 1965, Jim Drake directed boycott efforts. He deployed coordinators along the West Coast and later to Boston, New York, Philadelphia, Baltimore, Chicago, Toronto, and other cities. Local ministers and religious communities often provided office space. Rank-and-file church members also participated. Nuns, college students, and middle-class housewives picketed supermarkets. Incidents like the following were not uncommon:

> [In Chicago] there was a confrontation between women shoppers at a large co-op grocery market and an official from S&W Foods, which was being boycotted to put pressure on DiGiorgio Farms, the parent company. The women, as both consumers and owners of the Co-op, were going through the store removing all the S&W cans from the shelves. They were filling shopping carts with the cans and then putting leaflets on them telling other shoppers about the Delano strike and boycott of S&W products.
>
> An S&W official happened to come into the store at this time. "He got furious at the women, tried to put some cans back on the shelves, and finally, in desperation, shoved a loaded shopping cart at one of the women, who was seven months pregnant. She was knocked to the ground. Police soon arrived and escorted the S&W official out of the store." The store manager helped the women take the rest of the S&W cans off the shelves, leaving 59 feet of empty shelf space.[58]

The combined efforts of boycotters finally paid off as fewer consumers were willing to buy grapes. The union estimated that the 1968 table grape market had fallen 15 percent from the previous two years. A new season saw a further decline of 20 percent. On 10 May 1969 the union even sponsored an International Boycott Day. As a result of mass picketing, A&P supermarkets in Pittsburgh and Boston stopped selling grapes. Dominion Stores in Canada followed suit. Boycotters in Chicago, Columbus, Detroit, and New York doubled their efforts. In November of 1969 Drake and others launched a second offensive, that is, a Thanksgiving Day event known as "Fast—not Feast." Once again consumers rose to the occasion, and table grape sales sunk to an all-time low.[59]

Various church bodies also took a public stand. On 12 July 1968, the Board of Directors of the Northern California Council of Churches announced its official support of the grape boycott. It urged not only churches in the state but also entire denominations to refrain from buying California table grapes. Other religious organizations followed its lead, including the National Council of Churches and even the World Council of Churches. Locally, the ecumenical San Francisco Council on Race, Religion, and Social Concern soon endorsed the boycott. A few months later the Episcopal Diocese of Los Angeles issued a statement of support. But many church groups were horrified by these responses. Although a nonviolent measure, the boycott, they believed, inflicted economic harm on too many innocent parties. Member congregations of the Northern California Council protested the pro-boycott announcement. Judicatories such as the Synods of the Sierra and Southern California, United Presbyterian Church, U.S.A., offered counterresolutions. Some church executives who had previously stood behind the union questioned the ethics of the boycott. Some Protestant clergy even founded groups designed as alternatives or supplements to the California Migrant Ministry and were based on the traditional model of reconciliation instead of justice.[60]

As a religious defender of the union, migrant minister Chris Hartmire strode into a new round of paper duels. Opponents unsheathed their pens to assail him. In turn, he parried their verbal thrusts and took the offensive. His main adversary was Allan Grant, a fellow Presbyterian. He was president of the California Farm Bureau, president of the California State Board of Agriculture, and a member of the Board of Regents of the University of California. In December of 1968 an article by Grant appeared in *Presbyterian Life*. Drawing on a number of statistics, he calmly argued that most of the grape growers were small farmers who paid their workers just wages and provided adequate housing. He added that many state agricultural laws insured the well-being of laborers. He then depicted the union as an illegitimate group of outsiders, bent on exploiting both workers and growers. Hartmire demanded equal time. He quickly authored his own version of the grape strike and submitted it to the editor-in-chief of *Presbyterian Life*. Regretting that he had published Grant's essay, the editor nevertheless told Hartmire that a rebuttal was clearly out of the question. It would serve only to intensify the strife and ill will plaguing the denomination. Hartmire persisted. He contacted other church executives and promised a substantial revision of his essay, which the magazine then published. He stressed the hardships of farm workers, the need for churches to help create a level playing field between workers and growers, and the regrettable but unavoidable negative impact of the strike on small farmers.[61]

Tensions among Anglo Catholics

Catholics also engaged in a war of words. Conservative laity in California published pamphlets critical of the grape strike, including accusations of communist infiltration in the ranks of the union. Two men, Frank Bergon and Murray Norris, coauthored the booklet *Delano—Another Crisis for the Catholic Church!* Both of them were tied to agricultural interests. A resident of the Valley community of Madera, Bergon was a retired agent of the Federal Bureau of Investigation and a third-generation grape grower. Norris was employed as an associate editor of *California Farmer.* They lambasted anyone who favored the strike, including Catholic bishops and other "outsider" priests who visited Delano. Bergon and Norris reserved the worst of their vitriolic, however, for the union itself. They insinuated that communists regularly advised the farm workers. One other target of their pen was the editor of the Fresno Diocese's organ *Central California Register,* who refused to condemn the grape strike or censure news stories about it. Bergon, Norris, and many of the growers regarded this stance as a legitimization of the union and thus an act of treason. Several other Catholics also entered the fray. In particular, two Jesuits published diatribes against La Causa. Daniel Lyons, S.J., a columnist in the Catholic paper *Twin Circle,* asked a fellow Jesuit to investigate the strike. Perceptions of his trip were recorded in a booklet titled *Battle for the Vineyards.* Echoing Bergon and Norris, the author first asserted that the union had manipulated bishops and priests. Second, he dismissed out of hand the possibility that the majority of farm workers even desired or needed a union. Last, he used the worn-out ploy of red baiting in that he even likened Chávez to Fidel Castro.[62]

These claims did not go unchallenged. Labor priest George G. Higgins wrote rebuttals in his weekly column, which appeared in diocesan newspapers throughout the nation. He decried the personal attack on Chávez, holding "that even . . . the late Senator Joseph McCarthy might have blushed" at some of the words printed about the union leader. Higgins also protested Lyons's editorials denouncing the United States Catholic Bishops' Ad Hoc Committee on Farm Labor, on which Higgins served as an adviser. Lyons's diatribes eventually backfired. The board of *Twin Circle* became weary of his biased reports and finally relieved him of his editorial duties.[63]

The high pitch of this war of words suggested that the boycott was finally achieving its desired effect. Grape growers were feeling the economic pinch and were resorting to any and all means to discredit La Causa. The denunciations by Bergon, Norris, and others underscored the desperation felt by many growers. By 1969 some fissures even began to appear in the wall of grower intransigence. Several grape farmers quietly contacted local bishops about the possibility of mediation. This overture signaled a volte-face from the first four years of the strike, a time during which the relationship between the grape growers—most of them Catholics—and the institutional church had steadily deteriorated. Growers were incensed that the California prelates did not officially condemn the strike or at least regard it as an issue falling outside the realm of the church. Occasionally farmers and other laypersons voiced these feelings in public, usually criticizing the Catholic Church as a whole. More frequently these persons sent angry letters to bishops, threatening to withdraw financial support for diocesan projects and, in a number of cases, carrying out such threats. The strongest public outcry came from Delano grower Martin Zaninovich at a meeting in San Francisco:[64]

> I want to see elections held among the congregations of the churches in the country to determine if the philosophy church leaders are expounding today is representative of the attitudes of their flocks. I feel certain that Americans would reject these self-appointed leaders in the same manner our workers have rejected the agitators in Delano.
>
> As far as I am concerned, church leaders had better start looking for other financial means to carry out these radical theories they are attempting to force upon us.
>
> It is apparent to me that the need for churches to administer to the spiritual need of man has taken a back seat to the need to fight causes of various types. If the churches want this perhaps it is about time that they, like any other political organization, be relieved of their tax-exempt status and start paying their own way.[65]

The Diocese of Fresno, in which Delano is located, did in fact suffer severe financial repercussions. Three months after grape growers and farm workers signed their contract, diocesan chancellor Roger Mahony wrote a letter to the chief arbiter, auxiliary bishop Joseph Donnelly of New Haven, Connecticut: "since Catholic Charities suffered so very much because of our involvement in the farm labor issue, three of our best self-help programs are on the verge of termination. Our Appeal is down almost 50% this year . . . if you could give [Fresno] Bishop Donohoe some support and encouragement it would be very helpful." The diocesan paper, *Central California Register,* met an even worse fate: in the early 1970s it was discontinued altogether. Its editor wrote to Ad Hoc Committee adviser George Higgins: "I am of the opinion that unless the [diocesan] priests come around a lot more, we shall not be in existence next year. . . . The latent hostility to the Bishop for his role on the Bishops' Committee in the farm labor role is ever present. Many of them are just not cooperating because their friends, the farmers, have threatened to cut off collection money. It is as simple as that."[66]

Vastly different understandings of the Catholic Church's role in the world lay at the heart of such criticisms. Commercial farmers and others drew a sharp line between spiritual and secular matters. They regarded bishops, priests, and nuns as religious caretakers with no knowledge of or competence in economic affairs, much less any mandate to address them. On their own part, growers were essentially ignorant of or insensitive to Catholic social teachings that upheld the rights of workers. Or growers sometimes claimed that agriculture was a special exception. Mostly second-generation U.S. citizens, these growers were intensely proud men. Their parents and grandparents had emigrated from Italy and Croatia between the two world wars. Men with names like Dispoto, Sandrini, Caratan, and Radovich had built large enterprises from small beginnings. They believed they knew what was in the best interest of their workers and that the Catholic Church had no right to meddle in their affairs.[67]

The California Bishops and the Response of Other Anglo Catholics

The clergy themselves held a variety of views on the grape strike, depending on which interest groups they informally represented. Some priests and nuns marched or picketed with the workers. Others, such as Daniel Lyons, condemned such actions. Still others took a middle-of-the-road approach. For example, California prelates conspicuously refused to champion either the workers or the growers. Instead the California hierarchy usually walked a diplomatic tightrope, continually stressing the rights of both sides.[68]

Hugh A. Donohoe was first to issue a statement on behalf of his fellow bishops. He spoke at the March 1966 hearings of the U.S. Senate Sub-Committee on Migratory Labor. Both a long-standing supporter of organized labor and bishop of a heavily agricultural region, Donohoe was well positioned to comment on the farm labor issue. A former instructor in industrial ethics, he had helped to found a local chapter of the Associated Catholic Trade Unionists. After serving in administrative posts in the Archdiocese of San Francisco, he became the bishop of Stockton in 1962. In 1969 he was assigned to the Diocese of Fresno. His statement opened with excerpts of general principles from Vatican II's "Pastoral Constitution on the Church in the Modern World" and Pope John XXIII's *Pacem in Terris*. Both quotations highlighted the need for equitable relations between employers and workers and the active role that the government should play to insure such relations. Donohoe balanced his testimony to include the rights of both farmers and workers, although leaning in favor of the latter. In closing, he urged the extension of the National Labor Relations Act to agriculture, which would legally guarantee farm workers with "fair labor standards, non-discriminatory employment opportunities, adequate sanitation and physical safety, minimum wage, adequate social security, and unemployment insurance."[69] Two months after Donohoe spoke at the hearing, the bishop of the strike area released his own statement. Aloysius J. Willinger of the then Diocese of Monterey-Fresno issued a call for a free election among workers, in order to determine whether they wanted a union and, if so, which union. Although the document ostensibly took a neutral stand, newspaper reporters saw it as weighted in favor of the growers. So did farm worker advocate James Vizzard:

> Bishop Willinger insists that the "Church of the Diocese of Monterey-Fresno . . . does not endorse or align herself with a particular union, owner organization, or other secular enterprise." Despite that claim, both the workers and the owners have quite clearly understood that Bishop Willinger has, in fact, aligned himself with the owners. His whole statement has been rightly interpreted by both sides to be an open endorsement of the growers' views and propaganda.

Last week, using Bishop Willinger's statement as a spring board [*sic*] and justification, Di Giorgio [Corporation] unilaterally announced, and on very short notice (two days), conducted its own "election." The result was a farce and a fraud. Even Governor Brown, no stalwart friend of the farm worker, has publicly urged Di Giorgio and Teamsters (who, with the growers' open assistance, won the election) to suspend any contract negotiations until an impartial investigation is made on the "election."[70]

Besides Vizzard, other leaders of the Catholic Church supported the strikers. The activist role of Eugene S. Boyle, S.J., illustrates the tensions existing not only between local clergy and laity but also among the priests. Chair of a social-justice commission in San Francisco, he marched with the *peregrinos* in 1966. He also held a mass and even served as one of the speakers at the Easter Day rally at the Capitol. In 1967 he helped to negotiate an agreement between the union and a Delano vineyard. When Chávez broke his fast in March of 1968, Boyle was one of the priests who distributed the host. Boyle's superior, Archbishop Joseph T. McGucken, upheld the right of unionization among farm workers. Yet McGucken did not always take unequivocal positions on controversial issues. Instead he allowed "new-breed" priests to become involved in La Causa without necessarily granting his approval or setting specific limits to their activities. Not a few times this practice led to confusion and misunderstanding. For example, in May and June of 1966 McGucken was forced to defend Boyle's correspondence with some producers of sacramental wine. Boyle had advised the wineries to recognize the union. In turn, the food conglomerate DiGiorgio Corporation accused the archdiocese of extortion. McGucken quickly countered that no such pressure had occurred and that DiGiorgio was spreading vicious rumors.[71]

Amid negotiations between farm workers and one of the vineyards, yet other protests were lodged about the appropriateness of Boyle's involvement. This time, however, one of the voices belonged to John T. Dwyer, a fellow priest and Archdiocesan Director of the National Catholic Rural Life Conference. He and others had been holding dialogues with Catholic growers. When arbitrations between the union and a grower broke down, Boyle excoriated the latter who decided to maintain a sweetheart contract with the Teamsters. In response, Dwyer urged the archbishop to reprimand Boyle. Thus clergy who blazed the trail of social justice and those who preferred the traditional path of reconciliation often exchanged sharp words. Some bishops thereby functioned as referees, not only between clergy and laity but also among priests.[72]

In spite of internal problems, the California bishops reaffirmed in June of 1968 an earlier statement that the National Labor Relations Act should include agricultural laborers. The next autumn other U.S. bishops defended this proposal. Still others endorsed the grape boycott. Lawrence Cardinal Shehan of Baltimore, Maryland, declared his support in September of 1968. Similar statements soon followed, including those from the archbishops of Denver, San Antonio, St. Paul, and Portland, Oregon. The bishops of Buffalo and Detroit exhorted their priests and parishioners not to purchase table grapes or patronize grocers who carried them. A total of nearly twenty-five prelates approved the boycott, many of them located in the East and Midwest. One statement announced that a host of "diocesan papers, religious orders, lay organizations, priest's senates [*sic*], Catholic student organizations and individual Catholic lay leaders" had joined the boycott. This tidal wave of support for the farm workers had clearly spread over much of the nation.[73]

One of many persons who directed boycott efforts was Victor P. Salandini of the Diocese of San Diego, who was affectionately known as "the Tortilla Priest." In 1961 his bishop had granted him study leave, ostensibly to work on a master's degree at St. Louis University, but probably to remove him from the lettuce-strike controversy in the Imperial Valley. As a result of similar activities in 1965, a new bishop sent Salandini to the Catholic University of America in Washington, D.C., to pursue a doctorate in economics. Once there, however, Salandini conducted research for the union and staged local media events that spotlighted the grape boycott. In a dramatic move he even accompanied a replica of the Liberty Bell as it was paraded through several major cities. Donated by a foundry in London, the bell remained silent until the union had secured the right to organize and bargain collectively.[74]

In light of these developments, the National Conference of Catholic Bishops felt mounting pressure to issue a definitive statement on the strike. Such a pronouncement would reveal the degree of consensus among the bishops and the level of commitment of the Catholic hierarchy on behalf of the farm workers. Would the bishops choose strong words? Words that would even justify the secondary boycott? Or would they stress more conventional themes such as the mutual rights and obligations of both employers and workers? In 1968 several groups contributed to drafts of a proposed statement. Monsignor Roger Mahony of the Diocese of Fresno represented the California bishops. He suggested a moderate approach, which was reflected in an early draft submitted to the Social Action Department. in Washington. Its director, Monsignor George Higgins, favored a stronger stand that stood unequivocally on the side of the workers. So did the officers of the National Catholic Rural Life Conference and the Bishops' Committee for the Spanish Speaking. Opposing sides especially argued about the boycott. Bishop Manning of the Diocese of Fresno wanted to include the phrase, "We do not condone the boycott." Higgins vehemently objected, believing that failure to endorse the boycott would undercut statements already made by other bishops. Moreover, the National Council of Churches had recently approved the boycott. A considerably milder statement from the bishops might create a credibility problem with liberal Protestants. Mahony nevertheless pressed for exclusion of any position at all on the boycott. He argued that such an endorsement would destroy all hope of bringing growers to the bargaining table. Higgins finally agreed to modify that part of the draft but refused to strike it out completely—in spite of an eleventh-hour plea from Mahony. Yet, in the end, Mahony and the California bishops prevailed. On 13 November 1968, the National Conference published a brochure, titled "Statement on Farm Labor," which in most respects resembled the last draft prepared by the Social Action Department. The statement denounced past injustices suffered by farm workers. It also called for their inclusion in the National Labor Relations Act, the minimum-wage law, and the national unemployment insurance program. All references to the boycott, however, had been deleted.[75]

The United States Bishops Ad Hoc Committee and the 1970 Grape Contracts

In 1969 boycotters intensified their efforts, applying relentless pressure on supermarket chains. The union also unceasingly called for full and unqualified endorsement from Catholic bishops. Supporters like George Higgins turned to Catholic social theory to justify the boycott. Migrant Minister Jim Drake took a different tack, simply urging dozens of Protestant leaders to express their views to the president of the Bishops' Conference. Mexican American organizations, such as the Southwest Council de La Raza and a group of priests known as PADRES, also called the bishops. Union leaders joined the chorus.[76]

The Conference of Bishops met again in November of 1969, when a compromise was reached among the California prelates, Higgins, and AFL-CIO leadership. In lieu of endorsing the boycott, the bishops agreed to appoint a special committee to negotiate a grower-worker settlement. The head of the conference named Joseph F. Donnelly to chair the group, which became known as the United States Catholic Bishops Ad Hoc Committee on Farm Labor. As auxiliary bishop of Hartford, Connecticut, and a recognized expert on employer-worker relations, Donnelly had helped to establish a number of labor schools in the 1940s and had served twenty years on the state arbitration board. The new cardinal of Los Angeles also was appointed to the committee, as well as Donohoe and two other bishops. Higgins joined them as a special consultant, while Roger Mahony of the Diocese of Fresno served as the secretary.[77] According to Higgins, California bishops would have proceeded at a glacier pace. So Donnelly scheduled a meeting in January 1970. Soon afterward the committee, a dozen growers, and union officials gathered in Fresno. Most of the growers in attendance had negotiated briefly with the union a few months earlier. In early March Donnelly, Higgins, and Mahony decided to crisscross the San Joaquin Valley in order to meet with the Guimarra family in Bakersfield, farmers in Fresno, and several growers in Delano. Receptions ranged from politeness to open hostility. Donnelly was shocked to learn that most of the growers had never even met Chávez. He also was surprised that they believed in so many of the baseless rumors about the union.[78]

Despite these obstacles, the committee was able to arrange a second meeting between union leaders and growers. Among other things, Mahony knew that the staying power of the boycott was beginning to wane, which made the union willing to sit down with growers. So he recognized the unique role that the Catholic Church could play in bringing the strike to an equitable settlement. Beforehand, Mahony visited growers individually, which revealed the existence of three distinct groups. On the one hand, the Guimarras and other agribusinessmen appeared immovable. On the other hand, smaller commercial farmers seemed open to collective bargaining. Still other growers promised to recognize the union as long as others paved the way. So Mahony devised a strategy to capitalize on these differences. He counseled the committee to allow the most willing growers to speak directly to the union. Once these negotiations led to several contracts, then the vacillating group would be encouraged to enter talks. This strategy indeed bore fruit. Significantly, the first major breakthrough occurred not in Delano but in the Coachella Valley. This region always harvested the first grapes of the season and relied heavily on early retail sales. Thus local growers were highly motivated to settle with the union. Another important fact was that the first grower to sign with the union was not even a Catholic. Lionel Steinberg was a liberal Democrat and personal friend of the Kennedy family. He had wanted to negotiate with the union as early as 1968, but feared reprisals from fellow growers. On 1 April 1970, he and Chávez sat down in the chancery office of the Archdiocese of Los Angeles and signed a binding contract. The very next day two other Coachella growers expressed an interest in formal talks. One of them, K. K. Larson, was a Methodist and asked his minister and Mahony to witness union elections on 11 April. Workers voted almost unanimously in favor of collective bargaining. In early May a third Coachella Valley grower recognized the union.[79]

Simultaneously, two farms in the San Joaquin Valley had also entered into negotiations. In a secret meeting on 6 April 1970, a consultant represented the Dispoto and Bianco farms. The two sides encountered major difficulties and, for all practical purposes, recessed until mid-May. The Ad Hoc Committee then scheduled another meeting and, following some very tense bargaining, the union and growers signed a contract on 20 May 1970. While the base wage did not change, César Chávez and Dolores Huerta nevertheless gained other concessions, such as the exclusion of the use of several pesticides. Mahony and other committee members were ecstatic. They regarded the contract as a prototype for other growers, for the Bianco and Dispoto holdings resembled the typical size and operation of most of the other Delano vineyards. Three weeks later the committee was called to the Roberts Farms, where that enterprise and the union requested assistance during final talks. This contract signaled yet another major advance for the union. Although Hollis Roberts cultivated only several hundred acres of table grapes, he grew many other crops that totaled over forty-eight thousand acres. Soon thereafter two more Coachella Valley growers—Milton Karahadian & Sons of Thermal and Key-Kas Ranches of Indio—signed contracts.[80]

On 19 June 1970, the Ad Hoc Committee took part in negotiations between the union and two other Coachella grape growers, which culminated in contracts on 26 June 1970. Several other growers soon fell into line. As of 28 June 1970, table grapes were included in union contracts in 65 percent of the Coachella Valley, 60 percent in the Lamont-Arvin area, and 20 percent in Delano vineyards. As the harvest season loomed in Delano, the Ad Hoc Committee felt confident that the union would see even more arbitrations. The committee was not disappointed. On 9 July 1970, it contacted a labor-relations consultant representing twenty-six of the Delano grape growers, including Giumarra Vineyards. Their holdings consisted of 35 to 40 percent of the entire California table grape industry. The next day the consultant instructed the bishops to press the union to negotiate via the State Conciliation Service. The committee pursued this suggestion, but the union refused. Governor Ronald Reagan had earlier called for this approach, and union leaders feared that the service would arbitrate in favor of the growers. So the Ad Hoc Committee offered to bring the two parties together, although the consultant and a union organizer would be responsible for the actual negotiations. The talks commenced on 17 July 1970 in Bakersfield, but nearly broke down when philosophical differences surfaced. The union then demanded that its entire leadership attend subsequent meetings. On 20 July 1970, Chávez, Huerta, and others made new demands, including the dropping of existing lawsuits against the union. Although these matters were of minor importance to the growers, what truly concerned them were proposals for an overall economic package and the use of union hiring halls. Clearly, the farm workers were seeking wages and benefits beyond the Bianco and Dispoto contracts. The grower counsel told the Ad Hoc Committee that the farmers found the union's terms unacceptable and intended to break off negotiations. Donnelly, Higgins, and Mahony called his bluff, and everyone departed.[81]

A few days later, however, the growers returned to the bargaining table. John Guimarra Jr. contacted union attorney Jerry Cohen, and talks resumed. This time the counsel for the growers and the Ad Hoc Committee participated as observers, while the union and growers themselves ironed out remaining differences. On Wednesday, 29 July 1970, at 11:00 A.M.—nearly five years after grape pickers had first shouted "¡Huelga!"—a contract was signed with the majority of Delano vineyards. The farm workers demanded that it be held at union headquarters, which contributed to a visible uneasiness among the growers. Chávez and John Guimarra Sr. sat down together at a table. Donnelly, Higgins, diocesan newspaper editor Gerard E. Sherry, and John Guimarra Jr. stood behind them as twenty-five other growers, several hundred farm workers, and scores of reporters witnessed the event. Chávez and Guimarra signed the contract, shook hands, and smiled for the flashing cameras. Chávez then declared that all union grapes would indeed be sweet. Elated, farm workers broke out in thunderous cheers. They waved union flags wildly in the air and embraced one another. A new day had dawned for agricultural labor.[82]

The editor of the diocesan newspaper was among the first to applaud the efforts of the Ad Hoc Committee:

> the leadership of the Bishops Committee has been vital in bringing the [two] sides together in peaceful and fruitful negotiation. This was a task in which the state administration had failed; in which the politicians had failed, and which the parties involved in the dispute had found difficult to achieve.
> . . . Labor peace is almost with us, and we all should offer a prayer of thanksgiving for it. The Valley's sorrow has been turned into joy.[83]

His optimism was premature. Joseph Donnelly cautioned that the grape contract merely marked the beginning of efforts to organize farm laborers elsewhere. Although a momentous event, the agreement suggested only the first stage in a possible new relationship between growers and workers. The United Farm Workers hoped to attract tens of thousands of other agricultural workers, not only in California but also in Texas, the Midwest, and on the Atlantic seaboard. This feat could be accomplished only one painstaking step at a time. In fact, even as workers cheered in Delano, Chávez prepared to leave for the Salinas Valley. The union had recently begun to organize lettuce workers there, and their employers anxiously awaited the outcome of the Delano negotiations. On hearing the news of the contract, the lettuce growers quickly signed a sweetheart deal with the Teamsters. Chávez hardly paused to join the Delano victory celebration, but immediately set up picket teams in Salinas and converted the nationwide boycott from grapes to lettuce.[84]

The union's struggle in the lettuce fields lasted several years, enduring Teamster violence and even the deaths of two farm workers. In 1973 the grape contracts were reviewed. Delano and Coachella Valley growers had justifiably complained about the cumbersome and inefficient administrative procedures of the union's ranch committees. Of course, many employers also were inventing reasons not to renew union contracts. In 1975, however, the farm workers found an ally in Governor Jerry Brown.

He mediated extensively between the union and the growers, which led to a state law guaranteeing legal status for the union.[85]

Conclusion

The United Farm Workers succeeded where other agricultural labor unions had failed. It had not merely survived but also won major contracts. No one could dispute that Chávez and his fellow strategists had overcome what previously had seemed an insurmountable obstacle. Many factors were responsible for this milestone in labor history. The awakening self-consciousness of Chicanas/os and the extension of the civil rights movement to scores of Mexican American communities ranked high on the list. The economy also played an important role. By the mid-1960s a number of California farm workers enjoyed greater stability in their lives, although still significantly modest by middle-class Anglo standards. A third factor was a loosely held coalition that came to the aid of the union. College students walked the picket lines, distributed pamphlets, and telephoned potential donors. Various trade unions lent their support. Liberal politicians seeking Mexican American votes also became associated with La Causa.[86]

A number of religious individuals and organizations joined this coalition. Elements of an "East Coast and West Coast" Protestantism stood with the union throughout the strike. Chris Hartmire, Jim Drake, and others adopted a "servanthood" form of ministry, placing themselves at the beck and call of the farm workers. The Migrant Ministry's commitment of both funds and personnel insured the union's survival in the first few critical weeks and months of the strike. Hartmire's constant defense and interpretation of the struggle kept the lines of communication open to church leaders. He frequently reiterated the dictum that the growers would never come to the negotiating table until power between them and the workers had been equalized. In his eyes this obvious fact easily justified the use of the secondary boycott. Although many other Protestant clergy and laypersons disagreed with his views, they were seldom a match for the sheer logic and force of his arguments.[87]

Chávez played a religious role as well, inspiring fellow workers and supporters by means of his soft-spoken charisma. His masterful employment of an array of resources, including images of Mexican devotional

Catholicism, the ideal of Franciscan poverty, the Cursillo movement, Gandhian nonviolence, and even Latina/o Pentecostalism was unparalleled. The feelings that images such as the suffering Christ and La Virgen evoked in both male and female farm workers helped to reinvigorate the strike in its darker moments. A broad ecumenism born of necessity accompanied this practical spirituality, by means of which Chávez welcomed all religious groups that befriended the union. The regular participation of Catholics, Protestants, and Jews—even agnostics and atheists—attests to the interfaith dynamics of the strike.

Last, the institutional Roman Catholic Church acted as yet one more major player in the Delano victory. It was true that Catholic support in California often expressed itself only through individual priests, nuns, and laypersons. Still, local bishops eventually acquiesced to negotiations that led to the end of the grape strike, thanks to the mounting pressure exerted by other prelates and various Catholic organizations. By refusing or failing to endorse all aspects of the union struggle, the California bishops were perhaps inadvertently able to maintain fragile relationships with the growers. Longtime veterans of the Catholic labor tradition, Donnelly and Higgins of the Ad Hoc Committee used these relationships to reopen negotiations.[88]

Each of these aforementioned religious dimensions was indispensable for the temporary success of the farm worker movement in California. Yet none of them alone or together served as *sufficient* factors. They operated as only one cluster of a number of crucial elements. Nevertheless, the convergence of these three religious aspects functioned as a *necessary* factor in the victory of La Causa. If just one of these entities—the Migrant Ministry, César Chávez's spiritual leadership, or the institutional Catholic Church—had not acted in timely, determined, or creative ways, the United Farm Workers would not have won its history-making contracts with the grape growers.

Filipino farm workers meeting in a union hall. Courtesy TakeStock Photos, San Rafael, California, #3643507.

Workers marching in the 1966 Delano-Sacramento march. Courtesy Walter P. Reuther Archives of Labor and Urban History, Wayne State University, Detroit, Michigan.

Others on the march. Courtesy TakeStock Photos, San Rafael, California, #3624035.

Workers in front of the state capitol in Sacramento. Courtesy Walter P. Reuther Archives of Labor and Urban History, Wayne State University, Detroit, Michigan.

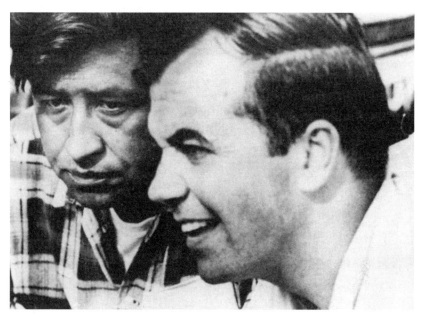

César Chávez and migrant minister Chris Hartmire. From *Ministry of the Dispossessed,* by Pat Hoffmann; photographer unknown.

UFW leader Dolores Huerta, migrant minister Jim Drake, and others, dancing and singing "De Colores." Courtesy TakeStock Photos, San Rafael, California, #3644732.

Spouses and daughters of growers counterprotesting. Courtesy TakeStock Photos, San Rafael, California, #3611821.

Dolores Huerta on the picket line. Courtesy TakeStock Photos, San Rafael, California, #3642017.

UFW chaplain, Father Mark Day, O.F.M., and two unidentified priests. Courtesy Walter P. Reuther Archives of Labor and Urban History, Wayne State University, Detroit, Michigan.

César Chávez breaking his 1968 fast—with Robert F. Kennedy, Helen Chávez, and Chávez's mother. Courtesy Walter P. Reuther Archives of Labor and Urban History, Wayne State University, Detroit, Michigan.

1970 Contract signing between UFW and grape growers. Seated, Chávez and John Guimarra Sr.; standing, left to right, unidentified union leader, Auxiliary Bishop Joseph F. Donnelly, Msgr. George G. Higgins, diocesan newspaper editor Gerard E. Sherry, and John Guimarra Jr. Courtesy Walter P. Reuther Archives of Labor and Urban History, Wayne State University, Detroit, Michigan.

Part 2: Texas

Chapter 5: Churches, Mexicans, and Farm Labor in Texas, 1930–60

As I look at the total scene, it seems to be that the local churches are doing the least to help. The County Public Health Department is doing something, though it knows it isn't enough. But it has no more funds. The schools are again doing something but not a complete job. They, too, are concerned about the whole problem. But the churches, what are they doing? Practically nothing. There are three [mainline] Protestant churches—and two Southern Baptist churches, the combined pressure of which could materially improve the whole outlook of this part of the [Rio Grande] Valley. However, the churches themselves, [sic] have a vested interest in a continuation of the status quo.
MIGRANT MINISTER, ALAMO, TEXAS, 1942

The lack of interest shown by our diocesan priests in our recent regional conference [on the Spanish speaking] was certainly discouraging. I remarked at the time that interested priests came to the congress from as far away as California and Michigan but most of our own priests did not show up.
ROBERT E. LUCEY, ARCHBISHOP OF SAN ANTONIO, 1958

Unlike California, Texas did not suddenly become populated by men seeking fortunes in gold. Nor did large groups of midwesterners pour into Texas in response to real-estate promotions. Instead, the Lone Star State received a steady stream of immigrants over the course of an entire century. Small Anglo-American colonies were first established in the 1820s and early 1830s. After winning independence from Mexico in 1836, the Republic of Texas encouraged not only old-stock Anglo-Americans to relocate from the lower and upper South but also Europeans. This trend continued after Texas was admitted into the United States. As in California, the early 1900s witnessed a flood of refugees escaping the economic and political hardships of the Mexican Revolution.

These groups all brought with them their various faith traditions. Plantation owners along the upper Gulf Coast were often Southern Episcopalians and Presbyterians, while many of their slaves often embraced revivalist Christianity. Yeomen from Kentucky, Tennessee, Missouri, and Arkansas settled in Central and Northern Texas. They subscribed to the Southern Methodist, Southern Baptist, and Church of Christ communions, or none at all. In contrast, the immense brush land of South Texas remained a stronghold for Tejana/o Catholics. Last were those who settled in the *shatter belt* of Texas, which stretched westward from Houston to San Antonio and southward to Corpus Christi. This geographical band defied ethnic and nationalistic homogeneity. It became home to nearly all of the aforementioned populations, including Europeans as well. Germans, Czechs, Irish, and Poles departed their ancestral homes to forge new lives in Texas. Most of them were Catholics, Lutherans, or Moravians, while a small percentage were Freethinkers.[1]

As Anglo-American Southerners settled in Texas, the region experienced a gradual but significant change in its religious census. Officially Catholic under the Mexican flag, the republic and then state of Texas soon compared favorably to the religious diversity of much of the rest of the United States. By the late 1800s, though, Catholicism appreciably declined as a percentage of the population, overtaken first by Southern Methodists and then by Southern Baptists. Reflecting a subtle but definite shift in demographics, this decline in no way suggested a lack of effort on the part of the Catholic Church. On the contrary, the U.S. hierarchy, which assumed local responsibility after 1836, conscientiously strove to meet the spiritual needs of this new part of its flock. As more European Catholics migrated to the state, however, the church instead focused on them and subsequently neglected Tejana/o Catholics. Only a handful of religious orders, notably the Oblates of Mary Immaculate, continued to labor faithfully among the Mexican apostolate in South Texas.[2]

While Texas Protestants cared mainly for their own groups, a few of them felt called to evangelize Mexican Americans. As early as the 1830s, Southern Presbyterians and Methodists distributed Spanish-language Bibles and later, along with Southern Baptists, held Sundays schools and revivals for Tejanas/os. Soon thereafter Mexican laymen were recruited as ministers. By the 1910s Methodists had founded a number of settlement houses and schools for the Spanish speaking. Finally, the National Migrant Ministry entered the Texas field in the early 1930s. As in California, however, no Protestant denominations related to Mexicans and Mexican Americans as organized workers. On the one hand, only when confronted with the melon-worker strike in the 1960s did some Texas Protestants acknowledge and address the longtime injustices suffered by farm workers. A Christian ethos based on a Southern, agrarian culture encouraged individual conversion and discipline but eschewed social action that challenged the status quo. Racial and religious prejudice played its part as well. On the other hand, the Texas Catholic Church occasionally publicized the plight of agricultural workers. Robert E. Lucey, archbishop of San Antonio, regularly spoke out in favor of unionism in a state that, like the South, was long known for its hostility to organized labor. Cofounder of the Bishops' Committee on the Spanish Speaking, Lucey pressed for programs among Mexican and Mexican American farm workers and *braceros*.

In summary, this chapter provides a general overview of the arrivals and interactions of some of the ethnic and religious groups in Texas from 1840 to 1960. Recounted also is the rise of commercial agriculture in the Rio Grande Valley, the establishment of Mexican American self-help organizations, and the perennial struggles of Tejana/o and Mexican farm workers.[3]

Prologue 1: The Roman Catholic Church and Home Missions in Texas, 1840–1930

Mexico's independence from Spain in 1821 left the local Catholic Church in disarray. Conditions were especially chaotic in Texas. Having always led a tenuous existence in a border region, Texas missions became bereft of any support from the Spanish Crown. As in California, a handful of priests and lay catechists continued to minister to thousands of Tejanas/os in San Antonio, Nacogdoches, and the Rio Grande Valley. Vast distances separated these faith communities from one another and the rest of Mexico. The Catholic Church in Texas was suspended in a state of limbo until Anglo-Americans fought for and created an independent republic in 1836. Only afterward did Rome respond to pleas for help from local Catholics, that is, Irish colonists. Recognizing new political realities, the Vatican sent personnel by means of the U.S. Catholic Church. Irish American John Timon, rector of a seminary in Missouri and a member of the St. Vincent de

Paul Society, canvassed the region. Beginning in Houston and Galveston, he traveled north to the historic missions of Nacogdoches and San Augustine. Then he made his way westward to the towns of Goliad, Refugio, Victoria, and San Antonio. Later he secured the services of two French priests from Louisiana and two Irish American priests from Kentucky. In 1840 Timon became Prefect of Texas, assisted by fellow Vincentian John Mary Odin who eventually served as Texas's first bishop.[4]

A native of France, Odin had lived in the United States since 1820. In Texas he faced a host of challenges. For example, he shepherded the state's Catholics as they survived the strains of both the Mexican-American War and the U.S. Civil War. He also coordinated relief efforts for victims of epidemics and hurricanes. Moreover, he was always recruiting priests for what was essentially a frontier region. As a Vincentian he naturally appealed to various religious orders. Ursulines and the Sisters of the Incarnate Word and Blessed Sacrament were among those who answered his call. By the late 1860s and early 1870s other organizations, such as the Benedictines and the Congregation of the Holy Cross, had also established local ministries. Above all others, however, the Oblates of Mary Immaculate distinguished themselves. Founded in Lyons, France, this missionary society responded wholeheartedly to Odin's invitation. Already active in Galveston and San Antonio, they soon dominated religious life in South Texas. They worked primarily among Mexicans between the Rio Grande and the Nueces River—a large spread of brush country known as "the Nueces Strip," which was regarded as disputed territory until 1848. Based in communities from Brownsville to Laredo, circuit-riding Oblates visited ranchos that spanned thousands of square miles. They braved the elements and were constantly on the lookout for bandits and unfriendly Indian tribes even as they heard confessions, said mass, baptized and confirmed children, and validated civil marriages.[5]

Although a populous group, Catholic Tejanas/os were soon marginalized. Protestant Anglos relocating from the U.S. South eventually outnumbered Texas Mexicans, who became a minority even in their own religious tradition. While a few Anglo-American Catholics arrived from the U.S. North, the majority of new Catholics hailed from Europe. Various societies helped to relocate Germans, Czechs, Irish, Poles, and others to the Lone Star State. These groups regularly entered Texas via the ports of New Orleans, Galveston, and Indianola, Texas. Some of them settled in towns and cities, but most founded agricultural colonies. These communities fanned out along the Gulf Coast from Galveston to Corpus Christi and extended as far as the region known as the Texas Hill Country, which lies beyond Austin and San Antonio. Odin quickly sent for priests from the homelands of these immigrants, and Rome soon had to divide the diocese into four chancellorships. San Antonio ultimately became the see of a new diocese, while Brownsville was designated a vicariate apostolic. In the 1880s the Vatican shifted Texas Catholic leadership from French Americans—including names such as Claude Marie Dubuis, Dominic Manucy, and Jean Claude Neraz—to Irish Americans, elevating Nicholas A. Gallagher as bishop of Galveston. As in California, this change reflected the growing numbers and influence of English-speaking Catholics in Texas. Thereafter Irish and Irish American priests dominated parishes, missions, and other religious institutions.[6]

Meanwhile, an indigenous clergy among Tejanas/os was virtually nonexistent. While several Spanish Vincentians accompanied Odin on his first trip to South Texas, Spanish-speaking priests remained in short supply. A refugee of the French-Mexican conflict of the 1860s, Pedro Verdaquer de Prat served first in Southern California and later as vicar apostolic of South Texas from 1890 to 1911. Although he ministered faithfully among Tejanas/os, the Catholic Church as a whole neglected them. For example, while Galveston benefited from an ambitious building program and a steady supply of priests and nuns, Brownsville suffered from both a lack of parishes and personnel. The diocese regarded a focus on Mexicans as a drain on scarce resources and an impediment to institutional growth. Yet national support finally reached Tejanas/os in the early 1900s, when the newly formed Catholic Extension Society disbursed funds for missions in the South and Southwest. Southwestern Catholics received a total of $1,141,655, some of which was distributed for the benefit of Tejanas/os. For instance, priests purchased two cars that they called "the St. Peter" and "the St. Joseph," in order to visit Mexican Americans on the remaining ranchos. Tejanas/os and Mexican refugees in the cities also benefited from some of these resources. At this time, the Sisters of Mercy entered the field, establishing a number of schools in the Rio Grande Valley. But these efforts were modest compared to those of the Los Angeles Diocese. Furthermore, resources slated for Texas benefited mostly English-speaking and immigrant European Catholics. For instance, the Anglo-American Diocese of Dallas, with 46,000 Catholics, received about the same amount of funds as the Diocese of Corpus Christi, home to approximately

428,000 Mexican Americans. This imbalance essentially held for years, in spite of the influx of the Spanish-speaking during the Mexican Revolution and the religious persecutions of the 1920s and 1930s. In addition to institutional neglect, many priests felt an antipathy toward the Spanish-speaking, not only as a poverty-stricken people but also as a group who, in their own eyes, seemed spiritually inferior. One author writes about Texas clergy whose forebears had been refugees of the French Revolution and thus could have identified to a degree with the plight of their Mexican American parishioners:

> Their rigidity helped make them strict disciplinarians, and they sometimes could not understand either the laity or the non-French priests with whom they came in contact. . . . When these clergy came into the Southwest, as was the case at least with Odin, they sometimes exhibited little understanding of Hispanic Catholicism and culture. Their answer was often to attempt to lay a French Catholic veneer over what[ever] they encountered.[7]

Prologue 2: Protestants and Tejanas/os, 1850–1930

Beginning in the 1840s, a familiar sight appeared on the front doors of abandoned cabins and houses throughout the U.S. South—signs that read "Gone to Texas."

Emigrants from the gulf states of Georgia, Alabama, Mississippi, and Louisiana usually settled in the cotton-producing region of East Texas, often accompanied by slaves. In contrast, subsistence farmers from Kentucky, Tennessee, Missouri, and Arkansas bought land in Central and North Texas on which to raise grain crops and livestock. Others looking for new economic opportunities included transplanted Northerners who opened businesses in growing towns and cities: "Typically, the Yankees were merchants in the port towns or professional soldiers at posts on the Indian frontier. . . . A much greater proportion of them lived in urban areas than was the case with upper southerners, Midwesterners, or lower southerners."[8]

The majority of these new residents were Anglo-Americans who practiced the Protestant faith. The Presbyterians, for example, established an early presence in Austin's Colony and East Texas, while Episcopalians established parishes primarily in coastal cities such as Houston, Galveston,

Corpus Christi, and Brownsville. Energetic colporteurs spread their expressions of Protestantism throughout the region. The Methodist Episcopal Church—after the schism of 1844 the Methodist Episcopal Church, South—was especially successful. Itinerant lay ministers held emotional revivals and weekly Sunday schools and helped to establish mission congregations. By the late 1840s Texas Methodists boasted two conferences, adding a third one ten years later. Their numbers grew at an exponential rate, in fact, sixfold by the advent of the U.S. Civil War: "Between 1846 and 1860 Methodist membership in Texas increased from 6, 693 to 39,021." Baptist preachers also entered the field, several of whom were arrested or otherwise discouraged in early years by the Mexican government. In spite of their efforts the Baptists grew at a slower rate, probably as a result of casual organizational practices. After the U.S. Civil War, they gained momentum and by 1890 even superseded the Methodists. Another group of Southern Protestants migrating to Texas at this time were members of the Church of Christ.[9] All of these preachers and evangelists naturally concentrated on their own people.

Yet there were exceptions. As early as the 1840s, Baptists proselytized Catholic and Lutheran Germans who were homesteading in the Texas Hill Country. Moreover, a few colporteurs for the American Bible Society shared the gospel with Tejanas/os. Still, no systematic evangelization occurred until after the Mexican-American War of 1848, when some military veterans and other Anglos colonized the Rio Grande Valley. Protestants immediately recognized the value of the region as a stepping-stone to missions in Mexico and even the rest of Latin America, much as their colleagues had regarded San Francisco in relation to the Far East.[10]

One of these evangelists was the ecumenical Melinda Rankin. A native of New Hampshire, she arrived in Brownsville in 1850. Her goal was to teach the Gospel south of the border, but Mexican law forbade Protestant missionaries. So she circumvented the law by establishing a Sunday school in Brownsville and then inviting girls who lived across the Rio Grande in nearby Matamoros. Although Rankin successfully enlisted the aid of local Anglos, she soon needed more funds. Traveling to Philadelphia, she convinced both the Presbyterian Board of Education and some private benefactors to sponsor her mission. Monies in hand, she returned to Brownsville and reopened the school as the Rio Grande Female Institute. It enjoyed modest success, but eventually became a casualty of the U.S. Civil War. In other words, Rankin and the local Presbyterian minister were at odds. He claimed that the school was the outpost of an "Abolition Society" and that Rankin was "not in sympathy with the Southern Confederacy." The Institute was subsequently closed. In the long run, however, this disappointment was only temporary. A new Mexican government sanctioned Protestant activity, and Rankin later founded a mission school in Monterrey, Mexico. She operated it for a number of years and finally turned it over to a denominational agency. In 1875, at the age of sixty-four, Rankin retired and moved to Illinois.[11]

After the U.S. Civil War, Southern Methodists began spearheading Tejana/o stations in the cities of San Antonio, Corpus Christi, and Laredo. In 1874 the local bishop founded the Mexican Border Mission District. He commissioned several Mexicans for this work, all of whom had studied under Rankin. Steady growth necessitated the creation of another district in 1880 and two more in 1882, at which time the territory became a full-fledged conference. Interestingly, its churches and schools in northern Mexico prospered much more than those in South Texas. Jealousies among Anglo church officials later undermined the work, causing Tejana/o missions to languish for a period of time.[12]

Southern Presbyterians also evangelized the Spanish-speaking. By the 1880s two indigenous ministers and one Anglo were working among Mexicans in Central Texas. Presbyterians later founded four Mexican congregations in the Valley: "By 1907 there were seventeen organized churches, nearly one thousand communicants, four ordained ministers, and four licentiates in the rapidly expanding Mexican mission field."[13] Southern Baptists were the last major Protestant group to evangelize Tejanas/os on a larger scale. First Baptist Church of San Antonio regularly sent missionaries to Mexico, who, on return visits, held Spanish-speaking Sunday schools and revivals. By 1888, Primera Iglesia Bautista of San Antonio had been chartered. That same year the Baptists officially founded a Mexican mission board, which sponsored churches in Corpus Christi, Laredo, and El Paso in 1903.[14]

Home missionaries often submitted glowing reports to conferences, presbyteries, and state conventions. In reality, these evangelists struggled constantly to minister effectively among Mexicans and Mexican Americans. In order to justify their proselytizing, they raised the specter of a people in need of deliverance from a papal religion reeking of ignorance, corruption, and political ambitions. Yet, in terms of financial support, these scare tactics seldom produced the desired results. As Southerners, most Anglo Texans regarded Mexicans much as they had African Americans, that is, "a pariah people" not worth the time, effort, or money of converting to the Protestant faith.[15]

Still, those who persevered increasingly practiced a two-pronged strategy among Mexicans and Tejanas/os: they supplemented personal testimonies and revivals with an educational ministry. Indeed, a fundamental principle underlying the work of tract societies and colporteurs was that a personal, unmediated encounter with the scriptures would appeal not only to the reader's heart but also his or her mind. Hopefully, such an experience would then prove the inherent superiority of the Protestant faith. Southern Methodists, Presbyterians, and Baptists extended this principle to the next logical step and began establishing schools as a means by which to reach the Spanish-speaking. In contrast to their northern counterparts in California and New Mexico, Texas church schools concentrated less on education as a means of assimilation and economic betterment as simply another tool leading to individual conversions. This latter emphasis reflected the more traditional ethos of Southern Protestantism. These schools included the Lydia Patterson Institute in El Paso, the Holding Institute in Laredo (both Methodist), the Texas Mexican Industrial Institute in Kingsville, the Presbyterian School for Mexican Girls in Taft (both Presbyterian), and the Mexican Baptist Institute in Bastrop.[16]

Nevertheless, the Social Gospel movement that influenced northern Protestants in the West and elsewhere also influenced some Texas Protestants. Church officials responded to the burgeoning population of Mexican refugees of the 1910s by founding settlement houses and medical clinics, perhaps even rivaling those in California. Southern Methodists dominated these institutions, thanks in large part to the leadership of Frank Onderdonk. Like his northern counterpart in California, Vernon McCombs, Onderdonk was a transitional figure insofar as he merged personal salvation with the new emphasis on social ministry. He first served as a missionary in Mexico, later directing home missions in Texas. He was responsible not only for launching several schools for Mexicans and Tejanas/os but also a number of community centers and "Wesley Houses." Reflecting again the more conservative ethos of Southern Protestantism, Onderdonk stressed social ministry less as a way to meet the material needs of poor people but more as a means by which to win their souls. In either case, the extremely paternalistic aspects of this ministry were conspicuous. Yet Tejanas/os and Mexicans often resisted the conversion and assimilation attempts of Anglo Protestants. Many Spanish-speaking Catholics undoubtedly used the services of community centers and clinics with no intention of leaving the church of their birth. Moreover, many of those who joined the Methodists, Presbyterians, Baptists, or some other such group were only partly Americanized. Last, more secular Tejana/o organizations fought for self-determination from the 1900s to 1930s, especially for economic betterment. An overview of their activities is now discussed within the context of the rise of commercial agriculture in Texas.[17]

Commercial Agriculture in South Texas and Organized Labor, 1900–1940

Early twentieth-century Mexican migration to Texas coincided with the evolution of commercial agriculture in the Rio Grande Valley. Before 1900 a rancho economy and culture prevailed on both sides of the border, not unlike that of the Southern Californios. Criollos and Mexicans raised cattle on the land from the mid-1700s to the end of the nineteenth century, during part of which even some Jesuits and Carmelites owned and operated ranches. After the Mexican-American War and the U.S. Civil War a number of Anglos settled in the Valley, many of whom worked as teachers, government employees, and traders. Some Anglo men married into the families of wealthy Mexicans. By the 1880s these newcomers owned a slim majority of the land. There were sometimes cases of Anglos acquiring land by extralegal means, but, by and large, economic changes such as dropping market prices for livestock and long-standing inheritance patterns had a much greater effect on Tejana/o ranchers. As Anglo Protestant landowners turned to farming, however, tensions grew between them and Tejana/o Catholic ranchers. According to at least one historian, the ideology of Manifest Destiny began to take hold in South Texas. Furthermore, transplanted Southerners tended to redirect their racist views from African Americans to Tejanas/os.[18]

In the early 1900s economic changes accelerated. Railroad companies laid tracks that linked the Valley to San Antonio and other destinations. Land corporations increasingly promoted the region's possibilities to farmers in states such as Minnesota, Wisconsin, and Indiana. Irrigation, hard-surface roads, and other improvements followed—all developments that paralleled California's Imperial Valley. For all practical purposes, South

Texas evolved from a Mexican cattle-grazing concern into a commercial farm economy dominated by Anglos. Early experimental crops included sugarcane, rice, and corn, while the area eventually specialized in cotton, garden vegetables, and citrus fruits. Produce was packed in nearby Valley towns and shipped to faraway markets. One writer has remarked on the geography and viability of large-scale farming in the Valley:

> It is bounded on the south by the Rio Grande, on the east by the Gulf Coast, and on the north by a strip of sandy land not suitable for agriculture. The area forms a triangle of about ninety miles along the river, sixty miles along the coast, and ninety miles on the north. It contains approximately one million acres. Abundant water supply and topography and soil fertility accounted in great part for the Valley's agricultural success. The surface is generally smooth except in the bottom lands along the river. . . . The climate in the area has been described as semi-tropical and is such that some crops can grow under irrigation every month in the year.[19]

As a result of this seismic shift from a relational ranch society to impersonal agribusiness, large numbers of Tejanas/os and Mexicans became seasonal contract laborers in the fields of South Texas. They responded to this new economic state of affairs as workers did elsewhere in the United States—by banding together into self-help groups. Workers in other parts of Texas had self-advocated from the 1880s. For example, in that decade over eight thousand laborers participated in nearly one hundred strikes, most of them led by the Knights of Labor. In the 1890s the populist Farmers' Alliance became active in East Texas. From 1885 to 1915 coal miners fought for their rights in the northern and western regions of the state, while the American Federation of Labor entered Dallas and San Antonio in the last decade of the century. Carpenters, hod carriers, and longshoremen had even organized in the Valley towns of Brownsville and Harlingen in the 1930s.[20]

Tejanas/os participated in some of these labor activities, even though as a racial minority they were officially banned from trade unionism through the First World War. More often they organized their own mutual-aid societies. Some of these *mutualistas* were religious confraternities, others were secular, and a few were even socialistic in ideology. Whatever their creed, a number of them resembled proto-unions, for instance, a group of Tejana/o agricultural workers in South Texas in the 1910s, known as La Agrupación Protectora. Seldom, however, could they claim any real

victories. As in California, several factors impeded them. First, they faced
a nationwide economic downturn following World War I. Next, competition with a second influx of Mexicans in the 1920s also dimmed their
prospects for bargaining power. Third, the aforementioned reality of racism and violence afflicted Tejanas/os, particularly in the Rio Grande Valley. Some Anglos lynched Mexican Americans from the 1880s and bru-
tally reacted when a handful of Tejanos hatched the Plan of San Diego
in 1915—a poorly conceived manifesto designed to create an independent
nation in the U.S. Southwest. The Texas Rangers were especially merciless
in crushing these uprisings. In light of this pattern of repression, it is not
surprising that farm worker militancy in the Lone Star State was small
when compared to California:

> Labor relations in Texas agriculture by the 1930s in many ways bore a strik-
> ing resemblance to those in California, and the similarity grew stronger
> during this decade. Farms were being mechanized rapidly, small operators
> were being displaced in great numbers, and land was being consolidated into
> larger holdings. New cash crops intensively grown for sale in distant markets
> had been introduced in many areas. A widespread system of factory farming
> had developed, and it was fully as dependent as that of California upon large
> and mobile supplies of cheap labor. . . .
>
> Although it surpassed most other States [sic] in the number of its agri-
> cultural laborers, Texas [nevertheless] remained relatively free of unionism
> and strikes in agriculture and allied industries. It was virtually untouched
> by the wave of farm labor outbreaks during 1933. Organized action on the
> whole continued to be local and infrequent throughout the decade.[21]

Significantly, the Catholic Church became involved in two conflicts
led by Tejanas/os in agriculturally related industries in the 1930s. The first
protest occurred in the Winter Garden District south of Laredo. Spinach
farmers in Crystal City had lowered wages in the early years of the Great
Depression. In response, Oblate priest Charles Taylor founded the Catholic Workers Union and helped laborers regain their former pay scale. He
was in an excellent position to accomplish this goal, shepherding a congregation made up primarily of Tejanas/os but including a few influential
Anglos. A longtime member of the community, he also was on very good
terms with Anglo Protestant businessmen. So he was a natural choice to
broker an agreement between growers and farm workers. A major motive
of resolving the conflict, however, may have had little at all to do with

the issue of worker justice. In other words, Taylor may well have feared that the repercussions of the strike would have doomed a major parish-building program his church had recently undertaken. After the contract was signed, the union soon disbanded. Taylor never again participated in labor activities, yet remained obsessed with construction projects. In the rest of his thirty-seven years as a priest—no matter where he served—he tried to erect new facilities, even when they were patently unnecessary. His "brick-and-mortar" mentality and incessant solicitation of funds became a frequent source of irritation among him, his fellow priests, and his provincials superior.[22]

Another priest who participated in a struggle of Tejana/o workers was Carmelo Tranchese, S.J. He was the senior priest of Our Lady of Guadalupe Church, a parish on the Spanish-speaking west side of San Antonio. An Italian, Tranchese had already served for years as a missionary in the United States when arriving in San Antonio in 1932. In contrast to Taylor, he constantly sought to improve both the spiritual and material lives of his parishioners, fighting for decent public housing, supporting organized labor, and addressing health crises such as the high rates of tuberculosis and infant mortality.[23]

Some of Tranchese's church members were migrant farm laborers, while most worked in factories. In 1933 employees of several pecan-shelling companies staged a strike, eventually securing modest wage increases. A large percentage of them were young, single Tejanas. Tranchese aided them by coordinating food and clothing drives. More strikes were held in the next two years. In 1937 the workers' organization, the Pecan Shelling Workers Union, was reconstituted as a chapter of a California-based union. Soon, however, labor leader Emma Tenayuca of the radical Workers' Alliance took over the reins of leadership. Although young, this experienced, dynamic, and fearless Tejana—known by her followers as "La Pasionaria"—led the newly merged group in a walkout of nearly ten thousand pecan shellers. The rest of the San Antonio community quickly reacted. Police tear-gassed and arrested pickets en masse. The city government, local newspapers, and middle-class Mexican Americans vilified strike leaders for their communist affiliations, accusing them of subversive political activities. The Catholic Church joined the chorus. Condemning what he believed was a communist insurgency, the local archbishop counteracted by establishing a Catholic labor union. He also censored *La Voz de la Parroquia,* a newspaper that Tranchese had founded for Tejana/o

Catholics. Although Tranchese also opposed communism and spoke only indirectly in behalf of Tenayuca and others, he nevertheless sympathized with them. In fact, he had printed not only Catholic social teachings in the paper but also the views of the pecan shellers. Ultimately, the workers gained several concessions. Yet their hard-won efforts ironically led to their downfall. Faced with a higher minimum wage, company heads decided to remechanize shelling operations they had discontinued in the late 1920s. Fortunately, the ever-resourceful Tranchese again came to the aid of his church members and others, successfully lobbying for 1,800 new jobs sponsored by the Works Progress Administration.[24]

The Migrant Ministry in Texas, 1930–60

As a whole, the Texas Catholic Church of the 1930s did not advocate for Mexican American farm workers. Only the aforementioned priests were conspicuous for their aid. Protestant denominations were even more oblivious to this segment of the Spanish-speaking population. Yet, as in California, one organization established a small but significant presence among Mexican American agricultural laborers. It began with a letter that Adela Ballard, Western Supervisor of the National Migrant Ministry, received from an Anglo minister in the Rio Grande Valley:

> If you will get a Texas county map and look up Brownsville, the southernmost point in the United States proper, then come up the Rio Grande and around, following the lines until you have located Cameron, Hidalgo and Willacy Counties, you will have a birdseye [sic] view of our country where more than 50,000 Mexicans need the work you are doing and which, when we get your vision, we can help you do. . . . Seventy-five per cent of these people are located more or less permanently in the many towns and little cities that dot this very rich, irrigated valley that is the wonder of the age in development. . . . This little territory is now the equal of Florida and will soon rival California in the production of oranges, grapefruit, avocadoes and all kinds of vegetables. . . .
>
> Some little Christian work is being done by a number of denominations but not touching the great need. The schools are doing considerable for these people but your work would very greatly supplement and help all this and should cause no friction even from the Catholic group which, of course, is closest to these people. . . . [T]hey live in cornstock [sic] hovels and tents but occasionally you will find a fairly good house and clean conditions. The

large per cent [*sic*] are filthy and diseased; morals and ideals are low, but the people are very responsive when once their confidences are gained.[25]

Ballard quickly responded. She surveyed the region, met with community leaders, and proposed a plan of action. The parent body of the Migrant Ministry, the Council of Women on Home Missions, secured a nurse for cotton pickers and their families. This staff person arrived in Hidalgo County, Texas, in October 1933. She not only stressed health needs such as prenatal care but also led children's activities and explored avenues for housing improvements. Religious education rounded out the program. The positive response of the community was unprecedented, prompting Ballard to suggest the creation of a local chapter of the Federated Church Women. She also scheduled a promotional tour, visiting Protestant women's groups in Chicago, St. Louis, Kansas City, Little Rock, and El Paso. By 1935 she recognized the need for modifications in the Valley program. So a nurse-teacher replaced the original staff member, tutoring families in nutrition, homemaking skills, and English. Meanwhile, local boards of education, county medical associations, and service clubs prepared plans for a tuberculosis camp for Mexican Americans.[26]

In the early 1940s the Migrant Ministry added lay and ordained pastors. They visited workers, held worship services, and sponsored recreational activities. The Council of Women purchased a house trailer for a staff member and his spouse, enabling them to live inside one of the camps and also join farm laborers in their annual trek. Increasingly, however, the Migrant Ministry sensed that community support was dwindling. In reality, Anglo churches had never assumed their fair share of responsibility. Their neglect toward Mexicans and Mexican Americans reflected the long-standing class and race structure of the Valley, especially in rural areas. Furthermore, Anglo Texans generally lacked a tradition of religious social reform. They practiced instead a quietist faith that was prevalent through most of the U.S. South. Although Texas Methodists had founded nearly twenty community centers and schools for Mexican Americans over the years, only two of them were located in the Rio Grande Valley. Even then they were not founded until after World War II.[27]

A second feature of Texas Protestantism, namely, anti-ecumenism, also revealed its Southern religious character and, again, its resistance toward the Migrant Ministry. A comparison to California highlights the abysmally low level of religious cooperation in Texas. As early as 1853, San

Francisco boasted chapters of several interdenominational groups, such as the American Bible Society, the American Tract Society, the American Sunday School Union, and the Young Men's Christian Association. By 1910 local Protestants had founded the San Francisco and Los Angeles Federations of Churches. Several years later these two bodies merged to become the California Federation of Churches. In 1918 it was one of only two state organizations with a full-time director, and by the 1940s it was staffed by nearly one hundred employees. In contrast, no state council even existed in Texas until 1954. Federated Women's groups followed a similar pattern. On the one hand, in the 1920s and 1930s, Adela Ballard related to dozens of chapters in greater San Francisco, Sacramento, Los Angeles, and smaller communities in the San Joaquin Valley. On the other hand, as late as 1941 only three such branches could be found in all of Texas. In short, West Coast Protestants mirrored the ecumenical identity of the Northeast and urban Midwest, while a Southern sectarianism prevailed in Texas. This dearth of cooperation in the Lone Star State could be attributed to isolationist Baptists and a predominantly rural population.[28]

Through the 1950s the Texas Migrant Ministry often struggled simply for its survival. Its staff continuously fought an uphill battle for local acceptance and financial support. One obstacle was that Valley Anglos had long regarded the poverty of Mexican Americans and Mexicans as an inevitable fact of life and regularly exploited it. Sensitive to this prejudice, Mexico even insisted that the U.S. government exclude Texas from participation in the Bracero Program, a policy that remained in effect through the late 1940s. In order to make amends and reverse this policy, the federal government's Office of Inter-American Affairs intervened. Designed to improve relationships among the U.S. and Latin American nations to counter possible Nazi influence, the Office persuaded Texas to found the Good Neighbor Commission. The ostensible purpose of the Commission was to encourage fair treatment of Mexican Americans and Mexicans in the state, which, among other things, might lift the ban on *braceros.* In spite of these actions, "discrimination and poor housing were still prevalent. Pressure from Valley growers forced the [Good Neighbor Commission's] secretary's resignation."[29] Nonetheless, Mexicans crossed the Rio Grande in record numbers. By the early 1950s tens of thousands of undocumented Mexicans had depressed Valley wages, forcing Mexican Americans to reenter the migrant stream. Although many of these Mexican Americans traveled to fields and orchards throughout the Midwest, others ventured closer to home and followed the cotton harvest from Corpus Christi to the Texas Panhandle. As early as 1949, migrant ministers set up welcome centers along this route. Not yet hardened by large numbers of migrant workers, Anglo churches in the Panhandle were particularly receptive. For example, Protestants in Lubbock virtually underwrote the cost of the local program. By the mid-1950s, however, attitudes had changed. Some West Texas farmers began recruiting Mexican nationals, claiming that domestic laborers would no longer perform stoop labor, that is, not cheaply enough. Grower arguments throughout the rest of the state echoed those of agribusiness in the Valley, complicating the work of the Migrant Ministry.[30]

Soon, however, greater cooperation among Methodists, Presbyterians, Episcopalians, and others finally breathed new life into the organization. In 1954 mainline Protestants founded the Texas Council of Churches. The midwestern supervisor of the Migrant Ministry hailed the new agency as a vital partner in meeting the religious and material needs of farm workers. Indeed, the Texas Council immediately joined hands with state branches of the interdenominational Church Women United to expand work among rural Mexicans and Mexican Americans. The Texas Migrant Ministry hired its first full-time director, while part-time staff laid the groundwork for new sites. A truly statewide program, however, remained a distant goal. As late as 1958, an estimated 240,000 field laborers sought work in Texas, compared to 281,000 in California. Although the needs in Texas nearly equaled those in the Golden State, its resources were meager by comparison. Although a staff of over sixty persons reached farm workers at sixty-three camps in California, a Texas staff of only seven was responsible for a total of twenty-six sites. The 1959 budgets for each state revealed a similar gap: $106,000 for California and $16,700 for Texas. Furthermore, Californians raised over $79,500 of their own funds, but Texans less than $7,000.[31]

This regional contrast in the strength of the Migrant Ministry held true not only for traditional work, such as religious education, day care, and recreation, but also for innovative programming. By the early 1960s rural fringe ministries were already well established and growing in California. The Migrant Ministry, however, did not introduce community organizing in Texas until 1961. Even then the impetus and monies came not from local sources but from New York. The Emil Schwarzhaupt Foundation had earlier awarded the Migrant Ministry about $120,000 to implement community organizing among agricultural workers and evaluate its effect. The parent body of the Migrant Ministry, the National Council of Churches, employed a social relations expert to direct the study, which was titled "the Migrant Citizenship Education Project." Three sites were selected—two of them in the Midwest and one in the Rio Grande Valley of Texas. Local staff became acquainted with both field laborers and year-round, middle-class residents. The staff then arranged opportunities for these two groups to meet and cultivate relationships with each other. The overall goal was to help agricultural migrants become a more integral part of each community and thereby empower themselves. Achieving this goal would also potentially transform the entire community. Attitudes of mutual indifference, suspicion, even hostility would ideally give way to greater sensitivity and cooperation. The project director reported that results in the midwestern sites, where staff used the "dual approach," ranged from satisfactory to excellent. "Working both sides of the track," they fraternized among both established citizens and migrants in order to open up lines of communication and help nurture a greater sense of inclusiveness. A different scenario, however, played out in the Rio Grande Valley. Betty J. Whitaker, who oversaw the project in Weslaco, Texas, eventually worked only with migrant laborers. The project director wrote: "There, the traditional breach between the Anglo community and its Mexican-American residents was so wide that the Project staff had no success at all in developing a cooperative community effort." On the positive side, Mexicans and Mexican Americans joined a citizenship-education club and sponsored a voter registration drive. Yet even these efforts collapsed as soon as the project ended. Such was the Migrant Ministry's introduction of community organizing to South Texas.[32]

The Roman Catholic Church and Farm Workers in Texas, 1940–60

Protestants in the postwar period never touched the issue of organized labor among Mexican and Mexican American farm workers. Neither did most Anglo Catholics, except for Robert E. Lucey, the new archbishop of San Antonio. Born, raised, and educated in California, Lucey was both a supporter of the policies of the FDR administration and a strict enforcer of papal encyclicals on labor. In the early 1930s, the Vatican appointed him as bishop of Amarillo, Texas, and, on the death of San Antonio's prelate in 1940, elevated him to that see. In order to systematize outreach to Mexicans and Mexican Americans in the U.S. Southwest, Lucey soon cofounded the Bishops' Committee on the Spanish Speaking. He outlined an ambitious strategy to contribute to social justice among Mexican Americans and bring them more into the life of the Catholic Church. A portion of this strategy was creating conditions that would lead toward greater economic self-determination.[33]

Most of Lucey's plan was never realized. Still, the dioceses of Texas strove to meet some of the needs of its Spanish-speaking members, including farm workers. Lucey addressed these needs in two ways. First, he and others engaged in a national campaign against the Bracero Program, which finally helped to terminate it in 1964. Second, the Texas Catholic Church continued traditional ministries among migrant agricultural laborers—whether they were Mexican Americans, *braceros,* or undocumented Mexicans. Given the numbers of workers, merely acknowledging the scope of this more modest objective could be overwhelming. Thus Lucey reported at an annual meeting of the Bishops Committee on the Spanish Speaking:

> Last year 143,000 Texas Mexicans joined the migrant stream. 210,000 Mexican nationals were imported, giving us a total of 353,000 Catholic Spanish-speaking migrants in the state of Texas alone. With all the good will in the world the Church in Texas has not been able to meet that challenge. The invading army is just too big.[34]

Yet the Catholic Church in Texas pressed on. In the mid-1950s, it found an ally in a major government agency—the U.S. Labor Department. The department had recently employed a Catholic layperson to arrange worship services for Mexican nationals in the Rio Grande Valley. His job was to help insure that farms, most of which were owned by local non-Catholics or even national companies, "protect the workers from evil and degrading influences." This mandate was a clause in the contract between Mexico and the United States. Although the representative of the Labor Department was ostensibly neutral in securing the services of various denominations, he favored the Catholic Church, and, besides, most of the workers were indeed Catholics. In effect, he sent dozens of priests into government reception centers and private labor camps. Reports in 1956 boasted an impressive response from *braceros,* noting that many of them not only had attended mass but also confessions, rosary devotions, and even first communions. Some Mexican priests accompanied laborers as they migrated northward, especially to the cotton fields in the Texas Panhandle, while laymen held *cursillo* retreats for workers. Lucey, however, continued to encounter obstacles. Although he urged Valley parishes to recruit laypersons—sometimes raising the specter of Protestant proselytizing in order to goad them—few volunteers answered the call. Furthermore, the Catechist sisters, upon whom overworked priests often relied, were in short supply. Most telling of all, the local prelate resented Lucey's interference. The bishop of the Diocese of Corpus Christi wanted only United States–born priests among the *braceros* and hardly warmed to the idea of lay involvement. For Lucey, encouraging even traditional ministry often seemed a Sisyphean task.[35]

Tens of thousands of Texas farm workers never received any ministrations at the hands of priests, catechists, or lay volunteers. Harvesting crops on large, isolated farms and constantly on the move, workers often relied on other resources for their spiritual well-being. Since most *braceros* and undocumented nationals had come from rural settings in which the institutional church was characteristically weak, they were already accustomed to practicing their own style of faith. They frequently prayed to the saints for strength and sustenance. While adoration of La Virgen de Guadalupe was common, other saints or manifestations of Christ were also venerated, for example, El Señor de los Milagros and Nuestra Señora de San Juan de los Lagos. In fact, these two objects of petition and thanksgiving were so important that shrines for them were "re-localized" in Texas. In other words, those who had visited such holy sites in Morelia and Jalisco, Mexico, respectively, recreated these sacred spaces in their new homes or places of work. Both Mexicans and Mexican Americans have traditionally prayed for healing in the Chapel of the Lord of Miracles, San Antonio, and pilgrims have worshipped at the shrine of Nuestra Señora de San Juan de los Lagos:

> [Our Lady], patroness of journeys—of the comings and goings of life—is a favorite in Texas. The shrine is located in San Juan, near the Rio Grande. This devotion came originally from Mexico, where Our Lady is honored in a popular shrine with the same title. People from all over south Texas, especially Mexican-American migrant farm workers, make the shrine the focal point of the beginning and the end of their long trips.[36]

Mexicans in the Valley have not limited their supplications only to saints recognized by the Catholic Church. They also have visited the tomb of Don Pedro Jaramillo in Falfurrias, Texas, a well-known, nineteenth-century *curandero* or faith healer. These devotions and other practices helped Mexican American and Mexican agricultural laborers to survive in the face of widespread racism, a nomadic existence, and backbreaking work.[37]

Conclusion

The ministries of the Texas Catholic Church and various Protestant denominations among Mexicans and Mexican Americans often mirrored those in California. In both states, the churches often neglected these groups, especially during the years as frontier institutions. When Catholic and Protestant leaders finally paid greater attention to the Spanish speaking—beginning with the mass migrations of Mexicans to the United States in the 1910s—they developed extremely paternalistic programs that stressed Americanization. In both Texas and California, the churches focused their efforts in the cities, while leaving work among rural Mexicans to various religious orders and the Migrant Ministry.

Yet significant differences distinguished efforts in Texas and California. For example, as in California, the San Antonio Archdiocese hosted Mexican priests and prominent laity who fled their homeland during the Mexican Revolution and, later, the Cristero Rebellion (1926–29). The Texas Catholic Church, however, failed to establish a social ministry that even remotely approached the scope of the Diocese of Los Angeles in the 1920s. Texas Protestants also lagged behind their counterparts in California. Although the Migrant Ministry was introduced to South Texas only a few years after the beginning of its work in the Imperial and San Joaquin valleys, it languished while the California program blossomed. Furthermore, the short-lived Weslaco Project in the Rio Grande Valley compared poorly to the flourishing rural fringe ministries planted in Central California in the 1950s. By the same token, Bishop Lucey spoke often about community organizing among Mexican Americans, but on a statewide level this goal was never actualized. In contrast, a small group of determined priests in the San Francisco Archdiocese, the Spanish Mission Band, introduced the principles of community organizing. These differences revealed a more conservative Catholic Church in the Lone Star

State. They also highlighted Southern Protestant sectarianism and social quietism in Texas compared to the East Coast–West Coast ecumenism and Social Gospel values practiced by many California Protestants. This Southern Protestant tradition strongly reacted to the melon workers' strike of the late 1960s and successfully turned back a northern incursion of new-breed clergy.

Chapter 6: The Church and the Farm Worker Movement in South Texas, 1966–69

. . . we may well be witnessing in the Valley the beginning of a sweeping social movement larger than growers or unions, fraught with peril and promise. Maybe it is not too late for the Church to be a part of it, struggling not to avoid its conflict, but to make it creative rather than destructive.

JORGE LARA-BRAUD, DIRECTOR OF THE
HISPANIC-AMERICAN INSTITUTE, AUSTIN, TEXAS, 1967

As in California, the lives of some Mexican Americans in Texas improved in the 1940s and 1950s. A number of them found work at the state's military bases and in manufacturing. Although often employed in unskilled jobs, they at least escaped dependence on part-time and exploitative farm labor. On the political front, the League of United Latin American Citizens (LULAC), the American G.I. Forum, and other traditional organizations continued to chip away at the state's Jim Crow laws. Sometimes they objected to harsh treatment of Mexican immigrants, as in Operation Wetback in 1954. In the presidential election year of 1960, progressive Anglo politicians recognized and courted the Mexican American vote. Several years later Latino candidates themselves made headway in some of the state's metropolitan centers. An emerging Chicana/o group even overturned the power structure in Crystal City, a town in the Winter Garden District. Chicanas/os such as José Angel Gutiérrez soon founded the Mexican American Youth Organization and the La Raza Unida Party, contributing to the abolishment of racial discrimination in public schools. Yet these gains failed to strike a deathblow to persistent racism or the cold war mentality held by many Anglo Texans that most social movements and unions were communist inspired.[1]

One expression of this newfound activism was a wildcat strike called by cantaloupe pickers in the Rio Grande Valley of Texas. In contrast to

California, they faced even greater obstacles. Although beginning on 1 June 1966 and surviving until the fall of 1967, the strike, which was held mostly in Starr County, faced seemingly insurmountable hurdles. It suffered from grossly inadequate organization, the easy availability of day workers from Mexico, the state's anti-labor laws, a fairly weak coalition of urban liberals, and the strikebreaking measures of the Texas Rangers. In short, the overall conservatism of the Lone Star State boded ill for the cantaloupe workers.[2]

The strike often mirrored earlier attempts by field laborers. In at least two respects, however, it also resembled events among farm workers in Delano. First, the Starr County strike enjoyed widespread publicity, especially during La Marcha, a four-hundred-mile trek from Rio Grande City to the state capitol in Austin, Texas. Second, the strike, or La Huelga, received substantial support from some of the state's religious groups. Catholic priests in San Antonio and Houston became deeply involved, as well as Protestant clergy, particularly those affiliated with the Texas Council of Churches. These clerics led marches and preached at outdoor gatherings. They also solicited financial contributions and helped to organize food caravans for the strikers and their families. The Council even sued the Texas Rangers for obstructing legitimate religious activity. In the end, though, this support failed to tip the balance in favor of the strike. Both Catholic and Protestant officials gradually withdrew their partisan support, seeking to extricate themselves from the "lost cause" of the farm workers. New-breed ministers who refused to be brought to heel were eventually disciplined or terminated from their positions. In protest, Mexican American laity picketed the residence of the Catholic archbishop and, later, the constituting convention of the Texas Conference of Churches, the successor body to the Council. By 1968 the union drastically scaled back operations. Its leaders turned mostly to traditional programs, such as establishing a credit union and a legal-aid office. Breathing a collective sigh of relief, Catholic and Protestant leaders then cosponsored a parallel organization whose noncontroversial approach reflected the overall religious and social climate of the state.[3]

The Beginning of the Starr County Strike of 1966–67

In the 1960s, civic boosters in Texas's four southernmost counties often promoted their home as the Magic Valley. Several factors had helped to transform this ranch country into an agricultural wonderland, including crop experimentation, irrigation, transportation improvements, and, not least of all, a steady supply of cheap labor. The counties of Willacy, Cameron, Hidalgo, and Starr boasted large farms that produced a variety of crops—grain, cotton, citrus fruits, and vegetables. Commercial ventures in Starr County—the most rural district in the Valley—grew celery, peppers, lettuce, honeydew melons, and cantaloupes. In addition to agriculture, the Magic Valley attributed a measure of its prosperity to tourism. Frequently known as "snowbirds" or "Winter Texans," retirees from northern states had discovered the mild winter climate and low living costs of South Texas. They flocked every winter to the cities of Brownsville, Harlingen, McAllen, and a host of smaller communities.[4]

Yet most Mexican Americans missed out on the economic boom of the Valley. Mexicans commuted daily across the border, thereby depressing wages for them. The latter earned only fifty to eighty-five cents an hour and averaged only one hundred workdays per year. Many of them still followed seasonal harvests, sometimes traveling as far north as Michigan. So the fact was not surprising that Starr County held the unflattering reputation as the most impoverished rural county in the state, indeed, in the entire U.S. Southwest. The annual median income of rural families in the county was only $1,535. In 1964 a national television program aired a scathing documentary on the Valley. The *Houston Chronicle* ran a similar set of stories titled "Texas' Magic Valley—Or Is It Miserable?"[5]

These were the region's economic realities that preceded the Starr County strike. Ignorant of these obstacles, an Anglo volunteer from California founded a farm workers' union and staged a strike against commercial growers. Eugene Nelson, a volunteer in the Delano grape strike, had been deployed by Chávez to lead Houston's boycott against Schenley Industries. Soon after Nelson arrived, however, the company signed a contract with the union. Local sympathizers urged him to organize workers in the Rio Grande Valley. In early May of 1966 he drove to the Valley and inquired about agricultural laborers. He was directed to two men, Margil Sanchez and Lucio Galván, the first of whom lived in Rio Grande City, the seat of Starr County. Neither of these men was employed in agriculture, but both had long expressed interest in a union. After meeting with them, Nelson began holding rallies in the downtown plaza.[6]

Acquaintances knew Nelson not for his quiet, painstaking organizational skills but for his flair and theatrics. The son of a former California citrus and vineyard grower, he lived on the road and was an aspiring writer. He spoke fluent Spanish and exhorted farm workers to claim their heritage of independence. Holding up a picture of the Mexican revolutionary Emiliano Zapata, he repeatedly shouted: "You are sons of Zapata! You must be brave!" He convinced about two hundred laborers to found the Independent Workers Association. On 31 May 1966 he announced that the union totaled six hundred to seven hundred members.[7]

The month of June was the cantaloupe harvest in South Texas. Workers had to pick the crop quickly in order to avoid spoilage. Nelson and others saw it as a perfect opportunity to declare a strike. On 1 June 1966—a scant week or so after Nelson had first recruited members—the union dispatched several picket teams. They drove to the fields of three commercial growers in Starr County—La Casita Farms, Los Puertos Plantation, and Sun-Tex Farms. Pickets convinced fellow workers to leave the harvest. Later that day strikers appeared at nearby packing sheds in order to block a shipment of melons. Nevertheless, a train filled with produce moved down the track. In dramatic fashion, Nelson ran ahead of the locomotive and, in doing so, allegedly caught his foot in a railroad switch. The engineer slammed on the brakes and the train grinded to a halt only four feet away from the labor organizer. A large crowd soon gathered. Two Texas Rangers finally arrived, freed Nelson from the track, and arrested him for instigating a riot. Thus ended the first day of the Starr County strike.[8]

On the second day, La Casita and other farms filed an anti-picketing injunction. Texas law forbade mass picketing, and the district judge immediately granted a restraining order. In response, strikers simply turned to the fields of other growers. Union members also assembled at the international bridges in the towns of Roma and Hidalgo, pleading with Mexican nationals, known as "green carders," not to break the strike. In sympathy, a number of packing-shed workers walked off their jobs, while the Political Association of Spanish-Speaking Organizations (PASSO), based in Houston, provided food and clothing to the strikers.[9]

The Early Involvement of the Roman Catholic Church

The Roman Catholic Church was a strong supporter of the strike. While still in Houston, Nelson had received financial aid from two church officials—the bishop of Galveston-Houston and a field representative of the Bishops' Committee for the Spanish Speaking. Public advocacy first appeared, however, when two diocesan priests arrived from San Antonio. Sherrill Smith and William Killian reached Rio Grande City on 6 June 1966. Both of them espoused the civil rights movement of the 1960s. A native of Chicago and a U.S. Navy fighter pilot in World War II, Smith had already marched in Delano, California, and in Selma, Alabama. The archbishop had earlier assigned him as the social action director in San Antonio, where the priest led labor strikes and school desegregation efforts. Originally from Connecticut, Killian had recently become editor of the archdiocesan newspaper, the *Alamo Messenger*.[10]

On their arrival, Smith and Killian immediately held a mass and rally on the plaza of Rio Grande City. On 7 June 1966, they led a five-mile march that was followed by another mass. They also joined pickets at the international bridges. The next week Smith and Killian returned to Starr County for more marches, rallies, and outdoor masses. The new executive secretary of the Bishops' Committee, the Rev. Henry J. Casso, provided material aid by coordinating a drive called Operation Foodstuff.[11]

These priests quickly clashed with conservative and moderate clergy in the Valley. On 17 June 1966, an *Alamo Messenger* editorial criticized local Catholics who were not helping the farm workers. Daniel A. Laning, a monsignor at St. Paul's Catholic Church in Mission, immediately reacted. He denounced Smith and Killian as outsiders who knew nothing about the Valley. He also objected to the marchers' use of a banner of La Virgen de Guadalupe. Other respondents, namely, the administrator and chancellor of the Brownsville Diocese, preferred quiet negotiations to their perception of grandstanding on the part of the San Antonio clergy. In turn, Archbishop Lucey defended the actions of his priests.[12]

The archbishop was responsible for much of the freedom that Smith and Killian enjoyed. A second factor was that the newly organized Diocese of Brownsville had recently lost its bishop to a fatal heart attack, which left a void of leadership Smith and Killian readily exploited. Less than two weeks later, however, the new bishop arrived. The installation service and banquet for Humberto S. Medeiros were scheduled for 29 June 1966, at the Brownsville cathedral. Clergy on both sides of the Valley conflict attended, which, under normal circumstances, would have been a gala affair. Laning served as the concelebrant, while another liturgist, the cathedral's pastor, had recently taken a stand on behalf of the farm workers. In terms of speaking opportunities, strike advocates clearly held the upper hand. The bishop of Corpus Christi, an ally of Lucey, gave the homily. He criticized those who believed that the Catholic Church should remain neutral in the conflict. Lucey himself spoke at the end of the mass. In characteristically bold language, he paraphrased Matthew 25: "I was a campesino near Rio Grande City. . . . I was tired and weary, and you did not comfort me." The cathedral priest continued the tongue lashing at the dinner, castigating local newspapers for their conservative editorials. Incensed, Laning rose from his chair to rebuke him, but was physically restrained. Finally, Medeiros spoke in general about the need for justice and thus ended the tumultuous evening.[13]

La Marcha

Even as Bishop Medeiros settled into his position, the union and its sympathizers were undertaking a new strategy. Since strikebreakers had harvested the cantaloupes, a new event was needed to bolster the workers' spirits and keep the strike before the public's eye. Taking a cue from Delano, the strikers planned a four-hundred-mile protest march—from the Valley to the state capitol in Austin. On 4 July 1966, about one hundred people set out from Starr County, winding their way through Valley towns, such as Mission, McAllen, and Edinburg. Several days later the marchers arrived at the Catholic shrine of Nuestra Señora de San Juan de los Lagos. Bishop Medeiros celebrated mass and shared words of encouragement. Heads of Mexican American organizations and trade unions also attended, including Dr. Hector Garcia of the American G.I. Forum and Henry Muñoz of the Equal Opportunity Department of the Texas AFL-CIO.[14]

Marchers were coolly received in some Valley communities but warmly in others, especially those with Mexican American mayors. After completing the first leg of their journey, the marchers turned northward. Although daily temperatures often exceeded one hundred degrees, a core group of ten to twenty workers pressed on. A cadre of students and professors at Texas A&I College welcomed them to Kingsville. While there the marchers adopted a burro as a mascot, which they named "$1.25," the state minimum hourly wage that farm workers and others were seeking. On 30 July the ragged entourage trudged into Corpus Christi. This coastal city, the midpoint of the march, was the first important stop since San

Juan, and a groundswell of support greeted the strikers. The Catholic bishop presided at a mass of over one thousand worshippers. Steelworkers hosted a noontime rally, followed by another in the evening. All these events boosted the morale of the tired *huelgistas*.[15]

Resting for the weekend, the marchers then proceeded on to San Antonio. On 17 August 1966, they entered Kenedy, Texas, and were publicly received by San Antonio priests. A few days later a mass and rally were held in Floresville, an agricultural town thirty miles southeast of San Antonio and the hometown of Texas Governor John Connally. As the California *peregrinos* had called for an audience with Governor Brown, so the Texas *huelgistas* hoped to meet Connally in Austin.[16]

On Friday, 26 August 1966, La Marcha reached the outskirts of San Antonio. Priests, nuns, and representatives of Mexican American groups greeted the farm workers and escorted them to a cheering crowd at the historic Mission San Juan Capistrano. Everyone worshipped, and the marchers were treated to dinner and local entertainment. On Saturday they attended mass at the downtown San Fernando Cathedral, during which Lucey gave the homily. Last, on Sunday evening, about one thousand people joined the marchers in a candlelight procession to the Alamo.[17]

On 29 August 1966, the *huelgistas* departed for the last leg of their journey, encountering a mixed reception in the city of New Braunfels. A Methodist minister welcomed them, while the Jaycees Club called them a gang of communists. A more serious incident occurred when a limousine pulled up to the procession, and Governor Connally stepped out. Smiling for the cameras, he exchanged greetings with a leader of the march, Father Antonio Gonzalez, who served as the chaplain of the Houston chapter of PASSO. Then Connally announced he would not hold a special legislative session on a minimum wage bill and, furthermore, would not meet the farm workers in Austin. He climbed back into his limousine, which sped away. Connally's rebuff initially discouraged the marchers, but they quickly recovered and vowed to redouble their efforts.[18]

The farm workers arrived in Austin on Sunday, 5 September 1966. Several thousand supporters were waiting for them at St. Edward's University, where the workers ate and slept. The next morning, Labor Day, the *huelgistas* finally marched to the Texas state capitol. An estimated ten thousand people soon filled the streets behind them, some singing the civil rights song "We Shall Overcome." They were a sea of colors—Mexican American and Anglo college students and a large group of African Americans—the last of which had just completed a two-hundred-mile solidarity march from Huntsville, Texas. Southern Christian Leadership Council field representative Booker T. Bonner and the civil rights group Huntsville Action for Youth coordinated this secondary march. Suddenly U.S. Senator Ralph Yarborough, a Texas progressive and longtime rival of Connally, jumped out from a side street. Joining the strike leaders, he then bounded up the steps of the capitol and delivered a stirring speech. As banners of labor unions and political organizations fluttered in the breeze, he chided the absent governor and predicted that the U.S. Congress would soon pass a minimum wage bill for farm labor. Spectators shouted, "¡Viva Yarborough! ¡Viva la Huelga! ¡Viva la Marcha!" Other speakers included U.S. Representative Henry B. Gonzalez, the president of the Texas AFL-CIO, Gene Nelson, and Father Gonzalez. Someone read a telegram of encouragement from U.S. Senator Robert F. Kennedy. César Chávez even flew in from California and addressed the crowd in nearby Zilker Park. Finally, two marchers—Reyes Alaniz and Benito Trevino—were assigned to keep a vigil at the capitol and pray their rosaries every hour until the state legislature passed a minimum wage bill.[19]

Although La Marcha seemed a great success, various problems plagued it from the beginning. For example, organizer Gene Nelson had to return to the Valley in order to quell union dissension. Physically and emotionally exhausted, he missed several speaking engagements in Corpus Christi. Rumors even circulated that he had left Texas. By default, march leader Father Gonzalez, O.M.I., had become the spokesperson for the *huelgistas,* a role in which he reveled. Wearing a cowboy hat, cowboy boots, a sign that read "Migrant Priest," and a Star of David, he fashioned himself a Latino version of Martin Luther King Jr. A major casualty of his leadership, however, was that the original purpose of the march was lost in a din of competing voices. Were the *huelgistas* marching to publicize the plight of farm workers in the Valley? Or for farm workers everywhere? Or for a minimum wage for all working-class people in Texas? Or something else? In a rambling interview Gonzalez seemed confused:

We are fighting for two million working men—not just Mexicans, but all working men in Texas . . . the anti-poverty program is part of why we march. The anti-poverty program is a slap in our face . . . the masses are on the march and they will march past the Church if the Church does not take the lead and go to the masses. This is why I march.[20]

Nelson complained to Archbishop Lucey, not only opposing Gonzalez's control of the march but also strike donations. Lucey and other church officials strategized to remove Gonzalez quietly from the farm worker dispute. The involvement of Texas AFL-CIO head, Hank Brown, was a problem as well. He had hoped to strengthen the union's presence along the Texas-Mexico border—all the way from El Paso to Brownsville. He came to the aid of the Valley farm workers, but, in so doing, contributed to the confusion over the march's original intent.[21]

Even though La Marcha resembled California's La Peregrinación in significant ways, it nevertheless lacked Chávez's tight control. He used the Delano-Sacramento event to appeal to the greatest number of people, but never allowed trade unions, state politicos, or others to co-opt or obscure the purposes and aims of the Lenten pilgrimage.

The Valley Strikers and the Shift of Support in the Catholic Church

Catholic clergy continued to argue about their churches' involvement in the strike. Archbishop Lucey, Smith, and Killian wanted to maintain an adversarial stance vis-à-vis corporate agriculture. Bishop Medeiros, his union liaison, and others closer to the scene preferred a moderate approach. Meanwhile, a new labor leader had arrived in the Valley—Antonio Orendain. Born and raised in Etzatlán, Jalisco, Orendain had first labored as an undocumented immigrant in Southern California in the late 1940s. He met César Chávez and eventually worked with him at the Community Service Organization from 1953 to 1962. He also was among those who left the agency to help Chávez build a farm workers' union and serve as one of its officers. He was usually clad in a black cowboy hat with matching shirt, trousers, and boots. He thus became easily recognized among strikers, farm managers, and law officers. He spoke English with a marked Spanish accent and, in the eyes of Anglos, sometimes conjured up the image of a Mexican revolutionary. Moreover, Orendain would not unequivocally rule out violence as a last resort for frustrated strikers and thus stood in stark contrast to the ostensibly self-effacing, saintly persona of Chávez.[22]

Orendain's first objective was to stop growers from using Mexican nationals to harvest the fall crops. His strategies soon spawned a rash of incidents. On 4 October 1966, *huelgistas* stopped a truck filled with Mexican laborers. State troopers, sheriff's deputies, and a Texas Ranger arrived, however, and defused a potentially explosive situation. Nearly two weeks later, on 24 October 1966, strikers blocked the international bridge at Roma, Texas. They refused to step aside for green carders headed for La Casita Farms. The sheriff eventually arrested Orendain, Nelson, and several others. The district judge granted a restraining order, which in effect forbade the union from interrupting bridge traffic. So, in a turnabout, on 31 October 1966, Orendain and two union sympathizers stood on the Mexican side of the bridge, stopped traffic, and were arrested by Mexican police.[23]

These confrontations soon escalated into an act of vandalism. On 3 November 1966, pickets at a packing shed in Rio Grande City convinced a train crew to abandon a load of produce. While the company dispatched a management team to move the cargo, someone discovered that the railroad trestle was on fire. Texas Rangers arrived and arrested the strikers, but no one was ever charged with the arson. The situation intensified. One week later authorities jailed nearly a dozen picketers. Other union members protested at the county courthouse, while a grand jury conspired how to close down the strike. Apprised of the circumstances, César Chávez sent a telegram to Archbishop Lucey and implored him to send Smith and Killian to help prevent an outbreak of violence. Instead, Bishop Medeiros sent his assistant to speak with the local priest, sheriff's deputies, La Casita's manager, and union members.[24]

Fortunately, hostilities subsided with the onset of the holidays. By this time strikers and their families had become preoccupied with the basics of food and clothing. So a new interfaith group sponsored two food caravans—one at Thanksgiving and another at Christmas. One of the leaders was Ernesto "Ernie" Cortes Jr., a graduate student at the University of Texas, who later distinguished himself as a community organizer throughout the Southwest. Students from Southwest Texas State College in San Marcos and Trinity University in San Antonio also collected foodstuffs and clothing, as well as the Bishops' Committee on the Spanish Speaking, the Texas Council of Churches, a Jewish organization, the Texas NAACP, and several Mexican American groups.[25]

The union's hiatus ended just before New Year's Day of 1967. On 29 December 1966, authorities arrested two strikers on charges of assault and battery and impersonating a law officer. Two weeks later a farm man-

ager reported that sugar had been poured into the tanks of several trac-
tors. So Chávez recalled Orendain and sent another organizer, Gilberto
Padilla, to the Valley. On 26 January 1967, he and others were arrested
for using a public address system while picketing. The presence of Smith
and Killian was again requested in order to quell any violence. Respecting
Bishop Medeiros's wishes, however, Lucey ordered the priests to remain
in San Antonio. Smith and Killian disobeyed, and on 1 February 1967 law
officers jailed them and several other priests for illegal picketing. In response, Bishop Medeiros released a statement. Interpreting Catholic social
teaching from a conservative point of view, he criticized the activist priests
for taking a direct role in labor strikes. Medeiros was especially upset with
Smith and Killian because he had recently approached growers and hoped
to arrange a meeting between growers and AFL-CIO representatives. Lucey then disciplined Smith and Killian by sending them to Via Coeli, a
New Mexico retreat center known for treating priests for sexual indiscre-
tions and psychological maladies. When the two clerics departed from the
airport, however, a group of supporters applauded them.[26]

Lucey's reprimand signaled not an about-face in his support for the
farm workers, but simply a means by which to control his priests. Although a liberal on many social issues, he clearly rejected any dissension
within the ranks. His purpose was to stem a growing loss of control over
priests involved in social action. Lucey believed that these "cowboys" were
tarnishing his reputation among other bishops and Catholic business people. Upholding the hierarchical structure of the Catholic Church, he was
widely known as an autocrat. In his opinion, his "new-breed" clergy had
taken matters into their own hands. While Killian readily accepted his
punishment, thereby keeping his editorial position, Smith was reassigned
to a parish on the outskirts of San Antonio and dismissed as the head of
the archdiocese's Social Action Department. Lucey also fired the executive
secretary of the Bishops' Committee of the Spanish Speaking and, later,
a lay worker on the committee. Yet Lucey's actions ultimately backfired.
Mexican American laypersons picketed both the chancery office and Lucey's residence. Other priests condemned his heavy-handed measures. In
September of 1968 the Archdiocesan Priests' Senate posted a letter to the
Vatican in which it called for Lucey's retirement. In June 1969, in his
twenty-eighth year as the archbishop, Lucey stepped down.[27]

The Catholic Church in Texas continued to aid the strikers, but with
less partisanship. First, a newly formed committee began investigating

conditions in the Valley. Second, Catholics participated in an Easter food caravan. Third, ten Texas bishops signed and published a statement in general support of the farm workers. Last, Bishop Medeiros quietly paid the medical bills of some of the workers. The Catholic Church's shift to moderate involvement may have further weakened the cantaloupe workers' strike, which from its very beginning struggled simply to survive. In the end, an act of nature dealt the deathblow to the *huelgistas*. In September of 1967, a powerful hurricane swept through the Valley, devastating towns and farms alike. Picketing in fields in which crops no longer existed was pointless, and strikers were forced to rely on odd jobs and charity.[28]

The Early Involvement of the Texas Council of Churches

In contrast to Catholics, Texas Protestants initially played a low-key role in the Starr County strike. Exceptions included James Novarro, a Baptist preacher from Houston, and Wendle Scott, a minister of a Mexican school of the Church of Christ. Both of them marched with the farm workers, which for Scott resulted in his firing. Institutionally, churches and denominations that were doctrinally conservative or sectarian never supported the strikers. Mainline Protestants instead took up this task, mostly through the auspices of the Texas Council of Churches. Like the Catholic Church, this ecumenical agency unsuccessfully embarked on a ministry of reconciliation among workers, growers, and other Valley residents.[29]

The first such individual to become involved in the strike was the Reverend Leo Nieto. He directed the Texas Migrant Ministry, which served as an arm of the Texas Council of Churches. He held master's degrees from Perkins School of Theology and Texas Christian University and belonged to the Rio Grande Conference of the United Methodist Church, the last remaining Mexican American judicatory of any major denomination. A few days after the beginning of the strike, Nieto received a letter from Gene Nelson, who requested food, money, and, if possible, "the presence of ministers in the strike area." Nieto proceeded cautiously, however, asking Valley pastors to gather facts. Then he visited Starr County to confirm the authenticity of the strike. Third, he sent an informational letter to board members of the Texas Migrant Ministry, members of the Department of Christian Social Relations of the Texas Council, and denominational executives in the region. Last, he tried to organize an interfaith fact-finding committee to investigate further the status of the strike. Three weeks later the Council released a carefully worded document in support of the farm workers:

> The Texas Council of Churches is a highly representative organization. Within its constituency are member denominational bodies whose churches embrace all parties in the current Valley labor situation. Most of these churches and the council repeatedly have cited the concern of the Church's Lord for all kinds and conditions of men and have expressed interest in all phases of human life—religious, social, and economic. In the present situation of human need, i.e. for a wage at least approximating that of minimum sustenance and health, the Church is afforded an opportunity to show empathy for the workers without explicit or implied condemnation of the growers. It should be understood quite clearly that ministering to workers and their families in their time of need is no act of partisanship. It is quite possible that some joining the march will be suffering not only with the workers but also may be suffering with the growers in their frequently difficult and unenviable situation of having no control over either costs of production or their market returns. It must be recognized that important social gains are rarely obtained without tension and perhaps controversy.[30]

Nieto and other council staff and board members stepped lightly, for the general manager of La Casita Farms worshipped at the Methodist church in Rio Grande City. Regional church leaders were well aware that many Anglo-Methodists belonged to the economic and political power structure of South Texas. The vast majority of these laypeople held conservative views. For example, they often accused the National Council of Churches of collusion with communists. In contrast, a number of younger ministers espoused the theological liberalism they had recently encountered in their seminary programs. Some of them even joined La Marcha, especially as it approached Austin. This dissonance between parishioners and pastors sometimes led not only to tensions but even overt acts of hostility. In an extreme example, in the Winter Garden District's political and racial strife of the 1960s, a "Methodist minister [recalled being] shot at and recognized the pickup from which the shot was fired as belonging to one of his laymen."[31]

Leo Nieto of the Texas Migrant Ministry was one of the pastors who became increasingly involved in the Valley conflict and faced possible retribution. By October of 1966 he had joined a committee to address the material needs of the strikers and their families. He helped to coordinate one of the holiday food caravans, while Starr County Anglos strongly opposed any church aid at all to the farm workers. Like congregations in Delano, California, First Methodist Church of Rio Grande City denied that any local Mexican Americans suffered from malnutrition. Furthermore, a rumor circulated that an Anglo vigilante group known as "the Minutemen" plotted to intercept the food distributors. The president of the Texas Council of Churches pleaded for peace, and the caravan finally reached its destination without incident.[32]

The Union, the Valley Team Ministry, and the Texas Rangers

In early 1967 the leadership and strategy of the Texas farm workers once again changed hands when Gilberto Padilla and Jim Drake arrived from California. Padilla had been serving as one of the union's vice presidents in Delano, while Drake, a United Church of Christ pastor and migrant minister, had been heading the table grape boycott. They quickly concentrated efforts on La Casita Farms, which was arguably the largest enterprise in Valley agribusiness. They gathered information about the California-owned corporation and discovered that supermarkets in Texas and Oklahoma carried 40 percent of its produce. So in early February the union announced a boycott of all La Casita fruits and vegetables. Clearly alarmed, company officials immediately protested the action as illegal and vowed to fight it.[33]

Simultaneously, the Texas Council of Churches took a more active role in the conflict. The Council decided to introduce a full-time team ministry to the Valley, whose quixotic quest was to reconcile opposing sides in the strike and, no less, within a reasonable time frame. The Council intended to recruit one person to relate directly to farm workers, other Mexican Americans, and middle-class Anglo churches. A second individual, ideally an expert in agricultural economics and rural sociology, would relate to farm managers, independent growers, and other business interests. Securing the second position was problematic since local agribusiness wanted no part of it. The first post, however, was quickly filled by Edgar A. Krueger. He had grown up in the German American Evangelical and Reformed Church and enrolled in its schools of Elmhurst College and Eden Theological Seminary, the same institutions attended by the famous Niebuhr brothers. As a seminarian Krueger met a supervisor of the National Migrant Ministry who persuaded him to pursue a vocation among Latinas/os. He eventually joined the Migrant Ministry and worked among farm laborers in the mid-1950s. Afterward, he served as a missionary in Honduras. Soft-spoken and unassuming, he had recently been teaching at a school in the Valley.[34]

Krueger's new duties commenced in March of 1967, only one month after the San Antonio priests had been sanctioned from further involvement in the Valley. Ironically, Texas Protestant leaders were forging a more direct link to the strikers even as the Roman Catholic Church was disengaging from such a relationship. Just a few months later the Texas Council of Churches found itself similarly enmeshed in the strife among the strikers, growers, and other Valley residents. Although the Council had hoped to serve as an agent of reconciliation, it was instead regarded as both a meddler and a betrayer. Conservative Anglo Protestants perceived it as an unwitting tool in the hands of the union. By the same token, Mexican Americans accused the Council of bending to economic and political pressures when it ultimately loosened ties with the strikers.

Krueger started out haltingly, due in part to a poorly written job description. For example, he was expected to relate both to Mexican Americans and other Anglos in a highly charged atmosphere. He also was called to a ministry designed for at least two staff persons. Nevertheless, he became acquainted with farm worker families who lived in the *colonias* and learned about the dynamics of the strike. Then he slowly introduced elements of community organizing. Last, he monitored roadside picketing, always reminding strikers to practice nonviolence.[35]

Still, Krueger's labors could not quell mounting tensions in the spring of 1967. Although La Casita Farms expected both a bumper crop and a large market for its melons, the company could not foresee the consequences of one other variable, namely, the strikers. Gil Padilla pledged that a refusal to recognize and negotiate with the union would lead to cantaloupes rotting in the fields. Local Two of the United Farm Workers Organizing Committee promised to prevent strikebreakers from entering the fields, to interfere with rail shipments, and, if necessary, to boycott Texas supermarkets. Padilla also vowed to expand union efforts into the citrus and vegetable industries in nearby Hidalgo, Willacy, and Cameron counties. Clearly, he was indulging in a show of bravado. Yet, as the manager of La Casita, Ray Rochester was worried. In his own bluff, he threatened to call the U.S. Justice Department. No federal agents were ever dispatched to Starr County, but the sheriff soon requested and received a reinforcement of Texas Rangers. Ultimately, the Rangers were the ones who engaged in violence.[36]

When the cantaloupe harvest opened in May of 1967, the union immediately unsheathed its new strategy. Padilla and others announced that a Mexican labor organization had agreed to honor the strike and prohibit its members from entering the fields. Thus, on 11 May 1967, this organization raised high a red flag on the Mexican side of the Miguel Alemán–Roma International Bridge, which signaled to day workers to return home. As a result, news reporters soon learned that La Casita Farms had received only 50 percent of the harvesters needed for that day. This international cooperation, however, was short-lived. By the end of the day Mexican pickets had left their post, and green-card workers crossed the bridge under the cover of night. Padilla declared that this seeming reversal was all a misunderstanding and that the Mexican union would begin monitoring bridge traffic around the clock. Yet a conflicting report claimed that Mexican authorities had expelled the pickets. In any event, Mexican solidarity with the strikers evaporated.[37]

Meanwhile, pickets on the U.S. side faced their own problems. They complained that the Texas Rangers were continually harassing them. Their list of grievances included the jailing of Gene Nelson for alleged threats, the arrests of over twenty union members and sympathizers, and, finally, on 26 May 1967, the charging of yet another group of pickets for unlawful assembly. The strikers had gathered near a set of railroad tracks to persuade a train crew to abandon a shipment of melons. Migrant minister Ed Krueger soon arrived, as well as a detail of Rangers. Krueger exchanged words with Captain A. Y. Allee, the head of deployment, who threatened: "You've been wanting to get arrested for a long time." Rangers then dragged Krueger and a striker to the track and held their faces within inches of a fast-moving train. Afterward, Allee threw Krueger into a patrol car, while other officers arrested Krueger's wife and the pickets.[38]

These confrontations climaxed in an event known as "the Dimas Affair." On 31 May 1967, just four days after the railroad-track incident, Texas Rangers and sheriff's deputies raided a house in Rio Grande City. They broke down the front door and apprehended two union members, purportedly for disturbing the peace and menacing law officers with a deadly weapon. After the strikers were jailed, a physician examined them and reported that both men needed hospitalization. One of them, Magdaleno Dimas, had been especially roughed up and was possibly suffering from a brain concussion. Allegations of police brutality gained national headlines. *Newsweek* even ran a story, accompanied by a photograph of a scowling Allee, complete with a white cowboy hat on his head, a cigar in his mouth, and a pearl-handled .45 revolver in his side holster. When asked about the strike, Allee, a veteran of numerous assignments, seemed bewildered by the turn of events: "Son, this is the goddamndest thing I've ever been in." In reality, the escalation of the strike into the Dimas Affair merely confirmed a long-standing tradition of racial violence among Texas Rangers and Mexicans and Tejanas/os, extending from "the Cortina Wars" of the 1850s and 1860s and resuming with the border skirmishes of the 1910s. Dimas indeed had a penchant for violence. Years earlier he had been convicted of murder in his native Mexico. Furthermore, when Tony Orendain arrived in the Valley, Dimas and others revealed to him a cache of weapons they wanted to use in an uprising against Anglos. Dimas eventually met an end that epitomized the aforementioned borderlands tradition of violence. In 1973 he was drinking in a bar and started arguing with a man whose father, a deputy sheriff, had once arrested strikers. According to a news account, Dimas pulled out a pistol and shot and wounded the man. Dimas himself was then shot and killed in the ensuing gunfire.[39]

After this latest round of arrests, the union decided to sue the Rangers. On behalf of Ed Krueger, the Texas Council of Churches filed a similar suit even as it scheduled a special meeting with union members and growers. Held in a Corpus Christi hotel on 8 and 9 June 1967, the meeting had a twofold purpose: it was both a fact-finding mission and a possible first step toward reconciliation of opposing groups. The Council had mailed invitations to local clergy, denominational executives, Anglo laity, and some of the strikers. Dr. Jorge Lara-Braud of the Hispanic-American Institute of Austin, a new Presbyterian agency, served as secretary of the proceedings. Born in Mexicali, Mexico, Lara-Braud was educated at Austin College, Texas A&I College, Austin Presbyterian Seminary, and Princeton Seminary. An active layperson, he sat on several national church committees. He also had been the dean at the Presbyterian Seminary in Mexico City and had taught at the Austin theological school. Last, he served on the Migrant Ministry Committee of the National Council of Churches of

Christ (NCCC) and on the Advisory Council on Inter-American Affairs, United Presbyterian Church, U.S.A.[40]

Church officials arranged first to interview farm laborers, but the workers had remained in the Valley to attend a rally for César Chávez. So religious leaders heard Ed Krueger and others describe the alleged collusion among farm managers, law enforcement agencies, and local courts to undermine the strike. Union sympathizers claimed that, in spite of Ranger provocation, strikers faithfully practiced nonviolence. The next morning, on 9 June 1967, the panel awaited the arrival of farm representatives, which had been in doubt. Although expecting a degree of hostility, church authorities were shocked when several agribusiness men, accompanied by an attorney, filed into the conference room. The presence of the lead counsel for La Casita Farms immediately set an adversarial tone. Indeed, it almost seemed a religious version of a federal inquiry, especially since departmental heads of denominational offices had traveled from as far away as New York and Washington, D.C. Participants soon seated themselves, and Leo Nieto of the Texas Council of Churches summarized recent events in the Valley. He had hardly finished when the lawyer abruptly questioned the purpose of the meeting. Nieto explained it was designed as an initial effort in a process of reconciliation between strikers and farm interests. A denominational executive then elaborated on the finer points of the concept of conflict resolution, all of which left the attorney unimpressed. Soon, however, a frank discussion followed. It turned on several questions, such as the use of green carders, the part the Rangers had been playing in the strike, and whether a bona fide strike even existed. Although growers, farm managers, and other agribusiness men themselves disagreed on some issues, they spoke in unison against any legitimate role of religion in economic affairs. They bitterly resented the involvement of the Texas Council of Churches. William Deines said:

> I've been quite active in the Church all my life, teaching teenagers, [serving as a] deacon, etc. I'm no longer as active because of positions taken by [the] TCC and NCC, leading [in] unionizing workers. You are going against [the] best interests of all, including [the] workers. I noticed in [the] *C[orpus] C[hristi] Caller-Times* statement by Nieto on [your] desire to ease [the Valley] situation. The best policy is for you to withdraw from the scene. I understand you are looking for a pastor for us to lead us out of the wilderness [a reference to the anticipated second specialist for the Valley Team Ministry]. It is beyond my comprehension you'd be willing to waste your money.[41]

The battle lines had been firmly drawn. Growers regarded the Texas Council and national church leaders not as agents of reconciliation but as meddlers and union partisans. This attitude was not completely unfounded. While not a striker, Krueger had come to empathize deeply with the cause of the workers. He said the Rangers' accusations that he was a union organizer were responsible in part for his growing militancy and identification with the workers. Second, both Jim Drake and Chris Hartmire of the California Migrant Ministry supported him, writing that, from an ethical point of view, he had no choice but to take up completely with the strikers. Third, Council members had signed a statement in March of 1967 that supported the rights of the unionists. Last, the Council had committed a tactical blunder insofar as it had filled the position of the Valley Team Ministry for the workers but not for the farm interests. By June of 1967 the recruitment of the second person had become a moot point.[42]

The fact-finding consultation not only further strained relations among Methodists but also highlighted tensions among Presbyterians. For example, Lara-Braud represented one side and William Deines the other. Harold Kilpatrick, another Presbyterian layperson and a moderate, was longtime Executive Director of the Texas Council of Churches. More than anyone else, with the possible exception of the Council president, Kilpatrick found himself in the unenviable role of defending the Council's actions to conservative Presbyterians and others. Anglo Protestant clergy in the Valley, including Presbyterians, may have sympathized with the farm workers but remained silent. Others, such as Howard C. Blake, Executive Secretary of the Presbytery of South Texas and brother of Eugene Blake of the World Council of Churches, also held a middle position. Initial funding for Krueger's position had even come from Presbyterian sources, which had been nearly depleted. Presbyterian Church–United States leaders discussed how to find more funding while bypassing the local presbytery.[43]

In addition to the consultation, another event further exacerbated ill will among growers, strikers, and religious groups. On 29–30 June 1967, the U.S. Senate Subcommittee on Migratory Labor held hearings in Rio Grande City and Edinburg, Texas. As in Delano, California, Harrison A. Williams Jr., presided. He was joined by fellow senator Edward Kennedy, as well as several others. Farm workers first testified, followed by a sheriff's deputy and various farm representatives. Ed Krueger, Sherrill Smith, Antonio Gonzales, and other religious figures also made statements. As a result, Williams concluded that the Texas Rangers had indeed committed acts of brutality.[44]

In the short term, however, the hearings were a hollow vindication of the strikers. The melon harvest had peaked, and so most of the Rangers had already left the Valley. In spite of union attempts to stop or at least slow down the harvest, Starr County farms celebrated a record crop. Growers were indebted to the easy availability of Mexican day workers, Rangers had intimidated strikers, farm managers and foremen had been deputized, local judges had doubled and tripled bail bonds for picketers, and the union lacked the necessary resources. Thus the rest of the summer passed quietly. Even a second Labor Day march, a seventy-mile walk between San Antonio and Austin, failed to draw much attention. The only noteworthy action was that Erasmo Andrade, an employee with the Bishops' Committee for the Spanish Speaking and state chair of the Valley Workers' Assistance Committee, was fired for having invited Reies Tijerina, the controversial land-grant activist in New Mexico, to participate in the march. The next major news story to break was not some novel strike strategy or strong-arm tactic by law enforcement. It was instead an act of nature—a powerful hurricane ripping through South Texas and ravaging the autumn crops.[45]

Hurricane Beulah

On 20 September 1967, Hurricane Beulah surged into the Valley, devastating homes, farms, and lives. Additional rains further swelled the banks of the Rio Grande and its tributaries. Floodwaters eventually covered more than 43,000 square miles. Hundreds of farm workers sought refuge in makeshift shelters, while growers grieved over ruined vegetable fields and citrus orchards. In response, church groups quickly transported food, clothing, and medicine to flood victims on both sides of the Rio Grande. Bishop Medeiros approved thousands of dollars for relief efforts. The New Orleans Federation of Churches sent $2,000, the Presbyterian Church, U.S., $2,500, and the United Church of Christ sent funds to victims on both sides of the border. The Texas Council of Churches and the Roman Catholic Diocese of Brownsville later established a joint program, the new Valley Service Committee, to disburse donations.[46]

Although immensely destructive, the hurricane actually inspired positive changes among the Mexican American population. Admittedly, the natural disaster delivered the deathblow to the farm labor strike. Picketing at farms with no crops was pointless. Yet the relief activity sparked a new sense of hope in the *colonias.* More residents attended house meetings to address everyday needs, such as lobbying local governments for paved streets and better water drainage. A new can-do spirit even took root among many people. The hurricane had seemingly swept away not only much of the physical landscape but also some of the psychological and social obstacles blocking the path to self-determination.[47]

In fact, the Valley Service Committee soon moved from relief efforts to community development. Consequently, Leo Nieto resumed the search for a second team minister. Since farm interests had rejected the possibility of an advocate on their behalf, the Texas Council of Churches tried another approach. While Krueger continued working in the *colonias,* another minister was secured to relate to Valley churches. Nehemias Garcia soon filled this post. He had previously served the Second Presbyterian Church of Harlingen, Texas, and before that churches in Mexico. Born in Chiapas, Mexico, Garcia had later studied both law and theology. As an added measure, Nieto and a field representative of the Migrant Ministry joined the team ministry as part-time staff.[48]

The Ranger Lawsuit, the VISTA Program, and the Firing of Krueger

Nehemias Garcia had barely assumed his new duties when the fifteenth annual assembly of the Texas Council of Churches convened in San Antonio, Texas. Gerald N. McAllister, outgoing president and canon of the local Episcopal diocese, addressed the delegates. Basing his message on St. Paul's theme of reconciliation in 2 Corinthians 5:14–15, 18–19, he offered one of the few theological reflections on the role of the Council in the Valley strike. He first acknowledged the relative neglect of mainline Protestant denominations toward minorities, especially Mexican Americans. Second, he reported that national church leaders had recently tried to right this wrong by launching more programs to attack the underlying causes of poverty and discrimination. He spoke as well about the economic difficulties that growers often faced. In short, McAllister presented a middle position vis-à-vis the strike: he upheld the right of farm workers to organize, but, as a former rancher in Central Texas and a onetime lay minister in the Valley, he also sympathized with agricultural interests. Specifically, he staunchly defended the actions of the Council. He stressed that Ed Krueger conscientiously performed his labors "as a minister of the gospel and not as an arm, tool or front for the union." On a final note, McAllister reviewed a timeline of events leading up to the Council's lawsuit against the Rangers. He explained that the Council had pursued all other avenues of redress and was still open to an out-of-court settlement. He was pessimistic, however, about such a resolution. For his actions and words, McAllister experienced the wrath of laypersons in the Valley. They vilified him for supporting the Council lawsuit against the Rangers. He has written: "I was savagely attacked at our Diocesan Council and branded as a communist and traitor to America. . . . In two Episcopal elections in [the Diocese of] West Texas, I was elected by the clergy to be the new bishop and soundly defeated by the laity who still remembered my days as T.C.C. prexy."[49]

Although McAllister upheld Krueger in his work, rumors spread that the pastor's days in the Texas Migrant Ministry were numbered. While McAllister and others espoused St. Paul's message of reconciliation, Krueger embraced St. Luke's preferential option for the poor and oppressed. This position hardly endeared Krueger to most Anglo Protestants in the Valley. In particular, his role in the Ranger lawsuit infuriated them. As early as February of 1968 a grower attorney and member of a Methodist church circulated a letter to the annual conference. He wrote that Krueger had directly supported the strikers and that the suit against the Rangers was a gross injustice. In retaliation, the attorney urged fellow Methodists to stop contributing funds to the Texas Council of Churches, thereby hoping to force Krueger's termination. This pressure, however, failed to stop legal proceedings. In May of 1968, a panel of federal judges heard testimony against the Rangers. Among those who gave depositions were Ed Krueger and his wife.[50]

During the hearing, the Texas Council became further involved with the federal government. The Council had applied for and recently received approval to participate in one of President Lyndon B. Johnson's programs in his War on Poverty, namely, the Volunteers in Service to America (VISTA). Designed as a means of uplifting economically depressed communities, VISTA contracted with various nonprofit groups to implement its objectives. In tandem with this program, the Council recruited several local Mexican Americans as employees and volunteers. These persons began teaching English and citizenship classes, managing recreational activities, establishing credit unions, and referring clients to other agencies. Many Valley Anglos deeply resented VISTA as one more government intrusion into local affairs. They naturally identified the program with the Texas Council, whose staff they continued to regard as outsiders and troublemakers.[51]

Simultaneously, tensions in the Council affected its work in the Valley. First, like Krueger, Leo Nieto of the Texas Migrant Ministry had become radicalized in the course of the strike, participating, for instance, in the Poor People's March in Washington, D.C., and eventually embracing the entire Chicana/o movement. Nieto's supervisor, Harold Kilpatrick, meanwhile, was first and foremost an ecumenist. He belonged to an older generation that held moderate and conciliatory views on most social issues. For example, as far back as 1937, he had attended a Conference on Church, Community, and State at Oxford, England, and a Faith and Order Conference at Edinburgh, Scotland. He hailed the creation of the Texas Conference of Churches in 1969—which included not only Protestants but also Roman Catholics, the Orthodox Church, and other Christian groups—as the high point in his career. When the union scaled back its operations, then, Kilpatrick hoped that fences could be mended between the Texas Council and Anglo Protestants in the Valley. As the commitments of Nieto and Kilpatrick diverged, however, their own relationship deteriorated. Nieto ultimately resigned from the Texas Council to take a position with his denomination's board of missions. Maintaining an office in Austin, Texas, he later funneled substantial church monies, known as the Fund for Reconciliation, to Texas farm workers.[52]

A second internal stress developed after the arrival of Nieto's temporary replacement, Jesse Reber. Recently retired from the Pennsylvania Council of Churches, the interim director set up his office in the Valley in order to supervise the VISTA workers. In step with Kilpatrick, Reber on the one hand preferred working with Anglo churches. On the other hand, Krueger continued organizing Mexican Americans in the *colonias*. Sparks sporadically flew between the two men. For example, they once faced off in the case of a Mexican American student who accused an Anglo teacher of physical abuse. Krueger upheld the student's allegations, while the director dismissed the incident. Relations between the ministers continually worsened, and by the end of the year Kilpatrick had advised the Council board to fire Krueger.[53]

In January of 1969 Krueger was indeed relieved of his duties. Kilpatrick charged that Krueger had failed to enlist the support of the Anglo laity and clergy of the Valley. Besides, Kilpatrick announced, the Council had changed its focus so that Krueger's services were no longer required. At the same time, Kilpatrick and others knew that the firing would draw a storm of protest. In fact, a scant week later a group of thirty to fifty Mexican Americans demonstrated outside of the First Methodist Church in Pharr, Texas, where, in an open meeting, Kilpatrick was explaining the dismissal. Advocates for the migrant minister believed that the real motive behind his firing was his refusal to drop his part of the lawsuit against the Rangers, which the Council itself had recently done. Officers and board members had been eager to withdraw from the suit for two reasons: first, they wanted to placate Anglo Protestants in the Valley; second, in the name of ecumenism, they wanted to end the lawsuit. In other words, the Council had voted to join hands with the Texas Catholic Conference, which would create one of the first ventures of its kind in the nation. Beforehand, however, each entity had to resolve any outstanding litigation. Although Krueger's refusal to withdraw from the lawsuit in no way prevented the merger—the Council had pled with him three times to do so—it nevertheless threatened to cast a shadow over the otherwise momentous event.[54]

Officials of the National Council of Churches were soon notified about Krueger's firing and immediately launched an investigation. Alfonso Rodriguez, Executive Secretary of the Council on Spanish-American Work, appointed a fact-finding committee. A few weeks later Rodriguez and others authored a document titled "Statement of Concern and Resolutions." This report strongly criticized the decision-making process of the Texas Council and urged that, in the future, the new Texas Conference of Churches include feedback from *colonia* residents and others when formulating strategies affecting them.[55]

Mexican Americans were not waiting, however, for a solicitation of their views. In late February, at the constituting convention of the Texas Conference of Churches, they expressed their opinion about the dismissal of Krueger. As leaders of several dozen church judicatories and ecclesiastical units gathered in Austin, Texas, on 24 February 1969, demonstrators picketed outside the building of the host congregation. In a scene eerily reminiscent of reactions to Archbishop Lucey's punishment of activist priests two years earlier, protesters waved placards condemning Krueger's

termination. Reynaldo de la Cruz, president of the grassroots organization Colonias of the Valley, declared that churches henceforth needed to
include the voices of the poor in any plans to improve their lives. In response, assembly delegates promised to take all such measures to that end.
Yet in light of all the polarization generated by the farm worker strike
and the churches' roles in it, defining, much less implementing, a genuine
ministry in the Valley remained a daunting task.[56]

In an editorial on the historic assembly of the Texas Conference of
Churches, Kilpatrick interpreted the Valley conflict in terms of Reinhold
Niebuhr's classic work *The Irony of American History*. He noted that the
Texas Council originally became involved in order to reconcile opposing
groups; yet it actually contributed to further polarization. He felt bitter
that the Council had aided Mexican American victims of Hurricane Beulah, only later to receive a tongue lashing by the same people. Yet since the
late 1950s Kilpatrick had defended the increasingly liberal policies of the
NCCC against the accusations of conservative Anglo Protestants, only ultimately to be investigated and criticized by an arm of the organization he
so dearly loved. After serving as the midwife for the new Texas Conference
of Churches, he retired as its acting executive director on 1 August 1969.[57]

And the strikers themselves? As the new decade succeeded the tumultuous 1960s, Local Two of the United Farm Workers languished. Its
onetime leader, Tony Orendain, later founded an independent union. In
the end, though, it hardly fared any better than its predecessor. A few
church officials, such as Leo Nieto, supported it, but most Protestant and
Catholic groups avoided distributing aid that even remotely suggested any
partisanship in favor of farm labor organizing.[58]

Conclusion

The farm worker strike in the Rio Grande Valley failed miserably. Nevertheless, it contributed to a series of events that led to a greater sense
of self-determination among Mexican Americans in Texas. For example,
the abolishment of the poll tax, the elections of Latinos to city councils,
student uprisings in public high schools and local universities, and the
founding of a host of Chicana/o civil rights organizations in the late 1960s
and 1970s. Groups such as the Mexican American Youth Organization
(MAYO), La Raza Unida Party, the Mexican American Legal Defense

and Education Fund (MALDEF), and the National Chicana Political Caucus became household names. William C. Velásquez, among the first members of MAYO, developed the Southwest Voter Registration Education Project. Ernie Cortes Jr., who had once coordinated food assistance for striking farm workers, helped to establish Communities Organized for Public Service (COPS) in San Antonio, as well as Valley Interfaith, which is largely a Catholic nonprofit group that advocates for *colonia* residents. As new legal rights were advanced by and for African Americans in the U.S. South, so a similar revolution swept across the Southwest. In the long run, demographic and economic changes also affected the lives of Valley residents, including farm workers. Growers accelerated the mechanization of crop production and harvesting, which displaced many laborers. In turn, tourism, building construction, and the establishment of *maquiladores*— small factories on both sides of the border—eventually supplanted much of the agribusiness of past years. To be sure, some Mexican Americans and Mexican nationals still worked in the fields, continuing to eke out a living that sometimes resembled third world conditions. Yet, practically speaking, their increasingly small numbers sidelined farm worker justice as an issue in the eyes of the public.[59]

The response of churches to the awakening of Mexican Americans in the Valley was mixed. In reaction to the South Texas strike, the leaders of the Roman Catholic Church and the Texas Council of Churches prematurely attempted a ministry of reconciliation, trying to relate both to farm workers and growers. This stance forced their new-breed ministers into impossible positions of supporting the farm workers and yet attempting to avoid partisanship. In contrast, the California Migrant Ministry unequivocally rallied behind the union, and representatives of the Roman Catholic Church finally helped to negotiate the table grape contracts. As the Starr County strike languished, Texas churches capitulated to the growers and other Anglo Valley residents. A Christian social justice rooted in northern Protestantism, liberal Catholicism, and an emerging Latin American theology of liberation ultimately withered in the face of a persistent southern ethos—one that tolerated only traditional ministries of mercy. In the end, the churches in Texas failed to live up to the expectations of persons such as Jorge Lara-Braud, who hoped it would struggle not to avoid the conflict of the growing Chicana/o movement, "but to make it creative rather than destructive."

Sympathy march coming into Austin from Huntsville, Texas, 1966. Courtesy Shel Hershorn photo collection at the Center for American History at the University of Texas, Austin.

Archbishop Robert E. Lucey. Courtesy Archdiocese of San Antonio archives.

Marchers approaching the Capitol in Austin. Courtesy Shel Hershorn photo collection at the Center for American History at the University of Texas, Austin.

U.S. Senator Ralph Yarborough joining 1966 march. Left to right, union leader Eugene Nelson, Protestant pastor James Novarro, Yarborough, PASSO priest Antonio Gonzales, O.M.I., and unidentified marcher. Courtesy Shel Hershorn photo collection at the Center for American History at the University of Texas, Austin.

Farm-worker "sentinels"
Reyes Alaniz and Benito
Trevino at the state Capitol
in Austin, 1966. Courtesy
Shel Hershorn photo collection at the Center for American History at the University
of Texas, Austin.

UFW union leader Tony Orendain in the Rio Grande Valley. Courtesy Alan C. Pogue, Texas Center for Documentary Photography, Austin, Texas.

Texas Council of Churches/ migrant minister Leo Nieto. Courtesy the General Commission on Archives and History, the United Methodist Church, Madison, New Jersey, Mission Education Records, Photograph Series.

Migrant minister Ed Krueger and unidentified mother with infant—Rio Grande Valley. Courtesy Alan C. Pogue, Texas Center for Documentary Photography, Austin, Texas.

Texas Ranger A. Y. Allee standing in front of a line of cars—Rio Grande Valley. Courtesy Mark St. Gil, BlackStar Photos, New York.

Chapter 7: Conclusion

. . . although the twentieth century has often been viewed as an age of impersonal institutions, I believe that human activity lies at the heart of any meaningful historical narrative.

FERENC MORTON SZASZ

This work has explored the roles played by and the interactions among several Christian traditions in the farm worker movement, culminating in events of the 1960s. In seeking to shed greater light on religious beliefs and practices in the context of this phenomenon, I have employed the interpretive lens of the (now Old) New Western History. This lens was sometimes filtered by the familiar perspectives of race, class, and gender. I also have borrowed a few insights from other disciplines, especially the subfield of geography known as regionalism. Comparisons of economic trends, shifting populations, and cultural realities in California and Texas have helped to illuminate why the efforts of farm workers temporarily succeeded in one region of the U.S. West but failed or were redirected in another. Moreover, what may have appeared as hazy images of religious identities, traditions, and strengths in the two states have been brought more clearly into focus. The field of sociology has helped as well to render more transparent the roles of religion in La Causa, specifically the theory of resource mobilization.

Farm Workers and the Churches has thus joined the corpus of the New Western History and perhaps also interdisciplinary studies. Among other things, this work recognizes the significance of the religious claims and practices of nonelites, such as those Mexicans and Mexican Americans who have struggled to climb beyond the lower rungs of economic, political, and cultural power. This book, then, may be counted as yet one more corrective to the once strongly held view that New England Puritanism and the westward expansion of its progeny constituted the heart and soul of American religion. As some recent historians have remarked, religious groups in the United States have moved not only from east to west—according to the ideology of Manifest Destiny—but also from west to east and from south to north. At the same time, I have in fact tended to spotlight the east-to-west movements of two forms of white Anglo-Saxon Protestantism and the differences between them, that is, a socially active northern version—along with liberal Catholicism—and a quietist southern version. I have shined much light on some of their organizations and the actions of some of their elites, such as church bureaucrats, ministers, and women leaders in home missions. Even so, ample attention also has been given to the various phenomena of Mexican devotional piety and their expression in La Causa. Much more work can and should be done in this area, especially in the use of oral history, cultural anthropology, and literary analysis. In short, *Farm Workers and the Churches* essentially serves as a "bridge" revision of Christian history in the U.S. West.[1]

Besides its contribution to the burgeoning literature of religion in the U.S. West, this book has focused on the faith efforts of individuals in helping to empower a particular population in the Southwest. This *who's who* list includes the following: sympathetic bishops, priests, and nuns; Anglo lay women and Anglo Protestant ministers (and some Latinos) in the home missions movement; new-breed ministers in both the Catholic Church and the National Migrant Ministry; national church executives and other leaders in both the Catholic Church and mainline Protestant communions; and, finally, the spiritual leadership of César Chávez. These persons and countless foot soldiers in Christian fellowships, church-related agencies, and other institutions—not to mention thousands of farm workers—all evidenced, in their own singular ways, a religious strength and commitment that transcended the organizations to which they belonged.

This transcendence evolved over time in three distinct phases. From the late 1800s through the early 1900s, Anglo Catholics intermittently ministered among a minority population within their own fold, even as a few Protestant evangelists were intent on winning Mexican souls for Jesus. From the early 1900s through the 1920s, Protestant organizations turned to a moderate Social Gospel as an approach in their work among farm laborers. Concurrently, modern Catholic social services were extended to Mexicans and Mexican Americans, especially in Southern California. From the 1930s through the 1940s, faint signs of applications of social encyclicals on organized labor were detected in the Catholic Church's relations with farm workers. As a result of the Bracero Program that commenced in

World War II, both the Catholic Church and the National Council of Churches advocated for legal redress among farm laborers. Finally, in the 1960s, a full-blown servanthood ministry—a precursor to the reflection/ action model of liberation theology—unconditionally expended its energies at the disposal of the United Farm Workers. Simultaneously, Chávez creatively combined Mexican devotional piety with strategies of the civil rights movement. From the 1920s, determined individuals often held accountable others in their respective religious organizations, challenging them to practice the beliefs that they all professed. At times such Christian activists were threatened, disciplined, ostracized, or even terminated for living in accordance with their faith commitments. Seldom, however, did Anglos face the level of retribution meted out to the farm workers themselves. Throughout a century of incremental change in the theologies and practices of religious elites, the majority of Mexicans and Mexican Americans doggedly held on to their own expressions of faith. These expressions included praying to the saints at home altars, participating in pilgrimages to beseech God for healing or in thankfulness for healing, observation of special events such as El Día de los Muertos and Las Posadas, and, of course, veneration of and supplication to La Virgen de Guadalupe.

La Causa emerged from the decades-old struggles of the farm workers. Yet it was certainly not limited to that one phenomenon of the Latina/o civil rights movement of the 1960s and 1970s. Instead, César Chávez and the United Farm Workers provided a focus, a base, a rallying cry from which dozens of other protest and/or self-help groups were born or at least were strengthened. The very term itself, *La Causa,* no longer belonged exclusively to the farm workers but was soon adopted by other Latinas/os throughout the West Coast and Southwest, even the entire United States. The farm worker movement thus inspired an entirely new generation, the members of which lived in mostly urban settings. The movement called them to both claim their rights as U.S. citizens and proudly celebrate their Mexican heritage.

A vivid example of this exponential growth is epitomized in the life of a Mexican American, who, like César Chávez, dedicated himself to La Causa. A student at St. Mary's University in San Antonio, William "Willie" C. Velásquez (1944–1988) directly participated in the struggles of the melon workers in South Texas and soon distinguished himself in other expressions of La Causa. A biographer writes:

He helped the United Farm Workers Union in organizing activities in the
Rio Grande valley [*sic*] in 1966–67 and left graduate school his last semester
to serve as boycott coordinator for the San Antonio area in the Starr County
Strike. While still a graduate student, Velásquez was hired as a consultant to
the executive director of the Bishop's [*sic*] Committee for the Spanish Speaking of the United States Catholic Conference. In March 1967 he helped
found the Mexican American Youth Organization at St. Mary's University,
and he also served as the first statewide coordinator of . . . the forerunner to
the Raza Unida Party. . . .

In 1969 Velásquez helped found the Mexican American Unity Council
and served as executive director. He was also a VISTA supervisor . . . In
June 1970 he became field director of the Southwest Council of La Raza in
Phoenix, the forerunner of the National Council of La Raza. In 1971 he became assistant director of field organizing and fundraising for the council's
national office. . . . Also in 1971 he organized [what later became known
as] the Southwest Voter Registration Education Project, [which] played a
fundamental role in the increase of Latino voters and officeholders in the
1970s and 1980s.[2]

Velásquez would certainly have risen as an indefatigable leader in the
Chicana/o or Latina/o civil rights movement regardless of whether farm
workers had been fighting for better wages and overall legitimacy in the
communities where they lived. Yet the fact remains that the melon worker
strike in the Valley galvanized and energized him into action, much as it
did for many other young Mexican Americans in Texas and as the grape
worker strike and boycott did for young Mexican Americans in California. Thus the farm worker movement ignited an economic, cultural, and
political blaze that swept across the Southwest and West Coast, the effects
of which are still being felt today. Another undisputed fact is that liberal
Protestants, Catholic labor advocates, and practitioners of Mexican devotional piety all played their own vital roles in those early years of La Causa.
Their combined efforts contributed significantly to the historic event of
the first major contract between California farm workers and growers.

Notes

Chapter 1: Introduction

1. "UFW Sets Off on Trek Back into the Fields," *Los Angeles Times,* 1 April 1994, A3; "Morning Edition," 1 April 1994, National Public Radio, Washington, D.C.

2. "Morning Edition," 1 April 1994, National Public Radio, Washington, D.C.

3. Ronald B. Taylor, *Chavez and the Farm Workers* (Boston: Beacon Press, 1975), 169, 173; Sam Kushner, *Long Road to Delano* (New York: International Publisher, 1975), 160; John Gregory Dunne, *Delano: The Story of the California Grape Strike* (New York: Farrar, Straus & Giroux, 1967), 130–35; Dick Meister and Anne Loftis, *A Long Time Coming: The Struggle to Unionize America's Farm Workers* (New York: Macmillan, 1977), 144–45.

4. Throughout this work *Chicana/o* denotes politically self-conscious Mexican Americans in the Southwest and on the West Coast who, beginning in the 1960s, founded organizations whose identity and goals contrasted with those of older, more traditional entities, such as the League of United Latin American Citizens (LULAC) and the American G.I. Forum (Rodolfo Acuña, *Occupied America: A History of Chicanos,* 3rd ed. [New York: Harper Collins, 1988], 338; Juan Gómez-Quiñones, *Chicano Politics: Reality and Promise, 1940–1990,* Calvin P. Horn Lectures in Western History and Culture [Albuquerque: University of New Mexico Press, 1990], 7; José Cuello, "Introduction: Chicana/o History as a Social Movement," in *Voices of a New Chicana/o History,* ed. Refugio I. Rochin and Dennis N. Valdes [East Lansing: Michigan State University Press, 2000], 12–15).

5. "Peregrinación, penitencia, revolución," Wayne State University Archives of Labor and Urban Affairs and University Archives, National Farm Worker Ministry, Box 14, File 1, Detroit, n.d., hereafter cited as NFWM.

6. Orlando Espín, "Popular Catholicism among Latinos," in *Hispanic Catholic Culture in the U.S.: Issues and Concerns,* ed. Jay P. Dolan and Allan Figueroa Deck, S.J., The Notre Dame History of Hispanic Catholics in the U.S., ed. Jay P. Dolan, vol. 3 (Notre Dame, Ind.: University of Notre Dame Press, 1994), 344.

7. Throughout the text *Latina/o* is used as an inclusive term referring to Spanish-speaking persons rather than *Hispanic,* which is an arbitrary label imposed by the U.S. government (Acuña, *Occupied America,* ix–xi; and José Angel Gutiérrez, *The Making of a Chicano Militant: Lessons from Cristal,* Wisconsin Studies in Autobiography, ed. William L. Andrews [Madison: University of Wisconsin Press, 1998], 12, 28–30).

8. Orlando Espín, *The Faith of the People: Theological Reflections on Popular Catholicism* (Maryknoll, N.Y.: Orbis Books, 1997): 163.

9. Espín, *The Faith of the People,* 92 (italics in original). Also see Virgilio Elizondo, *Galilean Journey: The Mexican-American Promise* (Maryknoll, N.Y.: Orbis Books, 1983), 12, 32–44; and Jeffrey S. Thiess, *Mexican Catholicism in Southern California: The Importance of Popular Religiosity and Sacramental Practice in Faith Experience,* American University Studies, Series VII, Theology and Religion, vol. 139 (New York: Peter Lang, 1993).

10. Throughout the text the term *Mexican American* denotes a U.S. citizen of

Mexican descent or a former Mexican immigrant who has become a naturalized citizen. This term describes someone who may or may not have been politically and socially active in the same sense as a Chicana/o.

11. The term *mestiza/o* refers to the new race produced by the mixing of Amerindian and Spanish blood.

12. Throughout the text the term *Anglo* refers not only to persons of strictly English descent but also all those U.S. citizens whose parentage can be traced to northern and central Europe—with apologies to Irish Americans and others.

13. David Montejano, *Anglos and Mexicans in the Making of Texas, 1836–1986* (Austin: University of Texas Press, 1987), 309–20; and Gutiérrez, *The Making of a Chicano Militant.*

14. W. K. Barger and Ernesto M. Reza, *The Farm Labor Movement in the Midwest: Social Change and Adaptation among Migrant Farmworkers* (Austin: University of Texas Press, 1994); Dennis N. Valdes, *Al Norte: Agricultural Workers in the Great Lakes Region, 1917–1970* (Austin: University of Texas Press, 1991), 84–86, 109–14, 155–56; and Patrick H. Mooney and Theo J. Majka, *Farmers' and Farm Workers' Movements: Social Protest in American Agriculture,* Social Movements Past and Present Series, ed. Irwin T. Sanders (New York: Twayne Publishers, 1995), 199–211.

15. D. W. Meinig, "American Wests: Preface to a Geographical Interpretation," *Annals of the Association of American Geographers* 62 (1972): 181. Also see Michael P. Malone and Richard W. Etulain, *The American West: A Twentieth-Century History* (Lincoln: University of Nebraska Press, 1989), 16–27, 217–18, 256–57.

16. Carey McWilliams, *Factories in the Field: The Story of Migratory Farm Labor in California* (Boston: Little, Brown, 1935); Carey McWilliams, *Ill Fares the Land: Migrants and Migratory Labor in the United States* (Boston: Little, Brown, 1942); Walton Bean, *California: An Interpretive History,* 6th ed., with James J. Rawls (New York: McGraw-Hill, 1993), 187–91, 364–76; Robert A. Calvert and Arnoldo De León, *The History of Texas,* 2nd ed. (Wheeling, Ill.: Harlan Davidson, 1996), 238–45, 346–52, 420–27; Glenna Matthews, "Forging a Cosmopolitan Culture: The Regional Identity of San Francisco and Northern California," in *Many Wests: Place, Culture, and Regional Identity,* ed. David M. Wrobel and Michael C. Steiner (Lawrence: University Press of Kansas, 1997), 211–34; Carl Abbott, *The Metropolitan Frontier: Cities in the Modern American West* (Tucson: University of Arizona Press, 1993); William Issel and Robert W. Cherny, *San Francisco, 1865–1932: Politics, Power, and Urban Development* (Berkeley: University of California Press, 1986); and Andrew Rolle, *Los Angeles: From Pueblo to City of the Future,* 2nd ed., Golden State Series, ed. Norris Hundley Jr. and John D. Schutz (San Francisco: MTL, 1995).

17. Laurie F. Maffly-Kipp, *Religion and Society in Frontier California* (New Haven, Conn.: Yale University Press, 1994); Harland E. Hogue, *Prophets and Paupers: Religion in the California Gold Rush, 1848–1869* (San Francisco: International Scholars Press, 1996); and Paul K. Shelford, *Protestant Cooperation in Northern California: The Historical Background of the Federation and Counciliar Movement, 1913–1963* (San Francisco: Northern California–Nevada Council of Churches, 1962), 48–51.

18. James P. Walsh, *Ethnic Militancy: An Irish Catholic Prototype* (San Francisco: R&E Research Associates, 1972); James P. Walsh, "The Irish in Early San Francisco," in *The San Francisco Irish, 1850–1976,* 2nd ed., ed. James P. Walsh (San Francisco: The Irish Literary and Historical Society, 1979), 9–26.

19. Terry G. Jordan, "The Imprint of the Upper and Lower South on Mid-

Nineteenth-Century Texas," *Annals of the Association of American Geographers* 57, no. 3 (1967): 667–90; Terry G. Jordan, "A Century and a Half of Ethnic Change in Texas, 1836–1986," *Southwestern Historical Quarterly* 89, no. 4 (1986): 385–422; Terry G. Jordan, John L. Bean Jr., and William M. Holmes, *Texas: A Geography* (Boulder, Colo.: Westview Press, 1984); and Harold Kilpatrick, "The Last That Became First," unpublished paper, February 1986 (copy in possession of the author).

20. Throughout the text the term *Tejana/o* refers to a Texas citizen of Mexican ethnicity and is most often used as an appellation for Texan Mexicans in the nineteenth and early twentieth centuries.

21. James T. Moore, *Through Fire and Flood: The Catholic Church in Frontier Texas, 1836–1900* (College Station: Texas A&M University Press, 1992); and James T. Moore, *Acts of Faith: The Catholic Church in Texas, 1900–1950* (College Station: Texas A&M University Press, 2002).

22. Patricia Nelson Limerick, *The Legacy of Conquest: The Unbroken Past of the American West* (New York: W. W. Norton, 1987).

23. Brian W. Dippie, "American Wests: Historiographical Perspectives," in *Trails: Toward a New Western History,* ed. Patricia Nelson Limerick, Clyde A. Milner, and Charles E. Rankin (Lawrence: University Press of Kansas, 1991), 114, 130; David Worster, "Beyond the Agrarian Myth," in *Trails: Toward a New Western History,* ed. Limerick, Milner, and Rankin, 7–11; Michael P. Malone, "Toward a New Approach to Western American History," in *Trails: Toward a New Western History,* ed. Limerick, Milner, and Rankin, 139–41; and Richard White, *"It's Your Misfortune and None of My Own": A History of the American West* (Norman: University of Oklahoma Press, 1991).

24. Limerick, *Legacy of Conquest,* 24–25; Patricia Nelson Limerick, "What on Earth Is the New Western History?" in *Trails: Toward a New Western History,* ed. Limerick, Milner, and Rankin, 83–84, 86; William G. Robbins, *Colony and Empire: The Capitalistic Transformation of the American West* (Lawrence: University Press of Kansas, 1994), 15–19; Dippie, "American Wests," 126–27; William G. Robbins, "Laying Siege to Western History," in *Trails: Toward a New Western History,* ed. Limerick, Milner, and Rankin, 186, 190, 196; and Michael C. Steiner and David M. Wrobel, "Many Wests: Discovering a Dynamic Western Regionalism," in *Many Wests: Place, Culture, and Regional Identity,* ed. Wrobel and Steiner, 9–11, 26. Also see Walter L. Buenger and Robert A. Calvert, *Texas History and the Move into the Twenty-First Century,* vol. 2, *Preparing for Texas in the Twenty-First Century: Building a Future for the Children of Texas* (Austin: Texas Committee for the Humanities, 1990); Walter L. Buenger and Robert A. Calvert, eds., *Texas through Time: Evolving Interpretations* (College Station: Texas A&M University Press, 1991); Arnoldo De León, "Topographical Identities in Texas," in *Many Wests: Place, Culture, and Regional Identity,* ed. Wrobel and Steiner, 259–70; Arnoldo De León, "Whither Tejano History: Origins, Development, and Status," *Southwestern Historical Quarterly* 106, no. 3 (2003): 349–64; and Laura Lyons McLemore, *Inventing Texas: Historians of the Lone Star State* (College Station: Texas A&M University Press, 2004).

25. Malone and Etulain, *The American West: A Twentieth-Century History,* 171–74.

26. Frederick Jackson Turner, "The Significance of the Section in American History," in *Rereading Frederick Jackson Turner: "The Significance of the Frontier in American History" and Other Essays* (New York: Henry Holt, 1994), 201–24, which originally was printed in *Wisconsin Magazine of History* 8 (March 1925), the quote appearing on p. 208.

27. H. Richard Niebuhr, *The Social Sources in Denominationalism* (Gloucester, Mass.:

Peter Smith, 1987; original copyright by Henry Holt, 1929); also see Peter E. Mode, *The Frontier Spirit in American Christianity* (New York: Macmillan, 1923); and W. W. Sweet, *The Story of Religion in America* (New York: Harper and Bros., 1930, 1939, 1950).

28. Earl Pomeroy, "Toward a Reorientation of Western History: Continuity and Environment," *Mississippi Valley Historical Review* 41 (March 1955): 592–93.

29. Michael P. Malone, "Earl Pomeroy and the Reorientation of Western American History," in *Writing Western History: Essays on Major Western Historians,* ed. Richard W. Etulain (Albuquerque: University of New Mexico Press, 1991), 325.

30. Jerald C. Brauer, "Regionalism and Religion in America," *Church History* 54 (1985): 375–77.

31. Edward J. Walsh, "Mobilization Theory vis-à-vis a Mobilization Process: The Case of the United Farm Workers' Movement," in *Research in Social Movements, Conflicts and Change,* vol. 1, ed. Louis Kriesberg (Greenwich, Conn.: JAI Press, 1978); John D. McCarthy and Mayer N. Zald, "Resource Mobilization and Social Movements: A Partial Theory," *American Journal of Sociology* 82, no. 6 (1977): 1212–42; J. Craig Jenkins, *The Politics of Insurgency: The Farm Worker Movement in the 1960s* (New York: Columbia University Press, 1985), 1–27; and Mooney and Majka, *Farmers' and Farm Workers' Movements,* xxvi–xxix.

32. The term *mujerista* refers to the feminist thought of Latina theologians.

33. Ferenc Morton Szasz, *Religion in the Modern American West,* The Modern American West Series, ed. Gerald D. Nash and Richard W. Etulain (Tucson: University of Arizona Press, 2000), xv.

Chapter 2

1. Francis J. Weber, *Encyclopedia of California's Catholic Heritage, 1769–1999* (Spokane, Wash.: Arthur H. Clark, 2000), 207, 262–63; Jose de la Guerra, "El Gran Capitan and the California Church, April 18, 1849," Santa Barbara Mission Archives, De la Guerra Papers, in *Documents of California Catholic History,* ed. Francis J. Weber (Los Angeles: Dawson's Book Shop, 1965), 58–61; Jeffrey M. Burns, *San Francisco: A History of the Archdiocese of San Francisco,* vol. 1, *1776–1884: From Mission to Golden Frontier* (Strasbourg, France: Editions du Signe, 1999), 16; and Moises Sandoval and Salvador E. Alvarez, "The Church in California," in *Fronteras: A History of the Latin American Church in the USA since 1513,* vol. 10, ed. Moises Sandoval (San Antonio, Tex.: Mexican American Cultural Center, 1983), 210–11.

2. John D. Stevenson, "Another Appeal from California, May 1, 1848," Archives of the Sacred Congregation of Propaganda Fide, in *Documents of California Catholic History, 1784–1963,* ed. Weber, 53.

3. Anthony Langlois, S.J., "Parochial Beginnings in San Francisco, 1849," cited in Joseph Riordan, S.J., *The First Half Century* (San Francisco, 1905), 19–20, in turn cited in *Documents of California Catholic History, 1784–1963,* ed. Weber, 55–56; also see Burns, *1776–1884: From Mission to Golden Frontier,* 17–21.

4. Jeffrey M. Burns, "The Mexican Catholic Community in California," in *Mexican Americans and the Catholic Church, 1900–1965,* vol. 1, ed. Jay P. Dolan and Gilberto M. Hinojosa, The Notre Dame History of Hispanic Catholics in the U.S., gen. ed., Jay P. Dolan (Notre Dame, Ind.: Notre Dame University Press, 1994), 134–35.

5. Weber, *Encyclopedia California's Catholic Heritage,* 287, 725, 753; "What the Catholic Church Has Done for San Francisco, 1907," *Overland Monthly* (November 1907), cited in *Documents in California Catholic History,* ed. Weber, 212–23; and Burns, *1776–1884: From Mission to Golden Frontier,* 22–47; the quotation is from p. 37.

6. "What the Catholic Church Has Done for San Francisco," 214–15; "Essentially a Churchman: Discourse Delivered at the Funeral of Archbishop Patrick W. Riordan, December 31, 1914," in *In Memoriam: Most Reverend Patrick William Riordan, D.D.* (San Francisco, 1915), cited in *Documents in California Catholic History, 1784–1963,* ed. Weber, 242–47; Jeffrey M. Burns, *San Francisco: A History of the Archdiocese of San Francisco,* vol. 2, *1885–1945: Glory, Ruin, and Resurrection* (Strasbourg, France: Editions du Signe, 1999), 2–18, 36–43.

7. "What the Catholic Church Has Done for San Francisco," 219.

8. Burns, *1885–1945: Glory, Ruin, and Resurrection,* 26–35.

9. Burns, "The Mexican Catholic Community in California," 135–36; and Sandoval and Alvarez, "The Church in California," 213–16.

10. Weber, *Encyclopedia of California's Catholic Heritage,* 230–31, 703, 714, 741–42, 754–55, 946–1022.

11. Ibid., 327–28; and Burns, "The Mexican Catholic Community in California," 136–37.

12. Weber, *Encyclopedia of California's Catholic Heritage,* 298–300, 699–700, 705, 726–27.

13. Aaron I. Abell, *American Catholicism and Social Action: A Search for Social Justice, 1865–1950* (Notre Dame, Ind.: University of Notre Dame Press, 1960); James E. Rooham, *American Catholics and the Social Question, 1865–1900* (New York: Arno Press, 1976; reprint of Ph.D. diss., Yale University, 1952); Henry J. Browne, *The Catholic Church and the Knights of Labor* (Washington, D.C.: Catholic University of America Press, 1939); Paul C. Stroh, "The Catholic Clergy and American Labor Disputes, 1900–1937" (Ph.D. diss., Catholic University of America, 1939); John A. Coleman, ed., *One Hundred Years of Catholic Social Thought: Celebration and Challenge* (Maryknoll, N.Y.: Orbis Books, 1991); Richard L. Camp, *The Papal Ideology of Social Reform: A Study in Historical Development, 1878–1967* (Leiden: E. J. Brill, 1969); and John F. Cronin, *Catholic Social Principles: The Social Teaching of the Catholic Church Applied to American Economic Life* (Milwaukee: Bruce Publishing, 1950).

14. R. A. Burchell, *The San Francisco Irish, 1848–1880* (Manchester: Manchester University Press, 1979), 3–14, 34–51, 65–66; James P. Walsh, "The Irish in Early San Francisco," in *The San Francisco Irish, 1850–1976,* 2nd ed., ed. James P. Walsh (San Francisco: The Irish Literary and Historical Society, 1979), 9–26; Issel and Cherny, *San Francisco, 1865–1932,* 5, 55–57, 125–30; Ira B. Cross, *A History of the Labor Movement in California* (Berkeley: University of California Press, 1935), 19–59; Bernard C. Cronin, *Father Yorke and the Labor Movement in San Francisco, 1900–1910,* vol. 12, Catholic University of America Studies in Economics (Washington D.C.: Catholic University of America Press, 1943), 37–38, 52–53, 55–60, 66, 75–83, 92–94, 111, 120–24, 145, 158–62, 224, 228; Joseph S. Brusher, *Consecrated Thunderbolt: Father Yorke of San Francisco* (Hawthorne, N.J.: Joseph F. Wagner, 1973), 57–63, 81–82, 108, 137–38, 172–74; Richard Gribble, *Catholicism and the San Francisco Labor Movement, 1886–1921* (San Francisco: Mellen Research University Press, 1993), 17, 21, 25–26, 36–47, 64–84, 114–17, 138–49, 163–67; Walsh, *Ethnic Militancy,* 20–27; Timothy J. Sarbaugh, "Father Yorke and the San Francisco Waterfront," *Pacific History* 25 (1981): 28–35; Mary E. Lyons, "Peter C. Yorke: Advocate of the Irish from the Pulpit to the

Podium," in *Religion and Society in the American West: Historical Essays,* ed. Carl Guarneri and David Alvarez (Lanham, Md.: University Press of America, 1987), 401–22; and quote coming from Weber, *Encyclopedia of California's Catholic Heritage,* 429.

15. Richard Gribble, C.S.C., *An Archbishop for the People: The Life of Edward J. Hanna* (Mahwah, N.J.: Paulist Press, 2006); Gribble, *Catholicism and the San Francisco Labor Movement, 1886–1921,* 138–49, 163–67; Mark Reisler, *By the Sweat of Their Brow: Mexican Immigrant Labor in the U.S., 1900–1940* (Westport, Conn.: Greenwood Press, 1976), 158; Antonio R. Soto, "The Chicano and the Church in Northern California, 1848–1978: A Study of an Ethnic Minority within the Roman Catholic Church" (Ph.D. diss., University of California at Berkeley, 1978), 137–38; Moises Sandoval, *On the Move: A History of the Hispanic Church in the United States* (Maryknoll, N.Y.: Orbis Books, 1990), 44; and Burns, "The Mexican Catholic Community in California," 207–8.

16. Reisler, *By the Sweat of Their Brow,* 14–17.

17. Soto, "The Chicano and the Church in Northern California, 1848–1978," 40–114; and Ricardo Romo, *East Los Angeles: History of a Barrio* (Austin: University of Texas Press, 1983), 80.

18. Samuel Ortegon, *The Religious Status of the Mexican Population of Los Angeles* (San Francisco: R&E Research Associates, 1972; reprint of 1932 master's thesis, University of Southern California), 50; compare to other figures for Los Angeles at 150,000 in 1923 and 230,000 in 1925–26 (Francis J. Weber, "Irish-Born Champion of the Mexican-Americans," *California Historical Society Quarterly* 69, no. 3 [September 1970], 234); the block quotation coming from Francis J. Weber, *John Joseph Cantwell: His Excellency of Los Angeles* (Hong Kong: Cathay Press, 1971), 39; also see Francis J. Weber, *Century of Fulfillment: The Roman Catholic Church in Southern California, 1840–1947* (Mission Hills, Calif.: Archival Center of the Archdiocese of Los Angeles, 1990), 424–26.

19. Weber, "Irish-Born Champion," 237.

20. Ibid., 235–42; Burns, "The Mexican Catholic Community in California," 148–55, 193; Romo, *East Los Angeles: History of a Barrio,* 145; "Missionary Sisters—Brawley, Annual Reports, September 1936–1954," Archives of the Diocese of San Diego, CA; and Elizabeth A. Clifford, *The Story of Victory Noll* (Fort Wayne, Ind.: Keefer Printing, 1981).

21. Burns, "The Mexican Catholic Community in California," 175; Cross, *A History of the Labor Movement in California,* 268; and Saul E. Bronder, *Social Justice and Church Authority: The Public Life of Archbishop Robert E. Lucey* (Philadelphia: Temple University Press, 1982), 11–12, 14–15, 21–38.

22. Maffly-Kipp, *Religion and Society in Frontier California,* 3, 37, 52, 66, 73–74; Sandra S. Frankiel, *California's Spiritual Frontiers: Religious Alternatives in Anglo-Protestantism, 1850–1910* (Berkeley: University of California Press, 1988), 1–6; Clifford M. Drury, "A Chronology of Protestant Beginnings in California," *California Historical Society Quarterly* 25, no. 2 (1947): 163–74; William D. Pond, *Gospel Pioneering: Reminiscences of Early Congregationalism in California, 1833–1920* (Oberlin, Ohio: News Printing, 1921); and Sandford Fleming, *God's Gold: The Story of Baptist Beginnings in California, 1849–1860* (Philadelphia: Judson Press, 1949).

23. Rolle, *Los Angeles: From Pueblo to City of the Future,* 1, 2, 77.

24. Remi A. Nadeau, *Los Angeles: From Mission to Modern City* (New York, 1960), 79, cited in Gregory H. Singleton, "Religion in the City of the Angels: American Protestant Culture and Urbanization, Los Angeles, 1850–1930" (Ph.D. diss., University of California at Los Angeles, 1976; University Microfilms International, 1979), 117.

25. Singleton, "Religion in the City of the Angels," 109; Leonard Pitt, *The Decline of*

the Californios: A Social History of the Spanish-Speaking Californians, 1846–1890 (Berkeley: University of California Press, 1966), 122–24, 131, 249, 274; Michael E. Engh, *Frontier Faiths: Church, Temple, and Synagogue in Los Angeles, 1848–1888* (Albuquerque: University of New Mexico Press, 1992), 9–11, 55–56, 192–93; Carey McWilliams, *Southern California Country: An Island on the Land,* American Folkways Series, ed. Erskine Caldwell (New York: Duell, Sloan and Pearce, 1946), 16, 205–17, 224, 275–77. William Deverell, "Privileging the Mission over the Mexican: The Rise of Regional Identity in Southern California," in *Many Wests: Place, Culture, and Regional Identity,* ed. David M. Wrobel and Michael C. Steiner (Lawrence: University Press of Kansas, 1997), 239; and the block quotation coming from Rolle, *Los Angeles: From Pueblo to City of the Future,* 76.

26. Engh, *Frontier Faiths,* 192–93, 198–202, 209; Walsh, *Ethnic Militancy,* 68–69; Issel and Cherny, *San Francisco, 1865–1932,* 103; Douglas F. Anderson, "Through Fire and Fair by the Golden Gate: Progressive Era Protestantism and Regional Culture" (Ph.D. diss., Graduate Theological Union, 1988; University Microfilms International, 1990), 863–79, 898–904, 938–42. On Prohibition in the Los Angeles area see Engh, *Frontier Faiths,* 193, 198–202, 209; Earl S. Pomeroy, *The Pacific Slope: A History of California, Oregon, Washington, Idaho, Utah, and Nevada* (New York: Alfred A. Knopf, 1965), 229–33; McWilliams, *Southern California Country,* 19; and Weber, *Century of Fulfillment,* 274, 276, 290, 308, 315, 317.

27. R. Douglas Brackenridge and Francisco O. García-Treto, *Iglesia Presbiteriana: A History of Presbyterians and Mexican Americans in the Southwest* (San Antonio, Tex.: Trinity University Press, 1974), 79–86; Engh, *Frontier Faiths,* 113–20; Edward D. Jervey, *The History of Methodism in Southern California and Arizona* (Nashville, Tenn.: Parthenon, 1960), 43–44, 90–91; Leland D. Hine, *Baptists in Southern California* (Valley Forge, Pa.: Judson Press, 1966), 133; Burns, "The Mexican Catholic Community in California," 158, 160–62; James A. Dombrowski, *The Early Days of Christian Socialism in America* (New York: Columbia Press, 1936), 60–73; C. Howard Hopkins, *The Rise of the Social Gospel in American Protestantism* (New Haven, Conn.: Yale University Press, 1940), 162–70; Aaron I. Abell, *The Urban Impact on American Protestantism, 1865–1915* (New Haven, Conn.: Yale University Press, 1940): 81–83, 224–45; Henry F. May, *Protestant Churches and Industrial America* (Cambridge, Mass: Harvard University Press, 1943; reprint, Hamden Conn.: Archon, 1962), 194–96; William King, "The Reform Establishment and the Ambiguities of Influence," in *Between the Times: The Travail of the Protestant Establishment in America, 1900–1960,* ed. William R. Hutchison, Cambridge Series in Religion and American Public Life, gen. ed. Robin W. Lovin (Cambridge: Cambridge University Press, 1989), 122; and William R. Hutchison, "Discovering America," in *Between the Times: The Travail of the Protestant Establishment in America, 1900–1960,* ed. Hutchison, 303–9.

28. Clifton L. Holland, *The Religious Dimension in Hispanic Los Angeles: A Protestant Case Study* (South Pasadena, Calif.: Carey McWilliams Library, 1974), 232, 268–69, 279, 294; Adam Morales, *American Baptists with a Spanish Accent* (Valley Forge, Pa.: Judson Press, 1964), 37–38; Brackenridge and García-Treto, *Iglesia Presbiteriana,* 140–47; Singleton, "Religion in the City of the Angels," 269–74, 282; Jervey, *The History of Methodism in Southern California and Arizona,* 93–99; Leo Grebler, Joan Moore, and Ralph Guzman, *The Mexican-American People: The Nation's Second-Largest Minority* (New York: Free Press, 1970), 491–92; and Vernon McCombs, *From over the Border: A Study of the Mexicans in the United States* (New York: Council of Women for Home Missions and Missionary Education Movement, 1925).

29. Grebler et al., *The Mexican-American People,* 491–92.

30. Ibid., 494–97, 502–4.

31. Allan Figueroa Deck, *The Second Wave: Hispanic Ministry and the Evangelization of Cultures* (Mahwah, N.J.: Paulist Press, 1989), 55–56; Orlando O. Espín, "Popular Catholicism among Latinos," in *Hispanic Catholic Culture in the U.S.: Issues and Concerns,* ed. Jay P. Dolan and Allan Figueroa Deck, S.J., vol. 3, The Notre Dame History of Hispanic Catholics in the U.S. (Notre Dame, Ind.: University of Notre Dame Press, 1994), 308–59; Espín, *The Faith of the People,* 32–62 and 111–55; Jeffrey Thiess, *Mexican Catholicism in Southern California: The Importance of Popular Religiosity and Sacramental Practice in Faith Experience,* in *American University Studies,* series VII, Theology and Religion, vol. 139 (New York: Peter Lang, 1993), 21–27; and Mark R. Francis, C.S.V., "Popular Piety and Liturgical Reform," in *Dialogue Rejoined: Theology and Ministry in the United States Hispanic Reality,* ed. Ana Maria Pineda, R.S.M., and Robert Schreiter, C.P.P.S. (Collegeville, Minn.: Liturgical Press, 1995), 162–77.

32. D. A. Brading, *Mexican Phoenix, Our Lady of Guadalupe: Image and Tradition across Five Centuries* (Cambridge: Cambridge University Press, 2001); Stafford Poole, *Our Lady of Guadalupe: The Origins and Sources of a Mexican National Symbol, 1531–1797* (Tucson: University of Arizona Press, 1995); Virgilio Elizondo, *Guadalupe: Mother of the New Creation* (Maryknoll, N.Y.: Orbis Books, 1997); and Edwin Sylvest, *Nuestra Señora de Guadalupe, Mother of God* (Dallas: Southern Methodist University Press, 1992).

33. Virgilio Elizondo, *La Morenita* (San Antonio, Tex.: Mexican American Cultural Center, 1980), 90.

34. For example, Jeanette Rodriguez, *Our Lady of Guadalupe: Faith and Empowerment among Mexican-American Women* (Austin: University of Texas Press, 1994); Daisy L. Machado, "Voices from *Nepantla:* Latinas in U.S. Religious History," in *Feminist Intercultural Theology: Latina Explorations for a Just World,* ed. María Pilar Aquino and Maria José Rosado-Nunes (Maryknoll, N.Y.: Orbis Books, 2007), 89–108; and Margaret Randall, "Guadalupe, Subversive Virgin," in *Goddess of the Americas: Writings on the Virgin of Guadalupe,* ed. Ana Castillo (New York: Riverhead Books, 1996), 113–23.

35. Espín, *The Faith of the People,* 23–24, 46–47, 72–73; Burns, "The Mexican Catholic Community in California," 182; and *Faith Expressions of Hispanics in the Southwest,* vol. 1, *Workshops on Hispanic Liturgy and Popular Piety* (San Antonio, Tex.: Mexican American Cultural Center, 1983?), 8.

36. Virgilio Elizondo, *The Future Is Mestizo: Life Where Cultures Meet* (Bloomington, Ind.: Meyer-Stone Books, 1988), 11, 19–20; *Faith Expressions in the Southwest;* and Burns, "The Mexican Catholic Community in California," 176–84.

37. Francis, "Popular Piety and Liturgical Reform in a Hispanic Context," 164–65; Burns, "The Mexican Catholic Community in California," 176–77, 187–88, 191; and Brading, *Mexican Phoenix,* 244–47.

38. Elizondo, *The Future Is Mestizo,* 24–25, 37, 53; and Burns, "The Mexican Community in California," 188–92.

39. John Leddy Phelan, *The Hispanization of the Philippines: Spanish Aims and Filipino Responses, 1565–1700* (Madison: University of Wisconsin Press, 1959), 3, 7, 41–44, 49–52, 64, 72–74, 78–79, 84–88, 157; David K. Yoo, *New Spiritual Homes: Religion and Asian Americans,* ed. David K. Yoo, Asian and Pacific American Transcultural Studies, gen. ed. Russell C. Leong (Honolulu: University of Hawaii Press, 2000), 10; Vicente L. Rafael, *Contracting Colonialism: Translation and Christian Conversion in Tagalog Society under Early Spanish Rule* (Ithaca, N.Y.: Cornell University Press, 1988), viii, ix, 12–19, 20, 105, 154; and Edwin B. Almirol, *Ethnic Identity and Social Negotiation: A Study of a*

Filipino Community in California, Immigrant Communities and Ethnic Minorities in the United States and Canada Series, no. 10 (New York: AMS Press, 1985), 183, 191–99, 203.

40. David W. Lantis, with Rodney Steiner and Arthur E. Karinen, *California: Land of Contrast* (Belmont, Calif.: Wadsworth Publishing, 1963).

41. Pitt, *The Decline of the Californios,* 84–103; Lawrence J. Jelinek, *Harvest Empire: A History of California Agriculture,* Golden State Series, ed. Norris Handley Jr. and John A. Schutz (San Francisco: Boyd and Fraser, 1979), 28–32; McWilliams, *Factories in the Field,* 12–27; Acuña, *Occupied America,* 112–18; and David G. Gutiérrez, *Walls and Mirrors: Mexican Americans, Mexican Immigrants, and the Politics of Ethnicity* (Berkeley: University of California Press, 1995), 22–24.

42. Jelinek, *Harvest Empire,* 33–52.

43. Ibid., 34–35, 52–55, 67–70; McWilliams, *Factories in the Field,* 53–55, 64–80, 85–89, 105–33; Gutiérrez, *Walls and Mirrors,* 43–45; Kushner, *Long Road to Delano,* 6–20; Richard Steven Street, *Beasts of the Field: A Narrative History of California Farm Workers, 1769–1913* (Stanford, Calif.: Stanford University Press, 2004), 3–88; Brett H. Melendy, *Asians in America: Filipinos, Koreans, and East Asians* (Boston: Twayne Publishers, 1977), 186–87, 228–332; Cletus Daniel, *Bitter Harvest: A History of California Farmworkers, 1870–1941* (Ithaca, N.Y.: Cornell University Press, 1981), 40–61.

44. Jelinek, *Harvest Empire,* 67.

45. Juan Gómez-Quiñones, *Mexican American Labor, 1790–1990* (Albuquerque: University of New Mexico Press, 1994), 76–77; and McWilliams, *Factories in the Field,* 99–102.

46. Kushner, *Long Road to Delano,* 39–54; Walton Bean, *California: An Interpretive History* (New York: McGraw-Hill, 1968; 6th ed., with James J. Rawls, 1993), 235–38; McWilliams, *Factories in the Field,* 153–63; and Daniel, *Bitter Harvest,* 81–86.

47. Burns, "The Mexican Catholic Community in California," 145–46; Barbara M. Posadas, *The Filipino Americans,* New Americans Series, ed. Ronald H. Bayor (Westport, Conn.: Greenwood Press, 1999), 24; Almirol, *Ethnic Identity and Social Negotiation,* 178–82; Mario Paguia Ave, *Characteristics of Filipino Social Organizations in Los Angeles* (San Francisco: R&E Research Associates, 1974; reprint of master's thesis, University of Southern California), 20–22; Kushner, *Long Road to Delano,* 70; Lantis, *California: Land of Contrast,* 56–68; and Kathryn Cramp, Louise F. Shields, and Charles A. Thomson, *Study of the Mexican Population in Imperial Valley, California* (New York: Committee on Farm and Cannery Migrants, Council of Women for Home Missions, 1926; Bancroft Library Collection, University of California at Berkeley), 1–3.

48. McWilliams, *Factories in the Field,* 124–25; Charles Wollenberg, "Huelga, 1928 Style: The Imperial Valley Cantaloupe Workers' Strike," *Pacific Historical Review* 38, no. 1 (1969): 46–65; James Gray, *The American Civil Liberties Union of Southern California and the Imperial Valley Agricultural Labor Disturbances: 1930, 1934* (San Francisco: R&E Research Associates, 1977), 1–2; and Devra Anne Weber, "The Organizing of Mexicano Agricultural Workers: Imperial Valley and Los Angeles, 1928–34: An Oral History Approach," Los Angeles, Reprints from *Aztlán—Chicano Journal of the Social Sciences and the Arts,* vol. 3, no. 2 (1972): 308–9, 313–14; Weber notes that two of the "seventy-four huge grower-shippers" were the Times-Mirror Company and the Southern Pacific Railroad (*Century of Fulfillment,* 314). Also see Daniel, *Bitter Harvest,* 108–9.

49. Daniel, *Bitter Harvest,* 109–64, 182, 195–201, 227–31, 246, 255, 257; McWilliams, *Factories in the Field,* 213–28, 229–68, the quote coming from p. 241; Mark Reisler, "Mexican Unionization in California Agriculture, 1927–1936," *Labor History* 14, no. 4 (1973):

573; Kushner, *Long Road to Delano,* 60–79; Louis Reccow, "The Orange County Citrus Strikes of 1935–1936: The 'Forgotten People' in Revolt" (Ph.D. diss., University of Southern California, 1972); Clark A. Chambers, *California Farm Organizations: A Historical Study of the Grange, the Farm Bureau and the Associated Farmers, 1929–1941* (Berkeley: University of California Press, 1952), 70; Gray, *The American Civil Liberties Union,* 31–33; Gutiérrez, *Walls and Mirrors,* 102–5.

50. Vicki Ruíz, *Cannery Women, Cannery Lives: Mexican Women, Unionization, and the California Food Processing Industry, 1930–1950* (Albuquerque: University of New Mexico Press, 1987), 92; and Devra Weber, *Dark Sweat, White Gold: California Farm Workers, Cotton, and the New Deal* (Berkeley: University of California Press, 1994), 95–97, and 265n93, the block quotation coming from p. 96.

51. Melendy, *Asians in America,* 33–43, 72–78; Posadas, *The Filipino Americans,* 15–20; Howard DeWitt, *Violence in the Fields: California Filipino Farm Labor Unionization during the Great Depression* (Saratoga, Calif.: Century Twenty-One Publishing, 1980), 4, 8–10, 30–48; Larry R. Salomon, *Roots of Justice: Stories of Organizing in Communities of Color* (Berkeley, Calif.: Chardon Press, 1998), 10–12; and Craig Scharlin and Lillian V. Villanueva, *Philip Vera Cruz: A Personal History of Filipino Immigrants and the Farmworkers Movement,* 3rd ed. (Seattle: University of Washington Press, 2000), 12–16.

52. DeWitt, *Violence in the Fields,* 11–16, 49–110; Posadas, *Filipino Americans,* 24; Salomon, *Roots of Justice,* 12, 18–20; and Melendy, *Asians in America,* 78–79.

53. DeWitt, *Violence in the Fields,* 102.

54. Robert T. Handy, *We Witness Together: A History of Cooperative Home Missions, 1900–1950* (New York: Friendship Press, 1956), xi–xiii, 7, 12, 54–59, 73–74, 86–98, 196–201; Samuel M. Cavert, *Church Cooperation and Unity in America: A Historical Review, 1900–1970* (New York: Association Press, 1968), 56–76, 236–39, 243–45; William R. Hutchison, "Preface," in *Between the Times: The Travail of the Protestant Establishment in America, 1900–1960,* ed. William R. Hutchison, Cambridge Series in Religion and American Public Life, gen. ed. Robin W. Lovin (Cambridge: Cambridge University Press, 1989), viii, xii; and William R. Hutchison, "Discovering America," in *Between the Times,* ed. Hutchison, 303–9; Patricia R. Hill, *The World Their Household: The American Woman's Mission Movement and Cultural Transformation, 1870–1920* (Ann Arbor: University of Michigan Press, 1985); Virginia Lieson Brereton, "United and Slighted: Women as Subordinated Insiders," in *Between the Times,* ed. Hutchison, 145–47; Susan M. Yohn, "'Let Christian Women Set the Example in Their Own Gifts': The 'Business' of Protestant Women's Organizations," in *Women and Twentieth-Century Protestantism,* ed. Margaret Lamberts Bendroth and Virginia Lieson Brereton (Urbana: University of Illinois Press, 2002), 213–35; and Wendy J. Diechmann Edwards and Carolyn DeSwarte Gifford, eds., "Introduction: Restoring Women and Reclaiming Gender in Social Gospel Studies," in *Gender and the Social Gospel* (Urbana: University of Illinois Press, 2003), 2–5.

55. Cavert, *Church Cooperation and Unity in America,* 236.

56. Elizabeth C. White, "Cranberries and Colony Contributions: Or the Appeal of the Colony to a Dweller in the Pines," read before the New Jersey Conference of Charities and Correction at Asbury Park, N.J., 21 April 1914 (National Council of Churches, Home Missions Council of North America Records, Records Group 26, Council of Women on Home Missions, "Migrant Work, New Jersey," April 1914–1931, Box 13, Folder 5, 1, hereafter cited as NCC, HMCNAR, RG 26, CWHM); Louisa R. Shotwell, *The Harvesters: The Story of the Migrant People* (Garden City, N.Y.: Doubleday, 1961), 176–77; Handy, *We Witness Together,* 96–98; Cavert, *Church Cooperation and Unity in America,* 243–44;

Jeanne Ellsworth, "Women, Children, and Charity in Migrant Labor Camps, 1919–1939" (Ph.D. diss., State University of New York at Buffalo, 1992); Cramp, Shields, and Thomson, *Study of the Mexican Population in Imperial Valley, California*, 1.

57. "Contract," NCC, HMCNAR, RG 26, CWHM, 15; the block quotation comes from 23; also see NCC, HMCNAR, RG 26, CWHM, 15, 28, "Migrant Work, Western Area Reports" (1926–33), February 1927, July–September 1927, December 1927, April 1928; and Cramp, Shields, and Thomsen, *Study of the Mexican Population in Imperial Valley, California*, 1; "Working Together!" NCC, HMCNAR, RG 26, CWHM, 15, 23: 2–3.

58. NCC, HMCNAR, RG 26, CWHM, 15, 28, "Western Area Reports" (1926–33), January 1929–1 March 1929, 1–4; and 25 March–8 May 1931; also see Carroll Smith-Rosenberg, *Disorderly Conduct: Visions of Gender in Victorian America* (New York: Oxford University Press, 1985), 16, cited in Brereton, "United and Slighted," 147–48; and Yohn, "Let Christian Women Set the Example in Their Gifts," 213–21.

59. NCC, HMCNAR, RG 26, CWHM, 15, 28, January 1929–1 March 1929: 5, the quotation coming from the January 1930 report: 2.

60. Ibid., 26, 15, 28: 2.

61. Ibid., 15, 28, December 1929: 2; NCC, HMCNAR, RG 26, CWHM, 15, 28, January 1930.

62. Francisco E. Balderrama and Raymond Rodriguez, *Decade of Betrayal: Mexican Repatriation in the 1930s* (Albuquerque: University of New Mexico Press, 1995), 50–64, 98–103, 108–11, and 120–22; and Reisler, *By the Sweat of Their Brow*, 209–18 and 231–32. David Gutiérrez estimates that from 1929 to 1937 nearly 80,000 Mexicans and Mexican Americans were annually repatriated, "with a reported 138,519 in 1931 alone" (*Walls and Mirrors*, 72).

63. NCC, HMCNAR, RG 26, CWHM, 15, 28, July–October Report, 1931: 3; ibid., 15, 29 May, ibid., May–November Report, 1936: 2; ibid., May–September Report, 1937: 2–3; Walter J. Stein, *California and the Dust Bowl Migration* (Westport, Conn.: Greenwood Press, 1973), 89–96, 171–73, 244–74; Robert Mapes Anderson, *Vision of the Disinherited: The Making of American Pentecostalism* (New York: Oxford University Press, 1979), 210–12, 221; and James N. Gregory, *American Exodus: The Dust Bowl Migration and Okie Culture in California* (New York: Oxford University Press, 1989), 139–68, the quotation coming from p. 81.

64. Stein, *California and the Dust Bowl Migration*, 60.

65. Ibid., 58–64, 182–83, the quote coming from p. 60; Gregory, *American Exodus*, 68, 100–113, 115, 154, 162, 165–69; and Walter Goldschmidt, *As You Sow* (Glencoe, Ill: Free Press, 1947).

66. NCC, HMCNAR, RG 26, CWHM, 15, 29, 1934 Report: 1; and 12 February 1935, Report: 1–2.

67. Ibid., "Report of Western Work, May–September, 1937": 2–3; ibid., "Report of Migrant Work—Western Area, 1938": 1; ibid., form letter by Velma Shotwell, 19 September 1938.

68. Jay P. Dolan, *The American Catholic Experience: A History from Colonial Times to the Present* (Notre Dame, Ind.: University of Notre Dame Press, 1992), 342–46; Joseph M. McShane, "The Bishops' Program of Social Reconstruction of 1919: A Study in American Catholic Progressivism" (Ph.D. diss., University of Chicago, 1981), 91–131, 286–315, 399–408, 429, 435, 457, 467; Abell, *American Catholicism and Social Action*, 88–89, 199–203, 210–16; Cronin, *Catholic Social Principles*, 351–52, 612–26; Aaron I. Abell, ed., *American Catholic Thought on Social Questions*, The American Heritage Series, ed. Leon-

ard W. Levy and Alfred F. Young (Indianapolis, Ind.: Bobbs-Merrill, 1968), 229–51 and 325–48; George G. Higgins with William Bole, *Organized Labor and the Church: Reflections of a Labor Priest* (New York: Paulist Press, 1993), 52–54; "Biography of Rev. R. A. McGowan, Director, Social Action Department," Archives of the Catholic University of America, Washington, D.C., National Catholic Welfare Conference Files, Social Action Department, Box 2, Folder 21, hereafter cited as ACUA, NCWC, SAD; and "Report of Social Action Department, National Catholic Welfare Conference, July 1931 to July 1932," ACUA, NCWC, SAD, 1, 47.

69. In California in the 1930s, the Catholic Church continued not to support Mexican American laborers but rather ethnic Irish, German, and Italian unionists concentrated in San Francisco (William Issel, "Faith-Based Activism in American Cities: The Case of the San Francisco Catholic Action Cadre," *Journal of Church and State* 50, no. 3 [2008]: 519–40).

70. "Linna Eleanor Bresette: A Biographical Sketch," ACUA, NCWC, SAD, 2, 14; letter to McGowan, 26 April 1930, ibid., 16, 8; "Report of Social Action Department, September, 1929–September 1930"; and "Report of Social Action Department, July, 1931–July, 1932," ibid., 1, 45 and 47, respectively.

71. Saul E. Bronder, *Social Justice and Church Authority: The Public Life of Archbishop Robert E. Lucey* (Philadelphia: Temple University Press, 1982), 59–60; Stephen A. Privett, S.J., *The U.S. Catholic Church and Its Hispanic Members: The Pastoral Vision of Archbishop Robert E. Lucey* (San Antonio, Tex.: Trinity University Press, 1988), 10–13.

72. See "Thomas J. O'Dwyer," in Weber, *Encyclopedia of California's Catholic Heritage,* 589–90.

73. Weber, *Century of Fulfillment,* 473, 476–77, the quotation coming from the Archives of the Archdiocese of San Diego, Buddy letter to Fumasoni-Biondi, 10 April 1940, cited in Burns, "The Mexican Catholic Community in California," 174.

74. Adam Morales, *American Baptists with a Spanish Accent* (Valley Forge, Pa.: Judson Press, 1964), 37.

75. Abraham Hoffman, *Unwanted Mexican Americans in the Great Depression: Repatriation Pressures, 1929–1939* (Tucson: University of Arizona Press, 1974), 127–30; Romo, *East Los Angeles: History of a Barrio,* 142–43; Gray, *The American Civil Liberties Union of Southern California,* 31–32; and McWilliams, *Factories in the Field,* 293–94.

Chapter 3

1. Maggie Rivas-Rodriguez, *Mexican Americans and World War II* (Austin: University of Texas Press, 2005); Matt S. Meier, ed., *North from Mexico: The Spanish-Speaking People of the United States,* by Carey McWilliams, 2nd ed., Contributions in American History, no. 140 (Westport, Conn.: Greenwood Press, 1990), 271–72; Gómez-Quiñones, *Chicano Politics,* 31–32, 41, 45–47, 53–61; Ernesto Galarza, *Merchants of Labor: The Mexican Bracero Story* (Charlotte, N.C. and Santa Barbara, Calif.: McNally and Loftin, 1964), 41–42; and Burns, "The Mexican Catholic Community in California," 196–97; Carl Allsup, *The American G.I. Forum: Origins and Evolution* (Austin: Center for Mexican American Studies of the University of Texas at Austin, 1982); and Robert A. Cuellar, *A Social and Political History of the Mexican-American Population of Texas, 1929–1963* (San

Francisco: R&E Research Associates, 1974, reprint of master's thesis, University of Texas at Austin, 1969?), 16–35.

2. David G. Gutierrez, *Walls and Mirrors: Mexican Americans, Mexican Immigrants, and the Politics of Ethnicity* (Berkeley: University of California Press, 1995), 134–35, 142; the quotation is from p. 133; U.S. Congress, House of Representatives, Committee on Agriculture, *Farm Labor and Production: Hearings,* 77th Cong., 2nd sess., 23 September, 25 September, 28 September, and 2 October 1942; the statement and testimony of Charles C. Teague, President of the California Fruit Growers' Exchange, in U.S. Congress, Senate, Committee on Appropriations, *Farm Labor Program, 1943: Hearings,* 78th Cong., 1st sess., March 1943: 151–69, all cited in Gutiérrez, *Walls and Mirrors,* 251.

3. The quotation comes from Acuña, *Occupied America,* 251. Also see Gómez-Quiñones, *Chicano Politics,* 31–34, 39–42; McWilliams, *North from Mexico,* 237–40; Matt S. Meier and Feliciano Rivera, *Chicanos: A History of Mexican Americans* (New York: Hill and Wang, 1972), 2nd ed., *Mexican Americans/American Mexicans: From Conquistadors to Chicanos,* American Century Series (New York: Hill and Wang, 1993), 309–17; Lawrence J. Jelinek, *Harvest Empire: A History of California Agriculture,* Golden Gate Series, ed. Norris Hundley Jr. and John A. Schutz (San Francisco: Boyd and Fraser, 1979), 83–84; Kushner, *Long Road to Delano,* 96–103; Galarza, *Merchants of Labor;* and Richard J. Coronado, "A Conceptual Model of the Harvest Labor Market, the Bracero Program, and Factors Involved in Organization among Farm Workers in California, 1946–1970" (Ph.D. diss., University of Notre Dame, 1980), 43–129.

4. Shotwell, *The Harvesters,* 183; Velma Shotwell, "Report of Work in Western Area, April, May, June, 1942": 1; Velma Shotwell, "July, August, September, 1942 Report": 1, both in NCC, HMCNAR, RG 26, CWHM, 15, 29.

5. Sydney D. Smith, *Grapes of Conflict* (Pasadena, Calif.: Hope Publishing House, 1987), 18–19.

6. "Report of Social Action Department," 1922, 1923, 1925?, ACUA, NCWC, SAD, 1, 38; SAD, 1, 40; and SAD, 1, 43, respectively; "Department of Social Action, 1937–1938," ACUA, NCWC, SAD, 1, 56: 2; Abell, *American Catholicism and Social Action,* 256–82; and Higgins and Bole, *Organized Labor and the Church,* 55, 63–64.

7. Privett, *The U.S. Catholic Church and Its Hispanic Members,* 56–60, the quote coming from p. 65; "Report of the Inter-American Seminar on Social Studies," 24 August–12 September 1942, ACUA, NCWC, SAD, 5, 29; "Social Action Department Annual Report, 1943–1944," ibid., 1, 62: 9–10; and "The Spanish Speaking of the Southwest and West, 20–23 July 1943," ibid., 21, 4; "Meeting of Archbishops of the Southwest," 17 November 1944, ibid., 21, 3; "Memorandum for Archbishops' and Bishops' Conference," 10–13 January 1945, ibid., 21, 4; "Letter of McGowan to Lucey," 8 December 1944, ibid., 21, 3; "Recommendations of the Seminars on Spanish-Speaking People," University of Notre Dame Archives, Robert E. Lucey Papers, Box 13, Folder 9, n.d., hereafter cited as UNDA, Lucey Papers; "Memo to Those Invited to the Seminar on the Spanish-Speaking, 17–20 October, Regis College, Denver, Colorado, to be held by the NCWC Social Action Department under the Sponsorship of Archbishop Vehr," n.d., ACUA, NCWC, SAD, 21, 4: 1–3.

8. Privett, *The U.S. Catholic Church and Its Hispanic Members,* 68–80, 91–97, 103–7; "Letter of Joseph McGucken to Lucey," 22 December 1944, UNDA, Lucey Papers, 13, 9; "Letter of John Cantwell to Lucey," n.d., ACUA, NCWC, SAD, 21, 3; and Grebler et al., *The Mexican American People,* 462; Albeus Walsh, "The Work of the Catholic Bishops'

Committee for the Spanish Speaking in the United States" (master's thesis, University of Texas at Austin, 1952), 80–104.

9. Josephine D. Kellogg, "Ministry, Hispanics, and Migrants: The San Francisco Mission Band, 1949–1961 (San Francisco: The Turlock Centennial Foundation, 1986, unpublished copy at the Archives of the Archdiocese of San Francisco), 24–70; Patrick H. McNamara, "Bishops, Priests, and Prophecy: A Study in the Sociology of Religious Protest" (Ph.D. diss., University of California at Los Angeles, 1968), 111–14, 126; Burns, "The Mexican Catholic Community in California," 215; Joan London and Henry Anderson, *So Shall Ye Reap* (New York: Thomas Y. Crowell, 1970), 79–82; "Priests' Conference on Spanish-Speaking, St. Charles Church," 10 February 1949, and "Priest's [*sic*] Conference on Spanish-Speaking People, Our Lady of Guadalupe Church 10 March 1949," both in Archives of the Archdiocese of San Francisco, Donald McDonnell Papers, hereafter cited as AASF, DMP; "Clinic Program"; "A Neighborhood Center for Minority Group Settlements"; and "Report on Work with Minority Groups in Santa Clara County," in AASF, DMP, 1952; and Antonio R. Soto, "The Chicano and the Church in Northern California, 1848–1978: A Study of an Ethnic Minority within the Roman Catholic Church" (Ph.D. diss., Catholic University of America, 1979), 178–87.

10. "Spanish-Speaking Migrants in the Archdiocese of San Francisco," AASF, DMP, 1955; Kellogg, "Ministry, Hispanics, and Migrants," 74–81, 86, 90–91; McNamara, "Bishops, Priests, and Prophecy," 116; "Report of the Catholic Rural Life Conference of the Archdiocese of San Francisco," 25 August 1955, AASF, DMP, National Catholic Rural Life Conference Files, 4–5; Galarza, *Merchants of Labor,* 89–97, 103–6, 131–55, 183–98, 200–218; London and Anderson, *So Shall Ye Reap,* 85; and De Prague Reilly, "The Role of the Churches in the Bracero Program in California" (master's thesis, University of Southern California, 1969), 114–17; Coronado, "A Conceptual Model of the Harvest Labor Market," 48–60, 71–90; and N. Ray Gilmore and Gladys W. Gilmore, "The Bracero in California," *Pacific Historical Review* 34 (1965): 266–82.

11. Donald H. Grubbs, "Prelude to Chavez: The National Farm Labor Union in California," *Labor History* 16 (1975): 454; Ernesto Galarza, *Workers and Agri-Business in California, 1947–1960* (Notre Dame, Ind.: University of Notre Dame Press, 1977), 9–13, 99–202; Jenkins, *The Politics of Insurgency,* 86–111; London and Anderson, *So Shall Ye Reap,* 39–45; Kushner, *Long Road to Delano,* 103–5; Gómez-Quiñones, *Mexican-American Labor,* 235–42; and Scharlin and Villanueva, *Philip Vera Cruz,* 16–18, 33–34.

12. Galarza, *Farm Workers and Agri-Business,* 103, 109, 163; Jenkins, *The Politics of Insurgency,* 91, 96–97; London and Anderson, *So Shall Ye Reap,* 43; Taylor, *Chavez and the Farm Workers,* 68–69; Kellogg, "Ministry, Hispanics, and Migrants," quotations on 72–74; McNamara, "Bishops, Priests, and Prophecy," 115–17; and letters, 4 April 1954 and 6 April 1954, AASF, DMP, 1954.

13. Kellogg, "Ministry, Hispanics, and Migrants," 78–79, 86–89, 92–94, 99–100; McNamara, "Bishops, Priests, and Prophecy," 118; London and Anderson, *So Shall Ye Reap,* 88–89; Gutiérrez, *Walls and Mirrors,* 169–72; Meister and Loftis, *A Long Time Coming,* 113–18; Taylor, *Chavez and the Farm Workers,* 78–88, 93; Jacques Levy, *Cesar Chavez: Autobiography of La Causa* (New York: W. W. Norton, 1975), 95, 97–107.

14. London and Anderson, *So Shall Ye Reap,* 90–94; Burns, "The Mexican Catholic Community in California," 219; Kellogg, "Ministry, Hispanics, and Migrants," 94–95; and Meister and Loftis, *A Long Time Coming,* 92.

15. London and Anderson, *So Shall Ye Reap,* 46–77, 95–97; Galarza, *Farm Workers,* 323–37; Kellogg, "Ministry, Hispanics, and Migrants," 101–3; Meister and Loftis, *A Long*

Time Coming, 92–94; Kushner, *Long Road to Delano,* 105–8; Jenkins, *The Politics of Insurgency,* 114–30; Taylor, *Chavez and the Farm Workers,* 96–102; and Victor P. Salandini, "An Objective Evaluation of the Labor Disputes in the Lettuce Industry in Imperial Valley, California, during January–March, 1961" (master's thesis, St. Louis University, 1964).

16. Kellogg, "Ministry, Hispanics, and Migrants," 104–20; Grebler et al., *The Mexican American People,* 463; London and Anderson, *So Shall Ye Reap,* 97; and Burns, "The Mexican Catholic Community in California," 220–21. "Letter from Thomas Mc-Cullough to [San Diego Bishop] Charles F. Buddy," 10 January 1961; "Letter from Donald McDonnell to Buddy," 11 January 1961; "Letter from Buddy to McDonnell," 13 January 1961; "Letter from Buddy to McCullough," 14 January 1961; "Letter from Victor Salandini to McDonnell," 15 January 1961, all in AASF, DMP, General Correspondence Files.

17. Kellogg, "Ministry, Hispanics, and Migrants," 55, 65, 84, 108, 114–18; McNamara, "Bishops, Priests, and Prophecy," 119–24; Burns, "The Mexican Catholic Community in California," 206–8, 220; Alberto Lopez Pulido, "Race Relations within the American Catholic Church: An Historical and Sociological Analysis of Mexican American Catholics" (Ph.D. diss., University of Notre Dame, 1989), 69–73; Charles F. Buddy, "The Catholic View," in *A Moral Look at Right-to-Work Laws* (San Francisco: California State Federation of Labor Pamphlet, 1958), the quote coming from NCWC, Bishops' Committee for the Spanish Speaking, Mexican Affairs: 1958–65, 8 March 1958, Archives of the Diocese of San Diego, cited in Pulido, ibid., 73. Also see Reilly, "The Role of the Churches in the Bracero Program in California," 95–99.

18. "Archbishop Lucey Scores U.S. Congress for Abuses in Migrant-Bracero Program," *Alamo Messenger,* 26 November 1959, 1, 11; "Archbishop Lucey Wires Views to Subcommittee Opposing any Further Importation of Braceros," *Alamo Messenger,* 31 March 1960, 1, 10; "Extension of Bracero Program Scored by Archbishop," *Alamo Messenger,* 28 April 1960, 1, 3; Privett, *The U.S. Catholic Church and Its Hispanic Members,* 115–18. Higgins to Lucey, 11 June 1958; Lucey to Higgins, 17 June 1958; Higgins to Lucey, 12 March 1959; Higgins to Lucey, 24 March 1959; Higgins to Lucey, 11 June 1959; Lucey to Higgins, 15 June 1959; Higgins to Lucey, 18 June 1959; Lucey to Higgins, 27 July 1959; Higgins to Lucey, 3 February 1960; Lucey to Higgins, 24 March 1960; and Lucey to Higgins, 29 March 1960, all in ACUA, George Gilmary Higgins Papers, "Migratory Labor," Box 37, Folders 1, 2, hereafter cited as ACUA, GGH. Higgins's "Yardstick" columns: 2 February 1959; 6 July 1959; 27 July 1959; 19 October 1959; 2 November 1959; 31 March 1960; 14 April 1960; 26 May 1960; 9 June 1960; 30 June 1960; 6 January 1961; 24 May 1963; and 16 August 1963. Also see Gerald M. Costello, *Without Fear or Favor: George Higgins on the Record* (Mystic, Conn.: Twenty-Third Publications, 1984), 92–93; Higgins, *Organized Labor and the Church,* 84–86; "Rural Life Bureau," 1 July 1923–1 July 1924, ACUA, NCWC/USCC, SAD, 1, 41; "The Rural Life Bureau" and untitled three-page document, 1925?, ACUA, NCWC/USCC, SAD, 1, 43; "History of the National Catholic Rural Life Conference," Annual Report, National Catholic Rural Life Conference, 1954–55, Department of Special Collections, Stanford University Libraries, James L. Vizzard Papers, M324, Box 12, Folder 10, hereafter cited as DSC, SUL, Vizzard Papers, M324, 10–11; "Manifesto on Rural Life," ACUA, NCWC/USCC, SAD, 15, 12, 56–59; Vizzard letters to Robert E. Lucey, 21 February 1961; Lucey, 2 June 1961; Secretary of Labor W. Willard Wirtz, 19 February 1963; BCSS Executive Secretary John A. Wagner, 17 January 1964; NCRLC Director Edward W. O'Rourke, 18 February 1964; U.S. Representative Henry B. Gonzalez, 25 May 1964; Gonzalez, 17 August 1964; President Lyndon B. Johnson, 20 October 1964; and California Governor Pat Brown, 1 December 1964, all in DSC, SUL, Vizzard Papers,

M324, 6, 3. Also see Reilly, "The Role of the Catholic Church in the Bracero Program in California," 107–11; "Churchmen Hit Extension of Bracero Labor Treaty," *Alamo Messenger,* 10 March 1961, 1, 9; "Calls for Justice for Farm Workers," *Alamo Messenger,* 15 December 1961, 1; "Bracero Labor Termed 'Crutch'; Request End of Program in U.S.," *Alamo Messenger,* 5 April 1963, 1; "Priest Warns of Bracero Revival," *Alamo Messenger,* 9 August 1963, 6; Burton H. Wolfe, "Father Vizzard: Enemy of Exploiters," *The Sign* (May 1966): 16–18; "Rev. James L. Vizzard, S.J., Biographical Sketch," 3 March 1967, and untitled three-page document, 1972, DSC, SUL, Vizzard Papers, M324, 2, 1.

19. Robert T. Handy, *We Witness Together: A History of Cooperative Home Missions, 1900–1950* (New York: Friendship Press, 1956), 196–99; Samuel M. Cavert, *Church Cooperation and Unity in America: A Historical Review, 1900–1970* (New York: Association Press, 1970), 247–49; *Western Harvester,* Western Area, Home Missions Council of North America (Fall 1947): 1, 3; *Western Harvester* (Spring 1948): 1; *Western Harvester* (Fall 1949): 1; "Letter from Mrs. F. E. Shotwell to members of the President's Commission on Migratory Labor," 11 August 1950, Wayne State University Archives of Labor and Urban Affairs, National Farm Worker Ministry, Part I, Box 4, Folder 1, p. 1, hereafter cited as NFWM, Part I.

20. Robert Wuthnow, *The Restructuring of American Religion: Faith and Society since World War II,* Studies in Church and State Series, ed. John F. Wilson (Princeton, N.J.: Princeton University Press, 1988), 81–82; Henry J. Pratt, *The Liberalization of American Protestantism: A Case Study in Complex Organizations* (Detroit: Wayne State University Press, 1972), 30–32, the quote coming from p. 19; Samuel M. Cavert, *The American Churches in the Ecumenical Movement, 1900–1968* (New York: Association Press, 1968), 209–34; "The Concern of the Churches for Migratory Farm Laborers," 19 September 1951, NFWM, Part I, 3, 11; "The Wetbacks: America's Displaced Persons Problem," 30 April 1954, NCC, Division of Home Missions Records, Records Group 7, Box 7, File 23; K. L. Billingsley, *From Mainline to Sideline: The Social Witness of the NCC* (Washington, D.C.: Ethics and Public Policy Center, 1990), 157–59. Also see Howard M. Mills, "The Department of the Church and Economic Life of the National Council of Churches, 1947–1966: A Critical Analysis" (Th.D. diss., Union Theological Seminary [New York], 1970), 74–109; and William M. King, "The Reform Establishment and the Ambiguities of Influence," in *Between the Times: The Travail of the Protestant Establishment in America, 1900–1960,* ed. William R. Hutchison, Cambridge Series in Religion and American Public Life, gen. ed. Robin W. Lovin (Cambridge: Cambridge University Press, 1989), 122–40.

21. Quarterly Reports of Western Area Supervisor Velma Shotwell, 1943–50, NCC, Home Missions Council of North America Records, RG 26, CWHM, 15, 30; Dean S. Collins, "Summary of the Western Region Summer Program," July 1955, NCC, Division of Home Mission Records, RG 7, 9, 4, 24–26; Smith, *Grapes of Conflict,* 42–43; Pat Hoffman, *Ministry of the Dispossessed: Learning from the Farm Worker Movement* (Los Angeles: Wallace Press, 1987), 9–13; and "Douglas M. Still, Biographical Sketch," NFWM, Part I, 3, 11.

22. Velma Shotwell, "Report of Migrant Work in Western Area," January, February, March, 1950, NCC, HMCNAR, RG 26, CWHM, 15, 30, 5–6; Dean S. Collins, "Items for the Agenda," 1 December 1953, NCC, DHMR, RG 7, 9, 4, 6; Dean S. Collins, "The Problem of the Rural Slums in California," 20 April 1956, General Files of the NCCC, RG 7, 22, 2, Presbyterian Historical Society, Presbyterian Church (U.S.A., Philadelphia); "Minutes of the California Migrant Ministry Committee," 5 May 1958, NFWM, Part I, 1, 1, 1–2; "Letter from Douglas Still to Carl Tjerendsen of the Emil Schwartzhaupt Foun-

dation," 8 February 1960, NFWM, Part II, 36, 11; Douglas M. Still, speech given to Triennium Assembly, NCCCUSA, 8 December 1960, NFWM, Part II, 3, 11; Louisa R. Shotwell, "Report on the Rural Fringe Ministry in California, Arizona, Texas" [Preliminary Draft], 1961, NCC, DHMR, RG 7, 11, 13, 17, 21, 25; Smith, *Grapes of Conflict*, 42–50; and Hoffman, *Ministry of the Dispossessed*, 13–15.

23. "Biographical Sketch of Edith Elizabeth Lowry," n.d., NCC, DHMR, RG 7, 12, 25. Edith Lowry, "Budget of Projected Needs, Migrant Work, 1957," 29 October 1957, ibid., 1, 1; "Minutes of Executive Board," 1 December 1957, ibid., 1, 1; and Lowry, "Budget of Projected Needs, Migrant Work, 1958," n.d., ibid., 1, 1.

24. Cavert, *Church Cooperation and Unity in America*, 249–50; Susan M. Hartmann, "Expanding Feminism's Field and Focus: Activism in the NCC in the 1960s and 1970s," in *Women and Twentieth-Century Protestantism*, ed. Margaret Lamberts Bendroth and Virginia Lieson Brereton (Urbana: University of Illinois Press, 2002), 50–51; Virginia Lieson Brereton, "United and Slighted: Women as Subordinated Insiders," in *Between the Times: The Travail of the Protestant Establishment in America, 1900–1960*, ed. William R. Hutchison, Cambridge Series in Religion and American Public Life, gen. ed. Robin W. Lovin (Cambridge: Cambridge University Press, 1989), 147, 157–64; Susan M. Yohn, "'Let Christian Women Set the Example in Their Own Gifts': The 'Business' of Protestant Women's Organizations," in *Women and Twentieth-Century Protestantism*, ed. Bendroth and Brereton, 213–35; Patricia R. Hill, *The World Their Household: The American Woman's Mission Movement and Cultural Transformation, 1870–1920* (Ann Arbor: University of Michigan Press, 1985), 6, 167; "Biographical Data: Rev. Jon L. Regier," n.d., NCC, DHMR, RG 7, 1, 1; "Minutes of Executive Board," 11 April 1958, ibid.; "Minutes, 'Future of the Vision of Home Missions,'" 12–13 November 1958, ibid.: 8–13; "Minutes of Executive Board," 10 December 1958, NCC, DHMR, RG 7, 1, 1; "Report of Executive Secretary," 6 October 1960, NCC, DHMR, RG 7, Executive Board, 1, 16: 2; Jon L. Regier paper, "Are the Boards Committed to This Call?" July 1961, DHMR, RG 7, Policy and Strategy Committee, 1, 11; "Minutes of the Reorganization Study Committee of the Policy Committee," 9 March 1959, ibid.: 2; "Minutes," 10 October 1962, ibid.: 12–13; Regier paper, "Structure and Function of Division of Home Missions," 21 November 1961, ibid.; "Minutes," 1 November 1963, ibid.; "Minutes," 11 March 1964, ibid.; and Pratt, *The Liberalization of American Protestantism*, 35–41.

25. Mills, "The Department of the Church and Economic Life," 387–98; and the quote comes from "Ethical Goals for Agricultural Policy," 4 June 1958, NFWM, Part I, 3, 11: 2.

26. "Child Labor, Particularly Child Workers in Agriculture," 2 February 1960; "The Future of the Mexican Agricultural Worker Importation Program," 2 February 1960; and "Agricultural Migratory Workers," 8 December 1960 (Mills, "The Department of the Church and Economic Life," 398–400). Also see "Cooperative Field Projects Committee," 1961–63, NCC, DHMR, RG 7, 2, 16; "Minutes of the California Migrant Ministry Committee," 5 May 1958, NFWM, Part I, 1, 1: 3; William E. Scholes, "Report of the Western Field Office to the Commission on Cooperative Field Projects," 12 March 1962, NCC, DHMR, RG 7, 2, 16: 4–5; Scholes, "Report of the Western Field Office," 8 October 1962, NCC, DHMR, RG 7, 2, 16: 4–5; and Smith, *Grapes of Conflict*, 23–24, 31.

27. "Finances—DJM from Dr. H. Conwell Snoke to Executive Board," 11 December 1961, NCC, DHMR, RG 7, 1, 14: 2.

28. "Appendix III-C," Executive Board Meeting, 10 October 1963, NCC, DHMR, RG 7, 1, 11: 2; Edith Lowry, "40th Anniversary of the Migrant Ministry" memo, 27 May

1959, ibid., 2, 7; the NCCC Newsletter Information Service, vol. 39, no. 19 (12 November 1960): 8 pp., NFWM, Part I, 2, 11; Shotwell, *The Harvesters;* "National Goals for the Fifth Decade," Fourth Draft, 2 February 1962, NCC, DHMR, RG 7, 2, 13, the list cited above found on pp. 1–2; and "Implementing the National Goals for the 5th Decade of the Migrant Ministry," 19–20 September 1962, NCC, DHMR, RG 7, 2, 16, the quotation cited above found on p. 5 (italics are author's). Also see Smith, *Grapes of Conflict,* 39.

29. Stanley Whitaker Thomas, "The Image of Labor Organization in Church and Trade Union, 1945–1955" (Ph.D. diss., Boston University, 1960), 147–243; and letter from William E. Scholes to author, 1 October 1994.

Chapter 4

1. Gutiérrez, *Walls and Mirrors,* 183–87, Gómez-Quiñones, *Chicano Politics,* 67–78, 96–97, 103–46; Acuña, *Occupied America,* 309–56, the quoted phrases from pp. 324–25; McWilliams, *North from Mexico,* 276–91; Meier and Rivera, *Chicanos: A History of Mexican Americans/American Mexicans,* 212–17; and Gutiérrez, *The Making of a Chicano Militant,* 98–183; Juan Gómez-Quiñones, *Mexican Students por la Raza: The Chicano Student Movement in Southern California, 1967–1977* (Santa Barbara, Calif.: Editorial La Causa, 1978).

2. Richard Griswold del Castillo and Richard A. Garcia, *César Chávez: A Triumph of Spirit* (Norman: University of Oklahoma Press, 1995), 114–15, 139; 151–54; Gutiérrez, *The Making of a Chicano Militant,* 222; and Gómez-Quiñones, *Chicano Politics,* 105–7.

3. Cletus E. Daniel, "Cesar Chavez and the Unionization of California Farm Workers," in *Labor Leaders in America,* The Working Class in American History Series, ed. Melvyn Dubofsky and Warren van Tine (Urbana: University of Illinois Press, 1987), 364.

4. Henry J. Pratt, *The Liberalization of American Protestantism: A Case Study in Complex Organizations* (Detroit: Wayne State University Press, 1972), 53–57, 158–86, 264–65; Robert Wuthnow, *The Restructuring of American Religion: Faith and Society since World War II,* Studies in Church and State Series, ed. John F. Wilson (Princeton, N.J.: Princeton University Press, 1988), 145–50 and 153–64; Jeffrey K. Hadden, *The Gathering Storm in the Churches* (Garden City, N.Y.: Doubleday, 1969); Dolan, *The American Catholic Experience,* 435–36; and Jan Hart Cohen, "To See Christ in Our Brothers: The Role of the Texas Roman Catholic Church in the Rio Grande Valley Farm Workers' Movement, 1966–1967" (master's thesis, University of Texas at Arlington, 1974), 12–18.

5. Levy, *Cesar Chavez,* 7–40, the block quotation coming from p. 38; and Daniel, "Cesar Chavez and the Unionization of California Farm Workers," 351–53.

6. Gutiérrez, *Walls and Mirrors,* 169–72; Fred Ross, *Conquering Goliath: Cesar Chavez in the Beginning* (Keene, Calif.: El Taller Gráfico Press, 1989); Levy, *Cesar Chavez,* 95, 129–44, 157–60, 162–63, 171, 173–76; Taylor, *Chavez and the Farm Workers,* 93–96, 107, 110–11, 115; Peter Matthiessen, *Sal Si Puedes: Cesar Chavez and the New American Revolution* (New York: Random House, 1969), 8, 51–53, 56–60; Kushner, *Long Road to Delano,* 117, 151; Smith, *Grapes of Conflict,* 78–82; Dunne, *Delano,* 72–76; London and Anderson, *So Shall Ye Reap,* 147–49; Meister and Loftis, *A Long Time Coming,* 117–19; Margaret E. Rose, "Women in the United Farm Workers: A Study of Chicana and Mexicana Participation in a Labor Union, 1950 to 1980" (Ph.D. diss., University of California at Los Ange-

les, 1988), 14–115; Richard A Garcia, "Dolores Huerta: Woman, Organizer, and Symbol," *California History* 72, no. 1 (1993): 57–71; and Griswold del Castillo and Garcia, *César Chávez: A Triumph of Spirit*, 31.

7. Levy, *Cesar Chavez*, 175, 184, the quote coming from p. 179; Taylor, *Chavez and the Farm Workers*, 115–16, 131; Matthiessen, *Sal Si Puedes*, 40–41; and Meister and Loftis, *A Long Time Coming*, 122.

8. "Biographical Sketch—The Rev. Wayne C. Hartmire, Jr.," February 1962, Walter P. Reuther Library of Labor and Urban Affairs, Wayne State University, Detroit MI: National Farm Worker Ministry Collection, Part I, 3, 11, hereafter cited as NFWM; and Wayne C. Hartmire Jr., "The Church Can Live through Mission," a two-page reflection as a 1959 Summer Area Leader for CMM, n.d., NFWM, Part I, 2, 12.

9. Pat Hoffman, *Ministry of the Dispossessed: Learning from the Farm Worker Movement* (Los Angeles: Wallace Press, 1987), 15–16, 101–4, 126; Smith, *Grapes of Conflict*, 18, 32–41, 60, 87, 104–5, 110, and 123–34; Taylor, *Chavez and the Farm Workers:* 103; Wayne C. Hartmire, "The Church and the Emerging Farm Worker's Movement: A Case Study," 22 July 1967, NFWM, Part II, 10, 13; Wayne C. Hartmire, "Death for the Sake of Life," *California Harvester* (Fall 1966): 1, NFWM, Part II, 1, 6; also see Dennis McCann, *Christian Realism and Liberation Theology: Practical Theologies in Creative Conflict* (Maryknoll, N.Y.: Orbis Books, 1981).

10. Hartmire letter to César Chávez, 5 June 1962, Walter P. Reuther Library of Labor and Urban Affairs, Wayne State University, Detroit MI, UFW Collection, Office of the President, Box 60, Folder 1, hereafter cited as UFW, President.

11. Alexandra Robbins, Director of the Kings-Tulare County Migrant Ministry, untitled four-page report, n.d., NFWM, Part II, 33, 38; "Rural Fringe Ministry in Tulare County," January 1962, ibid., 31; James Drake, "Report on Goshen Project, California," August 1964, ibid.; Hoffman, *Ministry of the Dispossessed*, 17–22; "Goshen Administrative Committee Minutes," 24 November 1964, ibid., 24; letter from Philip Farnham to Chris Hartmire, 27 July 1964, ibid., 29; "Goshen Project," February 1965, ibid., 26; Smith, *Grapes of Conflict*, 50–58; Steve Gibson, "The Rev. Jim Drake, Aide to Cesar Chavez," *The Sacramento Bee*, 5 September 2001: B5; "Goshen Administrative Committee Minutes;" and "Tulare County Administration Committee," 10 February 1965, both in NFWM, Part II, 33, 24; letter from Walter S. Press, Associate Conference Minister, to Gordon Johnson, Board Chair of the Northern California Conference of the UCC, 25 April 1966, ibid., 34; "Initial Proposal for Staff of Goshen Community Center Organization," 1 September 1965, ibid., 26; Philip Farnham, "[A Statement] Prepared for the Goshen Administrative Committee Meeting," 18 October 1965; and "Goshen-Tulare County Administrative Committee Minutes," 18 October 1965, both in ibid., 24.

12. Wayne C. Hartmire Jr., "Report on the Citizenship Education and Action Project in Tulare County," 12 November 1965, NFWM, Susan Drake Files, 1, 1; Taylor, *Chavez and the Farm Workers*, 117–23; Hoffman, *The Ministry of the Dispossessed*, 22–23; and Smith, *Grapes of Conflict*, 87.

13. Meister and Loftis, *A Long Time Coming*, 126–31; Taylor, *Chavez and the Farm Workers*, 120–21, 124, 127–28, 131; Jenkins, *The Politics of Insurgency*, 130, 145–46; Dunne, *Delano*, 77; Levy, *Cesar Chavez*, 184–86; Scharlin and Villanueva, *Philip Vera Cruz*, 31–51; and "Mabuhay Brother Pete Velasco," biographical sheet prepared by Velasco's widow, Dolores Ann Neubauer, n.d., copy in possession of author.

14. Levy, *Cesar Chavez*, 188–93, 204; Taylor, *Chavez and the Farm Workers*, 132–37,

156–60, 164–67; Meister and Loftis, *A Long Time Coming,* 134, 138–40; Matthiessen, *Sal Si Puedes,* 121–25; Jenkins, *The Politics of Insurgency,* 149–53; Dunne, *Delano,* 91–97; and Kushner, *Long Road to Delano,* 152–53.

15. Hartmire, "Report on the Citizenship Education and Action Project," 9; Hartmire, "The Church and the Delano Grape Strike—A Partial Report," February 1966, both in NFWM, Part II, 4, 4: 2–5; James L. Drake, "Statement of Ministry," May 1966, NFWM, Part II, 14, 1: 2–3; Hoffman, *Ministry of the Dispossessed,* 32–34; Taylor, *Chavez and the Farm Workers,* 142–44, 149; Jenkins, *The Politics of Insurgency,* 150–51; and Meister and Loftis, *A Long Time Coming,* 137.

16. Hartmire, "The Church and the Emerging Farm Worker's Movement," 8; the emphasis is original.

17. Letter from Roger A. Chute, First Baptist Church, Clovis, Calif., to Hartmire, 9 December 1965; and J. Leland Whitaker, First Baptist Church, Orange Cove, Calif., to Hartmire, 6 December 1965, both in NFWM, Part II, 14, 11; letter from Joseph M. Matthews, First United Presbyterian Church, Lindsay, Calif., to Drake, 7 October 1965, ibid., 11, 1; news clippings "Exeter [Methodist] Church Raps Ministry Role in Strike" and "Visalia Church [i.e., First Presbyterian] Drops Support of Migrant Clerics" reproduced in *Citizens for Facts from Delano,* n.d., both in ibid., 14, 6; the quoted phrase is from "Rev. [R. B.] Moore Criticizes 'Wild Attacks'" and "Migrant Ministers Pay NFWA Bills," reproduced in *Citizens for Facts from Delano;* "Visitors Refuse Suggestion at Meeting Then Leave Delano: Both Groups Present Views," *Delano Record,* 4 January 1966; Harry Bernstein, "Clergy Samples Grapes of Wrath Amid Strike," *Los Angeles Times,* 9 January 1966, unidentified page; Hartmire, "The Church and the Emerging Farm Worker's Movement," 24–25; Grebler et al., *The Mexican American People,* 511n49; also see William George Jeffs, "The Roots of the Delano Grape Strike" (master's thesis, California State College at Fullerton, 1969), 43–47.

18. Letter from Vizzard to George G. Higgins, 29 November 1965; letter from Vizzard to J. Walsh Murray, 6 December 1965; letter from Vizzard to Daniel Flaherty, 7 December 1965; letter from Vizzard to Edward W. O'Rourke, 7 January 1966; letter from Vizzard to Frederick W. Freking, 1 February 1966; letter from Vizzard to LeRoy Chatfield, 9 February 1966, all in Department of Special Collections, Stanford University Libraries, Vizzard Collection, M324, 6, 7, hereafter cited as JLV; "National Church Leaders' Statement," 14 December 1966, NFWM, Susan Drake Files, 1, 1; and "The Horn Blower of Delano," *The Central California Register* (official organ of Diocese of Monterey-Fresno), 6 January 1966, 1.

19. Untitled statement by the Episcopal Diocese of San Joaquin, approved and adopted at convention, February 1966; and "Resolution on Worker-Grower Issue," Board of Directors of the Fresno Area Council of Churches, 10 March 1966, both in NFWM, Part II, 4, 4.

20. "Motion to Be Referred to the Synod of California," Presbytery of San Joaquin, 14 June 1966, NFWM, Part II, 4, 6; letter from W. B. Yinger to Valley Ministers Association Members, March 1966, ibid., 14, 15; untitled statement by San Francisco Presbytery, January, 1966, ibid., 4, 4; "Protestants Plead in Grape Strike," *San Francisco Chronicle,* 10 March 1966, 50; "L.A. Presbytery Rejects Paper Supporting Migrant Ministry," *Southern California Presbyterian,* March 1966, 10; and untitled resolution, 13 November 1965, NFWM, Part II, 11, 3.

21. Levy, *Cesar Chavez,* quotation on 206–8; Dunne, *Delano,* 130–31; Matthiessen, *Sal Si Puedes,* 127–28; Taylor, *Chavez and the Farm Workers,* 171, 173; Daniel Ramirez,

Arizona State University, Responder, "Evangelicalism in Latina/o and Latin American Communities," American Academy of Religion, 2004 Annual Meeting, San Antonio Tex., 22 November 2004; and Ross, *Conquering Goliath*, 123–29.

22. César E. Chávez, *"Peregrinación, penitencia, revolucion"*; one-page march schedule titled, "Peregrinación Route"; one-page untitled handmade map of march route; one-page form titled "Registration for Peregrinacion"; one-page instruction sheet titled "Regulations for All Persons on Peregrinación to Sacramento," all in NFWM, Part II, 14, 2; César E. Chávez, "A Union in the Community," UFW, President, Part I, Box 9, File 7, Writings, 1969; Dunne, *Delano*, 130–34; Smith, *Grapes of Conflict*, 95; Hoffman, *Ministry of the Dispossessed*, 34–35; "Determination, High Spirits Mark Trek of Delano Farm Workers," *Fresno Bee*, 25 March 1966, 1, 2c; *"Misa de obreros,"* Walter P. Reuther Library of Labor and Urban Affairs, Wayne State University, NFWA, Box 8, File 25, hereafter cited as NFWA; *"Cantares de La Huelga,"* NFWA, Box 12, File 1; NFWM, Part II, 14, 15; NFWM, Susan Drake Files, 2, 14; and Jennifer Maura Sookne, "The Songs of the United Farm Workers in Their Socio-Cultural and Musical Contexts" (master's thesis, University of Texas at Austin, 1978); Levy, *Cesar Chavez*, 115–16, 209; Daniel Ramirez, "Borderlands Praxis: The Immigrant Experience in Latino Pentecostal Churches," *Journal of the American Academy of Religion* 67, no. 3 (1999): 573–96; Gaston Espinoza, "Borderland Religion: Los Angeles and the Origins of the Latino Pentecostal Movement in the U.S., Mexico, and Puerto Rico, 1900–1945" (Ph.D. diss., University of California at Santa Barbara, 1999); Victor De Leon, *The Silent Pentecostals* (Taylor, S.C.: Faith Printing Company, 1979); Matthiessen, *Sal Si Puedes*, 128–29; supplement of the SNCC publication *The Movement*, NFWM, Susan Drake Files 2, 5; and Taylor, *Chavez and the Farm Workers*, 168.

23. *Stockton Record*, 4 April 1966, 1, 14, 15; Newell Hart, "A Personal Account of the Farm Workers' Pilgrimage from Delano to Sacramento," Bancroft Library, University of California, Berkeley, 24–25, 37–40; and *The Movement* supplement cited in the previous note; also see Levy, *Cesar Chavez*, 212–14; Hoffman, *Ministry of the Dispossessed*, 35–36; Rosa Maria Icaza, "The Cross in Mexican Popular Piety," *Liturgy* 1 (1981): 27–34; "Marchers' Capitol Rally Draws Near," unidentified news clipping, NFWM, Part II, 14, 16; "Remarks by Wayne C. Hartmire, Jr.," 10 April 1966, ibid., 4, 4); the quotation from Albert Camus appeared in his *Resistance, Rebellion, and Death;* and Dunne, *Delano*, 134–35.

24. Letter of retired farm worker and union member María Saludado de Magaña to author, 26 November 2001; Gómez-Quiñones, *Chicano Politics*, 106; Hart, "A Personal Account," 40; and Hoffman, *Ministry of the Dispossessed*, 39. The quotation is taken from the Catholic Citizens of Delano ad, "And Then God Threw Dirt in Their Face," *Fresno Bee*, 2 May 1966; "Peregrinación for Publicity," a *Delano Record* story, and "Cancelled Mass," a *Central California Register* story, both reprinted in the newsletter *Citizens for Facts from Delano*, n.d., NFWM, Susan Drake Files, 2, 4; also see Andres G. Guerrero, *A Chicano Theology* (Maryknoll, N.Y.: Orbis Books, 1987), 96–117, 143–48; Brading, *Mexican Phoenix*, 238–54; and Elizondo, *La Morenita*, 110–13.

25. William Kircher, cited in Taylor, *Chavez and the Farm Workers*, 169.

26. Stan Steiner, *La Raza: The Mexican Americans* (New York: Harper and Row, 1969, 1970), 311–12; Donovan O. Roberts, "Theory and Practice in the Life and Thought of César E. Chávez: Implications for a Social Ethic" (Ph.D. diss., Boston University, 1978), 557–60; Paul A. Hribar, "The Social Fasts of César Chávez: A Critical Study of Nonverbal Communication, Nonviolence, and Public Opinion" (Ph.D. diss., University of Southern California, 1978), 214–19; Taylor, *Chavez and the Farm Workers*, 217–20;

Levy, *Cesar Chavez,* 256–68; Hoffman, *Ministry of the Dispossessed,* 39–41; and Anderson and London, *So Shall Ye Reap,* 182–83.

27. Levy, *Cesar Chavez,* 272–75; Matthiessen, *Sal Si Puedes,* 177–82, 185–86, the quotation coming from p. 182. A circular letter described the fourfold purpose of the fast: it "symbolizes the hardships" of farm labor; it "is a penance . . . for the faults of the Union members . . ."; it "reminds us that we are united . . ."; and it "calls Union members to rededicate themselves to the work and suffering which lies ahead." "The Fast of César Chávez," Walter P. Reuther Archives of Labor and Urban Affairs, Wayne State University, UFWOC, Box 2, File 2, n.d., hereafter cited as UFWOC.

28. Susan Samuels Drake, *Fields of Courage: Remembering César Chávez and the People Whose Labor Feeds Us* (Santa Cruz, Calif.: Many Names Press, 1997), 57–58, 61; Matthiessen, *Sal Si Puedes,* 183, 191; Kushner, *Long Road to Delano,* 165–66; Meister and Loftis, *A Long Time Coming,* 152–53; Steiner, *La Raza,* 321; Taylor, *Chavez and the Farm Workers,* 220 and 223, the reference to Chávez's room coming from p. 223.

29. Harry Bernstein, "Chavez Revolt Catching Fire across State," *Los Angeles Times,* 14 June 1970, 1.

30. Winthrop Yinger, *The Rhetoric of Nonviolence* (Hicksville, N.Y.: Exposition Press, 1975), 42.

31. Hribar, "The Social Fasts of César Chávez," 273; Yinger, *The Rhetoric of Nonviolence,* 43–44; Matthiessen, *Sal Si Puedes,* 194–97; Levy, *Cesar Chavez,* 285–86; Taylor, *Chavez and the Farm Workers,* 225–26; and Western Union Telegram from Martin Luther King Jr., to César E. Chávez, 5 March 1968, "Endorsements, Religious, 1968," UFW, President, Part I, 30, 15.

32. Taylor, *Chavez and the Farm Workers,* 223–24; and Levy, *Cesar Chavez,* 280–81.

33. Levy, *Cesar Chavez,* 273–78, 280–81, 282–83; Taylor, *Chavez and the Farm Workers,* 223–24, 225; Yinger, *The Rhetoric of Nonviolence,* 42; Matthiessen, *Sal Si Puedes,* 181, 191; and Kushner, *Long Road to Delano,* 174. Also see "Judge Denies Chavez Move," *Salinas Californian,* 27 November 1970, 1–2; "Judge Orders Chavez Jailed," *Salinas Californian,* 4 December 1970, 1; Eric C. Brazil, "Chavez Supporters Keep Vigil," *Salinas Californian,* 5 December 1970, 1–2; "Ethel Kennedy Ignores Taunts to March for Chavez in Salinas," *Salinas Californian,* 7 December 1970, 1A, 4A; and Eric C. Brazil, "Ethel Kennedy Visits Chavez," *Salinas Californian,* 7 December 1970, unidentified page.

34. Stephen R. Lloyd-Moffett, "The Mysticism and Social Action of César Chávez," in *Latino Religions and Civic Activism in the United States,* ed. Gastón Espinosa, Virgilio Elizondo, and Jesse Miranda (New York: Oxford University Press, 2005), 36–51, who claims that the sole source of Chávez's strength vis-à-vis the farm worker struggle came from his Catholic mysticism, as evidenced in his social fasts rather than from economic, political, and/or ethnic motives. Lloyd-Moffett provides a needed corrective but then indulges in hagiography (see Luís D. León, "César Chávez and Mexican American Civil Religion," in *Latino Religions and Civic Activism in the United States,* ed. Espinosa, Elizondo, and Miranda, 53–64, and 63n4).

35. Author interview with LeRoy Chatfield, 5 May 1994, Sacramento Calif.; Matthiessen, *Sal Si Puedes,* 184, 187; Taylor, *Chavez and the Farm Workers,* 223, 229; Yinger, *The Rhetoric of Nonviolence,* 59–61, 84–85; letter of retired farm worker and union member María Saludado de Magaña to author, 26 November 2001; letter of retired farm worker and union member Roberto Escutia to author, 20 November 2001; and letter of retired farm worker and union member Eloy Martinez to author, 25 November 2001; Drake, *Fields of Courage,* xiii–xiv; Levy, *Cesar Chavez,* 18, 91, 269–71; Anderson and London, *So*

Shall Ye Reap, 147–48, 183–84; Meister and Loftis, *A Long Time Coming,* 112–13; Roberts, "The Social Fasts of César Chávez," 295–304, 524–30; letters from Chávez to Dasgupta, 25 February 1969, and 23 July 1969, UFW, President, Part I, Box 33, File 4, "Gandhi, 1968–70"; letter from Chávez to Narayan Desai, 7 April 1970, Walter P. Reuther Archives of Labor and Urban Affairs, Wayne State University, United Farm Workers Collection, Administration Files, Box 9, File 28; "The Philosophy of Nonviolence and the Tactic of Nonviolent Resistance" of the SCLC, n.d., UFW, President, Part I, 46, 15, 5 pp.; and Griswold del Castillo and Garcia: *César Chávez: A Triumph of Spirit,* 5, 47.

36. Anthony M. Stevens-Arroyo, "Latino/a Catholic Theology," in *Handbook of Latina/o Theologies,* ed. Edwin David Aponte and Miguel A. La Torre (St. Louis, Mo.: Chalice Press, 2006), 175–76.

37. Gilberto M. Hinojosa, "Mexican-American Faith Communities in Texas and the Southwest," in *Mexican Americans and the Catholic Church,* ed. Dolan and Hinojosa, 116–19; Burns, "The Mexican Catholic Community in California," 222–24, 229; letter of Raymond J. Tintle, O.F.M., to author, 27 November 2001; letter of LeRoy Chatfield to Brendan Sexton, Director of Training, Citizens' Crusade against Poverty, 7 February 1968, Walter P. Reuther Archives of Labor and Urban Affairs, United Farm Workers, Information and Research Department Collection, Box 47, File 28. The block quotation comes from "Cursillo," "Notebook," 20, 21, 22 July 1962, UFW, President, Part I, 5, 5, 3.

38. Hribar, "The Social Fasts of César Chávez," 293–94; Levy, *Cesar Chavez,* 277; Yinger, *The Rhetoric of Nonviolence,* 66, 74–76; Matthiessen, *Sal Si Puedes,* 178, 187; and Anderson and London, *So Shall Ye Reap,* 182–84.

39. On the physical effect of the fast on Chávez see, for instance, Levy, *Cesar Chavez,* 276, 290–91. For an assessment of subsequent fasts see Hribar, "The Social Fasts of César Chávez," 276–89, 298–99, 372. The quote by Drake is cited in Hoffman, *Ministry of the Dispossessed,* 43 (ellipsis original).

40. León, "César Chávez and Mexican American Civil Religion," creatively and provocatively posits that Chávez actually developed a political and mythological religion set apart from traditional forms of Catholicism, that is, mysticism, social teachings of the institutional Catholic Church, and such (53–64).

41. Griswold del Castillo and Garcia, *César Chávez: A Triumph of Spirit,* 114–115, 152; Lloyd-Moffett, "The Mysticism and Social Action of César Chávez," 35–36, 41–43.

42. Edward J. Walsh, "Mobilization Theory vis-à-vis a Mobilization Process: The Case of the United Farm Workers' Movement," in *Research in Social Movements, Conflicts and Change,* vol. 1, ed. Louis Kriesberg (Greenwich, Conn.: JAI Press, 1978), 155–77; John D. McCarthy and Mayer N. Zald, "Resource Mobilization and Social Movements: A Partial Theory," *American Journal of Sociology* 82, no. 6 (1977): 1212–41; Jenkins, *The Politics of Insurgency,* 1–27; Mooney and Majka, *Farmers' and Farm Workers' Movements,* xxvi–xxix; and David Gates, "A Secular Saint of the '60s: Cesar Chavez, Farm Workers' Champion, 1927–1993," *Newsweek,* vol. 121, no. 18 (1993): 68; Drake, *Fields of Courage,* 106. The block quotation comes from the letter of Eloy Martinez to author, 26 November 2001.

43. Taylor, *Chavez and the Farm Workers,* 322–23; Daniel, "Cesar Chavez and the Unionization of California Farm Workers," 380; letter of David Train to César Chávez, 29 March 1977; letter of Deirdre Godfrey to Chávez, 18 April 1977; letter of Margaret Gavagan to Chávez, n.d.; letter of Roger H. Brooks to Chávez, 31 October 1978, all in UFW, President, II, 3, 22; letter of Doug Adair to Chávez, 7 April 1977, ibid., 23; Ben Bedell, "Shake-Ups Rattle Farm Union," *Guardian* (14 December 1977): 3; Edward L. Maillet, "Report on Research Visit to Synanon," June 1972, a forty-six-page document; How-

ard M. Garfield, "The Synanon Religion: The Survival Morality for the 21st Century," an eleven-page document, n.d., both in ibid., 24); Doug Cameron and Bonnie Benjamin, "Report on Field Trip to La Paz," a five-page document, n.d., UFW, President, II, 3, 25; "The Game," a one-page document, 28 October 1977; one-page memo of Chris Hartmire to César Chávez, 22 December 1977; "Emphases for the New, New Game," one-page document, July 1978; one-page, handwritten note, no author, n.d.: "Game is a tool for union—getting clean inside . . .", one-page memo of Hartmire to Chávez, 13 February 1978; and memo of Hartmire to Chávez, 23 February 1978, all in ibid., 9, 18; the poem comes from Drake, *Fields of Courage,* 106.

44. Letter from Dolores Huerta to César Chávez, n.d., "Since I had not heard from you," NFWA, Box 2, Folder: Correspondence, Huerta to Chavez (1962–64), Walter P. Reuther Archives of Labor and Urban Affairs, Wayne State University, Detroit Mich., cited in Rose, "Women in the United Farm Workers," 47–48, 51.

45. The term *mujerista* theology is similar to Latina/Chicana historiography in that it addresses not only gender, as (white) feminism does, but also class and ethnic issues. Furthermore, it focuses exclusively on religious understandings of and by Latinas, much as womanist theology does for African American women theologians (Stevens-Arroyo, "Latino/a Catholic Theology," 183); also see Ada María Isasi-Díaz, *En La Lucha/In the Struggle: Elaborating a Mujerista Theology/A Hispanic Women's Liberation Theology* (Minneapolis, MN: Fortress Press, 1993); and *A Reader in US/Latina Feminist Theology: Religion and Justice,* ed. Pilar Aquino, Daisy Machado, and Jeanette Rodriguez (Austin, Tex.: University of Texas Press, 2002).

46. Rose, "Women in the United Farm Workers," 17–25.

47. Ibid., 25–40. As of 1960, only 14.2 percent of U.S. Latinas graduated from high school and only 3.2 percent had entered college (*Who's Who in Labor* [Arno Press, 1976], 283, cited in Rose, "Women in the United Farm Workers," 27).

48. Rose, "Women in the United Farm Workers," 67–71, 74–95.

49. Ibid., 47–48, 57n25, 72–74, 94–103.

50. Ibid., 117, 130–34, and 139–51, 165–91.

51. Rodriguez, *Our Lady of Guadalupe: Faith and Empowerment among Mexican-American Women,* xviii–xxi, xxvi, xxxii, 48, 64, 69–72, 138, 160, the quotes coming from p. 48.

52. Ibid., 120–21, 128, 130–32, 135, 150–51, 154–55, 163–65, the quote coming from p. 130. Also see Kristy Nabhan-Warren, "Mary," in *Handbook of Latina/o Theologies,* ed. Edwin David Aponte and Miguel A. La Torre (St. Louis, Mo.: Chalice Press, 2006), 243–49.

53. Randall, "Guadalupe, Subversive Virgin," 113–23.

54. Daisy L. Machado, "Latinas in U.S. Religious History," in *Feminist Intercultural Theology,* ed. Aquino and Rosado-Nunes, 89–108, the quote coming from p. 100.

55. Conversation with Kathy Schmeling, Archivist, Walter P. Reuther Library of Labor and Urban Affairs, Detroit Mich., 4 August 1994.

56. Machado, "Latinas in U.S. Religious History," 101–2; and Lara Medina, "The Challenges and Consequences of Being Latina, Catholic, and Political," in *Latino Religions and Civic Activism in the United States,* ed. Espinosa, Elizondo, and Miranda, 97–110.

57. Taylor, *Chavez and the Farm Workers,* 150, 173, 217–20, 230–36; Levy, *Cesar Chavez,* 201–2, 267–68, 295; Meister and Loftis, *A Long Time Coming,* 140–41, 151–52, 154–60; and Kushner, *Long Road to Delano,* 156, 177–79.

58. *El Macriado* (June 1966), cited in Hoffman, *Ministry of the Dispossessed,* 63.

59. "National Grape Boycott Coordinators," n.d., NFWM, Part II, 38, 3; ibid., 39, 1–6; Hoffman, *Ministry of the Dispossessed,* 58–76, 130–32; circular letter titled "Attention Farm Workers," n.d., NFWM, Part II, 41, 3; untitled circular letter, 16 May 1969, ibid,, 39, 4; untitled circular letter, 14 June 1969, ibid., 38, 24; untitled news release, 6 November 1969, ibid., 38, 38; and letter titled "Boycott Staff Memo from Jim Drake," n.d., ibid., 38, 22.

60. "Resolution on Selective Buying of Table Grapes," Board of Directors of the Northern California Council of Churches, 12 July 1968, NFWM, Part II, 40, 4; "Resolution on Support of Farm Workers," General Board of the NCCC, 13 September 1968, ibid., 40, 4); "Statement in Support of the United Farm Workers Organizing Committee," Central Committee of the World Council of Churches, 22 August 1969, UFW, President, Part I, 70, 14; "A Push for S.F. Grape Boycott," *San Francisco Chronicle,* 31 August 1968, 10; "A Resolution in Support of Farm Workers Adopted by the Seventy-Fifth Convention of the Diocese of Los Angeles," 7 February 1970, NFWM, Part II, 40, 21; "[San Joaquin] Presbytery and the Northern California Council of Churches," 14 July 1968, ibid., 40, 3; *Sierra* [Synod] *Newsletter,* vol. 6, no. 6 (November 1968) in ibid., 40, 31; unidentified news clipping titled "[Southern California] Synod Asks Rights for Agriculture Workers," ibid., 40, 10; "Sanger [United Methodist] Church Urges Reconsideration of Church Council Boycott Resolution," 1 August 1968; the resolution of the board of Zion Reformed Church (UCC) of Lodi, California, titled "To the Northern California Council of Churches Board of Directors," n.d.; and St. Paul's Episcopal Church of Santa Paula's "Resolution on Strikes and Boycotts," 9 October 1968, all in ibid., 40, 4. Also see "Before the Official Church Board of the Belmont Christian Church of Fresno, California," 21 July 1968; and "Resolution Adopted by the First Congregational Church of Berkeley, California," November 1969, both in ibid., 40, 2; and Nazareth Lutheran Church, Turlock, California, "Resolution," n.d., ibid., 40, 3; letter of Everett C. Schneider, Superintendent, UMC, California Conference, Northern District, to Wayne C. Hartmire, 13 November 1968; and letter of Wayne C. Hartmire to Carl W. Segerhammar, President of the Pacific Southwest Synod, LCA, 30 August 1968, both in ibid., 40, 3; Smith, *Grapes of Conflict,* 163–67; and "The E.J.A.C. Proposal," 11 September 1968, NFWM, Part II, 40, 19.

61. Allan Grant, "California Grapes and the Boycott: The Growers' Side of the Story," *Presbyterian Life,* 1 December 1968, 20, 21, 35, 37–39; Allan Grant and Murray Norris, *Clergy Views of Delano and the Grape Boycott* (Fresno, Calif.: Rudell Publishing, 1969); Hoffman, *Ministry of the Dispossessed,* 81–82; Samuel R. Berger, *Dollar Harvest: The Story of the Farm Bureau* (Lexington, Mass.: D. C. Heath, 1971), 89–111, 140–71; letter of Robert J. Cadigan, editor-in-chief of *Presbyterian Life,* to Hartmire, 21 January 1969; and letter of Hartmire to Kenneth Neigh, Board of National Missions, UPCUSA, 23 January 1969, NFWM, Part II, 40, 12; Wayne C. Hartmire, "Servanthood among Seasonal Farm Workers—What Form?" *Presbyterian Life* (1 March 1969): 17–19, 32–33. Also see Wayne C. Hartmire, "The Delano Grape Strike: The Farm Workers' Struggle for Self Determination," Los Angeles, February, 1969 (NFWM, Susan Drake Files, 1, 2); editorial, "By Their Words," by Charles B. Shuman, President, American Farm Bureau Federation, *Nation's Agriculture* (March 1969): 4; and editorial in *The Christian Century* (19 March 1969).

62. Frank Bergon and Murray Norris, *Delano—Another Crisis for the Catholic Church!* (Fresno, Calif.: Rudell Publishing, 1968?); also see Murray Norris, "Chavez and the Catholic Church," *California Farmer* (20 July 1968): 5, 7; *The Delano Grape Story . . . from*

the Growers' View (Delano, Calif.: South Central Farmers Committee, n.d. [Diocese of Fresno Files, not cataloged, hereafter cited as DFF]); also see Gerard E. Sherry, "Farm Labor Problems: The Anguish of Delano," in *Central California Register* (copy in DFF); Cletus Healy, *Battle for the Vineyards* (New York: Twin Circle Publishing, 1969), 6, 23, 31–40; Gary Allen, "The Grapes: Communist Wrath in Delano," *American Opinion* (June 1966), the reference to Hartmire coming from p. 9; and Rex T. Westerfield, "Sour Grapes: The Move to Control Our Food Supply," *American Opinion* (December 1968).

63. George G. Higgins, press release for "The Yardstick," 15 September 1969, ACUA, George Gilmary Higgins Papers, 62, 2, hereafter cited as GGHP, the quotation coming from p. 3; also see the press releases for "The Yardstick," 10 November 1969 and 17 November 1969, GGHP, 62, 2; Higgins and Bole, *Organized Labor and the Church*, 93–95; letters from Higgins to Daniel Lyons, 11 May 1970, and to Dale Francis, editor-in-chief of *Twin Circle*, 23 June 1970, GGHP, 87, 5; NC News Service, "Five Bishops Charge Twin Circle Editorial a 'Gross Fraud,'" GGHP, 94, 1; Dan L. Thrapp, "Priest-Editor Resigns after Boycott Row," *Los Angeles Times*, 23 August 1970, A26; Daniel Lyons, *Twin Circle* (12 July issue); Daniel Lyons, "The Chavez Union is a Hoax," *Life Lines* 12, no. 84 (1970): unidentified page; Ralph de Toledano, *Little Cesar* (Washington, D.C.: Anthem Books, 1971); and press releases for "The Yardstick," 12 April 1970, 19 April 1970, and 10 May 1970, GGHP, 62, 2.

64. Anonymous letter to Leo Maher, Bishop of San Diego, 11 March 1970, Archdiocese of San Diego, Farm Labor—1966 through 1972, Box 30, hereafter cited as ADSD, FL; letter of Clyde E. Shields, Brawley, Calif., to Maher, 26 June 1970; letter of Mrs. W.W. Kelly, Indio, Calif., to Maher, 5 July 1970; letter of Pamela I. Miller, San Diego, Calif., to Maher, 13 May 1971, all in ADSD, FL, 30; letter of William R. Nager Jr., El Cajon, Calif., to Maher, 20 May 1971, Archdiocese of San Diego, United Farm Workers Organizing Committee (1971), 30; and letter of Richard T. Gilbert, Carlsbad, Calif., to Maher, 27 June 1971, ibid.

65. Martin Zaninovich, excerpt from the annual meeting of the Grape and Tree Fruit League, 24 March 1966, reprinted in *St. Joseph Magazine* 67, no. 6 (1966): 14–16.

66. Letter from Roger Mahony to Joseph Donnelly, 4 November 1970, GGHP, 87, 4; and letter of Gerard E. Sherry to George G. Higgins, 11 February 1971, ibid., 5.

67. Letter of grape grower Nick J. Canata, Earlimart, Calif., to Bishop Hugh A. Donohoe, Stockton, n.d., DFF; letter of Max Janes, Kern City, Calif., to Archbishop Joseph T. McGucken, San Francisco, 15 April 1966, Archives of Archdiocese of San Francisco, General Files; and letter of R. N. Blossom, Stockton, Calif., to Bishop Leo Maher, San Diego, 17 May 1971, ADSD, United Farm Workers Organizing Committee (1971), 30; also see Matthiessen, *Sal Si Puedes*, 64–67, 72–77, 246–52, 270–76; and Dunne, *Delano*, 9–10, 105–7.

68. Editorial titled "No Contest," *Catholic Herald* (16 December 1965): 4.

69. Issel, "Faith-Based Activism in American Cities," 525–31; Weber, *Encyclopedia of California's Catholic Heritage*, 254–55; Hugh Donohoe, "A Statement on the Farm-Labor Question," the quotation coming from p. 7, DFF; also see letter of James Vizzard to Donohoe, 9 March 1966, Stanford University Libraries, Department of Special Collections, James L. Vizzard Papers, M324, 7, 1, hereafter cited as JLVP; letter of Vizzard to Mother M. Assumpta, O.S.U., Los Angeles, 29 March 1966, JLVP, M324, 7, 1; and Harry Bernstein, "Catholic Leaders Urge Bargaining at Delano," *Los Angeles Times*, 17 March 1966, Part I, 4, 28.

70. Aloysius J. Willinger, C.Ss.R., "The Delano Strike—the Democratic Solution,"

15 June 1966; letter of Archbishop Joseph T. McGucken, San Francisco, to Willinger, 21 June 1966, both in AASF, General Files; James L. Vizzard, "Comments on Bishop Willinger's Statement: 'The Delano Strike—the Democratic Solution,'" 28 June 1966, and Vizzard, "Further Comments on Bishop Willinger's Statements," 19 July 1966, in JLVP, M324, 4, 10, the quotation above coming from p. 3 of "Comments" (ellipsis in original); also see editorial, "Farm Laborers and Just Wages," *Central California Register*, 14 October 1965; "Our Catholic Church is Involved," *Central California Register*, 21 October 1965, 1, 10, 11; and editorial, "Farm Labor: Church Role in Disputes," *Central California Register*, 4 November 1965, 1.

71. Joan Johnson, "The March Gathers Strength," *San Francisco Monitor*, 24 March 1966, unidentified page; Eugene J. Boyle, "Social Justice in the Archdiocese of San Francisco, 1962–1972—A Personal Reflection," 25–28, AASF, Eugene Boyle Papers; and Eugene J. Boyle, a two-page, untitled draft later published in *America* (Spring 1993) (draft copy in possession of the author); letter of Robert K. Ham, Assistant to the President, DiGiorgio Corporation, to McGucken, 5 May 1966; letter of Donald D. Connors Jr., to McGucken, 14 June 1966; letter of McGucken to legal counsel John F. Duff, 21 June 1966; and letter of McGucken to Donald D. Connors Jr., 21 June 1966, AASF, Boyle Papers, "Delano March"; and Dick Meister, "Delano Growers Blast Church," *San Francisco Chronicle*, 25 March 1966, 1. For biographical information on McGucken see the booklet titled ". . . As a Successor of the Apostles," prepared for the silver jubilee of his episcopal consecration, 19 March 1966, DFF.

72. "Report of the California Catholic Rural Life Directors Meeting, Newman Center, Fresno State College, Fresno, January 31, 1967," AASF, Boyle Papers; letter of John T. Dwyer to McGucken, 24 March 1967, and accompanying two-page document titled "Discussion"; "Minutes of Meeting of California Catholic Rural Life Directors," San Francisco, 30 March 1967; letter of J. Galen Wright, priest of St. Mary's Church, Delano, to McGucken, 12 July 1967; and letter of McGucken to Wright, 19 July 1967, all in ibid.; and "Church Now Tells Growers Which Union to Recognize," *California Farmer* (18 March 1967): unidentified page.

73. "Where Does the Roman Catholic Church Stand on the 'Delano Grape Strike?'" 4 October 1968, statement prepared by the Greater Washington "Don't Buy California Grapes" Committee, Washington, D.C., DFF, the quote coming from p. 5; news releases "Bishop Backs Grape Boycott," 3 July 1968, and "Backs Grape Boycott," 7 July 1968, ibid.; and Gerard E. Sherry, "Nearly 25 Bishops Support Grape Boycott," *Catholic Review* (4 October 1968): A1, 4; "Cardinal Cushing Backs Boycott," 26 November 1968, mimeographed flyer from the Dorchester, Mass., boycott office of the UFWOC AFL-CIO, DFF.

74. Letter of Salandini to César Chávez, 30 September 1965, Stanford University Libraries, Special Collections, Victor P. Salandini Papers, M249, Series I, 1, 16, hereafter cited as VPS; "Sympathy Pilgrimage and Mass, Washington, D.C.," *Washington Evening Star*, 11 April 1966, 1. The cities in which the bell appeared were New York, Newark, Baltimore, Washington, Pittsburgh, Chicago, Detroit, and St. Louis, VPS, M249, Series I, 3, 4.

75. Letter from Roger Mahony to John McCarthy (assistant to Higgins), 20 October 1968; letter from Mahony to McCarthy, 29 October 1968; letter from McCarthy to Mahony, 31 October 1968; letter from Mahony to McCarthy, 2 November 1968; letter from George G. Higgins to Mahony, 4 November 1968; letter from Mahony to Higgins, 6 November 1968; letter from Higgins to Hugh A. Donohoe, 11 November 1968; and two

different documents, both of which are titled "Draft: Proposed NCCB Statement on Farm Labor," n.d.; and brochure titled "Statement on Farm Labor," National Conference of Catholic Bishops, 13 November 1968, all in GGHP, 89, 7. Also see letter from John R. Quinn, Auxiliary Bishop of San Diego, to Timothy Manning, Bishop of Fresno, 28 October 1968, ADSD, FL, 30; "Resolution on Support of Farm Workers," General Board, NCCCUSA, 13 September 1968, Stitt Library Archives, Hispanic-American Institute Records, folder-Migrant Ministry-NCC; letter of Hartmire to Donohoe, 19 November 1968, NFWM, Part II, 40, 17.

76. Costello, *Without Fear or Favor,* 101–2; also see circular letter from Diana Chapman, National Boycott Coordinator, UFWOC, titled "More about the Bishops!" 29 October 1969, NFWM, Part II, 38, 21; letter of Donohoe to Higgins, 7 January 1969, DFF; A. V. Krebs Jr., "Bishop Donohoe Supports Chavez," *Monitor* (17 July 1969): 1, 3; and "Bishop Stresses Labor Union's Right to Exist," *Monitor, Special Farm Labor Supplement* (25 September 1969): 8. On PADRES, see Juan Romero, "Mexican American Priests: History of Padres, 1969–1989," in *Hispanics in the Church: Up from the Cellar,* ed. Philip E. Lampe (San Francisco: Catholic Scholars Press, 1994), 71–94; Antonio M. Stevens-Arroyo, *Prophets Denied Honor:* An Anthology on the Hispanic Church in the United States (Maryknoll, N.Y.: Orbis Books, 1980), 136–40; Moises Sandoval, ed., *Fronteras: A History of the Latin American Church in the U.S.A. since 1513* (San Antonio, Tex.: Mexican American Cultural Center, 1983), 397–403; Lawrence Mosqueda, *Chicanos, Catholicism, and Political Ideology* (Lanham Md.: University Press of America, 1986), 140–49; and Maria Eva Flores, C.D.P., "PADRES," *The New Handbook of Texas,* vol. 5 (Austin: Texas State Historical Association, 1996), 9–10.

77. Costello, *Without Fear or Favor,* 102–5; Higgins and Bole, *Organized Labor and the Church,* 55, 90–91; and Marco G. Prouty, *Cesar Chavez: The Catholic Bishops, and the Farmworkers' Struggle for Social Justice* (Tucson: University of Arizona Press, 2006), 31–66. Also see "Grape Strike Arbitrator Experienced as 'Oiler,'" *Tidings* (7 August 1970): 2; and Higgins, "Tribute to Bishop Joseph F. Donnelly," in "The Yardstick," news release (25 July 1977): unidentified page, GGHP, 62, 2; On Mahony see Charles McCarthy, "Fresno Priest Rolls up Miles, Years in Strike Solution Quest," *Fresno Bee,* 2 August 1970, A1, 18.

78. Levy, *Cesar Chavez,* 304–5; Costello, *Without Fear or Favor,* 103; and Higgins and Bole, *Organized Labor and the Church,* 91. Also see Memorandum of Donohoe to Ad Hoc Committee members, 26 January 1970; and memorandum of Mahony to Donohoe, 5 January 1970; "Report on Week of March 2," 11 March 1970, in DFF; Joseph F. Donnelly, "Report of Ad Hoc Committee on Farm Labor Dispute," Protocol Number 17, submitted to the NCCB conference in San Francisco in April 1970; and memorandum of Higgins to John Cosgrove, 27 February 1970, both in GGHP, 87, 4.

79. "Status report of Mahony to Ad Hoc Committee on Farm Labor," 21 March 1970, DFF: 3; and memorandum of Mahony to Donohoe, "Delano Farm Labor Issue," n.d., DFF. Also see "Antiboycott Moves Get NLRB Sanction," *Fresno Bee,* 20 March 1970, A1, 6; "U.S. Action in Grape Boycott," *San Francisco Chronicle,* 21 March 1970, unidentified page. On Steinberg see letter from Hartmire to Donohoe, 24 June 1968, DFF; letter from Steinberg to Donohoe, 5 July 1968, DFF; and circular letter from Hartmire to "Friends of the Union," 3 July 1968, NFWM, Part II, 41, 2; photocopy of two-page document signed by Chávez, Steinberg, and Donnelly, 1 April 1970, DFF; Levy, *Cesar Chavez,* 305–6; Mahony to Ad Hoc Committee, "Status Report: Farm Labor Dispute," 7 April 1970, DFF; Mahony to Ad Hoc Committee, "Status of the Farm Labor Problem in California," 9 April 1970, DFF; Mahony to Ad Hoc Committee, "Status of the Farm

Labor Problem in California," 12 April 1970, DFF; and "Two Ranchers Agree to UF-WOC Terms," *Fresno Bee,* 12 April 1970, A1, 4.

80. Ad Hoc Committee status reports of 7 April 1970, 9 April 1970, and 12 April 1970, cited in the previous note; Mahony to Ad Hoc Committee, 28 April 1970; Mahony to Ad Hoc Committee, 6 May 1970; Mahony to Ad Hoc Committee, 22 May 1970, all in DFF. Also see Ron Taylor, "Two Growers, Union Sign Grape Pact," *Fresno Bee,* 21 May 1970, A1; and "Big Grape Growers Sign with Union," *San Francisco Chronicle,* 22 May 1970, unidentified page; Ad Hoc Committee status reports of 28 April 1970 and 6 May 1970, cited above; Ron Taylor, "Farmer Says Union Pact Will Help Him," *Fresno Bee,* 3 May 1970, unidentified page; Mahony to Ad Hoc Committee, "Status Report," 17 June 1970: 1–2, DFF; Ad Hoc Committee, "Press Conference," 11 June 1970, DFF; Higgins and Bole, *Organized Labor and the Church,* 92; Costello, *Without Fear or Favor,* 107; Levy, *Cesar Chavez,* 308; Ron Hosie, "Two More Growers Recognize Union," *Press-Enterprise,* 13 June 1970, B1. For a negative experience for the Ad Hoc Committee in the Imperial Valley see "Status Report," 17 June 1970, cited in the previous note; letter of Mahony to Bishop Leo T. Maher, 14 June 1970; "Press Conference," 11 June 1970, both in ADSD, FL, 30; Harry Bernstein, "Growers Snub Bishops in Farm Labor Dispute," *Los Angeles Times,* 13 June 1970, 1, 8; and Richard Ruane, "Growers Criticized by Catholic Bishops," *San Diego Union,* 13 June 1970, 1; letter of John Hurtado to Leo T. Maher, "Brief Report on the Coachella and Imperial Valley," 17 June 1970; "Minutes of the Priests of the Imperial Valley," 22 June 1970; four separate letters of Priests of the Imperial Valley to Maher, all dated 29 June 1970, and signed by Daniel O'Callaghan, V.F., St. Mary's Church, El Centro; letter of O'Callaghan to Maher, 14 July 1970; and letter of Leo T. Maher to O'Callaghan, 15 July 1970, all in ADSD, FL, 30.

81. "Status Report," 6 May 1970: 2, in the aforementioned citation; "Status Report," 22 May 1970: 4, in the previous note; and Mahony to Ad Hoc Committee, "Status Report," 1 July 1970, DFF; also see Mahony to Ad Hoc Committee, "Status Report," 23 July 1970, DFF: 1; Mahony to Ad Hoc Committee, "Status Report," 23 July 1970, cited in aforementioned note; "Reagan Hits Lack of Choice Given Hands," *Los Angeles Times,* 30 July 1970, 2; "Clergy Plans to Maintain Role in Farm Labor," *Fresno Bee,* 30 July 1970, C1, 3; and Leo Rennert, "Bishops Rap Reagan, Murphy Charges in Grape Issue," *Fresno Bee,* 7 August 1970, unidentified page.

82. Ron Taylor, "Delano Grape Strike Ends in Pact Signing," *Fresno Bee,* 29 July 1970, A1, 4; Bill Boyarsky, "Handshakes Seal Pact Ending Grape Boycott," *Los Angeles Times,* 30 July 1970, 1, 28; Ron Taylor, "Chavez, Flushed with Strike Victory, Pledges to Make Grapes Sweet Again," *Sacramento Bee,* 30 July 1970, 2–3; Taylor, *Chavez and the Farm Workers,* 245–48; and Levy, *Cesar Chavez,* 312–14, 322–25.

83. *Central California Register,* 31 July 1970, 2; also see "Report, Bishops' Ad Hoc Committee on the Farm Labor Dispute to the National Conference of Catholic Bishops," 16–20 November 1970, DFF.

84. "Delano Grape Strike Over," *Central California Register,* 31 July 1970, 2; letter of Hartmire to Chavez, 11 May 1970, UFW, Office of President, 68, 10; "Chavez Will Shift Fight Center to Salinas," *Fresno Bee,* 3 August 1970, unidentified page; "Teamsters Claim Signup of Nearly All Major Growers," *Fresno Bee,* 5 August 1970, unidentified page; "'Huelga' is Readied for Lettuce Fields," *Fresno Bee,* 6 August 1970, D1, 6; and Harry Bernstein, "Battle between Teamsters and Chavez Looms," *Los Angeles Times,* 6 August 1970, 3, 20. Also see Mahony to Ad Hoc Committee, "Status Report," 10 August 1970, 18 August 1970, 26 August 1970, 19 October 1970, 18 January 1971, 8 May 1971, all in DFF;

Costello, *Without Fear or Favor*, 109–116; Higgins and Bole, *Organized Labor and the Church*, 97–100; and Levy, *Cesar Chavez*, 338–42, 353–57, 364–80, 391–93, 400–401.

85. Levy, *Cesar Chavez*, 327–36, 353–424, 434–39, 475–534; Taylor, *Chavez and the Farm Workers*, 248–62, 265, 272–79, 290–315, 318; Meister and Loftis, *A Long Time Coming*, 165–72, 215–18; and Kushner, *Long Road to Delano*, 207–12.

86. Jenkins, *The Politics of Insurgency*, 167, 173.

87. Hartmire, five-page document titled "Sharing Power"; also "The Church and the Delano Grape Strike—A Partial Report," 1, 7, 8; and "The Church and the Emerging Farm Workers' Movement," 1–4.

88. The Bishops' Ad Hoc Committee remained active until 1975 (Mahony to Ad Hoc Committee, "Status Report," 27 January 1975 [DFF]; and Costello, *Without Fear or Favor*, 116). Also see Ron Taylor, "Bishop Mahony Will Head State Farm Labor Board," *Fresno Bee*, 27 July 1975, 1–2.

Chapter 5

1. T. R. Fehrenbach, *Seven Keys to Texas* (El Paso: Texas Western Press, 1983; revised ed., 1986), 80; Jordan, "The Imprint of the Upper and Lower South on Mid-Nineteenth-Century Texas," 667–90; Carter E. Boren, *Religion on the Texas Frontier* (San Antonio, Tex.: Naylor, 1968); Daisy Machado, *Of Borders and Margins: Hispanic Disciples in Texas, 1888–1945*, AAR Academy Series, ed. Carole Myscofski (New York: Oxford University Press, 2003), 81–87; John W. Storey, "Baptist Church," *The New Handbook of Texas*, vol. 1, 375; R. L. Roberts, "Church of Christ," ibid., vol. 2, 105–6; A. G. Wiederaenders, W. A. Flachmeier, and Russell A. Vardell, "Lutheran Church," ibid., vol. 4, 340–41; Walter N. Vernon, "Methodist Church," ibid., vol. 4, 645–46; John R. Hendrick, "Presbyterian Church," ibid., vol. 5, 327; Lawrence L. Brown, "Protestant Episcopal Church," ibid., vol. 5, 359–60; and Terry G. Jordan, John L. Bean, William M. Holmes, *Texas: A Geography* (Boulder, Colo.: Westview Press, 1984), 115–22, in which the term *shatter belt* originates.

2. Linda K. Pritchard, "A Comparative Approach to Western Religious History: Texas as a Case Study," *Western Historical Quarterly* 19 (November 1988): 413–30; Samuel H. Lowerie, "Culture Conflict in Texas" (master's thesis, Columbia University, 1932), 52–58, 132–40; and Bernard Doyon, *The Calvary of Christ on the Rio Grande, 1849–1883* (Milwaukee: Bruce Publishing, 1956).

3. The term *Rio Grande Valley* of Texas refers to the southernmost part of the state, which is comprised of the present-day border counties of Cameron, Willacy, Hidalgo, and Starr.

4. Carlos E. Castaneda, *Our Catholic Heritage in Texas*, vol. 6, *The Fight for Freedom, 1810–1836* (Austin, Tex.: Von Boeckmann-Jones, 1958), 307–45; Carlos E. Castaneda, *Our Catholic Heritage in Texas*, vol. 7, *The Church in Texas since Independence, 1836–1950* (Austin, Tex.: Von Boeckmann-Jones, 1958), 7–43; and James T. Moore, *Through Fire and Flood: The Catholic Church in Frontier Texas, 1836–1900* (College Station: Texas A&M University Press, 1992), 3, 10–35.

5. Moore, *Through Fire and Flood*, 79, 83–96, 98–99; Carmen Tafolla, "The Church in Texas," in Sandoval, ed., *Fronteras*, 183–89; Doyon, *The Calvary of Christ on the Rio Grande*, 60–66, 83, 119–41, 164–75; Gilberto Rafael Cruz and Martha Oppert Cruz, *A Century of Service: The History of the Catholic Church in the Lower Rio Grande Valley*

(Harlingen, Tex.: United Printers and Publishers, 1979), 17–20; José Roberto Juárez, "La Iglesia Católica y el Chicano en Sud Texas, 1836–1911," *Aztlán* 4, no. 2 (1974): 217–55; and Randolph Campbell, *Gone to Texas: A History of the Lone Star State* (New York: Oxford University Press, 2003), the reference "the Nueces Strip" coming from p. 189.

6. Moore, *Through Fire and Flood,* 70–75, 102–11, 146, 166, 181; Donald Meinig, *Imperial Texas: An Interpretive Essay in Cultural Geography* (Austin: University of Texas Press, 1969), 51–54; Jordan et al., *Texas: A Geography,* 83–92, 120–22; Terry G. Jordan, "A Century and a Half of Ethnic Change in Texas, 1836–1986," *Southwestern Historical Quarterly* 89, no. 4 (1986): 408–14.

7. Moore, *Through Fire and Flood,* 150, 158, 173–74, the block quotation coming from p. 183; Hinojosa, "Mexican-American Faith Communities in Texas and the Southwest," 21–23, 66, 74; and Carmen Tafolla, "Expansion of the Church in Texas," in *Fronteras: A History of the Latin American Church in the USA since 1513,* ed. Moises Sandoval (San Antonio, Tex.: Mexican-American Cultural Center, 1983), 225–31; Castaneda, *The Fight for Freedom,* 165–205, 285–321, 387, 418–19; Abell, *American Catholicism and Social Action,* 157; Patrick H. McNamara, "Bishops, Priests, and Prophecy: A Study in the Sociology of Religious Protest" (Ph.D. diss., University of California at Los Angeles, 1968), 72–73; Moore, *Acts of Faith,* 17–18, 21–23, 83–85, 99–101, 110–14, 125–28, 133–39, 150–55, 160–77, the block quotation coming from p. 183; Richard Garcia, *The Rise of the Mexican American Middle Class: San Antonio, 1929–1941* (College Station: Texas A&M University Press, 1991), 161–62; Cruz and Cruz, *A Century of Service,* 26, 28–33; and Juárez, "La Iglesia Católica y el Chicano en Sud Texas, 1836–1911," 219–22, 224, 228–32, 234–42, 245, 246.

8. The "Gone to Texas" phrase serves as the main theme of Randolph Campbell's synthetic work *Gone to Texas;* also see Jordan, "The Imprint of the Upper and Lower South on Mid-Nineteenth-Century Texas," the quotation coming from p. 74.

9. Hendrick, "Presbyterian Church," 327; R. Douglas Brackenridge and Francisco O. García-Treto, *Iglesia Presbiteriana: A History of Presbyterian and Mexican Americans in the Southwest* (San Antonio, Tex.: Trinity University Press, 1974, rev. ed., 1989), 3; Brown, "Protestant Episcopal Church," 359–60; Vernon, "Methodist Church," the quotation is from p. 645. Also see Walter N. Vernon, *The Methodist Excitement in Texas* (Dallas: Texas United Methodist Historical Society, 1984); Story, "Baptist Church," 375; R. L. Roberts, "Church of Christ," 105–6; and Machado, *Of Borders and Margins,* 86–87.

10. Edwin Sylvest, "Hispanic American Protestantism in the United States," in *Fronteras,* ed. Sandoval, 291–95; Story, "Baptist Church," 375; and Grebler et al., *The Mexican American People,* 492.

11. John C. Rayburn, "Melinda Rankin—Crusader of the Rio Grande," *Journal of Presbyterian History* 40 (September 1962): 60–80, the references to the phrases "Abolition Society" and "not in sympathy with the Southern Confederacy" on pp. 167 and 168, respectively; Brackenridge and García-Treto, *Iglesia Presbiteriana,* 10–12; Grebler et al., *The Mexican American People,* 489–90; Martha Caroline Mitchell Remy, "Protestant Churches and Mexican-Americans in South Texas" (Ph.D. diss., University of Texas at Austin, 1970), 116–20; and Sylvest, "Hispanic American Protestantism in the Southwest," 296–97.

12. Alfredo Nañez and Clotilde Nañez, "Methodism among the Spanish-Speaking of Texas," in *The History of Texas Methodism,* ed. Olin Nail (Austin, Tex.: Capital Printing, 1961), 193–97; and Alfredo Nañez, "Methodism among the Spanish-Speaking People in Texas and New Mexico," in *One in the Lord: A History of Ethnic Minorities in the South Central Jurisdiction, The United Methodist Church,* ed. Walter N. Vernon (Bethany,

Okla.: Cowan Printing and Litho, 1977), 53–61; and Sylvest, "Hispanic American Protestantism in the United States," 298–308.

13. Brackenridge and García-Treto, *Iglesia Presbiteriana:*, 17–31, the quotation coming from p. 31; also see R. Douglas Brackenridge, "Botello, José Maria," *The New Handbook of Texas,* vol. 1, 659.

14. Joshua Grijalva, *A History of Mexican Baptists in Texas, 1881–1981* (Dallas: Baptist General Convention of Texas, 1982), 12–16; and Sylvest, "Hispanic American Protestantism," 315–16.

15. Grebler et al., *The Mexican American People,* 489–90, the term "pariah people" coming from p. 504; Brackenridge and García-Treto, *Iglesia Presbiteriana:*, 12–14, Remy, "The Protestant Church and Mexican-Americans in South Texas," 86–87, 117–20; Walter L. Buenger, "Texas and the South," *Southwestern Historical Quarterly,* vol. 103, no. 3 (2000): 309–23; and Campbell, *Gone to Texas,* 207, 214, 227–28, 232–34, 290–91, 325, 438.

16. Nañez and Nañez, "Methodism among the Spanish-Speaking of Texas," 206–7; Walter N. Vernon, "Lydia Patterson Institute," *The New Handbook of Texas,* vol. 4, 343; Brackenridge and García-Treto, *Iglesia Presbiteriana,* 33–62; 101–9; David Gifford, "Presbyterian Pan American School," *The New Handbook of Texas,* vol. 5, 328–29; Keith Guthrie, "Presbyterian School for Mexican Girls," ibid., 329; Ernest E. Atkinson, "Mexican Baptist Institute," ibid., 683; and Nañez, "Methodism among the Spanish-Speaking People in Texas and New Mexico," 71–78. Also see Paul Barton, "¡Ya Basta! Latino/a Protestant Activism in the Chicano/a and Farm Workers Movements," in *Latino Religions and Civic Activism in the United States,* ed. Espinosa, Elizondo, and Miranda, 127, 140; and Paul Barton, *Hispanic Methodists, Presbyterians, and Baptists in Texas,* Jack and Doris Smothers Series in Texas History, Life, and Culture, no. 18 (Austin: University of Texas Press, 2006).

17. Brackenridge and García-Treto, *Iglesia Presbiteriana,* 143; Seymour V. Connor, "Onderdonk, Frank Scovill," *The New Handbook of Texas,* vol. 4, 1153; and Machado, *Of Borders and Margins,* 97–98.

18. Armando C. Alonzo, *Tejano Legacy: Rancheros and Settlers in South Texas, 1734–1900* (Albuquerque: University of New Mexico Press, 1998), 5–12, 74–78, 96–98, 107–12, 128–43, 146–48, 162, 167, 171–72, 178–81, 223–28, 235–39, 251–56, 266–67. Also see Montejano, *Anglos and Mexicans in the Making of Texas,* 103–17; Edwin J. Foscue, "Agricultural History of the Lower Rio Grande Valley Region," *Agricultural History* 8 (March 1934): 124–38; and Arnoldo De León, *The Tejano Community, 1836–1900* (Albuquerque: University of New Mexico Press, 1982), 78–85.

19. Camilo Amado Martinez, "The Mexican and Mexican-American Laborers in the Lower Rio Grande Valley of Texas, 1870–1930" (Ph.D. diss., Texas A&M University, 1987), 22–48, 73–78, 89, 102, 125–32, the block quotation coming from p. 15. Also see Montejano, *Anglos and Mexicans in the Making of Texas,* 103–17; McWilliams, *North from Mexico,* 83–88; and J. Lee Stambaugh and Lillian J. Stambaugh, *The Lower Rio Grande Valley of Texas* (San Antonio, Tex.: Naylor, 1954), 160–238.

20. Ruth Allen, *Chapters in the History of Organized Labor in Texas* (Austin: University of Texas Press, 1941); and Ruth A. Allen, George N. Green, and James V. Reese, "Labor Organizations," *The New Handbook of Texas,* vol. 3, 1181.

21. Emilio Zamora, *The Mexican Worker in Texas* (College Station: Texas A&M University Press, 1993), 19, 40–53, 55–56, 58–62, 69–80, 110, 148–52, 162–93; Montejano, *Anglos and Mexicans in the Making of Texas,* 32–34, 117–19, 122–128; Campbell, *Gone to*

Texas, 193–94, 328; Acuña, *Occupied America,* 26–41; Robert M. Utley, *Lone Star Justice: The First Century of the Texas Rangers* (New York: Berkley Books, 2002); Benjamin Heber Johnson, *Revolution in Texas: How a Forgotten Rebellion and Its Bloody Suppression Turned Mexicans into Americans* (New Haven, Conn.: Yale University Press, 2003); Mary Margaret McAllen Amberson, *I Would Rather Sleep in Texas: A History of the Lower Rio Grande Valley and the People of the Santa Anita Land Grant* (Austin: Texas State Historical Association, 2003), 161–74, 463–97; Robert C. Overfelt, "Mexican Revolution," *The New Handbook of Texas,* vol. 4, 688; and Stuart Jamieson, *Labor Unionism in American Agriculture,* reprint ed., The Chicano Heritage Series (New York: Arno Press, 1976), the block quotation coming from p. 270.

22. Jamieson, *Labor Unionism in American Agriculture,* 270–78; Victor B. Nelson Cisneros, "La Clase Trabajadora en Tejas, 1920–1940," *Aztlán* 6, no. 2 (1975): 239–65; and Archives of the Missionary Oblates of Mary Immaculate of Texas, San Antonio, Texas, Charles Taylor Collection, Folder 1J1, letters to Provincial Superior Theodore Laboure, 10 April 1932, and 15 April 1932; letter from Laboure, 19 April 1932; letters to Provincial Superior J. W. Cozad, 24 December 1932, 28 December 1932, and 6 January 1933; and letter to Provincial Superior Arthur C. Dusseau, 27 December 1935.

23. J. Gilberto Quesada, "Toward a Working Definition of Social Justice: Father Carmelo A. Trancese, S.J., and Our Lady of Guadalupe Parish, 1932–1953," *Journal of Texas Catholic History and Culture* 4, no. 4 (1993): 44–64.

24. Quesada, "Toward a Working Definition of Social Justice," 46, 49–50; Jamieson, *Labor Unionism in American Agriculture,* 278–81; Cisneros, "La Clase Trabajadora en Tejas," 253–54; and Garcia, *The Rise of the Mexican-American Middle Class in San Antonio,* 63, 72–86, 158–74; Gutiérrez, *Walls and Mirrors,* 107–9; Castenada, *The Fight for Freedom,* 478; David Lewis Filewood, "Tejano Revolt: The Significance of the 1938 Pecan Shellers Strike" (master's thesis, University of Texas at Arlington, 1994), 85–87; Zaragosa Vargas, "Tejana Radical: Emma Tenayuca and the San Antonio Labor Movement during the Great Depression," *Pacific Historical Review* 66, no. 4 (1997): 553–80; and Roberto R. Calderon and Emilio Zamora, "Manuela Solis Sager and Emma Tenayuca: A Tribute," in *Chicana Voices: Intersections of Class, Race, and Gender,* ed. Teresa Córdova, Norma Cantú, Gilberto Cardenas, Juan García, and Christine M. Sierra (Austin: Center for Mexican American Studies, University of Texas, 1986; the National Association for Chicano Studies, 1990; Albuquerque: University of New Mexico Press, 1993), 30–41. Also see Teresa Palomo Acosta and Ruth Winegarten, *Las Tejanas: 300 Years of History* (Austin: University of Texas Press, 2003).

25. Letter of J. Marshall Janes of the People's Community Church to Adela Ballard, NCC, HMNNAR, RG 26, CWHM, box 15, folder 28, in "Report for March and April, 1932," 4–5.

26. "December 1932 Report," 2; "May–September 1933 Report," 1; "Migrant Work in Western Fields—1933," all in NCC, HMCNAR, RG 26, CWHM, 15, 28; "Report of Western Supervisor, February 1–March 15, 1934," ibid., 15, 29: 3; "Report of Western Supervisor, January, 1936, with Glimpses of November–December, 1935," 1; "Report of Western Supervisor, Council of Women for Home Missions, May to November, 1936," in ibid.

27. Verda Berge, "Report of Mid-West Work, Alamo, Texas, November, 1942"; and Emmett B. Waite, "Report of Mid-West Work, Weslaco and Harlingen, November 29, 1942," both in NCC, HMCNAR, RG 26, CWHM, 15, 16: 1–2 and 1–2, respectively; Helen White, "March–April, 1941 Report," ibid., 12, 25: 3; Helen White, "Migrant Work

Midwest Area Reports, February 1942," NCC, HMCNAR, RG 26, CWHM, 15, 16: 3 pp.; and Eugene Turner, "Report of Mid-West Work, Alamo, Texas, December, 1942," NCC, HMCNAR, RG 26, CWHM, 15, 16: 1. Also see Paul S. Taylor, *An American-Mexican Frontier: Nueces County, Texas* (Chapel Hill: University of North Carolina Press, 1934), 269–72, 296; and Ozzie G. Simmons, *Anglo Americans and Mexican Americans in South Texas: A Study in Dominant-Subordinate Group Relations* (Ph.D. diss., Harvard University, 1952; reprint ed., New York: Arno Press, 1974), 153–55, 460; Lewis L. Gould, "Progressives and Prohibitionists: Texas Democratic Politics, 1911–1921," *Southwestern Historical Quarterly* 75 (July 1971): 5–18; and Grebler et al., *The Mexican American People*, 499.

28. Shelford, *Protestant Cooperation in Northern California*, 23, 26–29, 31–34; Helen White, "March 1940 Report," NCC, HMCNA, RG 26, CWHM, 12, 25: 3–4; and "Report to the Executive Committee of the National Committee of Church Women, September 21, 1940," ibid., 3; and Harold Kilpatrick, "The Last That Became First: A History of the Texas Council of Churches, 1953–1969," unpublished paper in possession of author.

29. George N. Green, "Good Neighbor Commission," *The New Handbook of Texas*, vol. 3, 240; also see Gutiérrez, *Walls and Mirrors*, 138–40.

30. Acuña, *Occupied America*, 262–63; Dorothy Knowles [Eagle Pass], Veda Burge [Alamo], and Samuel Rocha [Harlingen and Brownsville], "Reports, 1945," NCC, HMCNA, RG 26, Box 15, File 16; Veda Burge, "Report, February 1943"; and Justa Campa, "Report, November 1945," both in ibid.; "Forward with Faith" document, 1949; Samuel Rocha, "Report: West Texas Areas, and Rio Grande Valley, Texas, November–December 1949"; "Report of Donald L. West, Beginning in the Southwest, October–November 1950"; and letter of Donald L. West to Mr. Ellis, 15 December 1950, all in ibid., 17; Monica B. Owen, "Report of the Migrant Work in the Midwest Area, 1951–1952"; W. E. Scholes, "1953 Preliminary Field Report, Midwest," both in NCC, DHMR, RG 7, 9, 2: 2–3 and 5, respectively; and "Minutes of the National Migrant Committee," 19 September 1952, ibid., 4, 22: 3–5; letter from Fred H. Husbands, Executive Vice President and General Manager of the West Texas Chamber of Commerce, to Edith E. Lowry, 2 September 1954; and letter from Harold Kilpatrick to Edith E. Lowry, 27 August 1954, both in ibid., 5, 3.

31. Letters from William E. Scholes to Edith E. Lowry, 21 November 1952; 14 March 1953; 7 October 1953; and Lowry to Scholes, 8 April 1954, all in ibid.; Scholes, "Annual Report of the Central Region Director for the Migrant Ministry," 12 November 1954, ibid., 9, 2: 7–8; letters from Scholes to Lowry, 23 December 1954; 4 January 1955; 23 February 1955; 18 March 1956, all in ibid., 8, 16; also see Kilpatrick, "The Last That Became First," 63–65; "1958 Farm Placement Estimates," ibid., 1, 17; and "California Harvester" newsletter, Fall 1958, ibid. 9, 8; Betty Whitaker, "Texas Migrant Ministry, 1958 Program, Part I, May–Sept. 12, 1958," ibid., 11, 5; "Texas Council of Churches, Sixth Annual Meeting, Minutes, Message to Churches, and Committee Reports," 10–12 March 1959, Texas Council of Churches General Files, 7; and "Minutes of the Semi-Annual Meeting of the General Board, Texas Council of Churches," 15 July 1959, ibid., 3.

32. Jon L. Regier and William H. Koch Jr., "Summary of DHM Movement in Citizenship Education-Fundamental Education-Community Development," Appendix C, 8 December 1961, NCC, DHMR, RG 7, 1, 14; "Minutes from the Commission for Cooperative Field Projects," 1 October 1961, ibid., 2, 16, p. 6; and William H. Koch Jr., "The 'Dual Approach'—an Alternative in Community Development," 3 July 1963, ibid., 3, 10; Louisa R. Shotwell, "Report on the Rural Fringe Ministry in California, Arizona, Texas," attached 30-page report subtitled, "Weslaco, Texas"; William H. Koch Jr., "Mi-

grant Citizenship Education: A Preliminary Report," 1 October 1960, ibid., Community Development, 1961–63, 3, 10, the quote coming from p. 3. Also see Donald E. Post and Walter E. Smith, *Clergy: Outsiders and Adversaries; The Story of Catholic and Protestant Clergy's Attempts to Relate the Gospel in Three South Texas Towns Experiencing Changing Mexicano/Anglo Relationships during the Period of 1945–1975*, National Endowment for the Humanities Grant, No. RS-26255–531, n.d., 37–102.

33. Theodore Radtke, Executive Secretary of the BCSS, "The Catholic Church and the Mexican Migrant Workers," May 1950, University of Notre Dame Archives, Lucey Papers, Bishops' Committee on the Spanish Speaking—Regional Office, 1945–1950, 17, 3, hereafter cited as UNDA, Lucey Papers, BCSS, 8.

34. "Report to Members of the American Hierarchy by Archbishop Robert E. Lucey for Bishops' Committee on the Spanish Speaking, Wednesday, November 14, 1956"; and "Our Catholic Southwest," n.d., both in UNDA, Lucey Papers, CLUC, 13, 8; Robert E. Lucey, untitled report, 12 November 1958, ibid., 13, 9: 2; and "Minutes of the Meeting of the Bishops' Committee for the Spanish Speaking, Catholic University, D.C., November 18, 1959," ibid., BCSS—General Correspondence, 18, 5: 3–6.

35. Letter from Robert E. Lucey to the Rev. William D. O'Connor and the Rev. Joseph H. Crosthwait, Field Representative, BCSS, n.d.; letter from Lucey to O'Connor and Crosthwait, 10 October 1956; "Father O'Connor's Talk to the Bishops," n.d.; letter from Lucey to O'Connor, 13 December 1956, all in UNDA, Lucey Papers, CLUC, 13, 8; letter from Crothwait to Lucey, 1 November 1957; letter from O'Connor to Lucey, 25 January 1957; untitled report of Crosthwait to Lucey, n.d., all in ibid., BCSS—Regional Office, 1957, 16, 4; and "Minutes of the Meeting of the Bishops' Committee for the Spanish Speaking, Catholic University [of America, Washington,] D.C., November 11, 1959," ibid., BCSS—General Correspondence, 1957–59, 18, 5; Robert E. Lucey's BCSS report of 15 November 1961, ibid., CLUC, 13, 8: 1–2; "Report to the American Hierarchy on the Work of the Regional Office of the BCSS by Most Rev. Robert E. Lucey, S.T.D., Archbishop of San Antonio, Executive Chairman of the Bishops' Committee on the Spanish Speaking, in Washington, D.C., November 17, 1954"; "Remarks of Most Rev. Robert E. Lucey, S.T.D., Executive Chairman of the BCSS, November 16, 1955"; "Report to Members of the American Hierarchy by Archbishop Lucey for Bishops' Committee for the Spanish Speaking, Wednesday, November 14, 1956"; "Meeting of the BCSS, Washington, D.C., Wednesday, November 12, 1958"; Robert E. Lucey, "Annual Report for Wednesday, November 18, 1959"; and Lucey's annual BCSS report, 1964, all in ibid., CLUC, 13, 8: 3, 1–2, 2, 1, 4, and 2–3, respectively; letter from Crosthwait to Lucey, 15 December 1956, ibid., CLUC, 13, 8; untitled report of Crosthwait to Lucey, n.d., ibid., BCSS Regional Office, 1957, 16, 4: 4; and "Minutes of the Meeting of the Bishops' Committee for the Spanish Speaking, Catholic University, D.C., November 18, 1959," ibid., BCSS—General Correspondence, 1957–59, 18, 5: 3–6. Also see Post and Smith, *Clergy: Outsiders and Adversaries,* 189–90; and Montejano, *Anglos and Mexicans in the Making of Texas,* 271–74.

36. *Faith Expressions of Hispanics in the Southwest,* vol. 1, *Workshops on Hispanic Liturgy and Popular Piety* (San Antonio, Tex.: Mexican American Cultural Center, 1983?), 16.

37. Ibid., 15–21; Karen Hastings, "Shrine's History Draws Faithful to Healing Mass," *Dallas Morning News,* 29 August 1999, A49, 51; and Dulcinea Cuellar, "Shrine of the Times: Visitors Flock to Basilica for Spiritual Needs," *The Monitor* [McAllen, Tex.], unidentified date in 2002, A1, 6. Also see "Don Pedro Jaramillo," Texas historical marker, Falfurrias, Tex.; Tafolla, "Expansion of the Church in Texas," 231–34; and Hinojosa, "Mexican American Faith Communities in Texas and the Southwest," 92–94.

Chapter 6

1. Montejano, *Anglos and Mexicans in the Making of Texas*, 262–64, 268–71, 274–84; Gutiérrez, *Walls and Mirrors*, 141–46, 152–55, 161–67, 176, 183–87; Acuña, *Occupied America*, 275–77, 282–84, 311–14; Gómez-Quiñones, *Chicano Politics*, 97–98, 129–31; and Gutiérrez, *The Making of a Chicano Militant*, 34–63, 101–4.

2. Ray Robert Leal, "The 1966–1967 South Texas Farm Worker Strike: A Case Study of Farm Worker Powerlessness" (Ph.D. diss., Indiana University, 1983; Ann Arbor Mich.: University Microfilms International, 1986), 110–17; Jan Hart Cohen, "To See Christ in Our Brothers: The Role of the Texas Roman Catholic Church in the Rio Grande Valley Farm Workers' Movement, 1966–1967" (master's thesis, University of Texas at Arlington, 1974), 110–12; Gómez-Quiñones, *Mexican American Labor*, 255; *Vernon's Annotated Civil Statutes of the State of Texas*, Art. 5154d and 5154f, cited in Ben Procter, "The Modern Texas Rangers: A Law-Enforcement Dilemma in the Rio Grande Valley," in *The Mexican-Americans: An Awakening Minority*, ed. Manuel P. Servin (Beverly Hills, Calif.: Glencoe Press, 1970), 222–23; and *Texas Government*, "Chapter 14: Labor Legislation and Administration," copy found in NFWM, Part II, Box 26, Folder 8: 264–81; and one-page handwritten document titled "Comments of Larry Goodwyn, former Executive Director of [the] Texas Democratic Coalition" (Texas version of C.D.C.), n.d., Walter P. Reuther Archives of Urban and Labor History, Wayne State University, UFW, Office of the President, II, Box 33, Folder 21, "Texas Organizing 1966–1967."

3. The phrase "lost cause" was used several times by Dr. Harold Kilpatrick, former Director of the Texas Council of Churches (in an interview with the author, 20 September 1994).

4. Bob McDonald, "Farming Big Valley Business," *Valley Evening Monitor*, 27 October 1965, A2; "Agriculture Income Up in Valley," *Brownsville Herald*, 30 June 1965, A16; "Midwesterners Flock into City, Send Registrations over 3,000," *Brownsville Herald*, 23 January 1966, A2; "Valley's 1966 Influx of Tourists Biggest in History," *Brownsville Herald*, 10 April 1966, A3; "Tourism Shows Big Increase Here," *San Benito News*, 23 January 1967, 1; Cohen, "To See Christ in Our Brothers," 23–24; and Charles Carr Winn, "The Valley Farm Workers Movement, 1966–1967" (master's thesis, University of Texas at Austin, 1970), 17–18.

5. Cohen, "To See Christ in Our Brothers," 23; "One Thousand Miles of Poverty," *Texas Observer*, 5 February 1965, 4–5. Also see "Houston Paper Does Its Annual Smear Job on Us," *Brownsville Herald*, 28 October 1965, A4; and "Hatchet Job on Life in Valley," *Valley Evening Monitor*, 28 October 1965, 4.

6. "Transcribed Recollection of Mr. Larry Skoog," Oral History 23, Labor Archives at the University of Texas at Arlington, November 1971, 1–7. Also see Cohen, "To See Christ in Our Brothers," 24–26; and Winn, "The Valley Farm Workers Movement," 20–23.

7. Leal, "The 1966–1967 South Texas Farm Strike," 254; and Winn, "The Valley Farm Workers Movement," 20–21; "A Long Struggle with La Casita," *Texas Observer* 50, no. 11 (1966): 1–5; and "On Being a Labor Organizer," *Texas Observer* 58, no. 16 (1966): 1, 3.

8. Cohen, "To See Christ in Our Brothers," 26–27; Leal, "The 1966–1967 South Texas Farm Strike," 255–56; and Winn, "The Valley Farm Workers Movement," 24–25.

9. Leal, "The 1966–1967 South Texas Farm Strike," 257; Winn, "The Valley Farm Workers Movement," 24–27; and Cohen, "To See Christ in Our Brothers," 27–28.

10. Cohen, "To See Christ in Our Brothers," 33–36, 40; and Saul Bronder, *Social Justice and Church Authority: The Public Life of Archbishop Robert E. Lucey* (Philadelphia: Temple University Press, 1982), 100–106.

11. "Priests and Strikers Picket Bridges at Hidalgo and Roma," *Brownsville Herald,* 8 June 1966, 1, 10; "Priests Lead Farm Picket Rights March," *Brownsville Herald,* 17 June 1966, 1–9; "Revolution Underway in Rio Grande Valley," *Houston Post,* 12 June 1966, 1, 14; "Viva la Huelga," *Alamo Messenger,* 17 June 1966, 4; and Cohen, "To See Christ in Our Brothers," 28–31, 33; also see Winn, "The Valley Farm Workers Movement," 29–30.

12. "Area Padres 'Hot under Collar' over Priests Joining Strikers," *Brownsville Herald,* 20 June 1966, 1, 8; editorial "Monsignor Speaks Out on Priests and Strike," *Brownsville Herald,* 20 June 1966, 3; "Msgr. Ralph Joins Protest on 'Marchers,'" *Valley Evening Monitor,* 20 June 1966, 1, 3; "Support Pours in for Laning Stand," *Brownsville Herald,* 21 June 1966, 1, 6; "Archbishop Supports Priests in 'Huelga,'" *Alamo Messenger,* 24 June 1966, 1, 10; Cohen, "To See Christ in Our Brothers," 35–39; Winn, "The Valley Farm Workers Movement," 34–35; and Patrick McNamara, "Bishops, Priests, and Prophecy: A Study in the Sociology of Religious Protest" (Ph.D. diss., University of California at Los Angeles, 1968), 149.

13. "Bishop Marx Appointed Head of New Brownsville Diocese," *Valley Evening Monitor,* 21 July 1965, 1; "New Brownsville Diocese Will Minister to 234,700 Catholics in Four County Area," *Brownsville Herald,* 1 September 1965, C6; "Bishop Marx, 50, Dies in Germany," *Valley Evening Monitor,* 1 November 1965, 1, 3; "Bishop Marx Is Dead," *Brownsville Herald,* 1 November 1965, 1, 10; "Msgr. Medeiros Named Bishop of Catholic Diocese of Brownsville," *Brownsville Herald,* 20 April 1966, 1; "New Brownsville Diocese Bishop is Consecrated," *Valley Morning Star* [Harlingen, Tex.], 10 June 1966, 1; "New Head of Diocese to Arrive in Brownsville," *Corpus Christi Caller,* 26 June 1966, 1, 10; "Leave Economic Details 'To Experts'—Medeiros," *Brownsville Herald,* 27 June 1966, 1, 3; "Clergy, Laymen Here for Bishop Medeiros' Installation," *Brownsville Herald,* 28 June 1966, A1, 8; "Medeiros Installed Here," *Brownsville Herald,* 29 June 1966, A1, 12; Cohen, "To See Christ in Our Brothers," 42–45; and Bronder, *Social Justice and Church Authority,* 113–14.

14. "Strike March Due in Mission Today," *Corpus Christi Caller,* 5 July 1966, 16; "Medeiros Asks Study by Church," *Corpus Christi Caller,* 7 July 1966, unidentified page; "Medeiros Readying Guidelines," *Corpus Christi Caller,* 8 July 1966, unidentified page; "Bishop Endorses $1.25 Minimum Farm Wage," *Corpus Christi Caller,* 9 July 1966, unidentified page; "Brownsville Bishop Backs Higher Pay," *Alamo Messenger,* 15 July 1966, 1, 10; Winn, "The Valley Farm Workers Movement," 42–47; Cohen, "To See Christ in Our Brothers," 46–50; and Jack Nathan Avant, "The 1966 Rio Grande Farm Workers Strike: Role of the Church" (master's thesis, University of Texas at Austin, 1967), 16–18.

15. "Ignoring Marchers Draws Raps," *Valley Morning Star,* 16 July 1966, 1, 3; "Strike Marchers' Boots Thin," *Valley Morning Star,* 20 July 1966, 1, 3; "Heat Takes Toll among Marchers," *Valley Morning Star,* 22 July 1966, 8; "Huelgistas Head for Corpus Christi," *Alamo Messenger,* 29 July 1966, 1, 10; "Eight of the Marchers," *Texas Observer.* 58, no. 14 (1966): 3; "The March into Corpus Christi," *Texas Observer* 58, no. 14 (1966): 4–5; Winn, "The Valley Farm Workers Movement," 47–50; Cohen, "To See Christ in Our Brothers," 57–58, 60; "Jackass Joins March to Austin," *Valley Morning Star,* 28 July 1966, 2; "Church Aids Huelgistas, Bishop Says," *Alamo Messenger,* 5 August 1966, 1, 10; "Weary Valley Marchers Get Big Spiritual Lift at Corpus," *Houston Post,* 31 July 1966, unidentified page; and "Labor Official Predicts National Farm Union Bid," *Corpus Christi Caller,* 31 July 1966, 1.

16. "Catholic Huelga Aid Hailed," *Alamo Messenger,* 12 August 1966, 1, 18; "Procession Continues to Push for 'Dignity, More Pay, Legislation,'" *Bee-Picayune* [Beeville, Tex.], 18 August 1966, 1; "Marchers Cross into Archdiocese," *Alamo Messenger,* 19 August 1966, 1, 14; and "Determined Farm Workers near Last Leg of Austin Trek," *Texas Catholic Herald* [organ of the Diocese of Galveston-Houston], 26 August 1966, 1, 10.

17. Kemper Diehl, "Marchers Greeted with Money in S.A.," *San Antonio Express-News,* 27 August 1966, A1, 6; "'Huelga' Comes to S.A.," *Alamo Messenger,* 26 August 1966, 1, 14; and "Archbishop Urges Connally: Meet Strikers," *Alamo Messenger,* 2 September 1966, 1, 9. Also see Winn, "The Valley Farm Workers Movement," 50–53; Cohen, "To See Christ in Our Brothers," 62–64; and "Sermon by His Excellency," August 1966, three-page speech, Archives of Archdiocese of San Antonio, Robert E. Lucey Papers, 39, 2.

18. "Priest Says Slap from Connally Put Spirit in Marchers," *Corpus Christi Caller,* 3 September 1966, unidentified page; Ernest Stromberger, "La Marcha: How a Strike Became a Cause," *Dallas Times Herald,* 4 September 1966, unidentified page; Bo Byers, "Farm Labor March Nearing Austin Goal," *Houston Chronicle,* 4 September 1966, 1, 10; and "The Confrontation," *Texas Observer* 58, no. 17 (1966): 9–11. On PASSO see Montejano, *Anglos and Mexicans in the Making of Texas,* 282, 284, 286; and Teresa Palomo Acosta, "Political Association of Spanish-Speaking Organizations," *New Handbook of Texas,* vol. 4, 256.

19. Ernest Stromberger, "Marchers at Capital," *Dallas Times Herald,* 5 September 1966, 1, 12; Tom Milligan, "Rally Climaxes March," *Dallas Morning News,* 6 September 1966, 1; "Huelgistas Push Strike," *Alamo Messenger,* 9 September 1966, 1, 14; Greg Olds, "Labor Day in Austin: A Bad Day for the Establishment," *Texas Observer* 58, no. 17 (1966): 6–8; "Huntsville Group Starts Austin March," *Houston Post,* 16 August 1966, unidentified page; "Huntsville Marchers Nearly Broke," *Houston Chronicle,* 19 August 1966, 1, 4; Bo Byers, "Two Wage Sentinels to Stand Vigil on Capitol Steps," *Houston Chronicle,* 6 September 1966, 1, 8; and "March Coordinators to Air Support for Minimum Wage," *San Antonio Express-News,* 7 September 1966, unidentified page.

20. "Melon Pickers Meet to Vote to Join NFWA," *Valley Morning Star,* 19 July 1966, 1; "Starr Union Reaffirms Affiliation with NFWA," *Valley Evening Monitor,* 19 July 1966, 1, 3; "Strike Marchers at Falfurrias," *Valley Morning Star,* 23 July 1966, 1; "Nelson Status Unclear," *Valley Morning Star,* 24 July 1966, A2; "New Group Reported Making Farm Union Try," *Valley Morning Star,* 28 July 1966, 1, 2; "Sanchez Asks Support for New Union," *Valley Morning Star,* 31 July 1966, A4; Kenneth J. Allen's transcribed interview with Antonio Gonzalez and James Novarro, cited in Avant, "The 1966 Rio Grande Farm Workers Strike," 32–43, the quotation coming from pp. 38, 40, 41. Also see Cohen, "To See Christ in Our Brothers," 61, 67–70, based partly on an interview with Sherrill Smith, Oral History, Archives of the University of Texas at Arlington, 19–24; and statement by Sherrill Smith, 9 September 1966, AASA, ARELP, 39, 2. Also see "At St. Mary's, San Antonio, Antonio Gonzales [*sic*] to Have First Mass," *Southern Messenger,* 23 March 1957, unidentified page; "More Priests Are Coming to Valley," *Brownsville Herald,* 21 June 1966, 1–6; "Clergy Probe Valley Strike," *Texas Catholic Herald,* 24 June 1966, 1, 6; Norman Baxter, "Valley March May Trigger Special Session," *Houston Chronicle,* 10 July 1966, 1, 26; "Priest, Minister Leading Worker March to Austin," *Texas Catholic Herald,* 15 July 1966, 3; Maury Maverick Jr., "Marching for a 'Ghastly Recompense' in Texas," *New Republic* (24 September 1966): 11. Also see Winn, "Mexican-Americans in the Texas Labor Movement," 79–80; "AFL-CIO Panel Votes to Back Valley March," *Houston Post,* 15 July 1966, unidentified page; "Union Council Backs 'Huelga,'" *Corpus Christi Caller,*

15 July 1966, 1, 16; "Union Men to Join March to Austin," *San Antonio Express-News,* 25 July 1966, unidentified page; and "Texas Labor Raises $5,000 for Marchers," *Houston Chronicle,* 26 July 1966, unidentified page.

21. Letter from Nelson to Lucey, 10 September 1966; memo from Chancellor Charles Grahmann to Lucey, 21 September 1966; letter from SAD field representative John Mc-Carthy to Lucey, 27 September 1966; letter from McCarthy to Lucey, 29 September 1966; and letter from Lucey to McCarthy, 5 October 1966, all in AASA, ARELP, 39, 2; "The Sleeping Dragon: South Texas, Valley Sown with Revolt," *Houston Post,* 11 August 1963, 1, 4; Fletcher Robertson, "Union Label on All Valley Products Avowed Aim of AFL-CIO," *Valley Morning Star,* 11 August 1963, A1, 2; Fletcher Robertson, "Economic Boost Aim Says Brown," *Valley Morning Star,* 12 August 1963, 1–2; "AFL-CIO Group Eyeing Valley as Fertile Organizing Territory," *Houston Chronicle,* 8 September 1963, unidentified page; "Texas AFL-CIO Readies Push for Valley," *Valley Morning Star,* 19 August 1964, 1–2; "Union Leaders Plan S. Texas Recruiting," *Houston Post,* 7 January 1966, unidentified page; "Union Officials Set Sights on 'Working Poor' in Valley," *Corpus Christi Caller,* 12 February 1966, unidentified page; and "Labor 'Conspiracy' Seen as Try to Take State," *San Antonio Express-News,* 31 March 1966, unidentified page.

22. Cohen, "To See Christ in Our Brothers," 73–74; Leal, "The 1966–1967 South Texas Farm Worker Strike," 128–34; "Mr. Antonio Orendain," a 1971 interview by Carr Winn, Oral History 7, Archives of the University of Texas at Arlington, 1–2, 5–6; and author's interview with Antonio Orendain, 3 June 2005, Pharr, Tex.

23. "Barricade Ends with 12 Arrested," *San Antonio Light,* 24 October 1966, 1; "Farm Union Pickets Are Arrested at Roma for Halting Bridge Traffic," *Valley Morning Star,* 25 October 1966, 1, 3; "Strike Leader Vows More Disobedience," *Alamo Messenger,* 27 October 1966, 1, 12; Cleveland Grammer, "Union Protests Green Cards," *Houston Post,* 30 October 1966, Sec. 2, 10; "More Efforts Due to Curb Green Cards," *San Antonio Light,* 1 November 1966, unidentified page; Winn, "The Valley Farm Workers' Movement," 56–58; and Cohen, "To See Christ in Our Brothers," 73–74.

24. "Bridge Fire Blocks Picketed Train," *Houston Post,* 4 November 1966, 1; "Valley Rail Trestle Destroyed by Fire," *Corpus Christi Caller,* 4 November 1966, 1, 14; "Rio Grande City Terrorism Charged," *San Antonio Express-News,* 8 November 1966, C1; "Starr County Asks Rangers to Stay On," *Valley Morning Star,* 8 November 1966, unidentified page; "'[Bell] Pepper Train' Still Stands on Rio Grande City Tracks," *Valley Morning Star,* 9 November 1966, 6; Winn, "The Valley Farm Workers Movement," 58–60; Cohen, "To See Christ in Our Brothers," 74–76; telegram from Chávez to Lucey, 9 November 1966; memo from Grahmann to Lucey, 10 November 1966; telegram from Lucey to Chávez, 10 November 1966; letter from Smith and Killian to Lucey, 10 November 1966; letter from Lucey to John McCarthy, 11 November 1966; letter from Lucey to Smith and Killian, 14 November 1966, all in AASA, ARELP, 39, 2; and Bronder, *Social Justice and Church Authority,* 122–23.

25. Cohen, "To See Christ in Our Brothers," 70–71, 76–78; Winn, "The Valley Farm Workers Movement," 60–61; "Plans for Farm Labor Mapped," *Corpus Christi Caller,* 10 September 1966, unidentified page; letter from McCarthy to Eugene Nelson, 8 November 1966, AASA, ARELP, 39, 2; Fred Pfeifer, "Starr County: To Lose a Strike, but Nurture an Awakening," *Texas Observer* 58, no. 23 (1966): 19–20; and Mary Beth Rogers, *Cold Anger: A Story of Faith and Power Politics* (Denton: University of North Texas Press, 1990), 60, 73–75, 93–125.

26. Letter from Tony Orendain to César Chávez, 7 December 1966, UFW, Office

of the President, Part 2, 33, 21; author's interview with Orendain; "5 S.A. Priests Seized in Valley Farm Pay Fuss," *San Antonio Express-News,* 2 February 1967, A1, 16; "10 Valley Pickets Arrested at Farm," *Corpus Christi Caller,* 2 February 1967, 1; Winn, "The Valley Workers Movement," 61–63; Cohen, "To See Christ in Our Brothers," 86–87; "Students Join Valley Pickets," *San Antonio Express-News,* 3 February 1967, 1; Letter from Lucey to Sherrill Smith, 2 February 1967; and letter from Lucey to Medeiros, 2 February 1967, both in AASA, ARELP, 39, 3; "Archbishop Lucey Sends Two Priests to a Monastery," *Valley Morning Star,* 4 February 1967, 1; "Priests Hailed as They Leave for Retreat," *Corpus Christi Times,* 6 February 1967, unidentified page; "Smith and Killian Welcomed on Return to San Antonio," *San Antonio Express-News,* 12 February 1967, A1, 13; Bronder, *Social Justice and Church Authority,* 124–26, 128; and McNamara, "Bishops, Priests, and Prophecy," 153–54; letter from Medeiros to Lucey, 2 January 1967; letter from Lucey to H. S. Brown, Pres., Texas State AFL-CIO, 3 January 1967; letter from Lucey to Medeiros, 9 January 1967; letter from H. S. Brown to Lucey, 23 January 1967; letter from Roy R. Evans, Secretary-Treasurer, Texas State AFL-CIO, 25 January 1967; and letter from Lucey to Evans, 30 January 1967, all in AASA, ARELP, 39, 3.

27. Cohen, "To See Christ in Our Brothers," 81–85, 88–90, 92–94, 116; Bronder, *Social Justice and Church Authority,* 123–24, 127–61; letter from Charles Grahmann, Chancellor of the Archdiocese of San Antonio, to Ramon Garcia, 22 February 1967, AASA, ARELP, 30, 3; Sylvia Springer, "Suspended Priests Get Smith's Support," *San Antonio Express-News,* 1 May 1967, A1, 13; "4 Suspended Priests Receive Rally Support," *Corpus Christi Caller,* 5 May 1967, unidentified page; Sylvia Springer, "Priest Reinstated, Other 2 Still Out," *San Antonio Express-News,* 7 May 1967, unidentified page; "Suspended Priests Transferred," *Corpus Christi Caller,* 15 June 1967, 1, 12; Mary Beth Rogers, "The Archbishop's Dilemma," *Texas Observer* 59, no. 16 (1967): 4–5; "Archbishop Picketed," *San Antonio Express-News,* 6 February 1967, A1, 12; letter from fifty-one priests of the Archdiocese of San Antonio [including Sherrill Smith and Henry Casso] to Pope Paul VI, 16 September 1968, AASA, Sherrill Smith Papers, uncatalogued; "Priest-Prelate Trouble Pinpointed," *Dallas Morning News,* 26 October 1968, unidentified page; "Anti-Lucey Pressure to Increase," *Fort Worth Star-Telegram,* 29 October 1968, C18; "Probe Rejected by 68 Priests," *Fort Worth Star-Telegram,* 18 November 1968, unidentified page; and Sylvia Springer, "Observer Meets 10 Dissenting Priests," *San Antonio Express-News,* 3 December 1968, A4.

In a related matter, Mexican Americans called for the retirement of conservative Francis Cardinal McIntyre of the Archdiocese of Los Angeles. The lightning-rod issue was the use of church funds. McIntyre had sponsored the building of a new worship facility, St. Basil's Cathedral. A religious Chicana/o group, Católicos Por La Raza, complained that the money should have been used for Mexican American social programs. Members of the group demonstrated at the opening service at St. Basil's—a Christmas midnight mass—and were quickly detained by off-duty police officers who were providing security. A similar protest was held when, after a fire in 1962, St. Mary's Cathedral in San Francisco was rebuilt with an ultramodern design (Mosqueda, *Chicanos, Catholicism, and Political Ideology,* 103–11; and Jeffrey M. Burns, *San Francisco: A History of the Archdiocese of San Francisco,* vol. 3, *A Journey of Hope: 1945–2000* [Strasburg, France: Editions du Signe, 1999], 22–25).

28. Cohen, "To See Christ in Our Brothers," 97–100, 105–12; Winn, "The Valley Farm Workers' Movement," 64; memo of McCarthy to Lucey, 7 March 1967; "Texas Bishops' Statement Concerns Farm Labor"; "The Rio Grande Valley of Texas: Report of

the Social Action Department of the Texas Catholic Conference to the Catholic Bishops of Texas Regarding Poverty and Socio-Economic Difficulties in the Rio Grande Valley Area and Some Suggested Church Programs," 16 June 1967, all in AASA, ARELP, 39, 3; and "Texas Bishops' Statement Hailed by Farm Labor Leaders," *Texas Catholic* [organ of the Diocese of Dallas], 22 April 1967, unidentified page. Also see letter from Mc-Carthy to Lucey, 2 February 1967, Catholic Archives of Texas, John E. McCarthy Papers, Box 4, Folder 6, hereafter cited as CAT; letter from McCarthy to Monsignor Quinn, BCSS office in Chicago, 8 February 1967, CAT, McCarthy Papers, 4, 2; letter from Mc-Carthy to Antonio Orendain, 15 February 1967, ibid., 6, 15; letter from McCarthy to James Drake, 21 February 1967, ibid., 6, 15; letter from McCarthy to Quinn, 3 March 1967, ibid., 4, 2; letter from James Drake to McCarthy, 5 March 1967, ibid., 6, 15; letter from Lucey to McCarthy, 7 March 1967, ibid., 4, 6; letter from McCarthy to Eugene Nelson, 20 March 1967; letter from Nelson to McCarthy, 28 March 1967; and letter from Mc-Carthy to Gilberto Padilla, 9 June 1967, all in ibid., 6, 15.

29. "Church Group Says Minister Acts Alone," *Valley Morning Star,* 13 July 1966, 1; Norman Baxter, "Church Halts Support of Marching Minister," *Houston Chronicle,* 5 July 1966, 1, 5; "Ministerial Teacher Loses Building for Joining March," *Valley Evening Monitor,* 5 July 1966, unidentified page; "Strike March Due in Mission Today," *Corpus Christi Caller,* 6 July 1966, 16; Ernest Morgan, "Church Role in Strike Disputed," *Corpus Christi Caller,* 7 July 1966, 1, 12; and "Fired Pastor Moving," *San Antonio Light,* 14 July 1966, unidentified page.

30. Kilpatrick, "The Last That Became First," 66; Avant, "The 1966 Rio Grande Farm Workers Strike," the quoted phrase coming from p. 23; Leo D. Nieto, "Letter from the Texas Council of Churches to Texas Council of Churches Members," 10 June 1966 (cited in Avant, "The 1966 Rio Grande Farm Workers Strike," Appendix A, 56–59). Also see Leo D. Nieto, "Letter from the Texas Council of Churches to Texas Council of Churches," 25 July 1966 (cited in ibid., Appendix B, 60–62); "Protestant Church Groups Take Look at Starr County Situation," *Brownsville Herald,* 29 June 1966, A12; "Church Group Mum in Starr County Probe," *Brownsville Herald,* 30 June 1966, 1; and "Statement of Church Concern for Farm Labor Relations," Texas Council of Churches, 19 July 1966 (cited in Avant, "The 1966 Rio Grande Farm Workers Strike," Appendix C, 68), from which the block quotation comes.

31. Nieto, "Letter from the Texas Council of Churches"; letter from Ted Richardson, Executive Secretary of the Conference Council of the Southwest Texas Conference of the Methodist Church, San Antonio, Tex., to Dr. Grover C. Bagby, Associate General Secretary of the Board of Christian Social Concerns, United Methodist Church, Washington, D.C., 18 July 1966; letter from Alfred T. Grout, District Superintendent, Southern District of the Rio Grande Conference, McAllen, Tex., to Bagby 19 July 1966; letter from Dr. Will Matthis Dunn Sr., pastor of First Methodist Church, Edinburg, Tex., to Bagby, 18 July 1966; and letter from Harold M. Griffith, then formerly of First Methodist Church, Rio Grande City, Tex., to Bagby, 20 July 1966, who identified the Methodist farm manager as Ray Rochester of La Casita Farms, all in Texas Council of Churches Dept. of Migrant Ministries, Folder 3: U.A.O. Unidentified, 1966–1969, the National Division of the General Board of Global Ministries, Accession 1980–038, United Methodist Archives, Madison, N.J. . Also see Grebler et al., *Mexican American People,* 499; "Procession Continues to Push for 'Dignity, More Pay, Legislation,'" *Bee-Picayune,* 18 August 1966, A1, 8; "Connally Silent as U.S. Labor Approves," *Texas Observer* 58, no. 16 (1966): 4; letter from Joe K. Ader, pastor of First Methodist Church, New Braunfels,

Tex., to Grover Bagby, 31 August 1966, accompanied by a manuscript of his rally speech, Texas Council of Churches Dept. of Migrant Ministries, Folder 3: U.A.O. Unidentified, 1966–1969, the National Division of the General Board of Global Ministries, Accession 1980–038, United Methodist Archives, Madison, N.J.; Kemper Diehl, "Church Group Endorses March," *San Antonio Express-News*, 27 August 1966, A6; and Avant, "The 1966 Rio Grande Farm Workers Strike," 31; "Clergy: Outsiders and Adversaries," 141–44, 147, 151, the quotation coming from p. 139. "Farm Worker Strike Starts with Bang, Then Coasts," *Fort Worth Star-Telegram*, 14 June 1966, unidentified page; "'Huelgistas' Receive Help as Strike Continues," *Alamo Messenger*, 17 June 1966, 1, 10; "Messages to the Churches of Texas," adopted by the Annual Assembly of the Texas Council of Churches, 9 March 1960, in *Texas Ecumenical Action* 5, no. 2 (1960), under caption titled "Protestants against Communism," 4; editorial titled "Protestantism under Attack," *Texas Ecumenical Action* 6, no. 1 (1961): 2; editorial titled "Church Planning and the Changing Texas Culture," *Texas Ecumenical Action* 6, no. 3 (1961): 2; "Church Hits NCC Support," *Valley Evening Monitor*, 16 July 1965, B10; and "Church Asks Withdrawal from Council," *Valley Evening Monitor*, 26 August 1965, 1.

32. Letter of Leo Nieto to Texas Council of Churches' Departments of Migrant Ministry and Christian Social Concerns, Judicatory Executives and District Superintendents, General Board Members, and South Texas Churches, 1 December 1966, NFWM, II, 26, 7; "Thanksgiving Caravan to Retrace Route of Starr County Farm March," *Valley Evening Monitor*, 22 November 1966, unidentified page; "Starr County Grand Jury Report Text," *Daily Review*, 17 November 1966, unidentified page; "Union 'Amazed' at Church Opposition," *Valley Evening Monitor*, 23 November 1966, 1, 3; "Texas Churches Ask Valley for Labor Peace," *Corpus Christi Caller*, 26 November 1966, unidentified page; and letter from Betty Whitaker, South Central Field Representative for the National Migrant Ministry, to William Scholes, Jack Alford, Chris Hartmire, Russell Carter, Isaac Igarashi, and Robert Kolze, 22 November 1966, NFWM, II, 26, 6. The reference to the vigilante group comes from the author's interview with Leo Nieto at the Hawthorne United Methodist Church, 26 April 1994, Los Angeles, Calif.

33. Unsigned letter [from Chris Hartmire?] to "Tony [Orendain], Bill [Chandler] and Gene [Nelson]," 2 February 1967, UFW, Office of the President, II, 33, 21; letter from Jim Drake to Chris Hartmire, 5 February 1967, NFWM, II, 26, 6; "La Huelga's New Look," *Texas Observer* 58, no. 27 (1967): 3–4; Sam Gerald, "Farm at Rio Grande City Prepared for Boycott of Its Fresh Produce," *Valley Morning Star*, 1 February 1967, unidentified page; Sam Gerald, "Injunction Action Is Contemplated by La Casita Farms," *Valley Morning Star*, 2 February 1967, unidentified page; "Court Action Threatened If Boycott Is Carried Out," *Corpus Christi Caller*, 2 February 1967, 2; and "Strikers Push Boycott," *Alamo Messenger*, 2 February 1967, 1.

34. "Report of the Director of Migrant Ministry and Mission to the Department of Migrant Ministry, Texas Council of Churches, for the Year 1966," 25 April 1967, NFWM, II, 26, 7; and "Proposal for the Texas Council of Churches' Valley Team Ministry," 6 March 1967, NFWM, II, 26, 7. Also see letter from Krueger to author, 23 September 1994; and Frank A. Kostyu, *Shadows in the Valley: The Story of One Man's Struggle for Justice* (Garden City, N.Y.: Doubleday, 1970), 18–20.

35. Letter from Hartmire to Krueger, 6 March 1967; letter from Hartmire to William E. Scholes, 7 March 1967; letter from Scholes to Hartmire, 18 March 1967, all in NFWM, II, 26, 6; Edgar A. Krueger, Report No. 2, Valley Team Ministry, Department of Migrant Ministry and Mission, 25 April 1967, Stitt Library Archives, Hispanic-

American Institute Records, Folder-Migrant Ministry, Texas Council of Churches; and Kostyu, *Shadows in the Valley,* 30.

36. Hoyt Hager, "Cantaloupe Harvest Prospects Excellent," *Corpus Christi Caller,* 3 May 1967, B16; Gary Garrison, "Negotiate or 'Rotten Melons,' Says Valley Farm Labor Group," *Houston Chronicle,* 7 May 1967, unidentified page; "Union Silent on Plans to Hit Starr Growers," *Valley Evening Monitor,* 9 May 1967, unidentified page; "La Casita May Ask Federal Help in Shipping Melons," *San Antonio Express-News,* 6 May 1967, A2; "Starr Grower Issues Warning to Union," *Valley Evening Monitor,* 7 May 1967, 1; "Valley Farmer Will Ask U.S. Aid in Labor Fight," *Houston Chronicle,* 7 May 1967, unidentified page; "Rangers Keeping Close Watch as Starr Harvest Season Underway," *Valley Evening Monitor,* 8 May 1967, unidentified page; "Starr Law Officers Outnumber Pickets," *Daily Review,* 8 May 1967, unidentified page; "Farm Union Planning to Extend Drive into Citrus Producing Region," *Valley Evening Monitor,* 4 May 1967, unidentified page; and "Union to Widen Effort to 3 Counties of Valley," *Corpus Christi Caller,* 4 May 1967, 1.

37. The Mexican Union was La Confederación de Trabajadores Mexicanos. See Kemper Diehl, "U.S., Mexico Unions to Join in Valley Ban," *San Antonio Express-News,* 8 May 1967, unidentified page; Gary Garrison, "Farm Union to Seal Off Roma Bridge," *Corpus Christi Caller,* 9 May 1967, unidentified page; "Mexican Union Halts Workers at Border," *Hidalgo County News,* 11 May 1967, 1–2; Gary Garrison, "Valley Union Claims Joint Effort Working," *Corpus Christi Caller,* 12 May 1967, unidentified page; Douglas E. Kneeland, "Mexican Union Joins Strike of Texas Farm Hands," *New York Times,* 12 May 1967, unidentified page; "Mexican Officials Break Picket Line," *Daily Review,* 11 May 1967, unidentified page; "Most 'Green Card' Workers Return to Starr Fields," *Valley Evening Monitor,* 12 May 1967, unidentified page; and Douglas E. Kneeland, "Farm Strike Stirs a County in Texas," *New York Times,* 19 May 1967, 41–42.

38. "Harvest Proceeding Quietly," *Valley Evening Monitor,* 14 May 1967, unidentified page; "'Activities' of Rangers at Site Protested," *Valley Morning Star,* 12 May 1967, unidentified page; Kemper Diehl, "Valley Probe Asked by Rights Official," *San Antonio Express-News,* 15 May 1967, unidentified page; "La Casita Manager Backs Union's Appeal for Civil Rights Probe," *Valley Evening Monitor,* 16 May 1967, unidentified page; Leo Nieto, "Migrant Ministry Newsletter," 19 May 1967, NFWM, II, 26, 7: 1; "Rangers, Deputies Arrest 22 Pickets," *Valley Evening Monitor,* 18 May 1967, 1; "Removal of Texas Ranger Asked," *Valley Morning Star,* 19 May 1967, 1; Gary Garrison, "Arrest of Starr Pickets Sets Valley Strike Mark," *Corpus Christi Caller,* 27 May 1967, 1, 16; Leo Nieto, "Migrant Ministry Newsletter," 5 June 1967, NFWM, II, 26, 7; "19 Freed on Bond after Arrest for Picketing Mo-Pac Railroad," *Valley Evening Monitor,* 28 May 1967, 1, 3; and letter from Gerald N. McAllister, then Episcopal canon and president of the Texas Council of Churches, to author, 5 October 1994.

39. "Senator Says 2 Men Beaten by Rangers," *Houston Chronicle,* 31 May 1967, 1; "Bernal Charges Rangers Beat Up 2 Union Men," *San Antonio Light,* 31 May 1967, unidentified page; "Texas; Trouble in the Melon Patch," *Newsweek,* 19 June 1967: 38, 40; interview with state senator Don Kennard, Fort Worth, Texas, 14 September 1967, in closed manuscript in possession of Ben Procter; and *San Antonio News-Express,* 11 and 12 May 1967, all cited in Procter, "The Modern Texas Rangers," 212–27; author's interview with Antonio Orendain; "Farm Workers' Leader Dies in Bar Shootout," *Lubbock Avalanche-Journal,* 9 May 1973, B8; "3 Senators Hear of Fear in Valley," *Dallas Morning News,* 7 June 1967, unidentified page; Z. Joe Thornton, "Ranger, Senators Clash on Charges," *Fort Worth Star-Telegram,* 7 June 1967, unidentified page; "Senators Find Rangers Necessary,"

Fort Worth Star-Telegram, 8 June 1967, unidentified page; "The Rangers and La Huelga," *Texas Observer* 59, no. 13 (1967): 13–28; Gary Garrison, "Federal Investigation of Rangers Continuing," *Corpus Christi Times,* 14 July 1967, 16; and Winn, "The Valley Farm Workers Movement," 65–67. For a contemporary, sympathetic treatment of the Rangers see Procter, "The Modern Texas Rangers," 212–27; and, conversely, Julian Samora, Joe Bernal, and Albert Pena, *Gunpowder Justice: A Reassessment of the Texas Rangers* (Notre Dame, Ind.: University of Notre Dame Press, 1979), 131–56.

40. "UFWOC Files Suit to Ban Actions of Lawmen," *Valley Evening Monitor,* 13 June 1967, unidentified page; "Farm Union Seeks Court Action to Guard Rights," *Corpus Christi Times,* 13 June 1967, 12; "Church Group Sues Rangers, Starr Officers," *San Antonio Express-News,* 28 June 1967, unidentified page; "Church Unit's Suit Names Rangers, Starr Officials," *Corpus Christi Times,* 28 June 1967, 1; "Council Sues Rangers to Establish Justice," *Texas Ecumenical Action* 12, no. 4 (1967): 1, 3; "Rangers, Texas Laws Hit by Trial Lawyers," *Rio Grande City Herald,* 13 June 1968, 1, 14; Gary Garrison, "Allee Testifies about Arrests," *Corpus Christi Caller,* 14 June 1967, A1, 16; "Council Lawsuit Aimed at Rangers Supported," *Alamo Messenger,* 6 July 1967, 8; "Protestants Accept Aid of Bishops," *Corpus Christi Caller,* 6 July 1967, unidentified page; David Dunnigan, "Gov. Connally Defensive on Ranger Issue," *Dallas Morning News,* 14 June 1967, unidentified page; "FBI Making Inquiry into Valley Dispute," *Dallas Morning News,* 14 June 1967, unidentified page; Gary Garrison, "Federal Investigation of Rangers Continuing," *Corpus Christi Times,* 14 July 1967, 16; Nieto, "Migrant Ministry Newsletter," 5 June 1967: 3; David Shute, "Churches' Council to Stay in Valley," *Alamo Messenger,* 29 June 1967, 2; vita, titled "Jorge Lara-Braud," Walter P. Reuther Library of Labor and Urban Affairs, Wayne State University, UFW, Office of President, Part II, 68, 4; and Barton, *"¡Ya Basta!"* 130–31.

41. Shute, "Churches' Council to Stay in Valley"; Jorge Lara-Braud, "Report on Farm Labor Relations in Lower Rio Grande Valley," n.d., NFWM, II, 26, 4: 5–10, which was published in *Texas Ecumenical Action* 1, no. 3 (1967). Also see Lara-Braud's fourteen pages of meeting notes, titled "Texas Council of Churches, Fact-Finding Consultation on Farm Labor Relations, Ramada Inn, Corpus Christi, 8–9 June 1967," Stitt Library Archives, Hispanic-American Institute records, folder-Huelga, hereafter cited as SLA, HAI, Huelga; the block quotation of William R. Deines, Executive Vice President of the Texas Citrus and Vegetables Growers and Shippers, appearing on p. 11 (bracketed words author's); Kemper Diehl, "Church Walks Tight Rope in Valley," *San Antonio Express-News,* 14 May 1967, A12; Kay Longcope, "Churches Try to Ease Tension as Farmers Face Union in Texas," *Presbyterian Life,* 15 July 1967: 23–24; David Shute, "Church Involvement in Huelga 'Misguided,'" *Alamo Messenger,* 17 November 1967, 11–12.

42. Kostyu, *Shadows in the Valley,* 133; letter from Drake to Hartmire, 5 February 1967; letter from Hartmire to Krueger, 6 March 1967; letter from Hartmire to William Scholes, 7 March 1967, all in NFWM, II, 26, 6. Also see "A Joint Statement of the American Jewish Committee (Southwest Region), the Texas Council of Churches, and the Texas Catholic Conference," 15 March 1967, SLA, HAI, Huelga; letter from Krueger to author, 23 September 1994; Grebler et al., *The Mexican-American People,* 511–12n49; letter from Harold Kilpatrick, Austin, Tex., to John F. Anderson Jr., Executive Secretary, Board of Church Extension, Presbyterian Church in the U.S., Atlanta, Ga., 19 June 1967; letter from Anderson to Howard C. Blake, Corpus Christi, Tex., 21 June 1967; letter from Jorge Lara-Braud to Anderson, 27 June 1967; letter from Kilpatrick to Anderson, 27 June 1967; letter from E. A. Dean, Stated Clerk and Executive Secretary-Treasurer, Synod of Texas, P.C.U.S., Austin, Tex., to Anderson, 27 June 1967; letter from W. Thad Godwin Jr., As-

sociate Secretary, Division of Home Missions and Christian Welfare, Board of Church Extension, P.C.U.S., Atlanta, Ga., to Dean, 15 August 1967, all in SLA, HAI, Huelga.

43. Letter from Krueger to author, 23 September 1994; Grebler et al., *The Mexican-American People,* 511–12n49; letter from Harold Kilpatrick, Austin, Tex., to John F. Anderson Jr., Executive Secretary, Board of Church Extension, Presbyterian Church in the U.S., Atlanta, Ga., 19 June 1967; letter from Anderson to Howard C. Blake, Corpus Christi, Tex., 21 June 1967; letter from Jorge Lara-Braud to Anderson, 27 June 1967; letter from Kilpatrick to Anderson, 27 June 1967; letter from E. A. Dean, Stated Clerk and Executive Secretary-Treasurer, Synod of Texas, P.C.U.S., Austin, Tex., to Anderson, 27 June 1967; and letter from W. Thad Godwin Jr., Associate Secretary, Division of Home Missions and Christian Welfare, Board of Church Extension, P.C.U.S., Atlanta, Ga., to Dean, 15 August 1967, all in SLA, HAI, Huelga.

44. "Witnesses Are Listed for Senate Hearing on Migratory Labor," *Valley Morning Star,* 27 June 1967, unidentified page; "Lucey, Smith Due at Senate Valley Meet," *San Antonio Express-News,* 27 June 1967, unidentified page; Kemper Diehl, "Evidence 'Persuasive,'" *San Antonio Express-News,* 1 July 1967, A1, 4; and "Little People's Day," *Texas Observer* 59, no. 14 (1967): 3–10.

45. "Ranger Force Cut in Starr County," *Fort Worth Evening Star-Telegram,* 15 June 1967, unidentified page; "Most Texas Rangers Withdrawn from Rio Grande City," *Houston Post,* 15 June 1967, unidentified page; "Half of Rangers Leave Valley," *San Antonio Light,* 15 June 1967, unidentified page; "'Brutality' Halts Starr Farm Pickets," *Corpus Christi Caller,* 15 June 1967, A1, 12; Hoyt Hager, "Valley Melon Crop to Total $7 Million," *Corpus Christi Caller,* 21 June 1967, unidentified page; "La Marcha II Doesn't Swing," *Texas Observer* 59, no. 18 (1967): 8–9; "Andrade Ousted as Leader of Farm Workers Group," *San Antonio Express-News,* 12 September 1967, unidentified page; and "VWAC Regroups," *Alamo Messenger,* 14 September 1967, 10.

46. Letter from Krueger to author, 23 September 1994; *Texas Presbyterian News Bureau,* 26 September 1967, Presbyterian Archives at Montreat, N.C., Box 209, Synod of Texas's Council 1968, Hurricane Beulah Disaster; "Church Forces Do Huge Relief Job after Beulah Hits Rio Grande Valley," *Texas Ecumenical Action* 12, no. 5 (1967): 1, 4; "Beulah Relief Work Continues with Valley and Mexican Churches," *Texas Ecumenical Action* 12, no. 6 (1967): 4; "Beulah Emergency Hangs On: TCC Asks for 'Second-Mile' Offering," *Texas Ecumenical Action* 13, no. 1 (1968): 1, 4; and "Churches Provide $1,000 Weekly for Valley Relief," *Texas Ecumenical Action* 13, no. 2 (1968): 4.

47. "In Hurricane Beulah's Wake," *Texas Observer* 59, no. 20 (1967): 4–5; E. B. Duarte, "Huelgistas Still Hopeful Despite Lull," *Alamo Messenger,* 12 January 1968, 1, 8; E. B. Duarte, "Chavez: Huelga Going On," *Alamo Messenger,* 19 January 1968, 1, 10; Leo Nieto to Dr. Harry Komuro, National Division, Board of Missions, The United Methodist Church, 30 November 1967, Texas Council of Churches Dept. of Migrant Ministries, Accession 1980–038, Folder 3-U.A.O. Unidentified, 1966–1969, United Methodist Archives, Madison, N.J.; letter from Ed Krueger to Harold Kilpatrick, 9 November 1967; letter from Krueger, Pharr, Tex., to Kilpatrick, Austin, Tex., 10 November 1967; and letter from Krueger to Kilpatrick, 11 November 1967, all in Walter P. Reuther Library of Labor and Urban Affairs, Wayne State University, UFW, Office of President, Box 70, Folder 1.

48. Letter from Leo Nieto to Harry Komuro, 16 August; and "Guidelines for Valley Ministry Staff," Texas Council of Churches, 20 December 1967, both in Texas Council of Churches Dept. of Migrant Ministries, Accession 1980–038; Folder-U.A.O. Unidentified, 1966–1969, United Methodist Church Archives, Madison, N.J.; "Rev. Ned Garcia

Joins Valley Staff," *Texas Ecumenical Action* 13, no. 1 (1968): 4; Leo D. Nieto, "Report of the Director of Migrant Ministry and Mission of the Department of Migrant Ministry, Texas Council of Churches for the Year 1967," 18 March 1968; and four-page memo from Leo D. Nieto to Valley Ministry Staff, 27 February 1968, both in Texas Council of Churches Dept. of Migrant Ministries, ibid.

49. Gerald McAllister, "President's Address to the Fifteenth Annual Assembly of the Texas Council of Churches," 19 March 1968, St. John Lutheran Church, San Antonio, SLA, HAI, Huelga, the quoted phrase coming from p. 6; vita of "The Right Reverend Gerald Nicholas McAllister," copy in possession of the author; and letter from McAllister to author, 5 October 1994. Also see "Episcopal Session May Grow Heated," *Brownsville Herald,* 2 February 1966, 1; "Episcopalian Council Opens Session Today," *Brownsville Herald,* 3 February 1966, 1; "Episcopal Council Tables Action on National Council," *Brownsville Herald,* 4 February 1966, 1, 3; "Mrs. Ray on Episcopal Diocese Executive Board," *Brownsville Herald,* 6 February 1966, A8; Brian Wallace, O.M.I., "Bishop [Harold C.] Gosnell [of the Diocese of West Texas] Resigns [from All Committees of the Texas Conference of Churches], Protests Boycotts," *Today's Catholic,* San Antonio, Tex., 14 March 1975, 1.

50. Letter from Ed Krueger to Leo Nieto, 20 February 1968; letter from John R. Moyer, United Church Board for Homeland Ministries, New York, to Harold Kilpatrick, Executive Director, Texas Council of Churches, Austin, Tex., 23 February 1968; and letter from Wayne C. Hartmire Jr., Los Angeles, to Krueger, Pharr, Tex., 1 March 1968, all in NFWM, II, 2, 3; letter from Krueger to author, 23 September 1994; and Kostyu, *Shadows in the Valley,* 165–67, 179. Also see Kenneth R. Clark, "Mrs. Krueger Reveals Document," *Valley Evening Monitor,* 6 February 1969, 1. On the Ranger lawsuit see "Suit Aimed at Rangers," *Alamo Messenger,* 17 May 1968, 1; E. B. Duarte, "Conspiracy Cited in Valley Huelga," *Alamo Messenger,* 14 June 1968, 1, 8; E. B. Duarte, "Ranger Captain Denies Plot in Farm-Labor Row," *Alamo Messenger,* 21 June 1968, 1, 8; "'Huelga' Trail to Resume Oct. 22," *Alamo Messenger,* 18 October 1968, 1, 10; E. B. Duarte, "Ruling Due Soon in 'Huelga' Suit," *Alamo Messenger,* 25 October 1968, 1, 10; and E. B. Duarte, "Restrain Rangers, Commissioner Asks," *Alamo Messenger,* 20 December 1968, 1, 11. The suit required federal judges since the union challenged the constitutionality of Texas laws on anti-mass pickets, secondary strikes and boycotts, disturbance of the peace, abusive language, unlawful assembly, and obstruction of a roadway. In 1972 a final ruling pronounced that all but one was unconstitutional ("State Laws Ruled Unconstitutional," *Corpus Christi Caller,* 27 June 1972, unidentified page).

51. "VISTA Project Approved for Valley Office," *Texas Ecumenical Action* 13, no. 3 (1968): 1–2; "Community Life Education Project: A Summary of an Economic Opportunity Proposal under Title III-B," n.d., SLA, HAI, Folder-Valley Assistance Committee; "The VISTA Minority Mobilization Project in Hidalgo County, Texas," 18 October 1968, SLA, HAI, Folder-Valley Service Committee; and Kostyu, *Shadows in the Valley,* 157–65.

52. "Late News Paragraphs," *Texas Ecumenical Action* 13, no. 3 (1968): 1; and Leo D. Nieto, "Involved in the Movement of La Raza," *Engage* 1, no. 21 (1969): 17–21; letter from McAllister to author, 5 October 1994; and letter from William Scholes, one-time Western Supervisor of the National Migrant Ministry, to author, 1 October 1994; letter from Kilpatrick to author, 21 September 1994; Kilpatrick, "The Last That Became First," 69; Harold Kilpatrick, "The Texas Council of Churches and the Valley Ministry: A Summary

Review," 20 September 1968 (in private folder of Kilpatrick, in possession of author); Judy Weidman, "Can There Be Peace in the Valley? Fund for Reconciliation Program Has Turbulent History," *Texas Methodist* (February 1972): 1–3; and Barton, "*¡Ya Basta!*" 131–33.

53. Harold Kilpatrick, "The Texas Council of Churches and the Valley Ministry;" and "Dr. Reber Takes MM-Valley Portfolios," both in *Texas Ecumenical Action* 13, no. 5 (1968): 1; Kostyu, *Shadows in the Valley,* 133–40, 160–61, 167–68, 170–73; and Kilpatrick, "The Last That Became First," 69. Also see "Testimony Given Edgar A. Krueger before the Committee on Wages and Employment of the State of Texas," October 1968, Texas Council of Churches; and "Valley Service Committee" meeting minutes, 25 November 1968, both in SLA, HAI, Folder-Valley Assistance Committee; letter of Krueger to author, 23 September 1994; and letter of Betty Whitaker to author, 8 October 1994.

54. Kostyu, *Shadows in the Valley,* 170–72, 180–82; and a three-page form letter from Harold Kilpatrick to Ministers and Churches in the Lower Rio Grande Valley, 10 February 1969 (in private folder of Kilpatrick, in possession of the author); Kilpatrick, "The Last That Became First," 69–71; "TCC Fires Figure in Valley Dispute," *Dallas Morning News,* 30 January 1969, unidentified page; "Plan to Kill Ranger Suit Confirmed," *Corpus Christi Caller,* 1 February 1969, A1, 16; "Krueger Fired," *Texas Observer* 61, no. 3 (1969): 10–11; "Crowd of Noisy Demonstrators Pickets TCC Meet in Edinburg," *Valley Evening Monitor,* 10 February 1969, unidentified page; E. B. Duarte, "Fired Minister to Stay with Poor in Valley," *Alamo Messenger,* 7 February 1969, 1, 8.

55. "NCC Official to Arrive to Probe Krueger Case," *Valley Evening Monitor,* 11 February 1969, unidentified page; "NCC Fact-Finders Due in Valley Today," *Valley Evening Monitor,* 13 February 1969, unidentified page; Kemper Diehl, "Church Council Warned on Valley," *San Antonio Express-News,* 24 March 1969, C4; "Rev. Krueger's Ministry Praised," *San Antonio Express-News,* 29 March 1969, unidentified page; Kostyu, *Shadows in the Valley,* 182; letter from Harold Kilpatrick to Alfonso Rodriguez, 17 March 1969; letter from W. Kenneth Pope (the new president of the Texas Conference of Churches) to Rodriguez, 18 March 1969; letter from Rodriguez to Kilpatrick, 25 March 1969; letter from Rodriguez to Pope, 26 March 1969, all in SLA, HAI, Folder-Texas Conference of Churches-File I.

56. "New Church Conference Given Birth," *Texas Ecumenical Action* 14, no. 1 (1969): 1, 4, the quoted phrase appearing on p. 1; Alyce Guynn, "Founding of Texas Ecumenical Group in Austin Marks Church Precedent," *Austin-American Statesman,* 23 February 1969, A26; Kilpatrick, "The Last That Became First," 70–71, 103–7; Sylvia Springer, "New Church Conference to Eye Valley Problems," *San Antonio Express-News,* 27 February 1969, unidentified page; Jean Kelly, "Ecumenical Group Stands Firm for Valley Ministry," *Dallas Morning News,* 3 March 1969, unidentified page; Spurgeon M. Dunnam III, "Council Dies, Pickets Protest, Conference Begins," *Texas Methodist* (7 March 1969): 1, 3; "TCC Challenge," *Alamo Messenger,* 7 March 1969, 9; Kay Longcope, "Confrontation: Texas Style," *World Outlook* (May 1969): 10, 12; and Kostyu, *Shadows in the Valley,* 186–88. Also see William Madsen, *Mexican-Americans of South Texas,* 2nd ed. (New York: Holt, Rinehart and Winston, 1973), 119; *Texas Ecumenical Action* 14, no. 1 (1969): 2; and letter from Kilpatrick to author, 20 September 1994.

57. *Texas Ecumenical Action* 14, no. 1 (1969): 2; and letter from Kilpatrick to author, 20 September 1994.

58. Texas Farm Workers Support Committee, *The Struggle of the Texas Farm Workers'*

Union (Chicago: Vanguard Books, 1977); Antonio Orendain, "Report of the Methodist Volunteers," July 1970, two-page report "Los Voluntarios del Valle Río Grande," n.d.; *La Voz del Campesino,* six-page report titled "The Spanish Speaking Task Force at Work," n.d.; letter from Los Voluntarios to Woodie W. White, Executive Secretary, Commission on Religion and Race, UMC, Washington, D.C., n.d.; letter from Orendain to the Spanish-Speaking Task Force, 16 January 1971, all in Walter P. Reuther Library of Labor and Urban Affairs, Wayne State University, UFW, Texas Collection, Box 12, Folder 15; "After Two and One-Half Years, Methodists Learn Some Facts about Controversial Reconciliation Fund," *Pharr Press,* 28 October 1971, unidentified page; and Virginia Armstrong, "Methodist Financial Support of Farm Union Activities Revealed," *Valley Evening Monitor,* 22 October 1971, A1, 3; and author's interview with Antonio Orendain.

For a more traditional, nonconfrontational approach on the part of churches toward farm workers, see "Valley Service Project Continues Work of Community Development and Reconciliation," *Texas Ecumenical Action* 14, no. 2 (1969): 3; H. S. Goodenough, "A Valley Pastor Reports," *Texas Ecumenical Action* 14, no. 3 (1969): 2; nine-page document "Committee to Study Program of Texas Conference of Churches in Rio Grande Valley—Report of Board of Directors, June 12–13 [1969], Brownsville, Texas," SLA, HAI, Folder-Texas Conference of Churches-File I; "Board of Directors Adopt Valley Committee Report," *Texas Ecumenical Action* 14, no. 4 (1969): 1, 4; and Norman D. Phillips, "Chicano Workers, Rio Grande Farmers Agree to Meet," *Christian Century* 88, no. 3 (1971): 84–87.

59. Madsen, *Mexican-Americans of South Texas,* 116–18; Montejano, *Anglos and Mexicans in the Making of Texas,* 262–307; Julie Leininger Pycior, "Mexican-American Organizations," *The New Handbook of Texas,* vol. 4, 660–62; Teresa Palomo Acosta, "Mexican American Legal Defense and Educational Fund," *The New Handbook of Texas,* vol. 4, 659; Teresa Palomo Acosta, "Southwest Voter Registration Education Project," *The New Handbook of Texas,* vol. 5, 1175–76; Cynthia E. Orozco, "Velásquez, William C.," *The New Handbook of Texas,* vol. 6, 720; "Valley Interfaith: Citizens in Action," fact sheet, November 18, 2002, Mercedes, Tex.; Robert Lee Maril, *Poorest of Americans: The Mexican Americans of the Lower Rio Grande Valley of Texas* (Notre Dame, Ind.: University of Notre Dame Press, 1989), 109–11, 171; "Domestic Farmworkers in America's Heartland: Weslaco, Texas, and the Lower Rio Grande Valley," in *Working Poor: Farmworkers in the U.S.,* ed. David Griffith and Ed Kissam (Philadelphia: Temple University Press, 1995), 89–122; "Hidalgo's Dubious Distinction: A Hot Spot for Colonias in Texas," *Austin American-Statesman,* 12 July 1998, A8, 10; Ralph K. M. Haurwitz, "After Tragedy, Years of Delay, Sewer Service Still but a Dream," *Austin American-Statesman,* 13 July 1998, A1, 4; and "Making Do without Basics Takes Grit," *Austin American-Statesman,* 13 July 1998, 5.

Conclusion

1. See, for example, Chris C. Park, *Sacred Worlds: An Introduction to Geography and Religion* (London and New York: Routledge, 1994), 21, 85–86; Thomas A. Tweed, "Introduction," in *Retelling U.S. Religious History,* ed. Thomas A. Tweed (Berkeley: University of California Press, 1997), 1–26; Laurie F. Maffly-Kipp, "Eastward Ho! American Religion from the Perspective of the Pacific Rim," in *Retelling U.S. Religious History,* ed. Tweed, 127–48; David K. Yoo, "Introduction: Reframing the U.S. Religious Landscape,"

in *New Spiritual Homes,* ed. Yoo, 1–15; Harry S. Stout and Robert M. Taylor Jr., "Studies of Religion in American Society," in *New Directions in American Religious History,* ed. Harry S. Stout and D. G. Hart (New York: Oxford University Press, 1997), 3–5; and Jay P. Dolan, "The New Religious History," *Reviews in American History* 15 (September 1987): 449–54.

　　2. Cynthia E. Orozco, "Velásquez, William C.," *The New Handbook of Texas,* vol. 6, 720.

Bibliography

Manuscript Sources

Arlington, Tex. Special Collections Department. University of Texas at Arlington Libraries. Oral History 23, "Transcribed Recollection of Mr. Larry Skoog." November
1971.

Arlington, Tex. Special Collections Department. University of Texas at Arlington Libraries. Oral History History 24. "Transcribed Recollection of the Rev. Sherrill Smith."
2 March 1972.

Austin, Tex. Catholic Archives of Texas. John E. McCarthy Papers.

Austin, Tex. Austin Presbyterian Theological Seminary. Stitt Library Archives.
Hispanic-American Institute Records.

Berkeley, Calif. Bancroft Library, University of California. Cramp, Kathryn, Louise
F. Shields, and Charles Thomson, "Study of the Mexican Population in Imperial
Valley, California." New York, N.Y.: Committee on Farm and Cannery Migrants,
Council of Women on Home Mission, 1926.

Berkeley, Calif. Bancroft Library, University of California. Hart, Newell. "A Personal
Account of the Farm Workers' Pilgrimage from Delano to Sacramento." n.d.

Detroit, Mich. Walter P. Reuther Library of Labor and Urban Affairs, Wayne State University. National Farm Worker Ministry Collection.

Detroit, Mich. Walter P. Reuther Library of Labor and Urban Affairs, Wayne State University. United Farm Workers Collection.

Fresno, Calif. Diocese of Fresno. U.S. Bishops' Ad Hoc Committee Files. Not
catalogued.

Madison, N.J. General Commission on Archives and History, The United Methodist
Church. Records of the National Division of the General Board of Global Ministries, Accession 1980–038.

Menlo Park, Calif. Archives of the Archdiocese of San Francisco. Eugene Boyle Papers.

Menlo Park, Calif. Archives of the Archdiocese of San Francisco. General Files.

Menlo Park, Calif. Archives of the Archdiocese of San Francisco. Donald McDonnell
Papers.

Menlo Park, Calif. Archives of the Archdiocese of San Francisco. National Catholic Rural Life Conference Files.

Notre Dame, Ind. University of Notre Dame Archives. Robert E. Lucey Papers.

Philadelphia, Pa. Presbyterian Historical Society. National Council of Churches of
Christ, U.S.A., Collection. Division of Home Missions Records 1950–1964. Record
Group 7.

Philadelphia, Pa. Presbyterian Historical Society. National Council of Churches of
Christ, U.S.A., Collection. Home Missions Council of North America Records
1903–1951. Record Group 26.

San Antonio, Tex. Archives of the Archdiocese of San Antonio. Archbishop Robert E.
Lucey Papers.

San Antonio, Tex. Archives of the Archdiocese of San Antonio. Sherrill Smith Papers.
San Antonio, Tex. Archives of the Missionary Oblates of Mary Immaculate of Texas. Charles Taylor Papers.
San Diego, Calif. Archives of the Diocese of San Diego. Missionary Sisters—Brawley, Annual Reports, September 1936–1954.
San Diego, Calif. Archives of the Diocese of San Diego. Farm Labor Files.
Stanford, Calif. Special Collections, Stanford University Libraries. Victor P. Salandini Papers, M249, Series I.
Stanford, Calif. Special Collections, Stanford University Libraries. James L.Vizzard Papers, M325.
Washington, D.C. Archives of The Catholic University of America. The Social Action Department of National Catholic Welfare Conference Collection.
Washington, D.C. Archives of The Catholic University of America. George Gilmary Higgins Papers.

Newspapers and Newsletters

Alamo Messenger (San Antonio, Tex.). 1959–70.
Brownsville Herald (Brownsville, Tex.). 1965–69.
Central California Register (Fresno, Calif.). 1965–71.
Corpus Christi Caller. 1966–69.
Corpus Christi Times. 1967.
Daily Review (Edinburg, Tex.). 1966–67.
Dallas Morning News. 1966–69.
Dallas Times Herald. 1966–69.
Fresno Bee. 1965–75.
Houston Chronicle. 1965–69.
Houston Post. 1966–69.
Los Angeles Times. 1965–70.
Salinas Californian. 1970.
San Antonio Express-News. 1966–69.
San Antonio Light. 1966.
San Francisco Chronicle. 1965–70.
Texas Ecumenical Action (Austin, Tex.). 1959–70.
Texas Observer (Austin, Tex.). 1966–69.
Valley Morning Star (Harlingen, Tex.). 1966–69.
Valley Evening Monitor (McAllen, Tex.). 1966–69.
Western Harvester (Chicago, IL). 1947–48.

Other Primary Sources

Books

Abel, Theodore F. *Protestant Home Missions to Catholic Immigrants.* New York: Institute of Social and Religious Research, 1933.

Alinsky, Saul. *Reveille for Radicals.* New York: Vintage Books, 1946; reprint edition in 1969 with a new introduction.

————. *Rules for Radicals: A Practical Primer for Realistic Radicals.* New York: Random House, 1971.

Bergon, Frank, and Murray Norris. *Delano—Another Crisis for the Catholic Church!* Fresno, Calif.: Rudell Publishing, n.d.

Citizens for Facts from Delano, n.d.

Day, Mark. *Forty Acres: Cesar Chavez and the Farm Growers.* New York: Prayer Publishers, 1971.

The Delano Grape Story . . . from the Growers' View. Delano, Calif.: South Central Farmers Committee, n.d.

De Toledano, Ralph. *Little Caesar.* Washington, D.C.: Anthem Books, 1971.

Dunne, John Gregory. *Delano: The Story of the California Grape Strike.* New York: Farrar, Straus and Giroux, 1967.

Galarza, Ernesto. *Merchants of Labor: The Mexican Bracero Story.* Charlotte, N.C. and Santa Barbara, Calif.: McNally and Loftin, 1964.

Gamio, Manuel. *The Mexican Immigrant: His Life-Story.* Chicago: University of Chicago Press, 1931.

Goldschmidt, Walter. *As You Sow.* Glencoe, Ill.: Free Press, 1947.

Grant, Allan, and Murray Norris. *Clergy Views of Delano and the Grape Boycott.* Fresno, Calif.: Rudell Publishing, 1969.

Gray, James. *The American Civil Liberties Union of Southern California and the Imperial Valley Agricultural Labor Disturbances, 1930, 1934.* San Francisco: R&E Research Associates, 1977.

Healy, Cletus. *Battle for the Vineyards.* New York: Twin Circle Publishing, 1969.

Jamieson, Stuart. *Labor Unionism in American Agriculture.* 1946. Reprint edition in the Chicano Heritage Series. New York: Arno Press, 1976.

Kostyu, Frank A. *Shadows in the Valley: The Story of One Man's Struggle for Justice.* Garden City, N.Y.: Doubleday, 1970.

Levy, Jacques. *Cesar Chavez: Autobiography of La Causa.* New York: W. W. Norton, 1975.

London, Joan, and Henry Anderson. *So Shall Ye Reap.* New York: Thomas Y. Crowell, 1970.

Matthiessen, Peter. *Sal Si Puedes: Cesar Chavez and the New American Revolution.* New York: Random House, 1969.

McWilliams, Carey. *Factories in the Field: The Story of Migratory Farm Labor in California.* Boston: Little, Brown, 1935.

————. *Ill Fares the Land: Migrants and Migratory Labor in the U.S.* Boston: Little, Brown, 1942.

————. *North from Mexico: The Spanish-Speaking People of the U.S.* 1948. Reprint edition in Contributions in American History. Edited by Matt S. Meier. Westport, Conn.: Greenwood Press, 1990.

———. *Southern California Country: An Island on the Land*. American Folkways Series. Edited by Erskine Caldwell. New York: Duell, Sloan and Pearce, 1946.

Pond, William D. *Gospel Pioneering: Reminiscences of Early Congregationalism in California, 1833–1920*. Oberlin, Ohio: News Printing, 1921.

Sherry, Gerard E. *Farm Labor Problems: The Anguish of Delano*. Fresno, Calif.: Diocese of Fresno, n.d.

Shotwell, Louisa R. *The Harvesters: The Story of the Migrant People*. Garden City, N.Y.: Doubleday, 1961.

Taylor, Paul S. *An American-Mexican Frontier: Nueces County, Texas*. Chapel Hill: University of North Carolina Press, 1934.

Taylor, Ronald B. *Chavez and the Farm Workers*. Boston: Beacon Press, 1975.

Articles and Chapters in Edited Books

Allen, Gary. "The Grapes: Communist Wrath in Delano." *American Opinion* (June 1966).

"Church Now Tells Growers Which Union to Recognize." *California Farmer* (unidentified issue).

Dunnam, Spurgeon M., III. "Council Dies, Pickets Protest, Conference Begins." *Texas Methodist* (7 March 1969): 1, 3.

Grant, Allan. "California Grapes and the Boycott: The Growers' Side of the Story." *Presbyterian Life* (1 December 1968): 20–21, 35, 37–39.

Hartmire, Wayne C. "Servanthood among Seasonal Farm Workers—What Form?" *Presbyterian Life* (1 March 1969): 17–19, 32–33.

"L.A. Presbytery Rejects Paper Supporting Migrant Ministry." *Southern Californian Presbyterian* (March 1966): 10.

Longcope, Kay. "The Changing Role of the Migrant Ministry." *Presbyterian Life* (15 November 1967): 12, 14–16, 38.

———. "Churches Try to Ease Tension as Farmers Face Union in Texas." *Presbyterian Life* (15 July 1967): 23–24.

———. "Protests Muddy Ecumenical Waters." *Together* (May 1969): 10, 12.

Lyons, Daniel. Editorial. "The Chavez Union Is a Hoax." *Life Lines* 12, no. 84 (17 July 1970).

Maverick, Maury, Jr. "Marching for a 'Ghastly Recompense' in Texas." *New Republic* (24 September 1966): 11.

Nieto, Leo D. "Involved in the Movement of La Raza." *Engage* 1, no. 21 (1969): 17–21.

Norris, Murray. "Chavez and the Catholic Church." *California Farmer* (20 July 1968): 5, 7.

Phillips, Norman D. "Chicano Workers, Rio Grande Farmers Agree to Meet." *Christian Century* 88, no. 3 (1971): 84–87.

Proctor, Ben. "The Modern Texas Rangers: A Law-Enforcement Dilemma in the Rio Grande Valley." In *Mexican-Americans. An Awakening Minority*, edited by Manuel P. Servin, 212–27. Beverly Hills, Calif.: Glencoe Press, 1970.

Shuman, Charles B. Untitled editorial. *Nation's Agriculture* (March 1969).

Westerfield, Gary. "Sour Grapes: The Move to Control Our Food Supply." *American Opinion* (December 1968).

Wolfe, Burton H. "Father Vizzard: Enemy of Exploiters." *Sign* (May 1966): 16–18.
Zaninovich, Martin. Untitled. *St. Joseph Magazine* 67, no. 7 (1966): 14–16.

Secondary Sources

Books

Abell, Aaron I. *American Catholicism and Social Action: A Search for Social Justice, 1865–1950*. Notre Dame, Ind.: University of Notre Dame Press, 1960.
———. *The Urban Impact on American Protestantism, 1865–1900*. Cambridge, Mass.: Harvard University Press, 1943. Reprint edition. Hamden, Conn.: Archon, 1962.
Abbott, Carl. *The Metropolitan Frontier: Cities in the Modern American West*. Tucson: University of Arizona Press, 1993.
Acuña, Rodolfo. *Occupied America: A History of Chicanos*, 3rd edition. New York: Harper Collins, 1988.
Allen, Ruth. *Chapters in the History of Organized Labor in Texas*. Austin: University of Texas Press, 1941.
Allsup, Carl. *The American GI Forum: Origins and Evolution*. Austin: Center for Mexican-American Studies of the University of Texas, 1982.
Almirol, Edwin B. *Ethnic Identity and Social Negotiation: A Study of a Filipino Community in California*. Immigrant Communities and Ethnic Minorities in the United States and Canada Series, 10. New York: AMS Press, 1985.
Amberson, Mary Margaret McAllen. *I Would Rather Sleep in Texas: A History of the Lower Rio Grande Valley and the People of the Santa Anita Land Grant*. Austin: Texas State Historical Association, 2003.
Anders, Evan M. *Boss Rule in South Texas: The Progressive Era*. Austin: University of Texas Press, 1979.
Anderson, Robert Mapes. *Vision of the Disinherited: The Making of American Pentecostalism*. New York: Oxford University Press, 1979.
Ave, Mario Paguia. *Characteristics of Filipino Social Organizations in Los Angeles*. San Francisco: R&E Research Associates. 1974 reprint of master's thesis, University of Southern California.
Balderrama, Francisco E., and Raymond Rodriguez. *Decade of Betrayal: Mexican Repatriation in the 1930s*. Albuquerque: University of New Mexico Press, 1995.
Bean, Walton. *California: An Interpretive History*. New York: McGraw-Hill, 1968; 6th edition, with James J. Rawls, New York: McGraw-Hill, 1993.
Berger, Samuel R. *Dollar Harvest: The Story of the Farm Bureau*. Lexington, Mass.: D. C. Heath, 1971.
Boren, Carter E. *Religion on the Texas Frontier*. San Antonio, Tex.: Naylor, 1968.
Brackenridge, R. Douglas, and Francisco O. García-Treto. *Iglesia Presbiteriana: A History of Presbyterians and Mexican Americans in the Southwest*. San Antonio, Tex.: Trinity University Press, 1974. Revised edition, 1989.
Brading, D. A. *Mexican Phoenix, Our Lady of Guadalupe: Image and Tradition across Five Centuries*. Cambridge: Cambridge University Press, 2001.

Bronder, Saul E. *Social Justice and Church Authority: The Public Life of Archbishop Robert E. Lucey*. Philadelphia: Temple University Press, 1982.

Brusher, Joseph S. *Consecrated Thunderbolt: Father Yorke of San Francisco*. Hawthorne, N.J.: Joseph F. Wagner, 1973.

Buenger, Walter L., and Robert A. Calvert. *Texas History and the Move into the Twenty-First Century*. Vol. 2 of *Preparing for Texas in the Twenty-First Century: Building a Future for the Children of Texas*. Austin: Texas Committee for the Humanities, 1990.

Burchell, R. A. *The San Francisco Irish, 1848–1880*. Manchester: Manchester University Press, 1979.

Burns, Jeffrey M. *San Francisco: A History of the Archdiocese of San Francisco*. 3 vols. Strasbourg, France: Editions de Signe, 1999.

Calvert, Robert A., and Arnoldo De León. *The History of Texas*. Wheeling, Ill.: Harlan-Davidson, 1995. 2nd edition, 1996.

Camp, Richard L. *The Papal Ideology of Social Reform: A Study in Historical Development, 1878–1967*. Leiden: E. J. Brill, 1969.

Candelaria, Michael R. *Popular Religion and Liberation: The Dilemma of Liberation Theology*. Albany: State University of New York Press, 1990.

Castenada, Carlos E. *Our Catholic Heritage in Texas*. Vol. 6 of *The Fight for Freedom, 1810–1836*. Austin, Tex.: Von Boeckmann-Jones, 1950.

———. *Our Catholic Heritage in Texas*. Vol. 7 of *The Church in Texas since Independence, 1836–1950*. Austin, Tex.: Von Boeckmann-Jones, 1950.

Caughey, John W., and Norris Hundley Jr. *California: History of a Remarkable State*. Englewood Cliffs, N.J.: Prentice-Hall, 1940, 1953, 1970, 1982.

Cavert, Samuel M. *The American Churches in the Ecumenical Movement, 1900–1968*. New York: Association Press, 1968.

———. *Church Cooperation and Unity in America: A Historical Review, 1900–1970*. New York: Association Press, 1970.

Chambers, Clark A. *California Farm Organizations: A History Study of the Grange, Farm Bureau, and the Associated Farmers, 1929–1941*. Berkeley: University of California Press, 1952.

Clifford, Elizabeth A. *The Story of Victory Noll*. Fort Wayne, Ind.: Keefer Printing, 1981.

Coalson, George O. *The Development of the Migratory Farm Labor System in Texas, 1900–1954*. San Francisco: R&E Research Associates, 1977.

Costello, Gerald M. *Without Fear or Favor: George Higgins on the Record*. Mystic, Conn.: Twenty-Third Publications, 1984.

Cronin, Bernard C. *Father Yorke and the Labor Movement in San Francisco, 1900–1910*. The Catholic University of America Studies in Economics Series 12. Washington, D.C.: Catholic University of America Press, 1943.

Cross, Ira B. *A History of the Labor Movement in California*. Berkeley: University of California Press, 1935.

Cruz, Gilberto Rafael, and Martha Oppert Cruz. *A Century of Service: The History of the Catholic Church in the Lower Rio Grande Valley*. Harlingen, Tex.: United Printers and Publishers, 1979.

Cuellar, Robert A. *A Social and Political History of the Mexican-American Population of Texas, 1929–1963*. San Francisco: R&E Research Associates. 1974 reprint of master's thesis, University of Texas, 1969?

Daniel, Cletus. *Bitter Harvest: A History of California Farmworkers, 1870–1941.* Ithaca, N.Y.: Cornell University Press, 1981.

Deck, Allan Figueroa. *The Second Wave: Hispanic Ministry and the Evangelization of Cultures.* Mahwah, N.J.: Paulist Press, 1989.

De León, Arnoldo. *The Tejano Community, 1836–1900.* Albuquerque: University of New Mexico Press, 1982.

———. *They Called Them Greasers: Anglo Attitudes toward Mexicans in Texas, 1821–1900.* Austin: University of Texas Press, 1983.

DeWitt, Howard. *Violence in the Fields: A Filipino Farm Labor Unionization during the Great Depression.* Saratoga, Calif.: Century Twenty-One Publishing, 1980.

Documents of California Catholic History. Edited by Francis J. Weber. Los Angeles: Dawson's Book Shop, 1965.

Doyon, Bernard. *The Calvary of Christ on the Rio Grande, 1849–1883.* Milwaukee: Bruce Publishing Press, 1956.

Drake, Susan Samuels. *Fields of Courage: Remembering César Chávez and the People Whose Labor Feeds Us.* Santa Cruz, Calif.: Many Names Press, 1997.

Elizondo, Virgilio. *The Future Is Mestizo: Life Where Cultures Meet.* Bloomington, Ind.: Meyer-Stone Books, 1988.

———. *Galilean Journey: The Mexican-American Promise.* Maryknoll, N.Y.: Orbis Books, 1983.

———. *Guadalupe: Mother of the New Creation.* Maryknoll, N.Y.: Orbis Books, 1997.

———. *La Morenita.* San Antonio, Tex.: Mexican American Cultural Center, 1992.

Engh, Michael E. *Frontier Faiths: Church, Temple, and Synagogue in Los Angeles, 1848–1888.* Albuquerque: University of New Mexico Press, 1992.

Ernst, Eldon G., with Douglas Firth Anderson. *Pilgrim Progression: The Protestant Experience in California.* Vol. 2 of *The Religious Contours of California: Windows to the World's Religions.* Edited by Phillip E. Hammond and Ninian Smart. Santa Barbara, Calif.: Fithian Press, 1993.

Espín, Orlando. *The Faith of the People: Theological Reflections on Popular Catholicism.* Maryknoll, N.Y.: Orbis Books, 1997.

Etulain, Richard. *Religion in the Twentieth-Century American West: A Bibliography.* Albuquerque: Center for the American West, Department of History, University of New Mexico, 1991.

Faith Expressions of Hispanics in the Southwest. Vol. 1 of *Workshops on Hispanic Liturgy and Popular Piety.* San Antonio, Tex.: Mexican American Cultural Center, 1983?

Ferriss, Susan, and Ricardo Sandoval. *The Fight in the Fields: Cesar Chavez and the Farmworkers Movement.* Edited by Diana Hembree. New York and San Diego: Harcourt Brace, 1997.

Frankiel, Sandra S. *California's Spiritual Frontiers: Religious Alternatives in Anglo-Protestantism, 1850–1910.* Berkeley: University of California Press, 1988.

Galarza, Ernesto. *Farm Workers and Agri-Business in California, 1947–1960.* Notre Dame, Ind.: University of Notre Dame Press, 1977.

García, Richard A. *The Rise of the Mexican-American Middle Class: San Antonio, 1929–1941.* College Station: Texas A&M University Press, 1991.

Gómez-Quiñones, Juan. *Chicano Politics: Reality and Promise, 1940–1990.* Calvin P. Horn Lectures in Western History and Culture. Albuquerque: University of New Mexico Press, 1990.

————. *Mexican-American labor, 1790–1990.* Albuquerque: University of New Mexico Press, 1994.

Grebler, Leo, Joan W. Moore, and Ralph C. Guzman. *The Mexican Americans: The Nation's Second Largest Minority.* New York: Free Press, 1970.

Green, George. *The Establishment in Texas Politics: The Primitive Years, 1938–1957.* Contributions in Political Science Series 21. Westport, Conn.: Greenwood Press, 1979.

Gregory, James N. *American Exodus: The Dust Bowl Migration and Okie Culture in California.* New York: Oxford University Press, 1989.

Gribble, Richard. *Catholicism and the San Francisco Labor Movement, 1886–1921.* San Francisco: Mellen Research University Press, 1993.

Griswold del Castillo, Richard, and Richard A. Garcia. *César Chávez: A Triumph of Spirit.* Norman: University of Oklahoma Press, 1995.

Grijalva, Joshua. *A History of Mexican Baptists in Texas, 1881–1981.* Dallas: Baptist General Convention of Texas, 1982.

Guerrero, Andres G. *A Chicano Theology.* Maryknoll, N.Y.: Orbis Books, 1987.

Gutiérrez, David G. *Walls and Mirrors: Mexican Americans, Mexican Immigrants, and the Politics of Ethnicity.* Berkeley: University of California Press, 1995.

Gutiérrez, José Angel. *The Making of a Chicano Militant: Lessons from Cristal.* Wisconsin Studies in Autobiography. Edited by William L. Andrews. Madison: University of Wisconsin Press, 1998.

Handy, Robert T. *We Witness Together: A History of Cooperative Home Missions, 1900–1950.* New York: Friendship Press, 1956.

Higgins, George G., and William Bole. *Organized Labor and the Church: Reflections of a Labor Priest.* New York: Paulist Press, 1993.

Hine, Leland D. *Baptists in Southern California.* Valley Forge, Pa.: Judson Press, 1966.

Hogue, Harland E. *Prophets and Paupers: Religion in the California Gold Rush, 1848–1869.* San Francisco: International Scholars Press, 1996.

Holland, Clifton L. *The Religious Dimension in Hispanic Los Angeles: A Protestant Case Study.* Pasadena, Calif.: Carey McWilliams Library, 1974.

Hoffman, Abraham. *Unwanted Mexican Americans in the Great Depression: Repatriation Pressures, 1929–1939.* Tucson: University of Arizona Press, 1974.

Hopkins, C. Howard. *The Rise of the Social Gospel in American Protestantism, 1865–1915.* New Haven, Conn.: Yale University Press, 1940.

Issel, William, and Robert W. Cherny. *San Francisco, 1865–1932: Politics, Power, and Urban Development.* Berkeley: University of California Press, 1986.

Jelinek, Lawrence J. *Harvest Empire: A History of California Agriculture.* Golden Gate Series. Edited by Norris Hundley Jr., and John A. Schutz. San Francisco: Boyd and Fraser Publishing, 1979.

Jenkins, J. Craig. *The Politics of Insurgency: The Farm Worker Movement in the 1960s.* New York: Columbia University Press, 1985.

Jervey, Edward D. *The History of Methodism in Southern California and Arizona.* Nashville, Tenn.: Parthenon, 1960.

Jordan, Terry G., John L. Bean Jr., and William M. Holmes. *Texas: A Geography.* Boulder, Colo.: Westview Press, 1984.

Kushner, Sam. *Long Road to Delano.* New York: International Publisher, 1975.

Lantis, David W., Rodney Steiner, and Arthur E. Karinen. *California: Land of Contrast.* Belmont, Calif.: Wadsworth Publishing, 1963.

Limerick, Patricia Nelson. *The Legacy of Conquest: The Unbroken Past of the American West*. New York: W. W. Norton, 1987.

Machado, Daisy. *Of Borders and Margins: Hispanic Disciples in Texas, 1888–1945*. American Academy of Religion Series. Edited by Carole Myscofski. New York: Oxford University Press, 2003.

Madsen, William. *Mexican-Americans of South Texas*. 2nd ed. New York: Holt, Rinehart and Winston, 1973.

Maffly-Kipp, Laurie F. *Religion and Society in Frontier California*. New Haven, Conn.: Yale University Press, 1994.

Malone, Michael P., and Richard W. Etulain. *The American West: A Twentieth-Century History*. Lincoln: University of Nebraska Press, 1989.

Maril, Robert Lee. *Poorest of Americans: The Mexican Americans of the Lower Rio Grande Valley of Texas*. Notre Dame, Ind.: University of Notre Dame Press, 1989.

Meier, Matt S., and Feliciano Rivera. *The Chicanos: A History of Mexican Americans*. American Century Series. New York: Hill and Wang, 1972. Revised edition, *Mexican Americans/American Mexicans: From Conquistadors to Chicanos*, 1993.

Meinig, Donald. *Imperial Texas: An Interpretative Essay in Cultural Geography*. Austin: University of Texas Press, 1969.

Meister, Dick, and Anne Loftis. *A Long Time Coming: The Struggle to Unionize America's Farm Workers*. New York: Macmillan, 1977.

Melendy, Brett H. *Asians in America: Filipinos, Koreans, and East Asians*. Boston: Twayne Publishers, 1977.

Montejano, David. *Anglos and Mexicans in the Making of Texas, 1836–1986*. Austin: University of Texas Press, 1987.

Moore, James T. *Acts of Faith: The Catholic Church in Texas, 1900–1950*. College Station: Texas A&M University Press, 2002.

———. *Through Fire and Flood: The Catholic Church in Frontier Texas, 1836–1900*. College Station: Texas A&M University Press, 1992.

Moore, Joan W. *Mexican Americans*. Englewood Cliffs, N.J.: Prentice-Hall, 1970.

Morales, Adam. *American Baptists with a Spanish Accent*. Valley Forge, Pa.: Judson Press, 1964.

Mooney, Patrick H., and Theodore J. Majka. *Farmers' and Farm Workers' Movements: Social Protest in American Agriculture*. Social Movements Past and Present Series. Edited by Irwin T. Sanders. New York: Twayne Publishers, 1995.

Mosqueda, Lawrence J. *Chicanos, Catholicism, and Political Ideology*. Lanham, Md.: University Press of America, 1986.

Nash, Gerald. *Creating the West: Historical Interpretations, 1980–1990*. Albuquerque: University of New Mexico Press, 1991.

One Hundred Years of Catholic Social Thought: Celebration and Challenge. Edited by John A. Coleman. Maryknoll, N.Y.: Orbis Books, 1991.

Phelan, John Leddy. *The Hispanization of the Philippines: Spanish Aims and Filipino Responses, 1565–1700*. Madison: University of Wisconsin Press, 1959.

Pitt, Leonard. *The Decline of the Californios: A Social History of the Spanish-Speaking Californians, 1846–1890*. Berkeley: University of California Press, 1966.

Pomeroy, Earl. *The Pacific Slope: A History of California, Oregon, Washington, Idaho, Utah, and Nevada*. New York: Alfred A. Knopf, 1965.

Posadas, Barbara M. *The Filipino Americans*. The New Americans Series. Edited by Ronald H. Bayor. Westport, Conn.: Greenwood Press, 1999.

Post, Donald E., and Walter E. Smith. *Clergy: Outsiders and Adversaries; The Story of Catholic and Protestant Clergy's Attempts to Relate the Gospel in Three South Texas Towns Experiencing Changing Mexicano/Anglo Relationships during the Period of 1945–1975.* National Endowment for the Humanities Grant. No. RS-26255–531, n.d.

Pratt, Henry J. *The Liberalization of American Protestantism: A Case Study in Complex Organizations.* Detroit, Mich.: Wayne State University Press, 1972.

Privett, Stephen A. *The U.S. Catholic Church and Its Hispanic Members: The Pastoral Vision of Archbishop Robert E. Lucey.* San Antonio, Tex.: Trinity University Press, 1988.

Prophets Denied Honor: An Anthology of the Hispanic Church in the U.S. Edited by Antonio M. Stevens-Arroyo. Maryknoll, N.Y.: Orbis Books, 1980.

Prouty, Marco G. *Cesar Chavez: The Catholic Bishops, and the Farmworkers' Struggle for Social Justice.* Tucson: University of Arizona Press, 2006.

Putnam, Jackson K. *Modern California Politics: 1917–1980.* Golden Gate Series. Edited by Norris Hundley Jr., and John A. Shutz. San Francisco: Boyd and Fraser Publishing, 1980.

Rafael, Vicente L. *Contracting Colonialism: Translation and Christian Conversion in Tagalog Society under Early Spanish Rule.* Ithaca, N.Y.: Cornell University Press, 1988.

Reisler, Mark. *By the Sweat of Their Brow: Mexican Immigrant Labor in the United States, 1900–1940.* Westport, Conn.: Greenwood Press, 1976.

Rodriguez, Jeanette. *Our Lady of Guadalupe: Faith and Empowerment among Mexican-American Women.* Austin: University of Texas Press, 1994.

Ross, Fred. *Conquering Goliath: Cesar Chavez in the Beginning.* Keene, Calif.: El Taller Gráfico Press, 1989.

Rogin, Michael, and John L. Shover. *Political Change in California: Critical Elections and Social Movements, 1890–1966.* Contributions in American History Series. Edited by Stanley I. Kutler. Westport, Conn.: Greenwood Publishing, 1970.

Rolle, Andrew. *California: A History.* New York: Crowell, 1963. 3rd edition. Arlington Heights, Ill.: Harlan-Davidson, I1978.

———. *Los Angeles: From Pueblo to City of the Future.* Golden Gate Series. Edited by Norris Hundley Jr., and John D. Schutz. 2nd edition. San Francisco: MTL, 1995.

Romo, Ricardo. *East Los Angeles: History of a Barrio.* Austin: University of Texas Press, 1983.

Rooham, James E. *American Catholics and the Social Question: 1865–1900.* New York: Arno Press, 1976.

Ruíz, Vicki. *Cannery Women, Cannery Lives: Mexican Women, Unionization, and the California Food Processing Industry, 1930–1950.* Albuquerque: University of New Mexico Press, 1987.

The Rumble of California Politics: 1848–1970. Edited by Royce D. Delmatier, Clarence F. McIntosh, and Earl G. Waters. New York: John Wiley and Sons, 1970.

Salomon, Larry R. *Roots of Justice: Stories of Organizing in Communities of Color.* Berkeley, Calif.: Chardon Press, 1998.

Samora, Julian, Joe Bernal, and Alberto Pena. *Gunpowder Justice: A Reassessment of the Texas Rangers.* Notre Dame, Ind.: University of Notre Dame Press, 1979.

Szasz, Ferenc Morton. *Religion in the Modern American West.* The Modern American West Series. Edited by Gerald D. Nash and Richard W. Etulain. Tucson: University of Arizona Press, 2000.

Scharlin, Craig, and Lillian V. Villanueva. *Philip Vera Cruz: A Personal History of Fili-*

pino Immigrants and the Farmworkers Movement. 3rd edition. Seattle: University of Washington Press, 2000.

Shelford, Paul K. *Protestant Cooperation in Northern California: The Historical Background of the Federal and Counciliar Movement, 1913–1963.* San Francisco: Northern California–Northern Nevada Council of Churches, 1962.

Simmons, Ozzie G. *Anglo-Americans and Mexican-Americans in South Texas: A Study in Dominant-Subordinate Group Relations.* Reprint edition. New York: Arno Press, 1974. Ph.D. dissertation, Harvard University, 1952.

Smith, Sydney. *Grapes of Conflict.* Pasadena, Calif.: Hope Publishing House, 1987.

Stambaugh, J. Lee, and Lillian J. Stambough. *The Lower Rio Grande Valley of Texas.* San Antonio, Tex.: Naylor, 1954.

Stein, Walter J. *California and the Dust Bowl Migration.* Westport, Conn.: Greenwood Press, 1973.

Steiner, Stan. *La Raza: The Mexican Americans.* New York: Harper and Row, 1969.

Street, Richard Steven. *Beasts of the Field: A Narrative History of California Farm Workers, 1769–1913.* Stanford, Calif.: Stanford University Press, 2004.

Texas through Time: Evolving Interpretations. Edited by Walter L. Buenger and Robert E. Calvert. College Station: Texas A&M University Press, 1991.

Thiess, Jeffrey S. *Mexican Catholicism in Southern California: The Importance of Popular Religiosity and Sacramental Practice in Faith Experience.* Vol. 139 of *Theology and Religion.* American University Studies. Series 7. New York: Peter Lang, 1993.

Trails: Toward a new Western History. Edited by Patricia Nelson Limerick, Clyde A. Milner, and Charles E. Rankin. Lawrence: University Press of Kansas, 1991.

Valdes, Dennis N. *Al Norte: Agricultural Workers in the Great Lakes Region, 1917–1970.* Austin: University of Texas Press, 1991.

Walsh, James P. *Ethnic Militancy: An Irish Catholic Prototype.* San Francisco: R&E Research Associates, 1972.

Weber, Devra. *Dark Sweat, White Gold: California Farm Workers, Cotton, and the New Deal.* Berkeley: University of California Press, 1994.

Weber, Francis J. *California Catholicity.* Los Angeles: Libra Press, 1979.

———. *California's Catholic Heritage.* Los Angeles: Dawson's Book Shop, 1974.

———. *Century of Fulfillment: The Roman Catholic Church in Southern California, 1847–1947.* Mission Hills, Calif.: The Archival Center of the Archdiocese of Los Angeles, 1990.

———. *Encyclopedia of California's Catholic Heritage, 1769–1999.* Spokane, Wash.: Arthur H. Clark, 2000.

———. *John Joseph Cantwell: His Excellency of Los Angeles.* Hong Kong: Cathay Press Limited, 1971.

Writing Western History: Essays on Major Western Historians. Edited by Richard W. Etulain. Albuquerque: University of New Mexico Press, 1991.

Wuthnow, Robert. *The Restructuring of American Religion: Faith and Society since World War II.* Studies in Church and State Series. Edited by John F. Wilson. Princeton, N.J.: Princeton University Press, 1988.

Yinger, Winthrop. *Cesar Chavez: The Rhetoric of Nonviolence.* Hicksville, N.Y.: Exposition Press, 1975.

Zamora, Emilio. *The World of the Mexican Worker in Texas.* College Station: Texas A&M University Press, 1993.

Articles and Chapters in Edited Books

Acosta, Teresa Palomo. "Mexican American Legal Defense and Educational Fund." In Vol. 4 of *The New Handbook of Texas,* edited by Ron Tyler. Austin: Texas State Historical Association, 1996, 659.

———. "Political Association of Spanish-Speaking Organizations." In Vol. 4 of *The New Handbook of Texas,* edited by Ron Tyler. Austin: Texas State Historical Association, 1996, 256.

———. "Southwest Voter Registration Education Project." In Vol. 5 of *The New Handbook of Texas,* edited by Ron Tyler. Austin: Texas State Historical Association, 1996, 1175–76.

Allen, Ruth A., George N. Green, and James V. Reese. "Labor Organizations." In Vol. 3 of *The New Handbook of Texas,* edited by Ron Tyler. Austin: Texas State Historical Association, 1996, 1181.

Anderson, Douglas F. "The Revered J. Stitt Wilson and Christian Socialism in California." In *Religion and Society in the American West: Historical Essays,* edited by Carl Guarneri and David Alvarez, 375–99. Lanham, Md.: University Press of America, 1987.

Atkinson, Ernest E. "Mexican Baptist Institute." In Vol. 4 of *The New Handbook of Texas,* edited by Ron Tyler. Austin: Texas State Historical Association, 1996, 683.

Barton, Paul. "*¡Ya Basta!* Latino/a Protestant Activism in the Chicano/a and Farm Workers Movements." In *Latino Religions and Civic Activism in the U.S.,* edited by Gastón Espinosa, Virgilio Elizondo, and Jesse Miranda, 127–41. New York: Oxford University Press, 2005.

Brauer, Jerald C. "Regionalism and Religion in America." *Church History* 54 (1985): 366–78.

Brereton, Virginia Lieson, "United and Slighted: Women as Subordinated Insiders." In *Between the Times: The Travail of the Protestant Establishment in America, 1900–1960,* edited by William R. Hutchison. Cambridge Series in Religion and American Public Life, edited by Robin W. Lovin. Cambridge: Cambridge University Press, 1989, 143–67.

Brown, Lawrence L. "Protestant Episcopal Church." In Vol. 5 of *The New Handbook of Texas,* edited by Ron Tyler. Austin: Texas State Historical Association, 1996, 359–60.

Buenger, Walter L. "Texas and the South." *Southwestern Historical Quarterly* 103, no. 3 (2000): 309–23.

Burns, Jeffrey M. "The Mexican Catholic Community in California: A Story of Neglect?" In Vol. 1 of *Mexican Americans and the Catholic Church, 1900–1965,* edited by Jay P. Dolan and Gilberto M. Hinojosa. The Notre Dame History of Hispanic Catholics in the U.S., edited by Jay P. Dolan, 129–233. Notre Dame, Ind.: University of Notre Dame Press, 1994.

Calderon, Roberto R., and Emilio Zamora. "Manuela Solis Sager and Emma Tenayuca: A Tribute." In *Chicana Voices: Intersections of Class, Race, and Gender,* edited by Teresa Córdova, Norma Cantú, Gilberto Cardenas, Juan García, and Christine M. Sierra. Austin: Center for Mexican American Studies, University of Texas, 1986. The National Association for Chicano Studies, 1990. Albuquerque: University of New Mexico Press, 1993, 30–41.

Cisneros, B. Nelson. "La Clase Trabajadora en Tejas, 1920–1940." *Aztlán* 6 (1975): 239–65.

Connor, Seymour V. "Onderdonk, Frank Scovill." In Vol. 4 of *The New Handbook of Texas,* edited by Ron Tyler. Austin: Texas State Historical Association, 1996, 1153.

Cuello, José. "Introduction: Chicana/o as a Social Movement." In *Voices of a New Chicana/o History,* edited by Refugio I. Rochin and Dennis N. Valdes, 1–23. East Lansing: Michigan State University Press, 2000.

Daniel, Cletus E. "Cesar Chavez and the Unionization of California Farm Workers." In *Labor Leaders in America.* The Working Class in American History Series, edited by Melvyn Dubofsky and Warren van Tine, 350–82. Urbana: University of Illinois Press, 1987.

De León, Arnoldo. "Topographical Identities in Texas." In *Many Wests: Place, Culture, and Regional Identity,* edited by David M. Wrobel and Michael C. Steiner, 259–70. Lawrence: University Press of Kansas, 1997.

De León, Arnoldo, and Robert A. Calvert. "Civil-Rights Movement." In Vol. 2 of *The Handbook of Texas,* edited by Ron Tyler. Austin: Texas State Historical Association, 1996, 118–20.

Deverell, William. "Privileging the Mission over the Mexican: The Rise of Regional Identity in Southern California." In *Many Wests: Place, Culture, and Regional Identity,* edited by David M. Wrobel and Michael C. Steiner, 235–58. Lawrence: University Press of Kansas, 1997.

Dolan, Jay P. "The New Religious History." *Reviews in American History* 15, no. 3 (1987): 449–54.

"Domestic Farmworkers in America's Heartland: Weslaco, Texas, and the Lower Rio Grande Valley." In *Working Poor: Farmworkers in the U.S.,* edited by David Griffith and Ed Kissam, 89–122. Philadelphia: Temple University Press, 1995.

Drury, Clifford M. "A Chronology of Protestant Beginnings in California." *California Historical Society Quarterly* 25 (June 1947): 163–74.

Elizondo, Virgilio. "Our Lady of Guadalupe as a Cultural Symbol: 'The Power of the Powerless.'" In *Liturgy and Cultural Religious Traditions,* edited by Herman Schmidt and David Power, 25–33. New York: Seabury Press, 1977.

Ernst, Eldon G. "American Religious History from a Pacific Coast Perspective." In *Religion and Society in the American West: Historical Essays,* edited by Carl Guarneri and David Alvarez, 9–39. Lanham, Md.: University Press of America, 1987.

———. "The Emergence of California in American Religious Historiography." *Religion and American Culture: A Journal of Interpretation* 11, no. 1 (2001): 31–52.

Espín, Orlando. "Popular Catholicism among Latinos." In *Hispanic Catholic Culture in the U.S.,* edited by Jay P. Dolan and Allan Figueroa Deck. Vol. 3 of *The Notre Dame History of Hispanic Catholics in the U.S.,* edited by Jay P. Dolan. Notre Dame, Ind.: University of Notre Dame Press, 1994, 308–59.

Flores, Maria Eva, C.D.P. "PADRES." In Vol. 5 of *The New Handbook of Texas,* edited by Ron Tyler. Austin: Texas State Historical Association, 1996, 9–10.

Foscue, Edwin J. "Agricultural History of the Lower Rio Grande Valley Region." *Agricultural History* 8 (March 1934): 124–38.

Francis, Mark R., C.S.V. "Popular Piety and Liturgical Reform." In *Dialogue Rejoined: Theology and Ministry in the United States Hispanic Reality,* edited by Ana Maria Pineda, R.S.M., and Robert Schreiter, C.P.O.S., 162–77. Collegeville, Minn.: Liturgical Press, 1995.

Garcia, Richard A. "Dolores Huerta: Woman, Organizer, and Symbol." *California History* 72, no. 1 (1993): 56–71.

Gifford, David. "Presbyterian Pan American School." In Vol. 5 of *The New Handbook of Texas,* edited by Ron Tyler. Austin: Texas State Historical Association, 1996, 328–29.

Guthrie, Keith. "Presbyterian School for Mexican Girls." In Vol. 4 of *The New Handbook of Texas,* edited by Ron Tyler. Austin: Texas State Historical Association, 1996, 329.

Gilmore, N. Ray, and Gladys W. Gilmore. "The Bracero in California." *Pacific Historical Review* 34 (1965): 266–82.

Green, George N. "Good Neighbor Commission." In Vol. 3 of *The New Handbook of Texas,* edited by Ron Tyler. Austin: Texas State Historical Association, 1996, 240.

Grubbs, Donald H. "Prelude to Chavez: The NFLU in California." *Labor History* 6 (1975): 453–69.

Gutiérrez, Ramon A. "Chicano History: Paradigm Shifts and Shifting." In *Voices of a New Chicana/o History,* edited by Refugio I. Rochin and Dennis N. Valdes, 91–114. East Lansing: Michigan State University Press, 2000.

Hartmann, Susan M. "Expanding Feminism's Field and Focus: Activism in the NCC in the 1960s and 1970s." In *Women and Twentieth-Century Protestantism,* edited by Margaret Lamberts Bendroth and Virginia Lieson Brereton, 49–70. Urbana: University of Illinois Press, 2002.

Hendrick, John R. "Presbyterian Church." In Vol. 5 of *The New Handbook of Texas,* edited by Ron Tyler. Austin: Texas State Historical Association, 1996, 327.

Hinojosa, Gilbert M. "Mexican-American Faith Communities in Texas and the Southwest." In *Mexican Americans and the Catholic Church, 1900–1965,* edited by Jay P. Dolan and Gilberto M. Hinojosa. Vol. 1 of *The Notre Dame History of Hispanic Catholics in the U.S.,* edited by Jay P. Dolan. Notre Dame, Ind.: University of Notre Dame Press, 1994, 1–125.

Hutchison, William R. "Discovering America." In *Between the Times: The Travail of the Protestant Establishment in America, 1900–1960,* edited by William R. Hutchison. Cambridge Series in Religion and American Public Life, edited by Robin W. Lovin. Cambridge: Cambridge University Press, 1989, 303–9.

Icaza, Rosa Marie. "The Cross in Mexican Popular Piety." *Liturgy* 1 (1981): 27–34.

Issel, William. "Faith-Based Activism in American Cities: The Case of the San Francisco Catholic Action Cadre." *Journal of Church and State* 50, no. 3 (2008): 519–40.

Jordan, Terry G. "A Century and a Half of Ethnic Change in Texas, 1836–1986." *Southwestern Historical Quarterly* 89 (April 1986): 385–422.

———. "The Imprint of the Upper and Lower South on Mid-Nineteenth-Century Texas." *Annals of the Association of American Geographers* 57 (September 1967): 667–90.

Juarez, José Roberto. *"La Iglesia Católica y el Chicano en Sud Texas, 1836–1911." Aztlán* 4 (1974): 217–55.

Killen, Patricia O'Connell. "Geography, Denominations, and the Human Spirit: A Decade of Studies on Religion in the Western United States." *Religious Studies Review* 21, no. 4 (1995): 277–84.

King, William. "The Reform Establishment and the Ambiguities of Influence." In *Between the Times: The Travail of the Protestant Establishment in America, 1900–1960,* edited by William R. Hutchison. Cambridge Series in Religion and American Public Life, edited by Robin W. Lovin. Cambridge: Cambridge University Press, 1989, 122–39.

León, Luís D. "César Chávez and Mexican American Civil Religion." In *Latino Religions and Civic Activism in the U.S.,* edited by Gastón Espinosa, Virgilio Elizondo, and Jesse Miranda, 53–64. New York: Oxford University Press, 2005.

Lloyd-Moffett, Stephen. "The Mysticism and Social Action of César Chávez." In *Latino Religions and Civic Activism in the U.S.,* edited by Gastón Espinosa, Virgilio Elizondo, and Jesse Miranda, 36–51. New York: Oxford University Press, 2005.

Lyons, Mary E. "Peter C. Yorke: Advocate of the Irish from the Pulpit to the Podium." In *Religion and Society in the American West: Historical Essays,* edited by Carl Guarneri and David Alvarez, 401–22. Lanham, Md.: University Press of America, 1987.

Machado, Daisy L. "Voices from *Nepantla:* Latinas in U.S. Religious History." In *Feminist Intercultural Theology: Latina Explorations for a Just World,* edited by María Pilar Aquino and Maria José Rosado-Nunes. Maryknoll, N.Y.: Orbis Books, 2007.

Maffly-Kipp, Laurie F. "Eastward Ho! American Religion from the Perspective of the Pacific Rim." In *Retelling U.S. Religious History,* edited by Thomas A. Tweed, 127–48. Berkeley: University of California Press, 1997.

Matthews, Glenna. "Forging a Cosmopolitan Culture: The Regional Identity of San Francisco and Northern California." In *Many Wests: Place, Culture, and Regional Identity,* edited by David M. Wrobel and Michael C. Steiner, 211–34. Lawrence: University Press of Kansas, 1997.

Medina, Lara. "The Challenges and Consequences of Being Latina, Catholic, and Political." In *Latino Religions and Civic Activism in the U.S.,* edited by Gastón Espinosa, Virgilio Elizondo, and Jesse Miranda, 97–110. New York: Oxford University Press, 2005.

Meinig, Donald W. "American Wests: Preface to a Geographical Interpretation." *Annals of the Association of American Geographers* 65 (1972): 159–84.

Montoya, Maria E. "Beyond Internal Colonialism: Class, Gender, and Culture as Challenges to Chicano Identity." In *Voices of a New Chicana/o History,* edited by Refugio I. Rochin and Dennis N. Valdes, 91–114. East Lansing: Michigan State University Press, 2000.

Moore, Joan W. "Colonialism: The Case of the Mexican American." In *Racism in California: A Reader in the History of Oppression,* edited by Roger Daniels and Spencer C. Olin Jr., 229–39. New York: Macmillan, 1972.

Nabhan-Warren, Kristy. "Mary." In *Handbook of Latina/o Theologies,* edited by Edwin David Aponte and Miguel A. La Torre, 243–49. St. Louis, Mo.: Chalice Press, 2006.

Nañez, Alfredo. "Methodism among the Spanish-Speaking People in Texas and New Mexico." In *One in the Lord: A History of Ethnic Minorities in the South Central Jurisdiction, The United Methodist Church,* edited by Walter N. Vernon, 53–61. Bethany, Okla.: Cowan Printing and Litho, 1977.

Nañez, Alfredo, and Clotilde Nañez. "Methodism among the Spanish-Speaking of Texas." In *The History of Texas Methodism,* edited by Olin Nail, 193–97. Austin, Tex.: Capital Printing, 1961.

Oropeza, Lorena. "Making History: The Chicano Movement." In *Voices of a New Chicana/o History,* edited by Refugio I. Rochin and Dennis N. Valdes, 197–230. East Lansing: Michigan State University Press, 2000.

Orozco, Cynthia E. "League of United Latin American Communities." In Vol. 3 of *The New Handbook of Texas,* edited by Ron Tyler. Austin: Texas State Historical Association, 1996, 129–31.

———. "Velásquez, William C." In Vol. 6 of *The New Handbook of Texas,* edited by Ron Tyler. Austin: Texas State Historical Association, 1996, 720.

Overfelt, Robert C. "Mexican Revolution." In Vol. 4 of *The New Handbook of Texas,* edited by Ron Tyler. Austin: Texas State Historical Association, 1996, 668.

Pomeroy, Earl. "Toward a Reorientation of Western History: Continuity and Environment." *Mississippi Valley Historical Review* (March 1955): 579–600.

Pritchard, Linda K. "A Comparative Approach to Western Religious History: Texas as a Case Study, 1845–1890." *Western Historical Quarterly* 19 (November 1988): 413–30.

Pycior, Julie Leininger. "Mexican-American Organizations." In Vol. 4 of *The New Handbook of Texas,* edited by Ron Tyler. Austin: Texas State Historical Association, 1996, 660–62.

Quesada, J. Gilberto. "Toward a Working Definition of Social Justice: Father Carmelo A. Trancese, S.J., and Our Lady of Guadalupe Parish, 1932–1953." *Journal of Texas Catholic History and Culture* 4, no. 4 (1993): 44–64.

Ramirez, Daniel. "Borderlands Praxis: The Immigrant Experience in Latino Pentecostal Churches." *Journal of the American Academy of Religion* 67, no. 3 (1999): 573–96.

Randall, Margaret. "Guadalupe, Subversive Virgin." In *Goddess of the Americas: Writings on the Virgin of Guadalupe,* edited by Ana Castillo, 113–23. New York: Riverhead Books, 1996.

Rayburn, John C. "Melinda Rankin—Crusader of the Rio Grande." *Journal of Presbyterian History* 40 (September 1962): 160–80.

Roberts, R. L. "Church of Christ." In Vol. 2 of *The New Handbook of Texas,* edited by Ron Tyler. Austin: Texas State Historical Association, 1996, 105–6.

Romero, Juan. "Mexican-American Priests: History of PADRES, 1969–1989." In *Hispanics in the Church: Up from the Cellar,* edited by Philip E. Lampe, 71–94. San Francisco: Catholic Scholars Press, 1994.

Rose, Margaret. "From the Fields to the Picket: Huelga Women and the Boycott, 1965–1975." *Labor History* 3 (1990): 271–93.

Sarbaugh, Timothy J. "Father Yorke and the San Francisco Waterfront." *Pacific History* 25 (1981): 28–35.

Steiner, Michael C., and David M. Wrobel. "Many Wests: Discovering a Dynamic Western Regionalism." In *Many Wests: Place, Culture, and Regional Identity,* edited by David M. Wrobel and Michael C. Steiner, 1–30. Lawrence: University Press of Kansas, 1997.

Stevens-Arroyo, Anthony M. "Latino/a Catholic Theology." In *Handbook of Latina/o Theologies,* edited by Edwin David Aponte and Miguel A. La Torre, 169–83. St. Louis, Mo.: Chalice Press, 2006.

Sylvest, Edwin, Jr. "Hispanic American Protestantism in the United States." In *Fronteras: A History of the Latin American Church in the U.S.A. since 1513,* edited by Moises Sandoval, 279–338. San Antonio, Tex.: Mexican American Cultural Center, 1983.

Tafolla, Carmen. "The Church in Texas." In *Fronteras: A History of the Latin American Church in the U.S.A. since 1513,* edited by Moises Sandoval, 183–94. San Antonio, Tex.: Mexican American Cultural Center, 1983.

Turner, Frederick Jackson. "The Significance of the Section in American History." In *Rereading Frederick Jackson Turner: "The Significance of the Frontier in American History" and Other Essays.* Originally in *Wisconsin Magazine of History* 8 (March 1925): 201–24.

Vargas, Zaragosa. "Tejana Radical: Emma Tenayuca and the San Antonio Labor Movement during the Great Depression." *Pacific Historical Review* 66, no. 4 (1997): 553–80.

Vernon, Walter N. "Lydia Patterson Institute." In Vol. 4 of *The New Handbook of Texas,* edited by Ron Tyler. Austin: Texas State Historical Association, 1996, 343.

———. "Methodist Church." In Vol. 4 of *The New Handbook of Texas,* edited by Ron Tyler. Austin: Texas State Historical Association, 1996, 645–46.

Walsh, Edward J. "Mobilization Theory vis-à-vis a Mobilization Process: The Case of the United Farm Workers' Movement." In *Research in Social Movements, Conflicts, and Change,* edited by Louis Kriesberg, 155–77. Greenwich, Conn.: JAI Press, 1978.

Walsh, James P. "The Irish in Early San Francisco." In *The San Francisco Irish, 1850–1976,* edited by James P. Walsh. 2nd edition. San Francisco: The Irish Literary and Historical Society, 1979, 9–26.

Weber, Devra Anne. "The Organizing of Mexicano Agricultural Workers: Imperial Valley and Los Angeles, 1928–34, An Oral History Approach." *Aztlán: Chicano Journal of the Social Sciences and the Arts* 3, no. 2 (1972): 307–47.

Weber, Francis J. "Irish-Born Champion of the Mexican-Americans." *California Historical Society Quarterly* 69 (September 1970): 233–50.

Wollenberg, Charles. "Huelga, 1928 Style: The Imperial Valley Cantaloupe Workers' Strike." *Pacific Historical Review* 38 (February 1969): 46–65.

Yohn, Susan. "Let Christian Women Set the Example in Their Gifts: The 'Business' of Protestant Women's Organizations." In *Women and Twentieth-Century Protestantism,* edited by Margaret Lamberts Bendroth and Virginia Lieson Brereton, 213–35. Urbana: University of Illinois Press, 2002.

Yoo, David K. "Introduction." In *Spiritual Homes: Religion and Asian Americans,* edited by David K. Yoo. Asian and Pacific American Transcultural Studies, ed. Russell C. Leong. Honolulu: University of Hawaii Press, 2000, 1–15.

DISSERTATIONS AND THESES

Anderson, Douglas F. "Through Fire and Fair by the Golden Gate: Progressive Era Protestantism and Regional Culture." Ph.D. dissertation, Graduate Theological Union, 1988; University Microfilms International, Ann Arbor, Mich., 1990.

Avant, Jack T. "The 1966 Rio Grande Farm Workers Strike: Role of the Church." Master's thesis, University of Texas at Austin, 1967.

Cohen, Jan Hart. "To See Christ in Our Brothers: The Role of the Texas Roman Catholic Church in the Rio Grande Valley Farm Workers' Movement, 1966–1967." Master's thesis, University of Texas at Arlington, 1974.

Coronado, Richard J. "A Conceptual Model of the Harvest Labor Market, the Bracero Program, and Factors Involved in Organization among Farm Workers in California, 1946–1970." Ph.D. dissertation, University of Notre Dame, 1980.

Ellsworth, Jeanne. "Women, Children, and Charity in Migrant Labor Camps, 1919–1939." Ph.D. dissertation, State University of New York at Buffalo, 1992.

Filewood, David Lewis. "Tejano Revolt: The Significance of the 1938 Pecan Shellers Strike." Master's thesis, University of Texas at Arlington, 1994.

Hribar, Paul Anthony. "The Social Fasts of Cesar Chavez: A Critical Study of Nonverbal

Communication, Nonviolence, and Public Opinion" Ph.D. dissertation, University of Southern California, 1978.

Janzen, Kenneth L. "The Transformation of the New England Religious Tradition in California, 1849–1869." Ph.D. dissertation, Claremont Graduate School, 1964.

Jeffs, William George. "The Roots of the Delano Grape Strike." Master's thesis, California State College at Fullerton, 1969.

Jones, Lamar Babington. "Mexican-American Labor Problems in Texas." Ph.D. dissertation, University of Texas at Austin, 1965.

Kellogg, Josephine D. "Ministry, Hispanics and Migrants: The San Francisco Mission Band, 1949–1961." Unpublished. Turlock Centennial Foundation, 1986.

Leal, Ray Robert. "The 1966–1967 South Texas Farm Worker Strike: A Case Study of Farm Worker Powerlessness." Ph.D. dissertation, Indiana University, 1983; University Microfilms International, Ann Arbor, Mich., 1986.

Lowerie, Samuel H. "Culture Conflict in Texas." Master's thesis, Columbia University, 1932.

Martinez, Camilo Amado. "The Mexican and Mexican-American Laborers in the Lower Rio Grande Valley of Texas, 1870–1930." Ph.D. dissertation, Texas A&M University, 1987.

McNamara, Patrick H. "Bishops, Priests, and Prophecy: A Study in the Sociology of Religious Protest." Ph.D. dissertation, University of California at Los Angeles, 1968.

McShane, Joseph M., "The Bishops' Program of Social Reconstruction of 1919: A Study in American Catholic Progressivism." Ph.D. dissertation, University of Chicago, 1981.

Mills, Howard M. "The Department of the Church and Economic Life in the National Council of Churches, 1947–1966: A Critical Analysis." Th.D. dissertation, Union Theological Seminary (New York), 1970.

Pulido, Alberto Lopez. "Race Relations within the American Catholic Church: An Historical and Sociological Analysis of Mexican-American Catholics." Ph.D. dissertation, University of Notre Dame, 1989.

Reccow, Louis. "The Orange County Citrus Strikes of 1935–1936: The 'Forgotten People' in Revolt." Ph.D. dissertation, University of Southern California, 1972.

Reilly, De Prague. "The Role of the Churches in the Bracero Program in California." Master's thesis, University of Southern California, 1969.

Remy, Martha Caroline Mitchell. "Protestant Churches and Mexican Americans in South Texas." Ph.D. dissertation, University of Texas at Austin, 1970.

Roberts, Donovan O. "Theory and Practice in the Life and Thought of Cesar E. Chavez: Implications for a Social Ethics." Ph.D. dissertation, Boston University, 1978.

Rose, Margaret E. "Women in the United Farm Workers: A Study of Chicana and Mexicana Participation in a Labor Union, 1950–1980." Ph.D. dissertation, University of California at Los Angeles, 1988.

Salandini, Victor P. "An Objective Evaluation of the Labor Disputes in the Lettuce Industry in Imperial Valley, California, during January–March 1961." Master's thesis, St. Louis University, 1964.

Singleton, Gregory H. "Religion in the City of the Angels: American Protestant Culture and Urbanization, Los Angeles, 1850–1930." Ph.D. dissertation, University of California at Los Angeles, 1976; University Microfilms International, Ann Arbor, Mich., 1979.

Smith, Rosemary E. "The Work of the Bishops' Committee for the Spanish-Speaking on Behalf of the Migrant Worker." Master's thesis, Catholic University of America, 1958.

Sookne, Jennifer Maura. "The Songs of the United Farm Workers in Their Sociological-Cultural and Musical Contexts." Master's thesis, University of Texas at Austin, 1978.

Soto, Antonio R. "The Chicano and the Church in Northern California, 1848–1978: A Study of an Ethnic Minority within the Roman Catholic Church." Ph.D. dissertation, University of California at Berkeley, 1978.

Stroh, Paul C. "The Catholic Clergy and American Labor Disputes, 1900–1937." Ph.D. dissertation, Catholic University of America, 1939.

Thomas, Stanley Whitaker. "The Image of Labor Organization in Church and Trade Union, 1945–1955: The Images of Labor Organization as Held by the American Federation of Labor, the Congress of Industrial Organizations, the National Catholic Welfare Conference, the Federal Council of Churches, and the National Council of Churches." Ph.D. dissertation, Boston University, 1960.

Walsh, Albeus. "The Work of the Catholic Bishops' Committee for the Spanish-Speaking in the United States." Master's thesis, University of Texas at Austin, 1952.

Winn, Charles Carr. "The Valley Farm Workers Movement, 1966–1967." Master's thesis, University of Texas at Austin, 1970.

Public Documents

"Abstract of Hearings on Unemployment before the California State Unemployment Commission, April and May, 1932." Berkeley: Bancroft Library, University of California at Berkeley, 1932.

Letters and Papers

Boyle, Eugene. "Social Justice in the Archdiocese of San Francisco, 1962–1972: A Personal Reflection," n.d.

De Magaña, María Saludado. Letter to author. Oakland, Calif. 26 November 2001.

Escutia, Roberto. Letter to author. Bakersfield, Calif. 20 November 2001.

Kilpatrick, Harold. "The Last That Became First." Austin, Tex. February 1986.

———. Letter to author. Austin, Tex. 21 September 1994.

———. Miscellaneous printed materials.

Krueger, Edgard A. Letter to author. Edinburg, Tex. 23 September 1994.

Martinez, Eloy. Letter to author. San Leandro, Calif. 25 November 2001.

McAllister, Gerald N. Letter to author. San Antonio, Tex. 5 October 1994.

———. "The Right Reverend Gerald Nicholas McAllister." Vita, n.d.

Neubauer, Dolores Ann. "Mabuhay Brother Pete Velasco." Biographical sheet, n.d.

Scholes, William E. Letter to author. Albuquerque, NMex. 1 October 1994.

Segerhammar, Ruth. Letter to author. Thousand Oaks, Calif. 19 January 1995.

The Rev. Raymond J. Tintle, O.F.M. Letter to author. Los Angeles, Calif. 27 November 2001.

Whitaker, Betty. Letter to author. Pharr, Tex. 8 October 1994.

Yinger, Winthrop. Letter to author. Port Charlotte, Fla. 28 February 1995.

Nonprint Sources

Chatfield, LeRoy. Interview with author. Sacramento, Calif. 5 May 1994.

Hartmire, Wayne "Chris." Interview with author. Sacramento, Calif. 5 May 1994.

Kilpatrick, Harold. Interview with author. Austin, Tex. 22 September 1994.

Krueger, Edgar A., and Betty Whitaker. Interview with author. Edinburg, Tex. 20 September 1994.

Nieto, Leo. Interview with author. Los Angeles, Calif. 26 April 1994.

Orendain, Antonio. Interview with author. Pharr, Tex. 3 June 2005.

Ramirez, Daniel. Responder. "Evangelicalism in Latina/o and Latin American Communities." Annual Meeting of the American Academy of Religion. San Antonio, Tex. 22 November 2004.

Transcript, "Morning Edition." National Public Radio. Washington, D.C. 1 April 1994.

Index

Congress of Industrial Organizations (CIO), 51, 56–57, 76, 145
Connally, John, 143
contracts with vineyards in California, 81, 82, 89, 101–5
Cortes, Ernie Jr., 162
Council of Trent, 2, 30
Council of Women for Home Missions, 39–41. *See also* Migrant Ministry
criollo landowners, 17–18, 31
Cruz, Reynaldo de la, 161
CSO (Community Service Organization), 55, 70
El Cursillo de Cristiandad, 85–86

Day, Mark, 83, *111*
Deines, William, 155
Delano, California grape strike, 5, 74–78. *See also* La Causa
Department of the Church and Economic Life, 62–63
deportation of Mexicans (1930s), 42–43
Depression, Great, 42, 45
Diego, Juan, 31, 87
Diego y Morena, Francisco García, 19–20
DiGiorgio Fruit Company, 54, 92, 98
Dimas, Magdeleno, 153
"Dimas Affair," 152–53
Dispoto farms, 102
Division of Home Missions, National Council of Churches. *See* Migrant Ministry
Doak, William N., 42
Donnelly, Joseph F., 101, 104, *112*
Donohoe, Hugh A., 97, 101
Drake, James: California ministry work, 73, 76, 92–93, 100–101; photos, *109;* Texas ministry work, 150, 155
Drake, Susan, 88
Duggan, Ralph, 53
dust bowl migrants from Mid-West, 43–44, 59
Dwyer, John T., 98

educational ministry to Tejanas/os, 123
Elizondo, Virgilio, 31
Emil Schwarzhaupt Foundation, 131–32
Espín, Orlando, 2–3
ethnic groups: cooperation in post-WWII farm labor movement, 54; diversity of South

Texas, 116; lack of cooperation among minority groups, 38; lack of minority representation in clergy, 32, 119, 120; Protestant pastor's denial of conflict, 76; WWII's contribution to mitigation of conflict, 48. *See also individual groups*
European Catholic immigrants to Texas, 118–19. *See also* Irish American Catholics

Farmers' Alliance, 125
farmers/growers. *See* growers/farmers
farm workers: governmental support for, 51, 133–34; influences on Mexican immigrant, 24–25; multiple immigrant wave challenge in Texas, 54, 126, 130–31; national/international scope of, 5; and poor rural habitation, 60–61; post-WWII continued exploitation, 48–49; reconciliation with agribusiness in Texas, 11; San Francisco (early 20th c.), 24. *See also* California; La Causa; religious dimension; Texas; union organizing
fast during strike, Chávez's, 82–85, 86
federal government: deportation of Mexicans (1930s), 42–43; and Good Neighbor Commission in Texas, 130–31; labor movement support from, 51; migrant labor management in Depression, 43; support for workers in Texas, 133–34; Texas Ranger brutality inquiry, 155–56; VISTA program, 158–59
feminists *(mujeristas)*, 12, 31, 88–91
Filipino immigrants: call of grape strike, 74; Catholicism of, 33–34; exploitation of, 37–38, 48–49, 59; loss of jobs to dust bowlers, 43; as migrant laborers in California, 35; photos, *107;* strikes by, 54–55; UFWOC leadership roles, 75; U.S. limitations on, 34
Filipino Labor Union, 38
financing of strike, challenges of, 75–76, 82
Frances DePauw Home, 29
Franciscan missions in California, 19
Fresno, California, La Causa march in, 80

Galarza, Ernesto, 56
Gallagher, Nicholas A., 119
Galván, Lucio, 139
Gandhi, Mahatma, 85
Garcia, John, 53

Garcia, Nehemias, 157
generational differences in labor activism support, 69
geographical differences in La Causa support, 69
Giumarra Vineyards, 103
Gonzales, Rudolfo "Corky," 68
Gonzalez, Antonio, 143, 144–45
Gonzalez, Henry B., 144
Goshen project, 73
Grant, Allan, 93–94
The Grapes of Wrath (Steinbeck), 43
grape strike and boycott, California, 5, 74–78. *See also* La Causa
grassroots organizing, Migrant Ministry's move into, 72
Great Central Valley of California, 34, 35. *See also* San Joaquin Valley
Great Depression, 42, 45
Green, Al, 75, 79
growers/farmers: boycott effect on, 95–96; contracts with farm labor in California, 81, 82, 89, 101–5; Depression's effect on, 42; exploitation of workers, 36, 37–38, 49, 54; and litigation against Texas Rangers, 154–55; pressure on churches to oppose unions, 69, *110*, 149; resentment of Huerta's leadership, 90; responses to Delano grape strike, 75, 81, 85; strike opposers as beneficiaries of, 94; Texas melon strike, 140, 149, 150, 151–52, 154–55; violence against farm workers, 36–37
Guimarra, John Jr., 103, *112*
Guimarra Vineyards Corporation, 92
Gutiérrez, José Ángel, 68

Hanna, Archbishop Edward J., 24–25
Hartmire, Wayne "Chris": and boycott of grapes, 93–94; Chávez's purge of, 87; La Causa role of, 76, 80; Migrant Ministry leadership role of, 72–73; photos, *109;* and Texas melon strike, 155; UFWOC leadership role, 75
Higgins, George G., 58, 94–95, 100, *112*
home altars *(altarcitos),* 32
home missions, 19–23, 28–30, 39–41, 122–23. *See also* Migrant Ministry

Huerta, Dolores: anniversary march, 1; background of, 71, 88–89; beginnings in AWOC, 54; in community organizing, 55–56; La Causa leadership, 80, 88–91; NFWA role of, 71, 79; photos, *109, 110;* UFWOC leadership role, 75
Huntsville Action for Youth, 144
Hurricane Beulah, 156–57

immigration: Anglo-Americans to Texas, 115, 116, 120–21; Europeans (besides Anglos) to Texas, 118–19; Mexican Revolution-era influx to California, 25; multiple waves of Mexicans, 25, 54, 58, 115, 126, 130–31; repatriation activities (1930s), 42–43. *See also individual immigrant groups*
"imperial states," California and Texas as, 5–6
Imperial Valley of California, 26, 35, 36–37, 40–42, 56–57
indigenous peoples of Latin America *(indios),* 3, 31, 32
Industrial Areas Foundation, 55
institutional Catholic Church: anti-communism in American, 127–28; contract mediation role, 98–99, 100–105; divisions over farm labor support, 39, 69, 77, 94–105, 141; ethnic/racial prejudices in, 18–19, 21–22, 32, 33, 120, 134; and immigrants in California (1850–1930), 17–27, 33, 44–46; influences on Latin American Church, 30–31; and Latina/o popular religion, 10–11, 22; neglect of support for the Spanish-speaking, 8, 18, 21–22, 23, 119–20; opposition to Bracero Program, 49; post-colonial development in Texas (1840–1930), 117–20; and Protestants, 26, 28, 79; rise and decline in Texas, 116; strike role of, 94–105, 106, 140–42, 145–48; support for farm labor, 44–47, 55–56, 61, 65–66, 126–27, 132–35; support for the Spanish speaking, 49, 50–58, 65–66, 77, 133, 141. *See also* clergy, Catholic
Irish American Catholics: institutional favoritism toward, 21, 119; and labor movement, 24; in San Francisco, 7, 17, 24; in Texas, 117–18
Itliong, Larry, 54, 74, 75